How Fa

to Amend the Constitution

Mobilize Political Change

How Failed Attempts to Amend the Constitution Mobilize Political Change

Roger C. Hartley

Vanderbilt University Press | Nashville

© 2017 by Vanderbilt University Press
Nashville, Tennessee 37235
All rights reserved
First printing 2017

This book is printed on acid-free paper.
Manufactured in the United States of America

Library of Congress Cataloging-in-Publication Data on file
LC control number: 2016042797
LC classification number: KF4555 .H39 2017
Dewey classification number: 342.7303/2—dc23
LC record available at *lccn.loc.gov/2016042797*

ISBN 978-0-8265-2148-4 (hardcover)
ISBN 978-0-8265-2149-1 (paperback)
ISBN 978-0-8265-2150-7 (ebook)

For Alice H. Cook and Herbert L. Sherman Jr.
Labor Educators

Contents

Acknowledgments ix
Introduction: The Problem 1

PART I. Lessons from the ERA

1 Amendment Efforts as a Movement-Building Resource 9
2 Amendment Efforts as a Resource for Expressing Dissent and Promoting Deliberation 34

PART II. Impact of Failed Amendment Efforts on Congressional Politics

3 Prodding Congress through Use of the Article V "Application Clause" 87
4 The Impact of Article V on Federal Legislation 109

PART III. Impact of Failed Amendment Efforts on Federal Executive Policy

5 Failed Amendment Efforts and the President's War-Making and Foreign Relations Powers 131

Conclusion 157
Cases Cited 163
Notes 165
Bibliography 225
Index 241

Acknowledgments

I am indebted to many people who assisted in this book's conception and completion. My late faculty colleague Professor Stephen Goldman deserves special thanks for his early encouragement to convert into a book preliminary ideas I initially thought were suited only for publication as a law journal article. Over countless afternoon discussions assisting me in refining my thesis, and by his reading and critiquing early draft chapters, Steve helped guide the structure and enhance the quality of the final version. In addition, I want to thank Steve Young, one of the extraordinarily talented reference librarians at Columbus School of Law of the Catholic University of America. Steve tracked down so many obscure references for me that I long ago lost count. For his talent and dogged persistence, I am both amazed and appreciative. I want to thank Deans Veryl Miles and Daniel Attridge and Associate Dean Marin Scordato who supported this effort by recommending and authorizing financial support from the Catholic University Faculty Research Fund. Countless friends and colleagues have encouraged me along the way. They include Bill Osborne (and the entire Osborne/McArdle family), Dos Hatfield, and Scott Shelley. I ask indulgence and understanding of any who have been supportive but whom I inadvertently have failed to list. Upon reading the initial manuscript, Michael Ames, the Director of the Vanderbilt University Press, appreciated immediately the political potency of failed constitutional amendment efforts and helped move this project expeditiously to completion. Michael's insights and masterful editing skills have left their tracings throughout the book. It is a markedly better book because of his input. And finally, without the patience and encouragement of my wife Catherine Mack this book could not have been written.

Introduction

The Problem

> The Congress, whenever two thirds of both Houses shall deem it necessary, shall propose Amendments to this Constitution, or, on the application of the Legislatures of two thirds of the several States, shall call a Convention for proposing amendments, which in either Case, shall be valid to all Intents and Purposes, as Part of this Constitution, when ratified by the Legislatures of three fourths of the several States, or by Conventions in three fourths thereof, as one or the other Mode of Ratification may be proposed by the Congress.
> —The Constitution of the United States, Article V

The provisions in Article V of the US Constitution are widely understood to perform the single function of providing a means for adding new language to the Constitution through the process of constitutional amendment. The goal of this book is to change that perception. The chapters that follow invite the reader to begin viewing Article V also as a tool that political and social reformers use to achieve a variety of other objectives.

A one-dimensional understanding of Article V's constitutional function is understandable. After all, Article V's text is limited to specifying the procedures for adding amendments to the Constitution. Moreover, media coverage of Article V is confined to discussions of newly proposed constitutional amendments or congressional hearings on a proposed amendment. And Article V's constitutional function in the public mind is defined by its most visible accomplishments—the twenty-seven constitutional amendments added over the past 225 years. These formal amendments have been transformative by defining goals and setting standards for America's public life.[1] Consider, for example, that but for Article V we would not have a Bill of Rights written into the Constitution. Nor would we have the Fourteenth Amendment's guarantee of due process and equal protection of the law. With the aid of Article V, the nation's political community has been expanded to include African Americans, women, those too poor to pay poll taxes, residents of the District of Columbia (at least in presidential elections), and citizens between the ages of eighteen and twenty-one.[2] But Article V's towering achievements may have distracted us from recognizing Article V's less obvious political functions.

Many outstanding books have analyzed either the amending process in general or the effects on our constitutional order of certain past successful amendment efforts.[3] By contrast, this volume primarily considers constitutional amendments that failed in the sense that they were proposed but never adopted. Fully alert to the reality that no constitutional amendment likely will result, individuals and groups nonetheless actively propose constitutional amendments in every session of Congress. Social activists support many of these proposed constitutional amendments as part of their reform-oriented strategy (or as part of a reform-impeding strategy). Sophisticated amendment supporters understand that proposing and championing adoption of a constitutional amendment can influence the political process by favorably altering institutional relations and practices. The amendment effort fails to add new constitutional text but introducing a proposed amendment gains ancillary advantages for the amendment proposers—creating the paradox of winning by losing.

Like baseball, the constitutional amendment process is a game of repeated failure punctuated by occasional success. During the approximately 225 years since the Constitution's ratification, members of Congress have introduced roughly twelve thousand proposals to amend the Constitution. In addition, states have filed several hundred petitions with Congress requesting the convening of a constitutional convention. Proposed amendments to restructure the government comprise the largest category of these proposals.[4] The pace of proposing amendments remains brisk. Members of Congress introduce nearly two hundred constitutional amendment proposals annually.[5] In recent years the flood of amendment proposals has been so great that some scholars have argued that a "constitutional amendment fever" had struck the land.[6] In April 2014, retired Supreme Court Justice John Paul Stevens published a book proposing political mobilization to adopt six additional constitutional amendments.[7] In June 2014, the Senate Judiciary Committee held hearings on a constitutional amendment to permit the federal government and the states to enact legislation to limit campaign spending.[8] In September 2014, eminent constitutional scholar and law school dean Erwin Chemerinsky published a book calling for a constitutional amendment providing eighteen-year terms for Supreme Court justices.[9] As recently as the summer of 2015, United States senator and presidential aspirant Ted Cruz staked his political career on excoriating the Supreme Court for its same-sex marriage and Affordable Care Act decisions and buttressed that attack on the Court by calling for a constitutional amendment requiring the justices to undergo periodic judicial retention elections.[10] Advocates continue to urge the state legislatures to act in concert to petition Congress to convene a constitutional convention.[11]

The contemporary amendment fever in Congress cannot be explained by any realistic likelihood that an amendment proposal introduced by a member of Congress will bear fruit in terms of being cleared in Congress, sent to the states for ratification consideration, and ultimately mature into a ratified constitutional amendment. Of the roughly twelve thousand amendment proposals that have been introduced, only seventeen have been adopted as constitutional amendments since ratification of the ten amendments comprising the Bill of Rights. Considering the Bill of Rights as a single "mega-amendment,"[12] that translates into a total of eighteen constitutional amendments adopted in about 225 years. In addition, Congress has proposed six additional amendments that failed to secure ratification by the requisite three-fourths of the states. For every amending proposal Congress has adopted by a two-thirds vote in each congressional chamber and forwarded to the states for ratification, hundreds have been introduced but were rejected. It has been estimated that the odds of an amendment proposal gaining congressional approval and being proposed to the states are roughly one in five hundred, and the chances that a proposed amendment will survive the gauntlet Article V erects and ultimately be ratified and added to the Constitution are about one in one thousand.[13] Article V's formidable procedural barriers largely explain the overwhelmingly low probability of success of efforts to add new constitutional text. Congress, by a two-thirds vote of each House, controls which amendments are proposed to the states unless two-thirds of the state legislatures petition for a constitutional convention to propose amendments—something that to date has never occurred. In either case, three-fourths of the states must ratify proposed amendments either through their legislatures or through state ratification conventions; which method is used is a decision left to Congress. This renders Article V extraordinarily undemocratic. Just thirty-four US senators can block Congress's ability to send a proposed amendment to the states for ratification. Moreover, the supermajorities required for state ratification empower a relatively small minority of the population to block constitutional change desired by substantial majorities.[14] The resulting difficulty of achieving constitutional amendment has spawned heated criticism.[15] Yet, counter-intuitively, constitutional amendments continue to be proposed by the hundreds in Congress each year.

The Article V amending process also appears to lack contemporary relevance because changes in constitutional text do not account for most contemporary changes in constitutional norms. The operative Constitution has changed fundamentally over the past eighty years. Since the New Deal, the changes in the structure of the federal government have been nothing short of dazzling. These changes in constitutional architecture have converted the federal government into a more centralized polity administering a far different activist administrative state than anything that the Founders could have imagined. Federal authorities are now charged with regulating a national banking system and complex multinational financial institutions; securing its citizens' legal equality and economic welfare; waging war and otherwise projecting global power; sustaining a massive and permanent national security state though maintenance of global military, intelligence, and diplomatic establishments; and regulating a transnational market economy.[16] The 1937 constitutional crisis that prompted the Supreme Court's famous "switch in time" decisions confirmed this nation's rejection of the 1789 Constitution's vision of a limited federal government. Since the New Deal, state governments, once the administrative and regulatory backbone of the country, have been forced to cede to the national government their pride of place as the primary economic regulators. In short, ours is a far different constitutionalism than the decentralized federal system that the "Four Horsemen" attempted in vain to preserve in the face of the changed, and ever-changing, political and economic environment of the early 1930s.[17]

The most stunning aspect of the late twentieth- and early twenty-first-century constitutionalism is that the fundamental restructuring of government during and following the New Deal and World War II occurred primarily "off-text"—through processes other than formal constitutional amendment. Indeed, of the twentieth century's twelve constitutional amendments, except for the provision for the direct election of senators, the income tax, and perhaps the 1951 addition of term limits for the president, none significantly changed the structural design for the national government from that provided in the Founders' Constitution.[18] To be sure, constitutional amendments expanded the franchise—for women, younger Americans, and the poor unable to pay a poll tax. But the crucial reality of constitutionalism over at least the past eighty years is that while the *structure of government* changed more than at any time in the history of the national constitutional order, constitutional text remained largely unchanged.[19] Indeed, because the last contested constitutional amendment was added in 1971, the vast majority of Americans have lived their entire lives having no political experience participating in a national dialogue resulting in ratification of a constitutional amendment.[20] Other than the sixty-one-year hiatus between the 1804 ratification of the Twelfth Amendment and the 1865 ratification of the Thirteenth Amendment, the present amendment drought is the longest in US history.[21]

Because the odds of successfully attempting to amend the Constitution are meager and because during the constitutional revolution of the past eighty years Article V appears to have been missing in action, many critics have concluded that Article V has become a pre-twentieth century constitutional relic. Taking a realpolitik view with respect to Article V's contemporary usefulness as a tool for social change, critics dismiss the formal amendment process as little more than a hoax. Their view is that Article V masquerades as an engine of change. Many contemporary critics have used quite sharp language. For example, in 2001 David Strauss wrote a widely respected article entitled *The Irrelevance of Constitutional Amendments*.[22] Article V has been labeled the Constitution's "Comatose Article,"[23] the "stupidest" constitutional provision,[24] and both a "virulent toxin" embedded within the political DNA of the Constitution and an "iron cage" with indestructible bars due to the near impossibility of effecting significant change through the constitutional amendment mechanism.[25]

Supporters of the failed Equal Rights Amendment (ERA) have been particularly critical of Article V, arguing that the ERA fell victim to the anti-majoritarianism inherent in our constitutional amendment procedures. Some ERA supporters are prepared to acknowledge the value of conditioning constitutional amendment on concurrence from supermajorities but argue that the requirement of concurrence from three-fourths of all of the state legislatures is excessive.[26] Professor Bruce Ackerman has offered perhaps the bluntest epitaph to Article V by describing Article V simply as a "road to nowhere."[27] One measure of the degree to which Article V currently is under attack is the brisk counter-effort to defend Article V from its critics.[28]

Given the improbability of any proposed amendment of real substance surviving the ratification gauntlet, why would members of Congress, advocacy groups, a retired Supreme Court justice, and one of the country's most highly respected constitutional scholars continue to urge activists to deploy the Article V amendment process as a means to achieve social change?

No doubt a member of Congress gains political advantage from hometown newspaper coverage when introducing a constitutional amendment having strong constituent appeal, such as banning flag burning, requiring a balanced budget, permitting prayer and Bible reading in public school, forbidding compulsory school busing to achieve school desegregation, or permitting regulation of campaign spending. Though probably futile, the act of introducing such a hot-topic constitutional amendment proposal is rationally calculated to raise one's political profile back home. Surely, posturing among one's constituents accounts for some of the constitutional amendments annually proposed in Congress.

But the desire to gain reelection by garnering hometown bragging rights hardly seems sufficient to account for the large number of amendment proposals introduced in Congress each term—especially because many are championed by citizens who are not seeking reelection, such as a law school dean and a retired Supreme Court Justice. The *opportunity to propose* constitutional amendments would seem to profit political actors and social reformers in additional ways.

The goal of this book is to demonstrate the political advantages that amendment adherents can gain when they propose and champion constitutional amendments. The following chapters contain twenty-five case studies that illuminate diverse pathways enabling political actors and social reformers to deploy amendment proposals to achieve an array of political and social reform objectives. There is no one-size-fits-all explanation. Credit claiming (posturing) has motivated members of Congress and the president to support proposed constitutional amendments, but there are many other political motivations. Some amendment proposals are used as a resource to build and sustain a social movement. Other proponents have used constitutional amendment proposals to prod Congress into action. A recurring strategic political use of Article V is to frame the debate during congressional consideration of pending legislation. In addition, proposing a constitutional amendment can influence the Supreme Court's determination of constitutional meaning through the catalytic effect amendment proposing can have on promoting democratic deliberation—an important factor discussed in the chapters that follow. This occurred, for example, during the failed ERA ratification effort as well as in the failed attempt to reverse *Roe v. Wade* by constitutional amendment.

This book's message is that Article V is alive and well. Article V is an institution of government that has been misunderstood and incompletely evaluated. Measuring its contemporary vitality simply by counting the number of amendments added to the Constitution is like judging the size of an iceberg by what protrudes above the sea's surface. The real significance of the Article V amendment process is best observed below the surface. Social change occurs through an intricate, interrelated national political process that has "many moving parts."[29] Article V endures as an important part of contemporary Constitutionalism because it is one of those "moving parts," even when it does not produce changes in constitutional text.

PART I

Lessons from the ERA

1

Amendment Efforts as a Movement-Building Resource

By the 1970s, the effort to add the Equal Rights Amendment (ERA) to the Constitution had attracted large numbers of engaged partisans on both sides. Few Americans were unaware of this amendment proposal. The ERA's substantive provision stated: "Equality of rights under the law shall not be denied or abridged by the United States or by any State on account of sex." Congress approved the ERA and sent it to the states for ratification in March 1972. The original seven-year expiration date for ratification was extended to June 30, 1982. By that date, the ERA had secured thirty-five state ratifications, three short of the required three-fourths of the states.

The ERA is an example of an unsuccessful constitutional amendment effort that nevertheless influenced a broad swath of US politics. Isolating the pathways through which political actors used the ERA as a resource to achieve a variety of political objectives opens opportunities for clarifying how other "failed" constitutional amendment efforts have provided amendment proponents similar political opportunities. The ERA was unique in the sense that it impacted US politics in several dimensions. One was using the ERA as a resource to help mobilize supporters favoring legal equality for women in general and building the feminist movement in particular.

Mass mobilization is normally necessary for generating the broad-based engagement, intense debate, and political agitation needed to stimulate significant political and social change. But such mobilization will seldom develop spontaneously. During times of "normal politics," people go about their business, remain relatively uninvolved in Washington, DC, politics, and only tangentially participate in political discourse.[1] To stimulate political agitation, a committed cadre must design a strategy that can first activate support from a small cohort of concerned citizens and then organize partisans into an effective social movement.[2] Existing scholarship demonstrates how asserting legal rights *through litigation* can serve as a resource for building a social movement. The "failed" ERA demonstrates that proposing a constitutional amendment similarly can and did operate as a resource for movement building—in the case of the ERA, serving as a catalyst for building the modern feminist movement and then creating a backlash countermovement.

Claiming Rights through Litigation as a Resource for Movement Building

Forty years ago Stuart Scheingold wrote the first edition of his important book *The Politics of Rights*. It describes how claiming legal rights through litigation can initiate and nurture political mobilization.[3] Scheingold was initially struck by the apparent paradox of American faith in law coexisting with the reality on the ground that law is often a feckless agent for effecting social change.[4] Americans are wedded to the idea that a legal right is an entitlement that courts will safeguard. But Scheingold's research, as well as research produced by later generations of scholars, confirms the existence of structural forces causing a disconnect between the law as extolled by judicial decisions and the law as it actually impacts individuals.[5] Scheingold coined the phrase "myth of rights" to describe this faith in law coexisting with a gap between the promise and the reality of law.

Scheingold's groundbreaking book advanced a second, even more powerful, insight. Since it is illusory to view judicially affirmed rights as self-implementing vehicles for achieving social justice, it is far more sensible to think of claims of legal rights not as ends in themselves but as a means to achieve the political mobilization that makes social justice achievable. Social movement organizers can exploit the "myth of rights"— the widely held perceptions that legal rights are entitlements that courts will enforce—both to initiate political mobilization (activation) and then nurture a fledgling rights-claiming campaign into an effective social movement (organizing). Scheingold called the power of rights claiming to catalyze social movement mobilization the "politics of rights."[6]

Activation

For political mobilization to commence, discontented people must cease thinking of their discontent as an individual problem and instead begin to perceive the injustices they see as social problems requiring a political solution.[7] For this to occur, individuals and groups must have their expectations altered to the point that they are able to conclude their grievance represents an indefensible deprivation and that redress through collective action is realistically possible.[8] A powerful way for social activists to alter expectations this way is through rights claiming—demanding official redress of grievances. Through reform strategies that demand official vindication of rights, social activists are able to accord grievances a measure of political legitimacy, which has the effect of raising expectations and activating individuals' and groups' political consciousness.[9] By providing a grievance the imprimatur of official acknowledgment and a measure of political legitimacy, rights claiming moves individuals from the view that they are isolated, atomized individuals with grievances to the view that it is politically legitimate and sensible to insist on official redress of grievances through mobilization for collective action.[10]

Scheingold, and subsequently others, have thus demonstrated that rights claiming might not succeed in effecting social change through judicial enforcement of the asserted right, but the process of rights claiming can become a resource for recruiting support for a social movement, and the resulting social movement may be successful in obtaining the desired social change through other political processes.

It is of critical importance to the present project of applying the politics-of-rights principles to efforts to amend the Constitution that subsequent research has demonstrated that Scheingold's politics-of-rights principles apply even to rights not yet formally recognized or enforced.[11] In other words, legal strategies centered on the contention that certain claimed rights should be acknowledged and respected can catalyze political mobilization.[12] And, of course, proposing a constitutional amendment is grounded in the assertion that a right not yet recognized should be acknowledged through a proposed amendment's ratification. Anything that validates a rights claim can activate rights consciousness. Even some relatively small departure from existing practice can serve to legitimatize a claim of rights and thus create connotations of entitlement.[13]

Organizing

Activation of political consciousness among the discontented is a necessary, yet insufficient, prerequisite for building an effective social movement. Rights claiming will not gain enough traction to influence changes in public policy absent effective political organizations that can maintain the momentum needed to press rights claims. Rights claiming can nurture a nascent social movement and assist in its development in several different ways.

First, rights claiming can promote movement growth by providing opportunities for movement organizers to develop a plausible legal logic for how change can occur. In order to take root and become effective, an incipient social movement and its members must be taken seriously. Only then can they expect to attract new members and powerful institutional allies and eventually gain sufficient influence to effect a favorable change in public opinion. When a social movement advocates a plausible legal logic for how change can occur, it is more likely to be taken seriously and inspire confidence among potential supporters that the organization has the capacity to become an effective change agent. That confidence facilitates the movement's effort to recruit new members and institutional allies.[14]

In addition, rights claiming permits an organization to benefit from a process known as "framing and naming." The social movement frames its goals as an effort to obtain official vindication of rights and names the right asserted in terms of some legally recognizable category. It makes a difference, for example, whether an asserted "right" is framed in terms of the right to life or a women's right to choose. In school prayer disputes, one might support the return of God to the classroom (connoting something has been taken away) versus an opponent's claim for respect for an individual's right to freedom of religion or separation of church and state. In desegregation and busing disputes, naming permits one to be associated with either the right to choose neighborhood schools versus the right to a racially integrated public education. By further example, in affirmative action disputes it makes a difference if the debate is framed within the ideological framework of eliminating effects of past racial injustice or in terms of white victimization resulting from a violation of the Equal Protection Clause's demand for color-blindness.[15] The point is that framing helps give social meaning to a discontent and empowers members by providing a conceptual context for making sense of the perceived injustice they feel. Naming helps sustain hope and confidence that change is possible because an individual's or a group's discontent can now be understood as a deprivation of a right described within a recognized legal category. Naming also provides groups the ability to coalesce around a mutually shared understanding of some perceived injustice and promotes cohesion by separating "us" (who all claim a discernible right) from "them" (who seek to deny "us" the right). And naming creates an easily administered litmus test for determining allies and opponents.[16] In short, rights claiming provides movement organizers creative opportunities to design a plausible legal strategy for how change can occur that frames its objective as insistence on official vindication of a right and names the claimed right in terms of a recognized legal category. Such framing and naming promotes cohesion among existing supporters and assists in recruiting new members and institutional allies.

Additionally, rights claiming can promote movement growth by providing media coverage. A nascent political movement gains organizational strength by aligning itself with affinity groups and elite activists in government, community groups, and the public at large.[17] A movement achieves leverage in its efforts to form such alliances when its agenda attains national prominence. This requires that a fledgling movement secure national publicity through media coverage. In addition to promoting favorable alliances, media coverage also educates the public, dramatizes the issues at stake, and can "awaken the 'sleeping giant' of protest" against a targeted perceived injustice.[18]

A rights-claiming strategy can provide a movement with valuable opportunities to generate national publicity. Preliminary litigation success, for example, has been shown to provide political legitimacy to a rights claim and concomitant mainstream media attention.[19] In a similar vein, proposing a constitutional amendment as a means to secure official redress of grievances is a dramatic political gesture that attracts media attention. The national media inevitably provides extensive coverage, particularly if congressional hearings are scheduled on the proposed amendment. This occurred in the spring of 2014, for example, when the Senate Judiciary Committee held hearings on a proposed constitutional amendment to authorize Congress and the states to regulate the raising and spending of money for political campaigns. These hearings received nationwide attention from both mainstream media and the internet.[20] Just writing a book proposing adoption of a constitutional amendment can land the amendment proposal on the editorial page of a major newspaper—at least if the author is a celebrated public figure.[21] Many examples of the media's attraction to amendment efforts can be seen in the history of the ERA, Prohibition, the proposed school prayer constitutional amendments, amendment proposals to ban flag desecration, balanced budget amendment proposals, and many more. The point is that generating media coverage, whether through litigation or proposing a constitutional amendment, operates as a movement-building resource and strengthens a movement organizationally.[22]

Moreover, rights claiming can promote movement growth by providing financial support. To stabilize and become an effective political organization, a social movement needs to mobilize financial support to fund activities such as internal and external publicity campaigns, lobbying, litigation, and so on. Designing a campaign strategy built around a claim of rights (including a "demand" for a constitutional amendment) is an effective way to mobilize financial support for all the reasons discussed so far. First, the movement members demonstrate that they take themselves seriously and therefore warrant being taken seriously. Second, discontents are named in terms of familiar legally derived categories of rights. This provides a conceptual frame for potential financial supporters to make sense of the perceived injustice the movement is seeking to redress and creates the opportunity for financial donors to coalesce around a mutually shared understanding of a perceived injustice.[23] Third, rights claims facilitate partnering with allies and gaining media coverage, both of which help secure national attention, public education, and exposure to potential donors.

Finally, rights claiming can operate as a resource for strengthening a social movement by creating a political legacy. Even when a struggle to redress grievances by vindicating a legal right fails, the movement that mobilized support for the struggle often endures. Despite a failure, the struggle can and often does transform movement members ideologically, and this metamorphosis outlasts the struggle that precipitated it. In addition, while a reform effort may have failed, its political consequences often live on in the form of a surviving political movement and a cadre of potential activists available to provide organizational support for the next struggle. A clear example of this is the pay-equity-for-women movement. That movement failed in achieving its primary objective that women should be compensated based on the theory of comparable worth, but the dramatic increase in rights consciousness created among women workers left a legacy of political empowerment and reform that was available for energizing subsequent struggles.[24]

Summary

Designing a social reform agenda around a strategy that asserts legal rights (even unsuccessfully) operates as a resource for building social movements. There are a number of important pathways that enable rights claiming to influence movement building:

Mobilizing supporters (activation): Rights claiming promotes transformation of legal consciousness by raising expectations and perceptions of entitlement

Recruiting new members: Rights claiming provides opportunities for a social movement to advocate plausible legal strategies for how change can occur and this attracts supporters

Promoting group cohesion by framing and naming: Framing the movement's claim as an insistence on official vindication of a right and naming that right in terms of a recognized legal category strengthens a movement by forging a group-based identity built upon a mutually shared understanding of a perceived injustice

Providing media coverage: Rights claiming attracts media coverage that in turn provides national prominence to a movement's agenda, promotes the view that the movement is advocating a credible cause for collective

action, mobilizes support from affinity group allies and powerful elites, and favorably shapes public opinion
- *Mobilizing financial support*: Through all of the above pathways, rights claiming facilitates the ability of a social movement to secure financial support
- *Creating* a *political legacy:* The social movement that mobilized political support for a failed claim-of-rights struggle endures, as does the raised political consciousness of its supporters, forging a legacy that is available as a resource for future struggles

The "Politics of Rights" Account of the ERA

The pathways discussed in the first section explain how a rights-based legal strategy that attempts to redress grievances through litigation can help build a social movement. Women's rights activists, using these same pathways, leveraged support for the ERA to assist in building the modern feminist movement.

Pre-1970 Support for the ERA as a Mobilization Resource

In the spring of 1970, Congress held hearings on the ERA. In 1972 Congress approved the ERA and sent it to the states for their consideration. Two factors might lead one to conclude that the ERA could not have contributed to building the women's movement prior to these early-1970s developments. First, by 1970, considerable public protest supportive of women's rights already had occurred,[25] thus the cause agent of this public action may have been something other than support for the ERA. Second, and related, until 1970 few among the rank and file potential supporters of the women's movement knew of the ERA.[26] These factors notwithstanding, compelling evidence demonstrates that support for the ERA did operate as a powerful resource that mobilized women and sustained the women's movement prior to 1970.

The Rift: Efforts to add an ERA to the Constitution began in the early 1920s. Most of the suffrage organizations withered after the Nineteenth Amendment was ratified but not the militant National Woman's Party (NWP). Alice Paul and her NWP drafted an Equal Rights Amendment that would have banned all gender discrimination, both private and governmental. As a symbolic gesture, this original ERA was introduced in Congress in 1923, again in 1925, and again in 1928.[27] In some form an ERA was introduced in every subsequent Congress until March 1972 when Congress finally approved and sent to the states a revised ERA that banned only governmental sex discrimination.[28]

During these early years following ratification of the Nineteenth Amendment, many women's rights advocates bitterly opposed the NWP's efforts to secure congressional support for the ERA. Florence Kelly and her allies in the National Consumers League, as well as many other women's rights activists, including Eleanor Roosevelt, opposed Alice Paul's ERA. These groups, with the strong support of organized labor, preferred pressing Congress and the states to enact protective labor legislation barring women from certain occupations, limiting the number of hours women could work either per day or per week, prohibiting night shift work for women, limiting the amount of weight women could be required to lift, requiring special accommodations for women such as seats and rest periods, and a host of other "protective" measures. For these reformers, the ERA was anathema because it endangered the constitutionality of these laws discriminating in favor of just one gender group. ERA supporters, however, came to exactly the opposite conclusion, viewing labor laws protecting women as causing more harm than good. Protective labor legislation treated women like children in need of protection, encouraged employers to prefer hiring men rather than women, served to subordinate women by enforcing and reinforcing a traditional sex-role structure that funneled men into high-paying jobs and women into low-paying jobs, and otherwise regulated men's and women's sex and family roles.[29]

Women's rights advocates fought one another to a stalemate for nearly half a century over the wisdom of having an ERA added to the Constitution. But these internecine struggles nevertheless contributed to movement building within each faction of the women's rights movement: in one group, enlisting adherents supportive of the ERA, and in the other, encouraging recruitment of women to oppose the ERA and instead work for women's rights through enactment of protective labor legislation. While this pre-1970 support (and opposition) for the ERA hopelessly divided feminist reformers, it also mobilized and politicized women for five decades.

Presidential Commission on the Status of Women: Support for some form of an Equal Rights Amendment grew during the 1930s as well as during and immediately following World War II. By the election of President Kennedy, the women's movement remained divided over the issue of preference for an ERA versus preference for protective labor legislation for women. President Kennedy expressed support for the ERA in a letter to a pro-ERA reformer but cleverly attempted to undercut the ERA by executive order when he created the Presidential Commission on the Status of Women. Kennedy primarily appointed longtime anti-ERA reformers to the Commission, such as Eleanor Roosevelt and Esther Peterson (head of the Women's Bureau and an Assistant Secretary of Labor). There is wide agreement that Kennedy created the President's Commission on the Status of Women as a strategy to blunt support for enactment of an ERA.[30] Peterson persuaded Kennedy to create the commission in order to focus attention on more achievable objectives and divert attention from the ERA, which she regarded as ill conceived.[31] Initially the ploy was successful. In 1963, the Commission issued its final report (*American Women*) documenting the ongoing denial of women's rights but concluding that because women were already entitled to constitutional protection against discrimination, women did not now need a constitutional amendment in order to establish equal rights.[32]

In one of the more interesting ironies in US political history, the President's Commission on the Status of Women, though created to undermine support for the ERA, became a vehicle for advancing the ERA's enactment and operated as a resource for building a strong women's movement that vigorously supported adoption of the ERA. This occurred because the President's Commission on the Status of Women created fifty state commissions to continue research into the status of women at the state level. In three significant ways these state commissions laid the groundwork for building the women's movement. First, sophisticated, politically active women agreed to work on these state commissions on the status of women. These women otherwise would not have had any reason to come together, meet one another, work together for the common cause of women's rights, and develop personal and professional ties useful a decade later when the feminist movement experienced its greatest growth. Second, these state commissions documented abundant evidence of discrimination against women. And finally, following publication of the state commissions' reports documenting rampant sex discrimination, women developed an activated political consciousness due to rising expectations that official remedial action would be forthcoming.[33]

In sum, the fifty state commissions on the status of women became causal agents that mobilized support for the ERA and the growing women's movement. But these state commissions would not have been created but for President Kennedy creating the President's Commission on the Status of Women at the urging of those who were attempting to undermine support for the ERA. Thus it was a twist of politics that turned opposition to the ERA in the 1960s into an unintended resource that helped build the women's movement.[34]

Enactment of the 1964 Civil Rights Act: The pre-1970s push to add an ERA to the Constitution influenced the growth of the women's movement in an additional way. This occurred during the Johnson administration and as a result of Congress's enactment of Title VII of the 1964 Civil Rights Act with its provision banning sex discrimination. That part of the story begins with a dark side of the ERA undertaking—deploying racist appeals as part of a strategy to secure support for the ERA.[35]

It was in the interests of the National Women's Party (NWP) and Southern segregationists to work together to defeat federal civil rights legislation. The NWP overwhelmingly favored the ERA and thus opposed legislative solutions remedying gender discrimination that might weaken arguments for securing gender equality through the addition of the ERA to the Constitution. In addition, by the mid-1960s many in the NWP who supported the ERA either were antagonistic to civil rights for African Americans or were tepid supporters. For years, therefore, the pro-ERA NWP worked with Southern segregationists to introduce amendments to civil rights bills that added protection for "white womanhood," the intent being to defeat pending civil rights legislation with killer amendments.[36]

During the legislative debate over the 1964 Civil Rights Act, ERA supporters in the NWP and Southern segregationists partnered to oppose the legislation.[37] Viewing the 1964 Civil Rights Act as a step undermining the passage of the ERA, the NWP requested Southern members of Congress to sponsor an amendment to Title VII banning sex discrimination, with the expectation that such an amendment would make the legislation a joke, subject the bill to derision, and kill it.[38] On the floor of the House, Rep. Howard W. "Judge" Smith (D-VA) proposed amending Title VII, adding sex as a prohibited category of discrimination. As expected, the amendment generated ridicule and laughter from many members of Congress.[39]

Of course, the NWP/Southern segregationist strategy to defeat Title VII backfired when Congress approved the amendment adding sex as a prohibited discrimination category and then enacted Title VII. Thus it was pre-1970s support for the ERA that greatly influenced adding a ban on sex discrimination to Title VII. But the ERA/Title VII connection does not end there. In several additional ways adding sex as a prohibited category of discrimination in Title VII helped build the women's movement.

First, the inclusion of the sex discrimination amendment in Title VII greatly alleviated racial tension that was impeding cooperation among women active in the women's movement and those active in the civil rights movement. Much of this racial tension was bound up in the view that, by proposing legislation without the sex amendment, Title VII activists were ignoring the interests of white Christian women. Inclusion of the Title VII sex amendment alleviated that source of racial tension because now all women, irrespective of race or religion, enjoyed equal statutory protection from sex discrimination.[40]

Second, the Title VII sex amendment also influenced the building of a coherent women's movement by eliminating the single greatest factor dividing that movement—the preference by some feminists for protective labor legislation favoring women rather than enactment of the ERA. Not many years after enactment of Title VII, both the Equal Employment Opportunity Commission's guidelines and court decisions banned state protective legislation singling out women for protection, permitting feminists to unite behind efforts to secure congressional backing for the ERA and support for the ERA in state legislatures.[41]

Of all of the ERA's influences on building the women's movement during the pre-1970s era, none is more significant than the crisis over the EEOC's initial refusal to take seriously Title VII's proscription on sex discrimination. That policy position by the EEOC created a crisis for women and a catalyst for the founding of the National Organization for Women (NOW). Title VII's prohibition on sex discrimination created in women the expectation that government would intervene to address sex discrimination in the private sector. Indeed, allegations of sex discrimination comprised more than one-third of the claims the EEOC received the first year following the effective date of Title VII.[42] The EEOC commissioners (mostly male) soon eroded this expectation by adopting attitudes ranging from overt hostility to treating the statute's sex discrimination ban as a joke.[43] In 1965, the EEOC announced that it would assign lower priority to sex discrimination than race discrimination complaints and ruled that the practice of sex-segregated job advertisements did not constitute prohibited sex discrimination.[44] This EEOC decision to under-enforce Title VII's proscription on sex discrimination contributed to building the women's movement in two related ways. First, the EEOC's under-enforcement policy and refusal to take sex discrimination seriously persuaded many feminist activists of the necessity to put aside their disagreements over the ERA sufficiently to enable them to mobilize politically and unite to vindicate women's economic equality at the workplace.[45] Second, many in the women's movement became convinced that women's rights would not be taken seriously until women created a formal organization similar to the NAACP to mobilize women and exert collective pressure on the government to enforce aggressively the ban on sex discrimination.[46]

Accordingly, in June 1966 Betty Friedan and a group of other activists attended the Third National Conference of Commissions on the Status of Women intending to introduce a resolution urging the EEOC to adequately enforce Title VII's sex discrimination provisions. When the resolution was ruled out of order, Friedan and a small group of other disappointed activists met and decided to form a more aggressive women's rights organization.[47] When an organizing conference was held in the fall of 1966, three hundred charter members formed the National Organization for Women (NOW), which was to go on to become the largest and most influential of the women's rights groups and the organization most identified with efforts to obtain ratification of the ERA.[48]

Post-1970 Support for the ERA as a Mobilization Resource

Recruiting Members: The congressional hearings on the ERA held in the spring of 1970, congressional adoption of the ERA in 1972, and subsequent efforts in the various states to secure the ERA's ratification produced a mass mobilization of women. Feminists with divergent points of view joined together and became politically active on behalf of women's rights.[49] This ERA ratification effort had the effect of activating the political consciousness of women. Many women were transformed by their engagement in the struggle to secure the ERA, especially as they responded to the need to publicly formulate their constitutional vision of women's rights.[50] Additionally, the ERA operated as a movement builder and momentum maintainer through its symbolic power, enhancing women's self-respect and proclaiming the nation's commitment to achieving effective legal equality for women.[51]

But women's rights groups in general and the National Organization for Women in particular used the ERA quite directly to mobilize support, recruit members, and build their organizations.[52] NOW initially promoted grassroots mobilization through consciousness-raising efforts that made the need for change more acute and predisposed women to view the ratification of the ERA as a common goal around which to organize.[53] NOW's aggressive role in the ratification effort swelled its membership, raising membership from about six thousand in 1971 to twenty thousand in just the next two years (1971–1973). The following year (1974), NOW membership doubled to forty thousand members. By 1982, the last year of the ERA ratification effort, NOW membership had swollen to 260,000 members.[54] NOW's various efforts to secure ratification account for much of its mobilization success,[55] an assessment confirmed by more recent case studies of NOW chapters throughout the United States whose memberships swelled the more the chapters expanded their efforts to work in behalf of ratification.[56] One reason people are drawn to a social movement is the sense of being able to make a difference,[57] and that is what the movement offered. Women joined the ERA's ratification movement out of profound belief in the cause and a conviction that their effort would make a material contribution to changing societal views regarding gender roles.[58]

Accordingly, while the ERA failed to achieve ratification, it served as a resource for building the women's movement by mobilizing movement members, by legitimizing the cause of women's rights, and by framing the claim for equality under law within the established, legally-derived category of securing ratification of a constitutional amendment.[59]

Salience, Media Coverage, Elite Support, and Mobilization of Funding: A rights-based social action strategy can become a resource for movement building by facilitating a favorable change in public opinion through media coverage, by adding public salience to a movement's agenda, by securing affinity group allies, and by mobilizing funding. These forces help build political movements, and the push for the ERA's ratification did all of these things.

With respect to media coverage and the desire to place gender equality prominently on the public agenda, ERA activists self-consciously chose the strategy of a constitutional amendment as a way to demonstrate the seriousness of their rights claiming. Mary Eastwood, an early ERA supporter, wrote an internal memorandum for NOW in 1967 in which she stated that whether or not the ERA is adopted by Congress and ratified by the states, vigorously pushing for it will show women are demanding equal rights and responsibilities under the law "by the most drastic legal means possible—a constitutional amendment."[60] As a means of adding salience to the cause of women's equality, the strategy of campaigning for the ERA was successful. By the early 1970s when Congress began to take the ERA seriously, NOW had become adept at getting publicity by taking advantage of a "press blitz" that focused on the ERA, which NOW had advanced as one of three principal initiatives.[61] NOW's executive director at the time stated that NOW had great difficulty keeping up with all of the media inquiries, and January through March of 1970, the months immediately preceding the first congressional hearings on the ERA, witnessed a barrage of press coverage.[62] Empirical evidence substantiates the conjunction of this surge in media coverage for the emerging women's movement and the intensification of the ERA push. For example, one study measured publicity for topics related to the women's movement by examining the *New York Times Index* and the *Readers' Guide to Periodical Literature* and concluded that listings were constant from 1965 to 1968 and then substantially increased after 1969 and into the 1970s.[63] This was exactly the time when the ERA most significantly gained legitimacy through the Senate hearings in May 1970, the fight to get the ERA to the House floor in August 1970, more Senate hearings and debate on the floor of the Senate in the fall of 1970, renewed hearings and votes in the House in 1971, and finally congressional approval of the ERA following the Senate's vote in March 1972.[64]

Additional research substantiates that the ERA gave the women's movement salience through soaring increases in media coverage. Research relying on *Readers' Guide* data and circulation data of major magazines demonstrates a sharp escalation in coverage of both women's rights issues and the women's liberation movement during the period 1970–1971, the time when Congress was most focused on the ERA and the ERA had gained national attention.[65] This increase in media coverage could not be explained by judicial opinions favorable to women's rights because the increase in media converge occurred before the Court had decided any major sex discrimination cases.[66] While the level of media attention on women's issues and the women's movement dropped off somewhat after 1971, it remained significantly higher over the next five years (1972–1976) than during any other comparable period going back to 1940.[67] This ERA-induced upsurge in media coverage coincided with a dramatic increase in 1971 (the year Congress most intensely was considering the ERA) in the numbers of those who favored efforts to strengthen and change women's status in society.[68] While much more was going on with respect to the women's rights movement in the early 1970s than just the ERA, the evidence is compelling that, through the expanded media coverage it generated, the ERA operated as a resource that provided the women's movement salience and prominence on the public agenda.

The effort to ratify the ERA also mobilized support for women's rights from influential allies.[69] Four presidents stated their support for the ERA: Eisenhower, Kennedy, Johnson, and Nixon. The number of votes in the House and the Senate in support of the ERA was far greater than the two-thirds vote needed for congressional passage of a constitutional amendment. Virtually all of organized labor (except the AFL-CIO itself) ultimately came to support the ERA. President Nixon's Task Force on Women's Rights supported the ERA, as did his Citizen's Advisory Council on the Status of Women. By 1970, dozens of governmental, labor, lay, and professional groups supported the ERA.[70] Moreover, every poll conducted by polling organizations, academic research institutes, and news organizations substantiated that national majorities favored the ERA.[71] One of the more notable decisions that NOW leadership made was to frame the pro-ERA agenda as a crusade benefitting both sexes. This helped women build a strong movement by encouraging partnership with men.[72] In terms of mobilizing public opinion generally and promoting elite support for the ERA in particular, the ERA ratification effort is a paradigmatic example of collective legal mobilization theory in action.

Additional evidence that the ERA operated as a resource for mobilizing women and building an effective movement is the increased revenue made available to women's rights organizations during the effort to ratify the ERA. Jane Mansbridge has reported that many ERA supporters concluded that their individual support was needed to avoid failure of the ERA ratification effort, motivating many women to make a contribution for a political cause for the first time in their lives. Sometimes the contributions were small and sometimes they were large, but the point is that the ERA increasingly helped women to view themselves as political actors advancing an important political cause.[73] Many studies show a growth in financial contributions to women's groups as these organizations mobilized to secure the ERA's ratification. For example, annual revenues at NOW increased from $26,000 in 1970 to $521,000 in 1974 as a result of recruitment successes built around support for the ERA.[74] The ERA ratification period also witnessed increases in the number and size of foundation grants to women's rights organizations.[75] A special direct mail fund-raising campaign by NOW in 1973 netted $150,000.[76] There can be little doubt that the ERA, and the ratification effort mounted in its behalf, were causal agents for mobilizing increased financial support for the women's movement.

Creating a Political Legacy: Another pathway through which a rights-based social action strategy can have a lasting political impact is that a movement that is built endures, as does the raised political consciousness of its supporters, creating a legacy that is available for future struggles. Here again the ERA ratification effort operated as predicted. Feminist groups helped raise consciousness about women's roles, sexuality, and family issues and converted women's individual discontent into a political issue.[77] These attitudinal transformations stimulated major advances toward legal equality that have endured, notwithstanding the failure to ratify the ERA. An excellent example of the ERA's political legacy can be found in the contemporary vibrancy of the National Organization for Women, which "cut its teeth," as it were, on the ratification effort. Following the defeat of the ERA, NOW transformed itself from a social movement to a fixture in the interest group community.[78] Mainstream forms of political action, such as financing political campaigns, dominate its agenda.[79] In recent years, NOW and a variety of other women's groups have formed coalitions with different and overlapping membership bases to pool resources and coordinate efforts to influence the legislative process.[80] Nor is the fight for constitutional change a dead letter at NOW, which continues to urge support for the Constitutional Equality Amendment (CEA).[81] In addition, the campaign to enact the ERA precipitated a national conversation regarding equal rights for women that has had a profound impact on contemporary legal doctrine and political attitudes regarding gender equality.[82] While the ERA's defeat disappointed its supporters, it awakened the need for more effective grassroots political organizing to elect profeminist candidates and attain advantageous social legislation. In short, many of the changes in social policy, law, and politics over the past thirty years can be traced to the social mobilization that the ERA's defeat inspired.[83]

Backlash: The ERA amendment effort, which operated as a resource for building the women's rights movement, had a quite similar effect on the politics of "counter mobilization"—the group-based resistance to the ERA. The anti-ERA movement also adopted a rights-claiming strategy, framing its claim as the right not to be burdened by the ill-effects of an ERA being added to the Constitution. ERA opponents were able to parlay their rights-claiming strategy into a resource for building an anti-ERA movement by deploying many of the same pathways used to build the pro-ERA movement.[84]

For example, anti-ERA activists were able to mobilize elite support for their anti-ERA movement by recruiting Phyllis Schlafly and her Stop ERA organization to lead this counter mobilization. Schlafly brought a national reputation to the anti-ERA effort: she had run for Congress, played a pivotal role in Barry Goldwater's campaign to gain the 1964 Republican nomination for president, and authored a monthly publication, *The Phyllis Schlafly Report*, that provided an intellectual and ideological foundation for the anti-ERA movement. Stop ERA recruited elite allies and formed coalitions with church groups, women's organizations, and pro-family groups. In addition, claiming the right not to be bound by the constitutional strictures that the ERA would impose operated as a catalyst mobilizing financial support through, for example, the Stop ERA PAC.[85] Finally, as with the pro-ERA ratification effort, the anti-ERA movement left a lasting political legacy. As many writers have noted, Phyllis Schlafly's involvement in the movement to defeat the ERA represented the conservative movement focusing on social issues and turning away from sole focus on traditional grassroots conservative issues such as anticommunism, fiscal restraint, and national defense.[86] In other words, successful opposition to the ERA not only represented an immediate political victory for the political right but also, in the process, revived political conservatism in ways that positioned it to become predominate in many aspects of US politics throughout the 1980s and beyond.

From the viewpoint of movement dynamics, the lesson is clear: the ERA debate that increasingly mobilized social movement activity was a double-edged sword. In other words, the ERA ratification effort shows how rights talk can not only mobilize support for a cause by focusing attention on certain beliefs and values and thereby activate political consciousness, but it can also mobilize a backlash.[87]

A "Politics of Rights" Account of Other Failed Constitutional Amendments

Amending the Constitution's Three-Fifths Clause

At the Founding, the Constitutional Convention struck a bargain with the Southern states. In return for their agreeing to join the new government, it was agreed that slaves must be counted for purposes of calculating representation in the House of Representatives and electors to choose the president. The negotiated compromise was that each slave would count as three-fifths of a person. This was referred to as the Three-Fifths Clause, also known as the federal ratio.[88] The greater the number of slaves in the state, the greater a state's national political influence would be.

The Constitution's Three-Fifths Clause secured Southern domination of national politics until the Civil War.[89] As Northern and Southern economic, social, and political cultures drew apart in the early nineteenth century, Northern resentment of the Clause soared. Especially in New England, Federalists viewed the Three-Fifths Clause and the resulting over-representation of the South in Congress and the Electoral College as the source of Southern dominance of the federal government and their own political displacement. The distress New England felt about this constitutional provision was exacerbated by the Louisiana Purchase and the resulting likelihood of the admission of even more slave states. Abolitionists concluded that upholding the Three-Fifths Clause enabled slavery by sanctioning it.[90] Accordingly, the Clause prompted many amendment attempts, none having a serious chance of succeeding when proposed, but all building a political case against Southern slave power and laying a foundation for an antislavery movement.[91]

For example, in the summer of 1804 the Massachusetts legislature adopted a resolution recommending repeal of the Three-Fifths Clause by constitutional amendment. Under this provision, congressional representation would be "apportioned among the several states according to the number of their free inhabitants. . . ." Called the Ely Amendment, two senators from Massachusetts introduced the proposal in Congress.[92] The proposed Ely Amendment generated heated debate. Ten state legislatures expressed their strong disagreement with the Massachusetts proposal. Contemporaries charged that Massachusetts proposed the Ely Amendment not as a good faith effort to amend the Constitution but rather "to gather public opinion on the fitness of dividing the Union."[93] To that portion of the accusation claiming that the amendment's introduction was designed to "gather public opinion," the amendment's sponsors no doubt happily would have pleaded "guilty as charged." For as they surely knew, and as collective legal mobilization theory developed more than a century later has verified, one link between amendment efforts (rights claiming) and movement building is its effect on raising the public salience of the cause.

The 1804 amendment effort to repeal the Three-Fifths Clause was renewed about a decade later when the Hartford Convention proposed a series of constitutional amendments. This time both the Massachusetts and the Connecticut legislatures supported the repeal proposal. These amendment proposals again operated as a catalyst for public debate, and again a majority of the states passed resolutions of disapproval.[94] The Hartford Convention's proposed repeal of the Three-Fifths Clause nevertheless was instrumental: it kept the issue of Southern slave power at the forefront of the political agenda.

The arousing-public-opinion effect of these failed amendment efforts to rid the Constitution of the Three-Fifths Clause reached a crescendo in 1843 when the Massachusetts legislature again adopted a repeal resolution and arranged for the introduction in Congress of a constitutional amendment repealing the Three-Fifths Clause. Herman Ames, the authoritative chronicler of attempted constitutional change during the Constitution's first century, reports that this time the proposal "awakened great excitement not only in Congress, but also in the Southern States." Its introduction in the House of Representatives generated much debate, and three Southern states proposed counter-resolutions that the House adopted. These counter-resolutions condemned Massachusetts for its resolution and provided that the House would refuse even to consider the Massachusetts resolution since it was "faithless to the compromises of the Constitution" and in truth was a proposition to dissolve the union. This prompted debate whether the right of the people to amend the Constitution extended to the Three-Fifths Clause on the same terms as it extended to most other constitutional clauses or whether the Three-Fifths Clause was immune from good faith attempts to repeal it through the Article V amendment process. Ames concluded that the vote of the House not to refer the Massachusetts Resolution for consideration ended efforts to repeal the Three-Fifths Clause but "indicated the presence of an 'irrepressible conflict.'"[95] With the benefit of collective legal mobilization theory, Ames might well also have added that the several amendments proposing repeal of the Three-Fifths Clause operated as resources in building public support for an antislavery movement. These failed amendment efforts were designed to raise public consciousness, arouse public opinion in opposition to slavery, move the slavery issue to the forefront of the public's attention, stir up controversy, promote debate, and enlist elite support. The amendments to eliminate the Three-Fifths Clause were paradigmatic examples of rights claiming designed to activate opposition to slavery and begin the process of building an effective antislavery movement.[96]

Antislavery Amendments

John Quincy Adams may not be our best-known former president but he is one of the more interesting ones. Following his 1825–1829 presidency, Adams was elected to the House of Representatives, began his service there in 1831, and served in that office until his death in 1848. While serving in the House following his presidency, Adams established an early precedent of using the constitutional amendment process as a resource for movement building, in his case two related movements—the antislavery movement and a new political organization that emerged as the Republican Party.

This narrative begins with the dominance of the Jeffersonian Republicans (which morphed into Jacksonian Democrats) in presidential politics during the sixty-four-year period from 1800 to 1864. During this period, the opposition Federalist-Whig political organizations were able to occupy the White House for only sixteen years and were able to elect only one president with a majority of the popular vote—William Henry Harrison.[97] In the early 1840s the Whigs attempted to revive their fortunes by building a coalition movement of Whigs and Northern Democrats around some version of antislavery. Adams's relentless denunciation of slavery became their voice of respectability and virtue as they attempted to organize around the concept of free soil.[98]

Initially, Adams was drawn to the fight against slavery through his opposition to restraints on free speech. By 1840 many Southern states had banned discussion of slavery.[99] During the 1835–1836 congressional session, the slave-power interests in the House of Representatives possessed sufficient influence to be able to impose a gag rule that automatically tabled all petitions to eliminate slavery, including those proposing constitutional amendments.[100] Viewing these restraints on free speech as a manifestation of slave power run amok, Adams increasingly devoted his time in the House of Representatives to the defeat of slavery.

For eight years Adams built opposition to the gag rule by deploying the twin strategies of Constitution amending and filing petitions on behalf of citizen groups. Prior to 1860, few constitutional amendments had been proposed addressing the question of slavery. One notable exception was Adams's introduction of a constitutional amendment in 1839 to abolish hereditary slavery after 1842, to forbid admission of slave states after 1845, and immediately to prohibit slavery and the slave trade in Washington, DC.[101] In addition, during the 1838–1839 congressional session alone, Adams introduced an amazing 693 petitions of various types that he had received from citizens throughout the United States. One commentator likened the aging Adams to "a dangerous old bear" whose modern equivalent might be Jane Fonda presenting petitions from Southeast Asians during the Vietnam War.[102]

As a political realist, Adams harbored no illusions of gaining congressional support for an amendment banning slavery.[103] Adams's introduction of a constitutional amendment providing for emancipation nevertheless had a serious political purpose—to raise the critical issue of how long the Democratic coalition of Northern and Southern agrarians could hold together in the face of increasingly expressed antislavery views. Adams's motivation was not so much a genuine attempt to amend the Constitution as it was an effort to politicize and publicize the view that slavery in the United States could not continue indefinitely.[104]

Adams's constitutional amendment and petition efforts in the House of Representatives had the intended effect of raising the public profile of the abolitionist viewpoint. For example, the struggle reversing the gag rule generated extensive press coverage that dramatized the widening rift regarding slavery.[105] Moreover, while Adams waged an attack on the gag rule out of conviction to vindicate freedom of expression, the attack also furnished moral support to those opposed to slavery and became an effective means to shape public opinion opposing slavery.[106] In addition, the public debate that resulted from Adams's campaign created many new converts to the antislavery cause and the American Anti-Slavery Society.[107] Southern slaveholders and their congressional allies desperately sought to banish discussion of the slavery issue from politics and the public square. Adams's use of the constitutional amendment process and other tactics dealt a crippling blow to the goal of erecting such a wall of silence.[108] Finally, in 1844 Adams was vindicated when the House repealed the gag rule.[109]

The importance of the consciousness-raising effect of Adams's constitutional amendment and petition proposals can be appreciated more fully when one understands the obstacles facing pre-Civil War abolitionists. Two of the more formidable hurdles were public apathy and the widely held attitude that helping slaves was an encroachment on society's established order. Because slavery had become so deeply rooted in American culture, even those not directly benefitting from its continuance were disinclined to assist abolitionists.[110] Veneration of the Constitution also contributed to public apathy regarding slavery, at least with respect to attacking the continuation of slavery in the states where it existed. Even among those who opposed slavery, the dominant ideology was that a constitutional bargain had been struck with the South in order to induce the Southern states to join the Union, which precluded federal interference with each state's autonomy to decide the slavery question for itself. To attack the constitutional bargain of 1787 was to attack the foundations of the Union. For this reason, at least initially, abolitionists demanding immediate emancipation of several million slaves were viewed as extremists and reviled for their unyielding commitment to the antislavery cause.[111] Moreover, it can be difficult for a twenty-first-century observer to appreciate that during the time that the antislavery movement was gaining strength, slavery was widely viewed by many as a respectable practice, even among those who would choose not to own slaves. Indeed, eight of the first twelve presidents were slaveholders. Until 1856, no major party at the national level had categorically opposed slavery.[112]

Adams's proposed constitutional amendment and petition efforts confronted these public attitudes supportive of slavery. John Quincy Adams, a former president, son of a president, and member of the House of Representatives, provided elite support to the antislavery point of view. Adams made open opposition to slavery a far more respectable activity and raised antislavery to the forefront of the public agenda. By the time the nation elected Lincoln as president, the Republican Party had branded slavery as an immoral and barbaric practice—perhaps a constitutional right but nevertheless a moral wrong that must be put on a course of extinction.[113] Deploying the constitutional amendment process as a tool to attack slavery thus provided the unique advantage of permitting one to challenge the slave system with honor: slavery would be eliminated not by breaking the 1787 constitutional covenants with the South but by renegotiating the constitutional contract. The point was not that the constitutional amendment effort would succeed but that the Article V strategy permitted honorable opposition to slavery to gain a footing.

One last point warrants consideration. Slavery had a corrosive effect on abolitionists. It caused them to lose faith in the constitutional system. For example, abolitionists such as William Lloyd Garrison argued that by countenancing slavery in the Constitution, the United States had made "a covenant with death, and an agreement with hell."[114] Garrison and his ilk basically gave up on the Constitution's redemptive capacity and lacked faith in the nation's ability to correct the Constitution. They argued that in order for the North not to be corrupted by the South and be consumed by the South's increasingly oppressive political demands that the institution of slavery be protected, it would be best for the South to secede and thus eliminate the scourge of slavery from our constitutionalism.[115]

With the benefit of hindsight, it becomes clear that Adams's introduction of a constitutional amendment resolution and other petitions to challenge the gag rule helped precipitate the efforts to find a long-range political solution to the problems created by the 1787 Constitution and fueled a powerful public debate that eventually fractured intersectional unity within the Whig party. This fracture accelerated the Whig party's dissolution in the 1850s, resulting in slavery opponents forming a coalition that began as the Free Soil Party and became the nucleus of the antislavery Republican Party.[116] Garrison may not have seen the oncoming demise of Jacksonian, Democratic slave power, but as early as 1847, the year prior to Adams's death, Democratic President Polk saw the writing on the wall. He attributed the consciousness raising over the antislavery issue to political opportunism by his political opponents but acknowledged that "it cannot fail to destroy the Democratic Party."[117]

Many forces contributed to building the antislavery movement and laying the foundation for the new political organization that became the Republican Party.[118] Reviewing the historical evidence, historian Daniel Walker Howe has concluded that Adams's above-described efforts as a member of the House of Representatives "proved an incalculable benefit" to the abolitionist cause.[119] American political history has tended to undervalue Adams's use of the Article V constitutional amendment process to bestow this incalculable benefit.

Prohibition and Its Repeal

Prohibition and its repeal, of course, are not examples of failed efforts to amend the Constitution. But they are added here because examining the twin efforts to enact Prohibition and then repeal it offers insight into the ways that attempting constitutional amending become a cause agent for both the consciousness activation needed to initiate a social movement and the movement organizing needed to build an effective movement.

The core of Scheingold's politics-of-rights idea discussed earlier is that, in order to mobilize individuals and groups, social activist cadres must modify how individuals understand their discontents.[120] Legal mobilization becomes possible once a citizen's discontent no longer is understood as an individual problem but rather as a social problem that has been accorded some form of political legitimacy and thus becomes a political problem requiring a political solution.[121] Scheingold might just as well have been referring to the collective mobilizations that helped build the Prohibition movement and later the movement for its repeal. In both cases, the amendment effort activated political consciousness. Discontent initially arose regarding the harmful societal effects of alcohol consumption, and later from the adverse societal effects caused by the government's ban on alcohol consumption. The constitutional amendment process assisted in converting each discontent into a perceived unjust denial of an entitlement—first the perceived entitlement to live in a society constitutionally shielded from the evils of alcohol consumption, and later the felt entitlement to be constitutionally protected from the government's intrusion on the free choice to consume alcohol.

The opportunity to amend the Constitution also facilitated organizing effective pro- and anti-Prohibition social movements. The national efforts, first to add the Eighteenth Amendment and then to repeal it, operated as resources for movement building by motivating citizens to engage in active political participation, many for the first time. Few Americans remained unaware of or indifferent to the constitutional changes being proposed. Indeed, Prohibition is on a short list, which also includes only the ERA, slavery abolition, and women's suffrage, of the constitutional amendment proposals that drew the most individuals into political activism.[122]

Activation: In terms of activating a political consciousness opposing alcohol consumption, Article V must share pride of place with political action opportunities made available under state law. This is because Prohibition had been debated in state legislatures for decades prior to the adoption of the Eighteenth Amendment. By the time the United States entered World War I in 1917 (thus prior to the 1919 ratification of the Eighteenth Amendment), twenty-six states had adopted Prohibition, mostly in the south and west.[123] Prohibition was an example of a states-first strategy having a bottom-up impact on national amendment politics.[124]

Having twenty-six states already in their pocket was a great asset for Prohibition supporters attempting to organize a nationwide constitutional amendment movement, but success required ratification from thirty-six of the then forty-eight states. Thus, to secure ratification of the Eighteenth Amendment, it became necessary for the existing grassroots support for state prohibition laws to morph into a national political movement. To activate the political consciousness of citizens in dry states and mobilize their support for national Prohibition through a constitutional amendment, it was necessary to design a strategy demonstrating that Prohibition was both desirable and plausible. The Article V constitutional amendment process became the means for accomplishing both of those goals by stimulating a nationwide democratic dialogue over the proposed Eighteenth Amendment.

Organizing: The successful effort to adopt the Eighteenth Amendment, and the subsequent successful repeal effort, developed a "template for political action" that influenced the structure of all subsequent social movement–building efforts.[125] First, the Prohibition controversy demonstrated the importance of building a reform movement around a specific reform goal (Prohibition or its repeal) rather than around several diffuse goals. Empirical research has substantiated the importance of selecting a well-defined, circumscribed issue that can unite potential supporters.[126] Second, the fight for adoption and then repeal of a Prohibition amendment demonstrated how constitutional amendment efforts can serve as a means for scattered and atomized potential reformers to settle on a unified protest theme, unite with others in a common cause, and gain emotional and intellectual support from association with other like-minded individuals. The single-issue reform movements that Prohibition and then its repeal spawned catapulted talented, energetic (and also many eminent, wealthy, and influential) persons to leadership positions, where they added respectability to the cause. For example, the Women's Organization for National Prohibition Reform (WONPR) was formed through the initiative of Pauline Morton Sabin, heiress to the Morton Salt fortune, a daughter of Theodore Roosevelt's secretary of the navy, wife of a J. P. Morgan partner, and the first female member of the Republican National Committee. The WONPR was able to pull in other socially prominent women such as Mrs. Archibald B. Roosevelt, Mrs. E. Roland Harriman, and Mrs. Coffin Van Rensselaer, among others.[127] The Prohibition controversy also illuminated the importance of forming alliances with other political groups as a way to create a catalytic effect for changing public sentiment.[128]

In addition, the Prohibition experience illustrated how constitutional amendment efforts can increase the public salience of a cause through media coverage. As the battle for repealing Prohibition progressed, the increasingly "wet" press provided support for repeal by actively reporting the substantial erosion of societal support for Prohibition.[129]

Finally, Prohibition proved how one reform effort can reinforce other reforms. For example, the effort to secure Prohibition added great support to the suffrage movement (and vice versa). The two movements resulted in a permanent shift in political activism by women's groups that manifested itself in women's opposition to the McCarthyite Red Hunts in the 1950s, coalesced in the Women's Movement of the 1970s and 1980s, and can be seen even today in the increased level of women's participation in business and elective politics.[130]

The Prohibition controversy exerted another well-documented effect on America's political and legal culture. It spawned the Back to the People constitutional amendment effort.[131] Opponents of Prohibition and women's suffrage endured twin defeats due to the 1919 ratification of the Eighteenth Amendment and the 1920 ratification of the Nineteenth Amendment. The opponents of these two amendments blamed the Article V amendment process for their defeats, instead of acknowledging that the proponents of these amendments had more effectively harnessed mass appeal and mobilized political power. The opponents of these two newly ratified amendments asserted that the existing Article V procedures for constitutional change failed to measure the will of the people accurately because state legislative ratification had determined the outcome rather than a direct vote by each state's citizens.

Immediate repeal of the Eighteenth and Nineteenth Amendments was politically unrealistic, so opponents of Prohibition and women's suffrage opted instead to propose that the Article V constitutional amendment procedures be changed through constitutional amendment. The goal was to amend Article V by reducing the role of the state legislatures and shifting more amendment authority to individual citizens. The Back to the People Amendment, introduced in Congress on April 13, 1921, proposed three major revisions to Article V procedure: 1) that at least one branch of the state legislature must have been elected after the submission of the amendment for state ratification; 2) that a state would be authorized to hold a popular referendum to affirm or overturn a state legislature's ratification;[132] and 3) that a state would be permitted to change its ratification vote until three-fourths of the states had ratified or one-fourth of the states had rejected the proposed amendment.

This amendment proposal has been characterized as a "quixotic gesture" designed to make it more difficult for Progressives to amend the Constitution.[133] The contempt for Article V's procedures expressed in this proposed amendment never matured into any subsequent alteration in Article V procedures, but it did serve as a symbolic conservative rallying point.

The proposed amendment also influenced adoption of the Twenty-First Amendment, which repealed Prohibition. The movement shaped the public debate through its repeated refrain that "the People" were never consulted adequately, they never wanted Prohibition in the first place, and the Eighteenth Amendment never would have been ratified but for the fact that Congress provided for ratification by state legislatures rather than a direct vote by each state's citizens. In response to this claim, Congress added a provision when approving the Twenty-First Amendment for ratification by state convention rather than by state legislatures. Article V provides for this but ratification by state convention had never previously been used and has never since been used.[134]

2

Amendment Efforts as a Resource for Expressing Dissent and Promoting Deliberation

Following the Supreme Court's decision in *Citizens United*,[1] grassroots activists called corporate abolitionists organized Move to Amend, a campaign to amend the Constitution to abolish corporate personhood. Such an amendment would reverse judicial decisions that interpret the Constitution to provide corporations the constitutional status of "persons," thereby investing these entities with constitutional rights such as the right to free speech and religious liberty.[2]

A mass movement attempting to amend the Constitution as a means to reverse a Supreme Court decision has been attempted successfully[3] and unsuccessfully[4] many times in the past; however, this particular constitutional amendment effort is noteworthy for its self-conscious motivation. Supporters have no illusion of any realistic likelihood that this effort will result in the adoption of their proposed constitutional amendment. Rather, their goal is transforming the meaning of the Constitution through the *process of attempting to amend* the Constitution, a strategy most famously deployed successfully by the women's movement through the failed ERA effort. Supporters of corporate abolitionists' Move to Amend campaign argue that constitutional amendment efforts can succeed in moving constitutional policy in a preferred direction, including inducing modification of judicial precedent, without the need to gain ratification of a constitutional amendment.[5]

Sometimes a constitutional amendment effort is simply a way to express dissent and anger, but leaves little if any trace on policy. However, the corporate abolitionist activists are correct that sometimes an effort to amend can shift constitutional meaning toward a position advocated by those seeking the amendment without the need for congressional approval of the amendment proposal.[6] There are many examples of proposed constitutional amendments that "failed" in the sense of not adding new language to the Constitution, but succeeded in modifying public policy, including the Court's constitutional jurisprudence. The corporate abolitionists have assembled a variety of arguments describing how their mobilization of dissent through championing a constitutional amendment can alter constitutional meaning. But fully understanding their viewpoint requires dissecting the operative processes that explain *how and why* a proposed constitutional amendment can serve as a transformative agent shifting public policy, including judicial policy.

The threshold argument that corporate abolitionists advance is that the Article V amendment process can be used to provide citizens a voice in law reform by creating opportunities to express opinions and outrage over established constitutional understandings.[7] This might profitably be understood as the *bully pulpit effect*, a way to inform the Court of strongly held disagreements with certain aspects of the Court's constitutional doctrine. The process of proposing a constitutional amendment may create opportunities to communicate group dissent, but what requires clarification are the operative mechanisms that can convert the bully pulpit's dissent, even thunderous dissent, into the Court's reconsideration of its constitutional views.

A second strand of the corporate abolitionists' account of how the act of proposing a constitutional amendment can influence constitutional meaning adopts the rhetoric of what is sometimes referred to as *popular constitutionalism*. Here, the claim is that courts do not have the final say with respect to constitutional interpretation. The Constitution belongs to "We the People," and the Supreme Court lacks institutional authority to entrench the Constitution's meaning.[8] Popular constitutionalists appropriate Sanford Levinson's groundbreaking book *Constitutional Faith* to adopt what Levinson calls a "protestant" constitutional view, one that accepts the legitimacy of individual interpretations of constitutional meaning and rejects a "catholic" view of the Constitution where the Supreme Court possesses exclusive and final authority to say what the Constitution means.[9] The rhetoric of popular constitutionalism proclaims that the Court may interpret but "the People" are the rulers in a democracy. When "the People" understand a Supreme Court decision as "judicial usurpation of the people's sovereignty," "the People" possess democratic authority to alter the judicial interpretation.[10] Whatever the normative merit (or lack of merit) of this version of popular constitutionalism, it presents formidable practical difficulties in operation. Left uncertain is who are "the People" whose constitutional understandings qualify as ones that trump the constitutional understandings of others? Moreover, how do "the People" go about claiming the power to be the "rulers" with final authority over constitutional meaning? And what are "the People" to do with the power to control constitutional meaning once they claim it?[11] In other words, how does this popular constitutionalism go about changing constitutional meaning on the ground, in terms of practical politics?

A third component of popular constitutionalism's account of how a proposed constitutional amendment can move judicial policy focuses on a proposed amendment's capacity to encourage citizens' participation in a *constitutional dialectic*. Robust reflection on the Constitution's proper interpretation helps maintain the Constitution's vitality among the citizenry in a variety of ways: constitutional issues are transposed from issues to be resolved by judicial technocrats to matters for citizen consideration; citizens become educated regarding constitutional meaning; and the process of debate and contention over constitutional understandings bonds citizens to our constitutional system and encourages respect for the Constitution. Thus, it is argued, under favorable circumstances social movements can become a catalyst for debate that shifts societal values.[12] Assuming for the moment the validity of that premise, what needs to be explained are the decisional mechanics used by Supreme Court justices that might illuminate how and why altering societal values can influence constitutional interpretation at the Court.

Proposing a constitutional amendment can have the effect of shaping the Court's constitutional interpretations. The notions of a bully pulpit, popular (protestant) constitutionalism, and alteration of societal values through the process of a dialectic provide helpful insights, but more is needed to explain how and why proposing a constitutional amendment can influence judicial doctrine. A fourth factor must be added: the *power of public opinion*, a force to which the Court responds when combined with the power of the bully pulpit, the ideological legitimacy of individual dissent (protestant constitutionalism), and the import of changing societal values. Understanding the interrelationship of these four political forces helps clarify how proposing a constitutional amendment can alter constitutional meaning over time.

Public Opinion's Influence on the Formation of Constitutional Meaning

The harmony between the Supreme Court's constitutional decisions and public opinion is empirically demonstrable. One of the more famous observations in this regard is that the public has historically shown great support for the Court because the Court generally has "told the country what it wanted to hear," and furnished the nation's dominant interests a constitutional justification to "do what they wanted to do."[13] This kinship between the Court's decisions and the desires of the country's dominant political actors has been tested empirically and verified repeatedly. An exhaustive survey of 231 policy changes between 1935 and 1979 found that US political institutions generally (at both the federal and state level) are responsive to public opinion when the public considers the issue important and when opinion does not fluctuate.[14] Moreover, empirical studies of the Supreme Court's decisions show they conform to public opinion in roughly the same ratio as do the decisions of the elected branches of government.[15] An analysis of the decisions of fifteen Supreme Court justices between 1953 and 1992 has confirmed the influence of public opinion on individual justices' decisions, either by altering their factual perceptions or by shaping their normative assumptions.[16]

These findings are not surprising given that the Court's sensitivity to public opinion is a historical fact. In 1924, Chief Justice William Howard Taft worked behind the scenes prodigiously with the popular press to fend off adverse public opinion and generate public support for the Court at a time when it was under attack for preferring the economic interests of business over the personal liberties of citizens.[17] Justice Benjamin Cardozo acknowledged that judges are influenced by contemporary beliefs and feelings because "the great tides and currents which engulf the rest of men do not turn aside in their course and pass the judges by."[18] With refreshing candor, Seventh Circuit Court of Appeals judge Richard Posner has acknowledged that judges face the possibility of reprisal should they too often rule contrary to strongly held public opinion.[19] When asked how far the Court could deviate from public opinion, Chief Justice Rehnquist responded that "we are not able to do so and it probably would be unwise to try."[20]

The weight of academic appraisal is that courts must be, and generally are, mindful of public opinion. One of the best-known studies is that of Robert McCloskey, who concluded that justices ignore public opinion at their peril, and history shows that the Court seldom has strayed significantly from mainstream American values.[21] Robert Dahl came to essentially the same conclusion, finding that federal judicial decisions generally conform to public opinion and that a close examination of the Court's decisions reveals a high correlation between the Court's dominant policy positions and the dominant policy preferences of the nation's lawmaking majorities.[22]

This same assessment prevails when one carefully examines the current work of the Court. Barry Friedman summed up the findings of a broad array of judicial experts, as well as his own, when he concluded that the

Court's constitutional work does not run contrary to the popular will because the court could not sustain itself in the face of popular opposition. Historically, and into the present, the Court generally has followed popular opinion, seldom veering far from the mainstream.[23] After examining the leading literature on the impact of public opinion on the Supreme Court's decisions, Keith Whittington has concluded that judicial decisions are shaped by many of the same forces that shape decisions of public officials—alterations of public opinion and political and social forces.[24]

The Court's historic acquiescence to popular opinion reinforces a strategic account of the Court's decision-making process. A strategic account assumes that judges are goal-directed actors whose choices are structured, at least in part, by their expectations about the preferences and choices of other actors who are in a position to frustrate or promote their goals, such as elected officials or the public.[25] The Court has an institutional stake in not venturing far from public opinion as it is expressed by the desires of the elected branches of the federal government. This occurs because the Court is both a judicial and a political institution, particularly when asked to render judgments on constitutional matters involving controversial questions affecting national policy such as religious freedom, race relations, gender equality, voting rights, and the like.[26] Over its roughly 225-year institutional life the Court has been part of the dominant national political alliance. The Court cannot sustain itself for long if it flagrantly opposes that alliance's major policies, and the Court is seldom tempted to do so.[27] The political branches of government have the means to discipline the Court if necessary and, in any event, lacking enforcement power, the Court's authority ultimately depends on support from the political branches.[28] The clear consensus among those who have studied the Court carefully is that the Court becomes the agent of its own preservation by resolving questions about the meaning of the Constitution in conformance with the dominant views of the ruling regime.[29]

Disputes over constitutional meaning thus are best understood as contests by political competitors over who possesses the institutional authority to enforce a particular constitutional vision. In such struggles, the Court normally is a side show. As political competitors vie for authority to interpret the Constitution, the audiences that most need convincing are powerful private interests and congressional leaders.[30] Transformative leaders are those who are able to "amend" the Constitution outside the procedures provided by Article V by overcoming institutional obstructions impeding acceptance of their constitutional visions.[31]

In short, the process of developing constitutional meaning entails powerful political actors deliberating until constitutional meaning is achieved through consensus.³² Because we have been taught to think that constitutional change occurs, and should occur, solely through the Article V formal amendment process, few Americans have pondered the operative constitutional political process, the paths that in fact account for most contemporary change in our constitutive rules. As scholars have struggled to capture the complex strategies employed in contemporary constitutional politics to achieve this consensus, the metaphors pile up. For example, the mechanism has been referred to as legal doctrine developing in a larger context composed of a "seamless web" of interconnected social and power processes.³³ Constitutional development has been visualized as dialogue between the Supreme Court and the American people.³⁴ Alexander Bickel called it a "continuing colloquy" between political institutions and the citizenry.³⁵ Rejecting the view that the process is linear with courts issuing the final word, other court observers have urged understanding the process as one that is more circular, constantly revolving around competing visions of the Constitution until a satisfactory outcome in achieved.³⁶ Prior to her elevation to the Court, Justice Ruth Bader Ginsburg also employed the dialogue metaphor, stating that courts do not alone shape legal doctrine but rather engage in an ongoing dialogue with the other branches of government and the citizenry.³⁷ Irrespective of the metaphor chosen, they share a common denominator: the Constitution is given meaning through collective responsibility among many participants using a variety of strategies in an intricate political process that has many moving parts.³⁸

The corporate abolition adherents referred to earlier have helpfully isolated some of the moving parts that make a difference. They are correct, for example, that using a constitutional amendment proposal as a bully pulpit is an important ingredient for effecting constitutional change. A bully pulpit assists in the process of moving public opinion, attracting media attention, inviting elite support for a preferred alteration of existing understandings of constitutional meaning, and informing the Court of the seriousness of the dissent to the Court's current judicial policies. Moreover, adoption of a protestant ideology of constitutionalism legitimates (and thus encourages) the formation of citizen movements to press their constitutional visions on governmental officials. And, of course, striving to shift societal values regarding constitutional meaning through proposing a constitutional amendment is a major goal in the effort to move public opinion. By shifting societal values, political elites and government officials are more likely to accept constitutional visions consistent with such value shifts. Political actors' transcending motivation is reelection, so they disregard shifts in societal values and public opinion at their peril. And as we have seen, when transformative federal officials, the president and congressional leaders, support an alteration in constitutional meaning, the Court will not, and cannot, long resist.

The crucial point is modest but essential. In the long run, the Court is not normally the major obstacle to constitutional change. Historically, its decisions will not long venture outside the mainstream of public opinion and the preferences of dominant political leaders. Of course text matters, but most of the text of the Constitution is written at a sufficiently high level of abstraction that its meaning must emerge through a dialectic, rather than be chosen from a limited menu among several dichotomous absolutes. Political events and textual authority combine to determine constitutional meaning. The Court normally will anticipate trends in prevailing public opinion that are firm and salient, reckon the interests of powerful political elites, and adjust its decisions accordingly. Thereby, the Court participates in the majoritarian political process as a partner with the national governing coalition.[39]

Failed constitutional amendment efforts play a vital role within this interactive process that results in alteration of constitutional meaning at the Court. The ERA is an excellent example.

A Democratic Deliberation Account of the ERA

It is all too easy to forget that the Court did not invoke the Equal Protection Clause of the Fourteenth Amendment to invalidate gender discrimination until 1971 in *Reed v. Reed*, where the Court merely applied a rational basis test to find that the classification at issue lacked a rational relationship to any legitimate governmental interest.[40] Three cases between 1870 and 1895 had upheld state-sponsored gender discrimination: two denying women the right to practice law and one denying women the right to vote. As recently as the immediate post–World War II period, the Court twice upheld discriminatory state laws: one barring women from working as bartenders and one barring women (but not men) from jury service unless women expressed a desire to be added to the jury roll.[41] In all of these cases, the state was required only to demonstrate some rational connection between the discrimination and some legitimate governmental interest such as protecting women, concern for their morals, and recognition of the "Divine Law of the Creator" that women "fulfill the noble and benign offices of wife and mother."[42]

Since *Reed*, two seemingly incongruous developments occurred with respect to constitutional recognition of gender equality. First, the country rejected the ERA, and second, the Court re-interpreted the Fourteenth Amendment's Equal Protection Clause by giving it meaning as if the ERA had been ratified. As early as 2001, Court watchers had demonstrated the ERA's effective triumph, pointing out that constitutional doctrine is virtually identical to what the ERA would have required, had it been adopted.[43] Today, there is no serious dispute that constitutional law absorbed the substance of the ERA incrementally. The ERA ratification effort actuated powerful changes in public attitudes regarding gender equality, contributing to a cultural equilibrium that prodded the Court to reshape its Equal Protection jurisprudence into what has been referred to as the *de facto* ERA.[44]

But lurking in this broad consensus that the ERA ratification effort influenced the development of Equal Protection jurisprudence with respect to gender discrimination are two matters that warrant close attention. First, the ERA ratification effort contains valuable lessons for better understanding the operative mechanisms that link proposing amendments with changes in the Court's constitutional jurisprudence. Second, only in recent years have Court watchers begun to understand that the national debate over the ERA did more than simply motivate the Court to adopt a heightened level of judicial scrutiny for sex discrimination cases.[45] Once the Court agreed to enlist in the cause of banning sex discrimination, it necessarily agreed to decide the contours of constitutionally proscribed sex discrimination. Understanding how the conflict over the ratification of the ERA influenced the outcome of that judicial task provides highly useful insights into understanding additional political roles played by failed efforts to amend the Constitution.

The ERA and the Court's Decision to Grant Heightened Judicial Scrutiny to Sex Discrimination

The Supreme Court's decision to apply heightened judicial scrutiny to sex discrimination cases can be traced to a self-conscious decision by the women's movement to agitate simultaneously for a constitutional amendment and judicial interpretation of the Fifth and Fourteenth Amendments that would ban government-sponsored sex discrimination. By the beginning of 1968, such a dual strategy had become the official position of the National Organization for Women.[46] One persuasive argument for such a dual strategy was that the ERA and a judicial approach to assuring gender equality were complementary. Even if the ERA failed, fighting for a constitutional amendment would demonstrate the seriousness of women's demand for equality, help move public opinion, and thereby improve the chances of prevailing on the Fourteenth Amendment cases before the Court. Conversely, the Court's willingness to find protection from sex discrimination in the existing Constitution was uncertain at best in the early 1970s. The possibility—perhaps the likelihood—of the failure of the Fourteenth Amendment litigation strategy would become a compelling argument for ratification of the ERA. Moreover, the dual strategy avoided the risk of the women's movement putting all its eggs in one basket. If one initiative failed (as, of course, the ERA did) the other might prevail (as the Fourteenth Amendment litigation strategy did).[47]

The Fourteenth Amendment wing of the feminist movement's dual strategy claimed its first major success in *Frontiero v. Richardson*,[48] decided in May 1973, a little more than one year after Congress proposed the ERA to the states. In *Frontiero*, petitioners challenged the constitutionality of a military rule requiring only female officers to prove their spouse's economic dependency to qualify for certain allowances for quarters and for medical benefits. The Court's several opinions in *Frontiero* reveal the advantages, as well as the pitfalls, of the strategy of advancing simultaneously a judicial and a constitutional amendment strategy. The ERA ratification effort weighed heavily in nearly all of the *Frontiero* opinions.

In *Frontiero*, Justice Brennan wrote a plurality opinion for four members of the Court that adopted strict judicial scrutiny for sex discrimination cases. Treating sex discrimination cases the same as race cases, both constituting "suspect classifications," represented a reinterpretation of the Constitution.[49] In effect, the Brennan decision would moot one of the chief aims of the ERA, the ratification of which was then pending before the state legislatures. In his plurality opinion, Justice Brennan cited the ERA, along with other legislation banning gender discrimination, to demonstrate Congress's "increasing sensitivity to sex-based classifications" and to demonstrate that Congress itself had concluded that gender classifications should be considered "suspect."[50] Justice Brennan's plurality opinion in *Frontiero* found support from the ERA ratification effort in yet another way. A wealth of academic literature had grounded its argument in support of the ERA's ratification on sharp criticism of the Court for its failure to find that the Fourteenth Amendment bans state-sponsored sex discrimination. Somewhat defensively, Justice Brennan argued that the Court should now address this academic criticism by finding sex a suspect classification.[51]

Justice White, who joined the Brennan opinion, wrote his colleagues during deliberations in *Frontiero* that he would conclude that gender is a suspect classification, for the sufficient reason that by sending the ERA to the states, Congress has determined that sex discrimination is unconstitutional.[52] It is difficult to imagine better evidence than this of a nexus between a failed constitutional amendment and framing constitutional meaning.

Notably, Justice Brennan penned a private communication to Justice

Powell, soliciting Justice Powell's support for finding that gender classifications are "suspect classifications." Brennan's communication to Powell argued that the justices ought not conclude that the Court can sit back and rely on the ERA to address gender inequality, because, as Justice Brennan presciently predicted, the ERA would fail to achieve ratification.[53] In his concurring opinion, which was joined by two members of the Court, Justice Powell acknowledged the significance of the then-pending ERA but concluded that the constitutional amending process *precluded* the Court from ruling that gender is a suspect classification since that was the whole point of the pending ERA.[54]

Justice Rehnquist dissented, so Justice Stewart was the crucial fifth vote Justice Brennan needed to assemble a five-vote majority in support of his historic opinion holding that gender classifications are "suspect classifications." Journalists Bob Woodward and Scott Armstrong report in their book *The Brethren* that Justice Stewart felt conflicted because his two best friends on the Court were Powell and Brennan. He disagreed with Justice Powell that the pending ERA precluded the Court from finding that gender discrimination is a suspect classification and stated that he was agreeable to following Brennan's proposal, but would not join the Brennan opinion due to his certainty that the states would ratify the ERA, relieving the Court of the political blame.[55] Justice Stewart thus declined to become the fifth vote Brennan needed for his opinion to be the Court's majority opinion.

Because the ERA was pending, gender never achieved suspect classification status at the Court. Yet the *de facto* ERA incorporated in contemporary Equal Protection doctrine finds its source in the failed ERA ratification effort. The ERA contributed to a national consensus supportive of gender equality as manifested by Congress's overwhelming endorsement of the ERA, the broad public support for the ERA, and the early state ratifications of the ERA. The Court's opinions in *Frontiero* acknowledged this emerging concern for women's equality, and within several years following its decision in *Frontiero*, heightened judicial scrutiny eventually gained the votes of Justices Burger, Blackmun, Stewart, and Powell.[56] Advocacy for the ERA and the development of the Fourteenth Amendment's guarantee of gender equality were inextricably intertwined.

The Impact of the ERA on the Constitutional Meaning of Sex Discrimination

Once the Court agreed to assume a more activist role in promoting gender equality, it implicitly agreed to become the arbiter of the contours of the Constitution's proscriptions of sex discrimination. These are policy choices, when, for example, it is alleged that sex discrimination includes government action burdening a woman's decision to have an abortion, government refusal to fund abortions, discrimination against those who are pregnant, refusing gay couples the status of marriage, or enactment of rape laws whose proscriptions are limited to males. The national dialogue spawned by the ERA ratification effort contributed to the shaping of a national consensus regarding the meaning of gender equality.

Early on, NOW's strategy to achieve the ERA's ratification entailed, first, partnering with male groups to provide women's groups the ability to combine their political strength with the political power of men, and second, attracting a broad-based coalition of women's groups. NOW's leadership reasoned that such a strategy would attract widespread national support. To create such a large tent under which diverse women's and men's groups could unite, NOW self-consciously limited the substantive scope of the proposed ERA to bans on formal governmental action (not private action). Adoption of such a relatively narrow scope for the ERA meant rejection of entreaties from many feminists who had hoped that NOW would lead a broad assault on gender inequality and join other women's groups and civil rights groups to advance arguments for gender equality beyond feminists' traditional concern with sex discrimination in employment and other aspects of the economy, to include issues such as reproductive rights, media imagery, and educational opportunities.[57] NOW's rather conservative approach with respect to the scope of the ERA's proscriptions shaped the subsequent debate, and ultimately the societal consensus, regarding the meaning of sex discrimination proscribed by the Fourteenth Amendment's Equal Protection Clause.

The ERA's ratification effort influenced the contours of constitutionally proscribed sex discrimination through the operation of "constitutional culture"—the mechanism for changing constitutional meaning through citizenry interaction with governmental officials.[58] Reva Siegel's extraordinary scholarship, which produced ground-breaking insights into the relationship between social movement conflict and social change, provided a compelling account of how conflict over the ERA's ratification shaped modern understandings of sex discrimination.[59]

Efforts to secure, and oppose, the ratification of the ERA changed the meaning of constitutionally prohibited sex discrimination in the following way.[60] As the dual ERA/Fourteenth Amendment campaign to secure gender equality matured, advocacy on behalf of the ERA produced a vigorous counter social movement. During ERA ratification battles in the various states, as well as in sex discrimination litigation, the pro- and anti-ERA social movements each competed to secure maximum public support for its constitutional vision of gender equality.[61] An ongoing dialogue with the American public and its political leaders thus developed, one that shaped each side's rationale and moderated its claims. Winning in the court of public opinion required that each movement advance a rationale that persuaded the maximum portion of the public that its constitutional interpretation best advanced the public interest and most scrupulously redeemed the enduring principles and values enshrined in our shared constitutional traditions.[62] To add to the public appeal of its arguments and gain the confidence of the American people, each movement was forced to respond to its opponents' arguments regarding the definition of equality for women and the meaning of sex discrimination. Sometimes a movement's best response to opponents entailed qualifying its own arguments in ways that acknowledged arguments advanced by the opposition. For example, the ERA's advocates could not simply ignore arguments championed by the traditional-family-values movement. ERA proponents thus were required to concede, for example, that the proposed ERA did not regulate matters concerning reproduction and sexuality—particularly homosexuality. By the same token, to answer arguments raised by the pro-ERA movement, many who opposed the ERA by advancing family values were compelled to acknowledge that roles of both women and men needed to be defined in more gender-neutral ways.[63] In short, during the ERA ratification battle, the adversaries each sought to sway public opinion by adjusting their arguments to address the most persuasive claims pressed by their opponents.

This process of each side honing its arguments in its quest for public support for its point of view created a convergent understanding, a sort of equilibrium, that has worked its way into sex discrimination constitutional law up to the present.[64] For example, legislation based on sex-role stereotyping that in the 1960s would have been viewed as constitutional because it was seen as rationally and accurately reflecting family roles, today is an unacceptable basis for treating persons differently based on their gender because of the egalitarian assumptions that increasingly dominate views of sex roles—exactly the fundamental argument advocated by ERA supporters. Meanwhile sex discrimination law has largely remained silent with respect to abortion regulation, childbearing, rape, and same-sex relations—concessions ERA supporters made during the ERA ratification debate.[65]

The social movement contestation generated during the ERA debate also facilitated societal acceptance of the boundaries the Court has adopted that now define constitutionally proscribed gender discrimination. If the end game during the ERA ratification era had consisted of nothing more than the Court choosing sides with respect to the meaning of the Fourteenth Amendment's Equal Protection Clause—preferring one constitutional vision over another—constitutional law would have become unstable. The American public widely accepts the core precepts of sex discrimination law as it has developed to the present.[66] The national debate over the meaning of sex discrimination that occurred during the ERA ratification debate mediated our understanding of constitutionally protected gender equality and thus helped bring about a cultural equilibrium resulting in public approval of the constitutional re-interpretation currently incorporated in the Court's sex discrimination doctrine. Those engaged in collective deliberation tend to accept outcomes even when they deviate from previously expressed preferences.[67] In other words, as counterintuitive as it may sound, social conflict and debate of the type generated from proposing and opposing a constitutional amendment "provide . . . the glue that binds us together."[68]

Jack Balkin has described these moderating effects of social movement contestation in a very useful way.[69] Balkin deploys the metaphor of a "spectrum of plausibility" to describe how political activism and advocacy move a claim that may be implausible ("off-the-wall") at a certain point of time to a position of ever-increasing plausibility ("on-the-wall").[70] Balkin demonstrates that an asserted constitutional understanding either gains little or no traction and languishes, or it progresses along the "spectrum of plausibility" until it gains sufficient widespread popular support and media support that cultural and legal elites (often lawyers) begin to give serious consideration to the claim and consider it reasonable. Balkin argues that the Constitution's current guarantee of sex equality is a paradigmatic example of a social norm that became reasonable while the counterview became unreasonable through the process of mobilization, countermobilization, and contestation processes that the ERA controversy induced and encouraged.[71] Once a public opinion consensus emerges from the national debate and a particular constitutional understanding is acknowledged as reasonable, most people accept that verdict because we are socialized to respect public opinion. Social movement contestation exerts a moderating influence that facilitates such acceptance of public opinion. Those who refuse to compromise during the national deliberations over constitutional meaning risk having their views rejected as unreasonable by political elites and the public generally.[72]

Democratic Deliberation and the Political Impact of Other Failed Constitutional Amendments

To function effectively as engines of social change, reform movements need to provide adherents and potential adherents something to rally around, a cause that articulates and hones the group's claims.[73] Advocating for a constitutional amendment can provide such a rallying cause. Indeed, it has been argued that Article V is most commonly deployed to provide a forum for voicing views regarding what the Constitution should provide.[74]

Sometimes Article V is deployed to create a forum to express majoritarian disapproval and defiance and assert leverage against the judiciary during periods of judicial resistance to strongly held majoritarian political preferences. Such offensive use of proposing constitutional amendments is relatively uncommon but occurred during the New Deal.

More often, partisans propose constitutional amendments to voice opposition to a Supreme Court decision when there is no national consensus regarding the correct reading of the Constitution. Public opinion remains fluid. At these times, constitutional amendments may be proposed with the objective that the amendment campaign will function as a catalyst for mobilizing mass opposition to the Court's decision, in the hope of turning public opinion against the Court's constitutional understanding. The strategy of such reform movements is to keep a particular point of view in the public eye, attract supporters, have the movement's views accepted as being within the spectrum of reasonable opinion, and attempt to change attitudes (especially elite attitudes) over time. The pro-life opposition to *Roe v. Wade* may be the paradigmatic example of a protest movement using proposed amendments defensively in this way. An analogy might be a third-party run for president, not undertaken so much for its chances of winning as for the opportunity to create a bully pulpit providing partisans a means to promote their points of view, in the hope that potential supporters will be attracted to the validity and wisdom of the arguments and ideologies advanced and that over time public opinion will accept the point of view.

At other times, mobilizing a mass protest movement is not required to organize opposition to the Court because wide-ranging antipathy to a Supreme Court decision develops spontaneously. Then amendment proposals are introduced to voice protest, gain media attention, and help sustain existing antipathy to a Supreme Court decision, rather than create it. Good examples are the spontaneous eruptions of protest precipitated by the Court's decisions banning government-sponsored school prayer and Bible reading in public school and the Court's decision in *Texas v. Johnson* finding that flag burning is speech protected by the First Amendment.

Offensive Use of Proposed Amendments: Majoritarian Defiance of the Court during the New Deal

During the New Deal period, the American electorate gradually developed a defiant attitude toward the Court's decisions overturning state and federal social and economic legislation. The conventional externalist account of that discord and the famous "switch in time" by Justice Roberts and Chief Justice Hughes focused on the Roosevelt administration's pressuring the Court through its proposed Court-packing legislation, introduced in February 1937. Recently, arguments have been advanced that the Court's abrupt conversion sustaining New Deal legislation had internal origins—it was merely one phase of an ongoing collapse of laissez-faire constitutionalism that was underway by 1934.[75] But the Court's switch was more than simply a natural progression of constitutional doctrine that would have occurred in the absence of external forces working on the Court.[76]

Lost in nearly all of the competing accounts of the switch-in-time narrative is the impact of constitutional amendments pending in Congress in the spring of 1937 when the famous judicial switch occurred.[77] Yet considerable evidence sustains the view that the judicial switch in 1937 more likely than not was influenced by the then-pending Wheeler-Bone constitutional amendment. The Wheeler-Bone Amendment would have radically restructured the institutional relationship of the Court and the political branches of the federal government by providing for a congressional override of the Court's decisions invalidating federal legislation. Also lost in most accounts of the New Deal constitutional crisis is Roosevelt's self-conscious decision to gain political leverage by publicly hinting that he might support a constitutional amendment as a way to remedy the Court's nullification of New Deal legislation. Finally, anticipating the possibility that the Congress might approve a constitutional amendment as a means of disciplining the Court, conservatives organized a countermovement designed to thwart ratification of such an amendment. Because all of these political developments can be traced to the impact created by the prospect that Roosevelt and/or the Congress would deploy a constitutional amendment to resolve the constitutional crisis of 1937, the various amendment proposals during this period deserve close examination.

Roosevelt's Use of Article V for Political Purposes: The story of the constitutional crisis of the mid-1930s has been told often and well.[78] But most standard accounts ignore Roosevelt's use of Article V for political purposes. The classic version is that FDR, who had no Supreme Court appointments during his first term, inherited a Court dominated by Republican appointees and composed of three blocs: four conservatives, three liberals, and a two-justice set of swing votes—Chief Justice Charles Evans Hughes and

Justice Owen Roberts. The Supreme Court's reversal of New Deal legislation during a seventeen-month period (from the second half the 1934 term of the Court and throughout the 1935 term) frustrated Roosevelt.[79] FDR won the 1936 presidential election by a landslide and then sent Congress proposed Court-packing legislation in early February 1937. That legislation provided for the addition of one Supreme Court justice for every sitting justice who had reached the age of 70 and chosen not to retire, but the composition of the Court could not exceed a maximum of fifteen justices. This Court-packing proposal would have afforded FDR four immediate appointments to the Court.[80] According to the conventional rendition, in the face of this legislative threat to the Court's institutional relationship with the political branches of the federal government, Justices Hughes and Roberts shifted their positions in the spring of 1937 and thereafter consistently supported New Deal legislation.[81]

Most commentators add to their account of the switch-in-time saga FDR's self-conscious rejection of various proposals to amend the Constitution as a way to stem the Court's nullification of New Deal legislation.[82] Lost in most accounts of the Court-packing story, however, is that up to the day that Roosevelt announced his proposed Court-packing legislation, he publicly kept open the possibility of his administration supporting a constitutional amendment. How FDR used the *hint* of his possible support for a constitutional amendment for his own political purposes provides one more insight into the political uses of constitutional amendment proposing.

That part of the tale begins with so-called Black Monday, May 27, 1935. On that day, by unanimous vote, the Court invalidated three key provisions of the New Deal recovery plan, including the National Industrial Recovery Act (NIRA), in the famous *Schechter Poultry* (sick chickens) case.[83] The Black Monday decisions appeared to cripple the New Deal by signaling the Supreme Court's determination to attack Roosevelt's legislative agenda for leading the country out of the Depression. The Roosevelt administration viewed this renunciation by the Court as thwarting the will of the People and an affront to the Constitution. The invalidation of the NIRA was not FDR's greatest concern; it was unpopular and its reauthorization by Congress was in doubt anyway.[84] The more troubling aspect of the Black Monday decisions was that the rationale the Court used to invalidate three New Deal initiatives rendered other New Deal legislation vulnerable, including the all-important Social Security Act and the National Labor Relations Act (Wagner Act).[85] Within twenty-four hours of Black Monday, members of Congress introduced an avalanche of amendment proposals, so many that the *New York Times* printed a guide for its readers.

-The prospect for constitutional change through amendment was problematic since congressional leaders remained cool to the idea.[86]

Congressional reticence to amend the Constitution began to change following a May 31, 1935, FDR press conference. At this press conference, FDR launched a trial balloon to test whether citizens would rally to a constitutional amendment providing the federal government enhanced centralized power to apply national solutions to national problems. Roosevelt read telegrams from constituents outraged by the invalidation of the NIRA. These included telegrams from owners of small businesses, pleading for federal assistance from the ravages of the Depression. Two of these telegrams called upon Roosevelt to curb the Supreme Court's power, one suggesting that Congress enact legislation stripping the Supreme Court of appellate jurisdiction over legislation such as the NIRA, and one suggesting a constitutional amendment to accomplish this. When asked at the press conference whether he supported such a constitutional amendment, FDR simply stated that the Court's decisions on Black Monday, "relegated [the country] to the horse and buggy definition of interstate commerce [power]" and that he could not immediately think of any solution to that problem other than a constitutional amendment.[87]

The strategic thinking at the White House was that agitation for some amendment was far more useful to FDR than public support for any specific amendment proposal. Public discussion of a constitutional amendment could both bring public pressure to bear on the justices and promote public awareness of the need for action.[88] FDR's sophisticated hint at the need for a constitutional amendment solution to the Black Monday debacle served him well as a political device to test, mobilize, and shape public opinion. Overnight, FDR had his answer. Following the May 31 news conference, newspapers characterized Roosevelt's receptiveness to supporting a constitutional amendment option with headlines stating that Roosevelt had advocated constitutional changes.[89] Senators heard from constituents through a deluge of telegrams supporting constitutional amendments of various sorts. Congressional leaders—both Democratic and Republican—responded to this constituent fervor by expressing a new openness to the idea of constitutional amendment to reverse the Black Monday decisions' adverse effects on constitutional doctrine. The media reported this development, describing it as a dramatic change by leaders of both political parties.[90] The May 1935 press conference thus well illustrates Article V's powerful political utility as a means to test and influence public opinion and congressional attitudes.

FDR understood that while public support for a constitutional amendment was growing, an amendment effort's success was largely driven by mass mobilization of citizens. Accordingly, in September 1935, FDR decided to use Article V again to test public opinion. This time FDR agreed to an interview published in *Collier's* weekly magazine written by George Creel, a Washington correspondent with whom FDR was friendly. In a portion of the article written verbatim by FDR, he stated that in the coming 1935 term (1935–1936), the administration might again "take a licking" from the Court. In that case, FDR stated, he would "have no other alternative than to go to the country with a Constitutional amendment." The piece generated little public interest, which furnished FDR the invaluable insight that, without some new provocation, there was no mass public support for a constitutional amendment. By disclosing publicly the *possibility* that he *might* decide to support a constitutional amendment to redress the Court crisis, Roosevelt strategically deployed the Article V amendment process as an instrument to gauge public opinion.

The Backlash: FDR's various public pronouncements of his openness to the amendment option generated another, perhaps unanticipated, political impact: a conservative backlash. Conservative groups began to organize an opposition to what they viewed as radical amendments they feared were on the horizon. These countermobilization initiatives against an amendment developed prior to the coalescence of any mass mobilization in support of a constitutional amendment. FDR's mere saber rattling that an amendment might prove necessary was sufficient to help launch a powerful political countermobilization.[91]

Impact of the Wheeler-Bone Amendment on the Court's Switch: The main event in the story of Article V's influence on the resolution of the New Deal constitutional crisis is the impact of the pending Wheeler-Bone constitutional amendment on Justice Hughes, and particularly on Justice Roberts, persuading each to reverse course and uphold the constitutionality of New Deal legislation. The judicial and political developments during the roughly eighteen months prior to the Court's switch clarify the impact of the pending Wheeler-Bone Amendment.

The Court's October 1935 term (1935–1936) brought a new wave of legislative invalidations by the Supreme Court. Two of the more important administration losses that term were a 6–3 vote invalidating the Agricultural Adjustment Act of 1933 (AAA)[92] and a 5–4 vote in *Carter v. Carter Coal Co.*, invalidating the Bituminous Coal Conservation Act.[93] These cases inaugurated an unprecedented period of attacks on the Court and calls for Court-curbing constitutional amendments.[94] Roosevelt took heart in the fact that Chief Justice Hughes had joined the liberal judges' dissent in *Carter*. If the switch by Hughes were permanent (but that hardly was assured), Justice Owen Roberts represented the swing vote.

The Court's last decision of the 1935 term, *Morehead v. Tipaldo*,[95] generated additional condemnation of the Court. In *Tipaldo*, the Court struck down (5–4) a New York minimum wage statute for women and children that was drafted with great care to help ensure its constitutionality. Justice Roberts added his vote to the four votes of the conservative "four horsemen" to provide the majority that invalidated the New York minimum wage statute in *Tipaldo*. State minimum wage laws were overwhelmingly popular; more than one-third of the states had such laws. The majority opinion's rationale in *Tipaldo* rendered them all unconstitutional as repugnant to the Constitution's requirement of due process. Of the many unpopular decisions of the 1935 Supreme Court term, *Tipaldo*'s unpopularity was unsurpassed.[96] Even the Court's normal defenders expressed indignation. By one count, of 344 editorials, only ten supported the Court's decision in *Tipaldo*.[97] *Tipaldo* made it clear that if neither the federal nor the state governments could remedy the inequities of the free enterprise system, then there was no governmental remedy.

By the end of the 1935 term, the Court's nullification of state and federal socioeconomic legislation had generated a level of scorn rare in the Court's history. Resentment grew among members of Congress who increasingly were discussing measures to restrain the Court, including calls for a constitutional amendment.[98] Highly influential Montana senator Burt Wheeler, an early Roosevelt supporter and ardent New Deal liberal, stated that he had concluded that amending the Constitution may be the only effective way to curb the Court.[99]

At Roosevelt's insistence, the Democratic Party's 1936 presidential election platform did not explicitly call for a constitutional amendment. Nor did it preclude that option in the circumstance that no other accommodation with the Court could be found. Through this language, the Democratic Party platform publicly hung a constitutional amendment sword of Damocles over the head of the Court. Roosevelt won the 1936 election by the widest margin of victory in the electoral college since 1820, winning 46 states (losing only in Maine and Vermont), garnering a staggering 61 percent of the popular vote, and amassing a better than three-fourths Democratic majority in both chambers of Congress.[100] With this landslide victory, Roosevelt made the political judgment that he could successfully take on the Court and considered, but ultimately rejected, several different constitutional amendment options, choosing instead his famous Court-packing plan.[101]

The Court-packing plan startled Congress when Roosevelt announced it in a special message on February 5, 1937. The plan created a bombshell and precipitated a clash that raged until the midsummer of 1937. Opposition was widespread and came from both sides of the political spectrum: Republican leaders of the bar, conservatives, moderate Southern Democrats in Congress, newspaper editors, state legislatures, and even members of the president's own party in Congress.[102] In a word, the Court-packing plan was Roosevelt's greatest political miscalculation.[103]

FDR's Court-packing plan seemed, therefore, to be dead on arrival, so the underlying problem of judicial nullification continued as a political crisis requiring a solution. Most commentators have overlooked the influence of swelling support in Congress during the spring of 1937 for a constitutional amendment solution to the crisis. In the weeks preceding FDR's February 1937 announcement of his Court-packing plan, both the Speaker of the House, William Bankhead, and the Senate majority leader, Joseph Robinson, publicly expressed support for a constitutional amendment to address the crisis created by judicial nullification of New Deal legislation.[104] Nearly fifty constitutional amendment proposals were introduced in Congress, most designed one way or the other to impair the powers of the Court.[105] None of the proposed constitutional amendment solutions gained as much traction in Congress as a proposed amendment introduced by Senator Burton Wheeler, Democratic senator from Montana (along with Senator Homer Bone). This amendment was introduced just twelve days after FDR's February 5, 1937, announcement of his Court-packing plan and became the preferred alternative among many in Congress who opposed Court-packing. The Wheeler-Bone Amendment provided for a "suspensive veto" by Congress of the Court's invalidation of federal legislation. That is, it provided that in any case where the Court declares federal law unconstitutional, the Congress by two-thirds vote of each chamber could override the Court's decision and declare the law constitutional, but this congressional override could occur only following an intervening election for members of the House of Representatives.

There is ample evidence that Wheeler's proposed amendment influenced the Court's "switch in time." First, Burton Wheeler was a powerful and influential leader in the Senate and was widely recognized as such. Wheeler was Roosevelt's first supporter among the western progressives, the first member of the Senate to endorse Roosevelt for president, and an ardent New Dealer.[106] Wheeler opposed the Court's invalidation of New Deal legislation as fervently as did Roosevelt but broke with Roosevelt over Court-packing and led the opposition as a matter of principle.[107] Because Wheeler was a liberal Democrat on domestic issues, his support for a constitutional amendment option was taken seriously by other New Dealers and could not be dismissed as a cynical conservative ruse. Moreover, Republicans in Congress were strongly opposed to Court-packing because of its effect of handing Roosevelt so many immediate Supreme Court appointments, a power that FDR would use to create a liberal majority dynasty on the Court. Accordingly, on March 2, 1937, just two weeks after Wheeler proposed his amendment, Republican leader Arthur Vandenberg announced his support for the Wheeler-Bone Amendment in a national radio broadcast. On March 29, the day that the Court announced its first switch-in-time decision in *West Coast Hotel v. Parrish*, the *New York Herald Tribune* reported that Republican leaders in the Senate had agreed to consolidate their opposition to Court-packing by supporting a constitutional amendment.[108] It thus is clear that powerful forces in Congress were poised to act if the Court did not switch, not by legislating Court-packing but rather by proposing the Wheeler-Bone Amendment to the states.

On March 29, 1937, however, Chief Justice Hughes, and particularly Justice Roberts, intervened in *West Coast Hotel v. Parrish*, by upholding a state minimum wage law for women.[109] In a 5–4 decision in *Parrish*, the Court upheld a statute that was almost identical to that invalidated in a 5–4 decision in *Morehead v. Tipaldo*,[110] decided just ten months previously. Justice Roberts had switched his vote to provide the Court a 5–4 majority in *Parrish*, leading some to quip that Roberts's vote was a "switch in time that saved nine."[111] The *Parrish* decision has been called "the greatest constitutional somersault in history."[112]

With the assistance of Roberts's fifth vote, the Court claimed the initiative and decisively took control of the political agenda, rather than lodging it with the president as Court-packing would have done, or with the Congress as a hostile Wheeler-Bone constitutional amendment proposal would have done.[113] The following weeks witnessed a Court that was in full retreat as it upheld the constitutionality of the National Labor Relations Act (NLRA) in *NLRB v. Jones and Laughlin Corporation*[114] and then upheld the constitutionality of the Social Security Act in two related cases. Through its timely decision to sustain New Deal legislation, the Court shrewdly outmaneuvered both Roosevelt and congressional proponents of a constitutional amendment. A Court majority concluded that it was unwilling to continue its resistance to majority will by wagering its institutional future on the hope that neither Court-packing nor any of the various proposed constitutional amendments, including Wheeler-Bone, would gain the necessary political support to prevail. That much seems self-evident.[115] The question that needs resolution is which of these forces operated to cause the Court's switch—the Court-packing plan or the Wheeler-Bone Amendment (or both).

It has been widely argued that the proposed Court-packing legislation influenced the Supreme Court to reverse itself.[116] This view is plausible and controversial. On the one hand, FDR's Court plan may well have seemed dead on arrival when first announced, as evidenced by poll data demonstrating unfavorable public reaction to Court-packing out-polled favorable reaction by 78 percentage points. Yet the public opinion division over Court-packing had become more nearly equal by the time the Court announced the *Parrish* decision in late March 1937.[117] Thus, the claim advanced is that the Court surely knew that the president was gaining on the Court in terms of public opinion and might have won the Court-packing battle had the Court remained obstructionist. The Court likely responded by calling retreat, or so the argument goes.[118]

It has been counterargued, however, that the Court had little to fear from the Court-packing plan. First, FDR's Court bill could not have motivated Justice Roberts's "switch in time" in the *Parrish* case.[119] The Court-packing plan was not made public until February 5, 1937, and the decisive vote on *Parrish* was taken on December 19, 1936, when Roberts joined the liberals to uphold the statute.[120] Moreover, in the spring of 1937, when Hughes and Roberts switched to support federal New Deal legislation consistently, they would reasonably have concluded that the firestorm of protest over Court-packing either would have doomed the Court-packing proposal in the Senate or that opponents of Court-packing had sufficient support to sustain a successful filibuster against the bill.[121] At a minimum, both justices knew that passage of the Court-packing legislation was far from a sure thing. Accordingly, it is argued, the Court-packing proposal is a weak candidate for explaining the shift by Hughes and Roberts in the spring of 1937.[122]

If one is inclined to question the likelihood that FDR's Court-packing proposal alone explains the Court's shift in 1937, the question becomes what other externalities can plausibly explain the shift and thus deserve close examination as a likely change agent? The prospect of a constitutional amendment solution generally, and the probability of Congress's adoption of the Wheeler-Bone Amendment proposal in particular, deserve careful consideration.

Much evidence supports the conclusion that, following Roosevelt's landslide victory in 1936, Justice Roberts, who voted in December 1936 to abandon his position in *Tipaldo* to join the majority *Parrish*, would have understood that the Court's continued resistance to progressive social legislation would precipitate accelerating demands for a constitutional amendment solution. First, until Roosevelt's Court-packing plan was announced, it was kept secret and thus could not have influenced Roberts's December 1936 vote in the *Parrish* case. By contrast, a constitutional amendment option was widely discussed during the 1936 presidential election campaign, well before the December 1936 vote in *Parrish*, and it was widely rumored that after his smashing victory in November 1936, Roosevelt was now ready to take on the Court.[123] Moreover, the 1936 Democratic Party platform had essentially threatened the Court by announcing that if a satisfactory accommodation could not be worked out with the Court, the Democrats would seek a "clarifying [constitutional] amendment as will assure to . . . Congress . . . the power to enact those laws which . . . the federal legislature . . . shall find necessary . . . to regulate commerce, protect public health and safety, and safeguard economic security."[124] In addition, by mid-December 1936, just as *Parrish* was being considered by the Court, the influential National Consumers League announced its support for a constitutional amendment that would expand congressional power to enact the type of legislation that the Court had been declaring unconstitutional. At that same time, a leadership group representing fifteen states had begun a highly publicized effort to organize political support for a constitutional amendment. Leadership on the Democratic National Committee expressed encouragement for these amendment efforts. During the waning days of 1936, following Roosevelt's reelection, members of Congress increasingly were advocating for an amendment solution, and liberal political activists were optimistic of success.[125] During this time, and until announcing his Court plan, Roosevelt always publicly left open the possibility of his support for an amendment solution.

In short, in the weeks immediately following FDR's landslide victory in the 1936 elections, no member of the Court could miss this coalescence of support for a constitutional amendment solution to the problem of the Court's nullification of legislation designed to ameliorate the adverse economic effects of the Depression. *Parrish*, of course, upheld a state minimum wage statute. But the ever-more-widening chorus of demands for a constitutional amendment to address judicial nullification of federal law, combined with the near-universal denunciation of the Court's *Tipaldo* decision ten months previously, surely placed Justice Roberts under great pressure to switch his *Tipaldo* vote when the Court considered the *Parrish* case in December 1936. Justice Roberts was aware that the political branches of the federal government most likely had the ability to carry out the threat of a constitutional amendment.[126] Jeff Shesol reports that Chief Justice Hughes "nearly hugged" Roberts when he learned how Roberts would vote in *Parrish*. It is easy to understand why. Events had forced Roberts (and Hughes) to face the political reality of the peril confronting the Court. *Parrish* offered the court a second chance, an opportunity for the justices to redeem themselves and the Court by taking control of the political agenda, pulling the Court back from the brink, and avoiding a potentially institutionally disastrous self-inflicted wound.[127]

Putting aside whether Roberts's switch in *Parrish* could have been influenced by threats of a constitutional amendment, Hughes and Roberts knew that during the spring of 1937 they would need to vote on the other cases challenging New Deal legislation, such as the constitutionality of the National Labor Relations Act and the Social Security Act. When the voting took place in these cases, in February and March 1937, Hughes and Roberts were the swing votes and each surely knew that the Wheeler-Bone Amendment proposal was then pending in Congress and had been introduced in an atmosphere of a national mass mobilization in support for some amendment solution.[128] Wheeler-Bone thus deserves the closest scrutiny as a force that influenced Hughes and Roberts in the spring of 1937, but it has gone unmentioned in most accounts of the 1937 Constitutional Revolution.[129]

Wheeler-Bone quickly emerged in Congress as a serious alternative to the Court-packing plan. Both Republicans and Democrats in Congress preferred some amendment solution over Court-packing and supported the Wheeler-Bone Amendment, in part because Senator Wheeler was one of the Senate's most respected and influential members. As the Court was considering the New Deal cases before it in the spring of 1937, Hughes and Roberts could not have failed to realize that Wheeler-Bone likely enjoyed overwhelming support in Congress and would be adopted, especially if the president decided to endorse it.[130] Indeed, on March 25, 1937, the Senate Judiciary Committee heard testimony from Columbia University law school dean Young B. Smith, who voiced strong opposition to the Court-packing plan but forcefully argued that a constitutional amendment was a preferred solution to the Court's recalcitrance. Dean Smith predicted success of an amendment solution if the president were to add his support.[131] Prominent coverage of this testimony ran the next day in the *New York Times*, just three days before the Court announced its decision in the *Jones and Laughlin* case. Reports described the growing enthusiasm for an amendment and argued that this emerging coalescence needed only presidential support to give an amendment option political traction.[132]

It thus is not credible to dismiss out of hand the Wheeler-Bone Amendment's probable influence on Justices Hughes and Roberts while they were contemplating their votes in the New Deal cases during the spring of 1937. By giving the Congress veto power over Supreme Court declarations that federal law is unconstitutional, Wheeler-Bone would have fundamentally restructured the institutional relationship between the Court and the Congress, thus threatening the Court with far more permanent institutional damage than legislation permitting FDR to nominate four additional justices. Court-packing had occurred in the past and the Court had survived. Wheeler-Bone was different because it would have forged a permanent constitutional rearrangement that in effect would have eviscerated the core of the power that Chief Justice Marshall claimed for the Court in *Marbury v. Madison*,[133] that "the federal judiciary is supreme in the exposition of the law of the Constitution." The Court continues as a powerful political institution only as long as its decisions continue to be viewed as the supreme law of the land, thus obliging government officials to follow these decisions because each is "solemnly committed by the oath taken pursuant to Article VI, § 3 to support this Constitution."[134] Hughes and Roberts surely were aware of the transcending harm to the Court as an institution if Wheeler-Bone were added to the Constitution. Wheeler-Bone would have lacked influence on these two justices only if they reasonably could have concluded that there was little likelihood that such an amendment could achieve ratification from two-thirds of the membership of each house of Congress and the state legislatures in three-quarters of the states. All of the evidence points in the opposite direction.

Bruce Ackerman has closely examined the question of Wheeler-Bone's ratification prospects. Agreeing with others,[135] he concludes that its ratification was very much a realistic expectation. Two days after proposing his amendment, Senator Wheeler gave a radio address, during which he argued that ratification of his amendment proposal was likely because Roosevelt carried forty-six of the forty-eight states, thirty-eight states had Democratic governors, three others had liberal governors, and if Roosevelt supported the amendment it would achieve ratification in short order.[136] Wheeler failed to add the most compelling statistic demonstrating the excellent prospects for his amendment's ratification, that in thirty-three states both houses of the legislature were in Democratic hands. And of the remainder, two states were nonpartisan, seven had one chamber controlled by Democrats, and in only six states were both chambers controlled by Republicans.[137] Moreover, as with the repeal of Prohibition, which required only ten months, Congress had the choice of providing for amendment ratification by specially called conventions in each state rather than ratification by each state's legislature. The point is not that ratification of Wheeler-Bone was a certainty, but rather that both Hughes and Roberts were aware of the depth of the Roosevelt landslide victory and the domination of Democrats in state government following the 1936 election and that the prospects for ratification were excellent. Their "switch in time" may well have preserved the institution of judicial review as we know it and thus saved the Court from an irrecoverable blow.

It should be noted that it is not necessary to understand Article V in the blatant political terms discussed above to agree that the Article V amendment process impacted the outcome of the 1937 constitutional crisis. The "switch" forever enshrined in the phrase "switch in time" represented not only a switch for the Court but more fundamentally a switch for the country. Americans had been acculturated to the doctrinal legacies of laissez-faire constitutionalism—sanctity of contract, substantive due process protection of property, strict limitations on government power, and so on. Changes regarding these constitutional principles, even when they arise in response to pressing social and economic exigencies, are weighty matters for a democracy to process. People who are asked to make a switch, such as Americans were asked to make during the New Deal, need time to deliberate, to "catch their breath" as one observer has put it.[138]

By provoking debate, the Article V amendment process helped provide the country an opportunity to engage in the creative process of constitutional dialogue. Years later, Justice Roberts reflected on the spring of 1937, concluding that he found it difficult to understand how the Court could have been successful in opposing the "popular urge" favoring the emerging national economy.[139] But this "popular urge" had to congeal in the public mind following a period of protagonists grappling with the issue. The proposed constitutional amendments precipitated debate and fostered democratic deliberation over competing visions of constitutional meaning. Wheeler-Bone in particular was hotly debated, with supporters speaking out in national primetime radio broadcasts,[140] and Roosevelt arguing against an amendment solution in a primetime address to the nation, advocating instead for his Court-packing legislation. A dialectical process, so important for mediating change, thrived at rallies, countless assemblies, the mass media, and radio. Only then did the "popular urge" to which Justice Roberts referred emerge. The point is not that this necessary democratic deliberation could not have occurred without pending constitutional amendments but rather that it did occur in the presence of, and with an assist from, pending constitutional amendments.

Disagreement over the causes of the Constitutional Revolution of 1937 will persist.[141] It is likely that many external factors contributed to convincing some members of the Court to intervene to end the debate over Court-packing and constitutional amending: Roosevelt's smashing November 1936 victory, rumors of FDR's willingness to take on the Court, introduction of the Court-packing plan just weeks before the

Jones and Laughlin decision, the gathering support in the Congress and throughout the country for a constitutional amendment solution generally and the substantial congressional support for the Wheeler-Bone Amendment in particular, and public opinion that change was needed to address the economic crisis that the New Deal legislation sought to redress.[142] It is appropriate that we understand and acknowledge the contribution of the heretofore generally underappreciated but important Article V amendment process during the Constitutional Revolution of 1937.

Defensive Use of Proposed Amendments to Challenge Disfavored Court Decisions

THE PRO-LIFE ATTACK ON *ROE V. WADE*

The Court's 1973 *Roe v. Wade* decision remains on everyone's short list of the most controversial Supreme Court decisions of the twentieth century.[143] In *Roe*, the Court concluded (7–2) that, prior to viability, a pregnant woman has a fundamental constitutional right to choose whether or not to terminate her pregnancy.[144] Accordingly, *Roe* held that prior to viability government may not prohibit abortions and may not regulate abortions except as necessary to advance a "compelling" governmental interest (strict judicial scrutiny). *Roe* had the effect of invalidating the abortion laws of forty-six states.[145] By 1992 the political terrain had shifted, and the Court with it. In *Planned Parenthood of Southeastern Pennsylvania v. Casey*,[146] the Court retreated substantially from its approach in *Roe*. *Casey* reaffirmed the core holding of *Roe* (5–4), that government may not *ban* abortions prior to viability. However, the government gained a far greater right to *regulate* abortions prior to viability. Such regulation, even if not necessary to advance a compelling governmental interest, is now constitutional unless the regulation creates an "undue burden" on a woman's access to an abortion.

Roe became *Casey* in the span of nineteen years. Change occurred through the process of a rich democratic dialogue animated by what has been aptly described as "*Roe* rage"[147]—a pro-life countermovement designed to reverse *Roe*, or at least undermine and cabin it.[148] This backlash to *Roe* polarized millions and precipitated a mass conservative countermovement that has developed a commanding presence in contemporary American politics.[149] One observer's view is that the *Roe v. Wade* decision helped convert a slumbering giant into what we today refer to as the Religious Right.[150]

The backlash to *Roe* may or may not have constituted a major setback for American liberalism, as has been argued,[151] but it certainly was *not* a setback for American constitutionalism. The national conversation and debate over abortion in general, and the political sustainability of the *Roe v. Wade* approach to abortion policy in particular, influenced a mediated outcome, a settlement, that the Court adopted in *Casey*.[152] *Casey* modified *Roe* to permit greater governmental regulation of abortion while reaffirming *Roe*'s basic holding regarding a woman's fundamental right to choose whether to terminate a pregnancy prior to viability. The *Roe v. Wade* literature well establishes the doctrinal shift from *Roe* to *Casey*, the "*Roe* rage" that animated it, and the benefits to our constitutional democracy from the ensuing debate over abortion. But largely absent from these contemporary accounts of the *Roe*-to-*Casey* metamorphosis is the influence of the many constitutional amendment proposals that were advanced between *Roe* and *Casey*.

Constitutional amendment proposals are the strategy of choice for modern judicial antagonists who are determined to overturn a Supreme Court decision.[153] The backlash to *Roe* was no exception. Initially, many local governments manifested their hostility to *Roe* legislatively and administratively in an effort to undermine the *Roe* decision.[154] Relatively common was new anti-abortion state legislation that some have interpreted as expressly designed to thwart women's ability to obtain an abortion.[155] Moreover, state and local governments widely banned access to public hospitals for women seeking to obtain abortion counseling and medical procedures and refused to fund abortions.[156]

At the federal level, the Nixon, Ford, and Carter administrations largely avoided the abortion issue, adopting the position that abortion was a state issue.[157] The exception was the Carter administration's endorsement of the right of states to refuse to fund abortions, a view upheld in *Maher v. Roe*.[158] The Carter administration also supported the Hyde Amendment. Upheld in *Harris v. McCrea*,[159] the Hyde Amendment banned federal funding of abortions that virtually eliminated Medicaid funding of abortions.

Congressional opposition to *Roe* in the immediate aftermath of the decision manifested itself primarily through the repeated introduction of constitutional amendment proposals to reverse *Roe*. These amendments benefitted the *Roe* countermobilization movement institutionally. The pro-life movement, initially disorganized and internally conflicted over strategy,[160] was able to achieve a measure of institutional coherence through consensus that the single best strategy for achieving its overarching goal of reversing *Roe* was ratification of a constitutional amendment.[161] The opposition to *Roe* was thus able to use the constitutional amending process as a resource to provide it something to cling to during the lean years, time to stabilize itself, and the ability to maintain momentum while forging a more unified political response to *Roe*. Within roughly a year from the Court's 1973 decision in *Roe*, members of Congress had proposed fifty-eight amendments of various types, all of which would have reversed *Roe*. Hearings on some of these amendment proposals were held in March 1974.[162] At that time, Roman Catholic clergy (three Cardinals) testified in favor of amending the Constitution, but religious leaders (both Christian and Jewish) representing forty religious groups supported *Roe*. Given this palpable lack of consensus within the American religious community, none of the proposed amendments had any realistic chance of clearing committee and gaining the requisite congressional support. No congressional action was taken on the anti-*Roe* constitutional amendment proposals in 1974.[163]

President Ronald Reagan embraced the cause of the right-to-life movement and offered a new perspective on the abortion debate. Carter had expressed a personal objection to abortion but opposed a constitutional amendment.[164] By contrast, Reagan embraced the pro-life movement and its constitutional amendment strategy.[165] Within days following his first inauguration, Reagan met with the pro-life movement's leaders, which added additional elite support and salience to the anti-abortion amendment effort.[166] Unlike Carter, who argued that abortion was a legal dispute for the courts to resolve, Reagan's view was that abortion was an issue to be resolved through the democratic process.[167] By 1980, twenty states had petitioned Congress to hold a convention to consider a constitutional amendment that proponents labeled the Human Life Amendment.[168] During Reagan's first term, the Senate held a vote on the Hatch-Eagleton "Human Life Federalism Amendment." It provided that "[a] right to abortion is not secured by this Constitution." The proposed amendment was defeated by a vote of forty-nine yes to fifty no.[169] The Republican Party platform continued to support a human life amendment to the Constitution,[170] but by the mid-1980s informed amendment advocates had concluded that obtaining the supermajorities needed for a constitutional amendment was unlikely.[171] Polls uniformly showed an absence of consensus for an amendment denying women reproductive choice.[172] Thereafter, while amendment proposals continued to be introduced to keep the issue alive and satisfy those insisting on a constitutional amendment reversal of *Roe v. Wade*, the political focus shifted to legislative and executive strategies to render obtaining an abortion increasingly difficult and persuading the courts to endorse these restrictions.[173]

In short, initially the pro-life movement's failed constitutional amendment proposals predominated its strategy for reversing *Roe*. But for several reasons these failed constitutional amendment efforts influenced the *Roe*-to-*Casey* transformation of abortion policy.

First, in order to subvert *Roe* politically, it was essential that the pro-life movement be able to achieve two initial goals: advance a bold, aspirational reform agenda and frame the abortion issue as a political issue rather than a legal issue reserved exclusively for the judiciary. Proposing constitutional amendments in the years immediately following *Roe* assisted the pro-life movement in achieving both goals.

Bold Reform Agenda: Generating and maintaining momentum for a fledgling reform movement often is a major challenge. In order for *Roe*'s opponents to prevail, therefore, they were required to develop strategies designed to attract, organize, and maintain a broad-based resistance opposing abortion. This in turn required that they advance a bold reform agenda centered on a symbol, a threat of crisis.[174] For potential pro-life adherents, there is hardly a bolder, more dramatic, or more aspirational reform proposal designed to portray *Roe* as creating an immediate crisis than a proposal responding to the dire need to protect the life of the unborn through amendment of the US Constitution.[175] The pro-life movement's constitutional amendment strategy produced the intended result in the sense that proposing amendments became an important resource in the effort to mobilize opposition to a woman's right to choose an abortion. The amendment campaign attracted considerable grassroots support. *Roe*'s opponents, who coalesced around the pro-life constitutional amendment strategy during the middle and late 1970s, were estimated to have organized themselves into three thousand chapters with eleven million members. Those supporting a pro-life constitutional amendment became a formidable constituency, one that members of Congress could ignore only at their peril. Members of Congress supported the demands of the anti-abortion constituency due to their high degree of mobilization, their single-issue focus, their ability to place the defeat of *Roe* at the forefront of the political agenda, and the intensity of their commitment to the defeat of *Roe*.[176] In short, the mobilization to reverse *Roe* by amending the Constitution was an effective agenda setter and organization builder during the mid- and late-1970s.

Framing the Abortion Issue as a Political Issue: Proposing constitutional amendments also assisted the pro-life movement in denominating abortion as a political, and not just a legal, issue. Immediately following *Roe*, the pro-life side was confronted with the liberal account of *Roe* that abortion was entirely a judicial issue and, therefore, access to an abortion was not a right requiring a political defense.[177] Proposing constitutional amendments was a vehicle for answering this liberal critique of abortion and for politicizing the abortion debate.[178] During the eight years from the January 1973 decision in *Roe* until the February 1981 inauguration of Reagan, the pro-life movement had a particularly acute need to propose amendments as a way to emphasize that the defeat of *Roe* was a political issue. The disorganized and strife-ridden pro-life movement had few available options at the federal level for politicizing abortion and maintaining momentum for the movement. Having members of Congress introduce repeated amendment proposals helped the pro-life movement survive these lean years by focusing media attention on the issue of the need to reverse *Roe*.[179]

The right-to-life movement's early constitutional amendment strategy also was instrumental in advancing the goal of attacking *Roe* by assisting the pro-life movement in recruiting elite support during that debate. Thomas Keck's insights help explain the process.

Keck has explained that in large part, Supreme Court justices respond to emerging ideas regarding constitutional meaning that are the product of national political deliberation and discussion.[180] The goal of any reform movement, therefore, is to advance a rationale that persuades the maximum portion of the public that the movement's constitutional interpretation is correct and thereby succeed in gaining the maximum number of supporters. Minor political dissenters often mount an opposition to Supreme Court decisions, but successful opposition requires support from a political system's dominant political players.[181] The pro-life movement used the constitutional amendment strategy effectively to gain support for its cause from dominant political actors and influential institutional allies.[182] In particular, Republican members of Congress became intensely committed to the demise of *Roe* early on through their arguments in favor of a constitutional amendment. The pro-life movement gained additional elite political support during the Reagan administration, support that coalesced around arguments for the demise of *Roe* that had its source in the early efforts to mobilize members of Congress to introduce and support pro-life amendments.[183]

Prevailing in the all-important ongoing national debates over abortion policy requires not only gaining the support of political elites, but also advancing "a coherent constitutional vision."[184] Proposing a constitutional amendment can be an effective means to invigorate an aroused public, gain control of the political agenda, and decenter the political establishment through its effect of visibly advancing a coherent call for political and policy-based change.[185] It might be useful to think of group mobilization that proposes a constitutional amendment as a stage in disputing that sounds the alarm, like placing a 911 call to alert the police to the presence of a crime. Advocates of a constitutional amendment to reverse *Roe* used their amendment proposals to raise the public and political salience of the need for change. These amendment proposals called upon the public and the political establishment to support an alternative constitutional vision in the hope of raising the public's, Congress's, the president's, and indeed the Court's, political stake in the outcome.[186]

The strategy was successful. There were twelve years between Ronald Reagan's first election in 1980 and the Court's 1992 decision in *Casey*. Many forces worked on the Court to bring it to the compromise position it adopted in *Casey*. Certainly, by the second Reagan administration, the political component of the backlash against *Roe* had engulfed presidential and Supreme Court appointment politics.[187] But much of this political movement toward the compromise in *Casey* finds its ideological foundation in the arguments developed by anti-*Roe* advocates who first sounded an alarm by urging adoption of a constitutional amendment. In the debate over reversing *Roe* by constitutional amendment, *Roe*'s opponents honed an ideology that would sustain the *Roe* backlash movement thereafter, such as advancing the concept of the constitutional "personhood" of the fetus, conceptualizing life as beginning at conception, promoting an ideology grounded on the sanctity of human life, condemning of abortion as a reflection of secular humanism, and associating abortion with the demise of the family, unwelcome changes in family roles, and the place and meaning of motherhood.[188] These arguments, perfected during the fight to reverse *Roe* through constitutional amendment, shaped the social meaning of opposing abortion. The effort to reverse *Roe* by constitutional amendment thus might be best understood as one important dimension, a phase, in a larger dynamic and multistage reform-oriented process. Another way of thinking about the proposed anti-*Roe* amendments is that they were part of a larger strategy to leverage and shape a court-approved constitutional settlement, one that the majority of the Court adopted in *Casey*.

Finally, perhaps the best evidence of the political functionality of the proposed anti-*Roe* constitutional amendments can be found in the *Casey* decision itself. In *Casey*, the Court's joint opinion famously emphasized that "the Court's legitimacy depends on making legally principled decisions in which their principal character is *sufficiently plausible to be accepted by the nation*,"[189] that is, only if it comports with the citizenry's emerging views regarding constitutional meaning.[190] Citizens' emerging awareness of constitutional meaning is communicated to the Court in a variety of ways, but certainly one method is through the dialectic created by a broad-based effort to amend the Constitution. The communicative function of the many proposed amendments to reverse *Roe* was never, therefore, to threaten the Court that unless it yielded by reversing *Roe* (or weakening it) the pro-life movement would somehow see that the Constitution was amended. Rather the function of these amendment proposals, like so many other proposed amendments that sound an alarm over some disfavored Supreme Court decision, was to generate debate that precipitates and contributes to democratic deliberation. As Ronald Kahn has eloquently explained, it is through democratic dialogue, and other means, that the Court determines the importance and contemporary scope of the rights at issue and the extent to which the American people have integrated certain notions of rights into their daily lives. In this way, the Court develops its understanding of constitutional meaning through the lens of its citizens' "lived lives."[191]

In sum, if it is true, as is widely understood, that constitutional rights are socially constructed, then the debate over abortion contributed to that construction by shaping public views about abortion, informing the emerging compromise among the citizenry of the scope of constitutional protection to be afforded women desiring to choose to have an abortion, and ultimately influencing the terms of a mediated truce reflected in the *Casey* decision. After reviewing polling data on Americans' views regarding abortion, Barry Friedman concluded that the joint opinion in *Casey* fully conforms to public sentiment in terms of being in agreement with popular opinion as evidenced in numerous opinion polls.[192] *Casey* shows once again that the world outside the Court factors into the Court's decisions. The proposed anti-*Roe* amendments were important during the journey from *Roe* to *Casey* because they were an integral part of that world during a generation of vibrant public debate over abortion.

PRAYER AND BIBLE READING IN PUBLIC SCHOOLS

In 1962, in *Engel v. Vitale*, the Court struck down New York's so-called Regents' Prayer.[193] The state required that this prayer be repeated in unison by public school students at the beginning of each school day. The *Engel* decision provoked a spontaneous public reaction and a sustained drive to amend the Constitution to return prayer to the public schools, an amendment effort that did not meaningfully subside until the mid-1980s. Indeed, between 1962 and 1987, members of Congress introduced more than 600 resolutions proposing constitutional amendments designed in various ways to return prayer and other forms of devotional activities to the nation's public schools.[194] The conventional narrative is that the Court in *Engel* heroically defended students' right of conscience (and the constitutional ban on the establishment of religion) by striking down the state-drafted school prayer; that a minority of "religious zealots" attempted to impose their will on the nation through a variety of strategies, including the proposal to reverse *Engel* through constitutional amendment, but in the end the Court prevailed because a majority of the country agreed with the Court.[195] So told, this story becomes little more than another morality play of the Supreme Court vanquishing its opponents who invoked the Article V amendment process when those opponents never really had a chance of surmounting the gauntlet Article V erects.

But the conventional narrative depicting the Article V amendment process as not much more than a device for venting frustration obscures the amendment's true political impact and tactical and strategic functions because the school prayer dispute lingered for two decades until a settlement was finally reached during the Reagan administration. First, the use of the Article V amendment process by opponents of the Court's school prayer decision moved the Court to initiate its own dialogue with the citizenry. Second, the amendment process bought time for cooler heads to prevail. Third, congressional hearings on the proposed amendment promoted democratic deliberation that uncovered for early amendment proponents compelling reasons for *opposing* any amendment. Fourth, even after it was clear that the constitutional amendment effort had no chance of securing a two-thirds vote of support from Congress, it continued as a means to keep the school prayer issue alive in an effort to secure an alternative legislative solution. Finally, usually lost in the conventional narrative is a dark side of the failed use of the Article V amendment process—a disturbing level of ongoing defiance against the Court's school prayer decision in some parts of the country as an alternative strategy to the failed school prayer amendment effort. Examining the school prayer fight in these terms invites a far more instrumental account of Article V's role in American politics than generally is acknowledged.

School Prayer, *Engel*, and Unprecedented Public Fury: At the turn of the twentieth century, public school policy was to impart shared societal values through daily Bible reading from the Protestant King James version of the Bible (not the Catholic Douay version) and a non-sectarian school prayer (though some schools required recitation of the Lord's Prayer). As the decade of the 1960s began, most public elementary and secondary schools continued to require devotional practices of one kind or another.[196]

Catholics unsuccessfully complained that at their core these devotional practices were inherently Protestant sectarianism.[197] And, of course, by promoting a Christian viewpoint, the school prayer policies discriminated against Jews, other non-Christians, and atheists. Accordingly, some school officials, such as the Regents for the New York public schools, crafted a nondenominational prayer to be recited in public school each day. The

New York Regents' Prayer was drafted in 1951, during the height of the Cold War, when the Pledge of Allegiance was changed to add the words "under God," and when a Law Day observance was initiated in paired opposition to the socialist's May Day. All of this was part of a larger effort to distinguish this nation from the "Godless Communists."[198]

This Regents' Prayer was at issue in the Court's 1962 decision in *Engel v. Vitale*.[199] Public school students recited the prayer daily, but participation was voluntary in the sense that any student wishing not to recite the prayer was permitted to refrain from doing so. To the great dismay of many religious persons, by a vote of 6–1 the Court struck down New York's state-authored and sanctioned prayer to "Almighty God."[200] The Court chose a historically focused approach for its *Engel* decision, relying greatly on the history of social conflict and religious divisiveness prior to the adoption of the First Amendment and implicitly concluding that conflict is inevitable *whenever* religion and government get involved with one another.

Engel stirred up a hornet's nest of protest, especially among conservative Christians. No case prior to *Roe v. Wade* generated more hostile mail sent to the Court—five thousand letters in the first month.[201] Many in Congress branded *Engel* as unconscionable and outrageous, a decision that represented a premeditated conspiracy to secularize and communize the country.[202] Unsuccessful efforts were made in Congress to earmark funds to purchase a Bible for each member of the Court. Three months after the *Engel* decision, the House voted (unanimously) to place the motto "In God We Trust" behind the Speaker's desk.[203] It remains there today.

The *New York Herald Tribune* viewed most of the media coverage as excessive emotionalism by newspapers that had lost their normal objectivity.[204] Underlying this media sensationalism was the sense, as the *Wall Street Journal* described it, that the Court was poised to eradicate all references to religion in the public schools.[205] A year after *Engel*, the *Washington Evening Star* editorialized a more pointed accusation at the Court when it concluded that while it may not have been intentional, the Court's rulings had created an environment of hostility to religion.[206] The media's sensationalization of the *Engel* ruling created two serious misimpressions: first, that the Court had ruled that all religious activity in public schools was now banned, thus prohibiting children from praying in school on their own if they wanted to, and, second, that national life was now to be secularized—all commingling of church and state would now be unconstitutional.[207] The Court, of course, had done nothing of the sort. It merely struck down a New York law that required public school students to begin each school day by uttering in unison a government-drafted prayer to a deity. *Engel* was despised for what the mass of Americans and a large percentage of the media mistakenly thought it said, that the Court had expelled religion from public life.[208] It was this broader understanding of *Engel* that fed the fire of revolt that erupted.[209]

Schempp, Article V, and Buying Time for Democratic Dialogue and Deliberation to Take Hold: Corinna Barrrett Lain has persuasively argued that the most important lessons to be gleaned from *Engel* are to be found in what occurred following the announcement of the decision.[210] That observation is particularly apropos with respect to Article V's politically instrumental role in the school prayer controversy.

A Gallup poll found that 79 percent of Americans approved of prayer and Bible reading in public schools.[211] *Engel*, therefore, spawned an unprecedented initial cascade of proposed constitutional amendments to reverse the decision. New York State Republican representative Frank J. Becker introduced a proposed amendment to reverse *Engel* the day after the case was announced. With only the abstention of Governor Rockefeller, the National Governors' Conference unanimously called for a constitutional amendment to reverse *Engel*. In addition, former President Hoover called for a constitutional amendment.[212] In 1962 alone, members of Congress introduced fifty-six amendment proposals designed to reverse the Court's decision. The John Birch Society paid for hundreds of billboards across the country clamoring for the impeachment of Chief Justice Earl Warren.[213]

During the term following *Engel*, the Court heard arguments in *School District of Abington Township v. Schempp*,[214] a case that considered the constitutionality of compulsory Bible reading and recitation of the Lord's Prayer in public school. *Schempp* was thus decided by a Court under siege by *Engel* opponents who had launched repeated Article V salvos as a means of registering uncompromising dissent. On the one hand the Court held firm in *Schempp*, deciding the case as a straightforward application of *Engel*. Applying the *Engel* principle of banning state-sponsored daily devotionals in public schools, the Court struck down a Pennsylvania law requiring that each school day begin with a reading, without comment, of verses from the Bible and a Baltimore rule that each school day begin with a recitation of the Lord's Prayer.[215] However, the Court found itself in a defensive posture due to the onslaught of Article V amendment proposals, which attacked the *Engel* decision specifically and the Court generally. Supreme Court historian Lucas Powe concludes that the justices worried that those who were promoting school prayer constitutional amendments were intransigent partisans whose dissent could harm American politics.[216] Through its several opinions in *Schempp*, the Court self-consciously attempted to communicate to the American people in an effort to mobilize resistance to the Article V–led assault on the Court and to mediate the dispute.

The Court's opening move was an appearance by Justice Tom Clark at the American Bar Association's August meeting during the summer following the term when *Engel* was decided. There, Justice Clark faulted the press for seriously misstating what the Court had decided and mounted a nearly unprecedented defense and clarification of the Court's *Engel* decision.[217] Justice Hugo Black responded to much of the mail the Court received following *Engel* by enclosing a copy of the *Engel* decision and inviting the person with whom he was corresponding to write again if he or she wished, but only after first having read the decision.[218] At the justices' conference on *Schempp*, Justice Arthur Goldberg reminded the other justices of how heated the school prayer issue had become and counseled that the citizenry needed reassurance.[219] Chief Justice Earl Warren, heeding that advice, assigned Justice Clark to write the opinion in *Schempp* in an effort to soothe the public furor over *Engel*. Clark had defended *Engel* at the ABA meeting and he was a conservative Southerner, known as a calm and balanced voice on the Court.[220] Clark had earned his spurs as an anti-Communist during his tenure as Attorney General, so no Court critic could claim that the Court was acting as a pawn to the atheistic communists. Justice Clark was an inspired choice, not only because he was regarded as a centrist who would draft a careful opinion that would avoid misunderstanding and emphasize the narrowness of the Court's holding, but also because his distress over media misrepresentation of *Engel* assured that he would appreciate the public relations implications of what the Court added to its *Schempp* decision.[221]

Justice Clark did not disappoint. His *Schempp* opinion exalted the revered place of religion in American culture; it showed respect for religious practice by acknowledging the myriad of historically settled religious aspects to public life, such as legislative chaplains and the oath of office; and it celebrated the First Amendment's commitment to religious freedom. Justice Clark argued that it was the Constitution's required deference to each individual's right to religious freedom, not scorn for religion, that required striking down state-sponsored and mandated Bible reading and prayer recitation in public school.

But the Court's public relations campaign with the American people, in the midst of the Article V bombardment of the Court, did not end with the Court's majority opinion in *Schempp*. Justice Brennan, the Court's only Catholic at the time, drafted a preemptive seventy-page concurring opinion in *Schempp* defending the Court's decision on historical grounds. It was clearly designed as a Catholic talking to other lay Catholics and the Roman Catholic hierarchy, entreating them to understand *Engel* and *Schempp* as grounded on constitutional principle and not on either secularism or an anti-religion philosophy. Justices Goldberg and Douglas also wrote concurring opinions. Together with the Brennan opinion, the Court in *Schempp* symbolically presented the American public concurring opinions from a Protestant, a Jew, and a Catholic.

In short, doctrinally, the Court held fast to the *Engel* neutrality principle in *Schempp*, but the justices wrote the *Schempp* opinions in a style that any Madison Avenue account executive would have applauded. In its *Schempp* opinions, the Court marketed its "product" to the American people, the Court's customers as it were, who had expressed profound disappointment with the Court through a deluge of proposed constitutional amendments. It is highly unlikely that the public relations content found in the various *Schempp* opinions would have been added as they were had Article V not provided the Court's *Engel* critics such an effective vehicle to mount a visible attack on the Court.

Further evidence of Article V's impact on the school prayer / Bible reading controversy can be found in the 1964 House hearings on proposed constitutional amendments. *Schempp* was decided in 1963. Even though the tone of public disapproval was far less virulent than the public reaction to *Engel*, the *Schempp* decision precipitated many more constitutional amendment proposals than did *Engel*. In the 1963–1965 Eighty-Eighth Congress alone, House and Senate members introduced approximately 265 joint resolutions proposing constitutional change related to religious practices in public schools.[222] This increased number of proposed constitutional amendments may have been because the ban on Bible reading and recitation of the Lord's Prayer affected many more state educational programs than did *Engel*'s ban on the Regents' prayer. Also, 1964 was an election year, and submitting a constitutional amendment proposal is an efficient, very public way for a member of Congress to signal policy alignment with constituents. Whatever the reason, by the spring of 1964 when the House Judiciary Committee scheduled a hearing, Congress had been deluged with constitutional amendment proposals, a majority proposed by members of Congress from the states constituting the former Confederacy.[223]

Representative Becker's amendment proposal had the greatest support in the House, but it had great difficulty overcoming the opposition of Emanuel Celler, chair of the House Judiciary Committee. The Becker Amendment's legislative journey appeared to be headed for success once Celler was forced to agree to hold hearings in the spring of 1964.[224] Pressure was great in the House to pass some version of a constitutional amendment. Prior to the beginning of the House hearings on the proposed amendments, a majority of the House Judiciary Committee members supported a constitutional amendment to reverse *Engel* and *Schempp*. The media published predictions that an amendment easily would pass the House if the House Judiciary Committee could agree on the language of an amendment.[225]

But the effect of House hearings was the opposite of what amendment supporters had hoped for and had anticipated. The hearings were held over the period of eighteen days, the House Judiciary Committee heard from nearly two hundred witnesses, and the testimony consumed 2,774 pages.[226] These hearings evolved into an exquisite exemplar of democratic deliberation as they moved the House Judiciary Committee members, the Congress, the religious establishment, and many attentive citizens from a position supportive of a constitutional amendment to strong opposition.

First, the hearings demonstrated to everyone, and particularly religious leaders, that writing an amendment to permit a prayer that would be acceptable to everyone was a highly complex, and perhaps impossible, task given the nation's commitment to religious pluralism. In other words, the Article V House hearings forced people to move past the sound bites of opposition and begin the tedious task of working together in an effort to govern.

Second, early in the hearings many witnesses from a broad spectrum of religious faiths testified in opposition to any amendment, concluding, on reflection, that an amendment could actually be detrimental to their interests. Not the least of their concerns was the realization that if the nonsectarian prayer had to be one that met the needs of all faiths it would meet the needs of no faith—it would become a meaningless ritual. Through these hearings the leaders of the nation's religious establishment largely concluded that, contrary to their earlier view, they now opposed any amendment. Mainstream Protestants became uniformly opposed.[227] Even the Catholics turned away from strong support for an amendment.[228] Once the religious leaders came out against a school prayer amendment, it became safe for the politicians to follow suit.

Compelling evidence of the contribution that these Article V hearings made to democratic deliberation can be found in the language of the amendment proposal that finally emerged from the hearings. After all the interested parties had completed their backroom discussions, negotiations, and compromising with one another, what emerged as the consensus amendment is one that closely tracked the Court's view of religious liberty in *Engel*.[229] The Article V–generated legislative hearing, designed as a majoritarian assault on the Court, had the opposite effect of vindicating the Court, at least to anyone sufficiently open to being persuaded. It is with no small degree of irony that the 1964 Republican Party platform contained a plank supporting a religious freedom amendment, but its essence was merely that individuals and groups, on their own and without the participation or coercion of government, are free to "choose to . . . exercise their religion freely in public places."[230] That, of course, did not reverse a word of either *Engel* or *Schempp*. In the end, no amendment ever reached the House floor from these 1964 hearings held by the House Judiciary Committee.[231]

Article V thus left three undisguised traces on the school prayer debate. First, the Court's overt dialogue with the American people in *Schempp* can be traced to the Article V constitutional amendments hurled at the Court by dissenters immediately following the *Engel* decision. Second, Article V provided a cooling off period of about one year prior to the commencement of the spring 1964 House Judiciary Committee hearings, providing time for those so inclined to evaluate their true interests rather than simply react to sensationalized media accounts of *Engel* and *Schempp*. Third, through a process of clarification and reflection, the House hearings on proposed constitutional amendments had a mediating effect on the crisis. Congress scheduled those hearings only because Article V in effect required them because Congress needed to formulate an informed judgment whether to propose a constitutional amendment to the states.

Defiance: State and local governmental officials not only bitterly denounced but also widely ignored *Engel* and *Schempp*.[232] Unwilling to abandon practices in place for many decades, local boards of education resisted both *Engel* and *Schempp* through a combination of trickery and stubbornness.[233] Robert Birkby's study of 121 Tennessee school districts' compliance with *Schempp* two years after the Court's decision documents that this resistance was widespread.[234] The practice of school prayer and Bible reading continued in many other parts of the country, especially in the South and East, due in part to encouragement from political leaders and the public perception that the school prayer question remained unresolved due to the congressional efforts to reverse *Engel* and *Schempp* by constitutional amendment.[235] For example, just one year following its decision in *Schempp*, the Supreme Court was required to decide yet another school prayer / Bible reading case. In *Chamberlin v. Dade County Board of Public Instruction*, the Court reversed a Florida Supreme Court decision that had upheld teachers reading Bible verses to students and participating in regular recitation of the Lord's Prayer and other religious sectarian prayers at school assemblies and in the classroom, rejecting the argument that the purpose and effect of these practices was secular.[236]

After the 1964 House hearings on the school prayer amendments, prayer temporarily subsided as hot-topic political issue in Congress until the 1970s when evangelicals revived it as a political cause célèbre. Thereafter, three times in fifteen years the Court was required to revisit the school prayer issue and push back local opposition to officially condoned school devotionals: first in 1985, striking down (6–3) a provision in an Alabama law requiring a minute of silence for "meditation or voluntary prayer";[237] next in 1992, striking down (5–4) a policy permitting clergy-led prayer at school graduations in Providence, Rhode Island;[238] and then in 2000, striking down (6–3) officially condoned student-led prayers at high school football games in New Mexico.[239] Nevertheless, particularly in some Southern schools, school-sanctioned prayer continues as an ongoing reality.[240]

Constitutional Amendment Revival in the 1980s and the Current Accommodation: Though a school prayer amendment has never cleared Congress to be sent to the states, it is a mistake to conclude that the public outcry and efforts to secure a constitutional reversal of *Engel* and *Schempp* ended in the 1960s, bore no subsequent fruit, and had no further impact on American politics. For example, it was hardly possible to miss the impact of the 1960s school prayer debate, the public fury, and the constitutional amendment campaign mounted against *Engel* and *Schempp* during Ronald Reagan's 1979–1980 presidential race. Indeed, Reagan was elected in 1980 on a platform that included a call for restoration of "the right of individuals to participate in voluntary nondenominational prayer in schools."[241]

The highly visible use of Article V by politicians running for elected office offers insight into an important, but often obscured, political function of Article V—posturing. David Mayhew coined the phrase "position taking" to connote taking action without policy implications, motivated by a desire to align one's public image with constituents' sentiments without the need for anything consequential to happen and therefore without the risk of adverse political consequences.[242] There is strong evidence that elected officials used the school prayer amendment proposals to engage in "position taking" with constituents by supporting school prayer amendment proposals when in fact they either opposed them or at least knew there was no chance that Congress would enact them. Defending school prayer in those circumstances is a cinch: it gains support from some voters with virtually no risk of antagonizing others.[243] Members of Congress thus get free political benefits with no worry about consequences.[244] Ronald Reagan, a consummate politician, appreciated the posturing potential of supporting a school prayer amendment. Looking to reelection in 1984, Reagan in 1982 declared a "National Day of Prayer" and backed a school prayer constitutional amendment even though it had little or no chance of adoption.[245] For Reagan, Article V became a useful, cost-free tool to deflect political heat generated from a Religious Right that was frustrated by a perceived lack of attention to its political agenda.[246]

In the wake of the renewed support for school prayer in the 1980s, the Court conspicuously retreated from a strict separationist approach to the Establishment Clause, which was the underpinning of *Engel* and *Schempp*, to a view that now incorporates a much more accommodating judicial attitude regarding public support for religion.[247]

Moreover, in 1984, Congress defused the controversy over school prayer and Bible reading in public school by enacting the Equal Access Act, which bars public schools from discriminating against meetings of student groups on school grounds on the basis of "religious, political, philosophical or other content" of the students' speech.[248] The continuing introduction of constitutional amendment proposals aided in securing enactment of the Equal Access Act.

First, these many constitutional proposals permitted supporters of the Equal Access Act to seize the moral high ground by being able to argue that they had tried in good faith, but in vain, to use the Constitution's Article V amendment process and now they required a different solution. The amendment proposals also became an effective vehicle to demonstrate that many in Congress supported the objective of returning religion to the schools. And the repeated introduction of constitutional amendments kept the issue alive among the electorate and thus kept pressure on members of Congress to enact a legislative solution.[249] Opponents of the Equal Access Act well understood this linkage between school prayer constitutional amendment efforts and enactment of the legislation, for they protested that the Equal Access Act was "nothing more than a school-prayer amendment in sheep's clothing."[250] Today, the Equal Access Act is understood as a statutory substitute for a constitutional amendment enacted by proponents of a school prayer constitutional amendment who had concluded that obtaining such an amendment was not politically feasible.[251]

Moreover, supporters of the Equal Access Act in Congress calculated that the legislation would provide members of Congress political protection from disgruntled constituents vexed over Congress's failure to pass a school prayer constitutional amendment.[252] This political calculation proved prescient. By protecting the right to engage in extracurricular religious activities in public schools, the Equal Access Act has sapped support for constitutional amendments reversing *Engel* and *Schempp*.[253]

There is one final Article V radiation from the failed school prayer amendment effort that warrants consideration. A strong case has been made that the diminished appetite among religious conservatives to keep fighting for school prayer is due largely to Congress's repeated refusal to adopt and send to the states a school prayer amendment and to the Supreme Court's resolute stand opposing government-sanctioned religious devotions in public schools.[254] So understood, the Article V amending efforts might profitably be conceptualized as laboratory experiments: some succeed and some fail. But repeated failure can be productive in the sense that it signals the need to move on and pursue alternative strategies.[255]

FLAG DESECRATION

The constitutional status of flag desecration was squarely addressed for the first time by the Supreme Court in *Texas v. Johnson*.[256] During the 1984 Dallas Republican National Convention, Gregory Lee Johnson burned a flag on a street adjoining the convention hall as a means to protest the policies of President Reagan. A Texas appellate court reversed Johnson's conviction imposing a sentence of one year in prison for violating a Texas statute prohibiting intentional desecration of a flag (state or national). The Supreme Court agreed that Johnson's actions constituted a form of symbolic speech protected by the First Amendment.

Criticism of the Court's decision in *Texas v. Johnson* was immediate and volcanic. *Newsweek* characterized the firestorm of public indignation across the country as "stunned outrage."[257] Senator Strom Thurmond (R-SC) interpreted the Court's decision as having unleashed a torrent of emotion nationwide that demanded immediate remedial action.[258] Cries for constitutional amendment reform were immediate. Within a week of the *Johnson* decision both the House and the Senate, by a nearly unanimous vote, expressed their profound disapproval. President George H. W. Bush went to the Iwo Jima Memorial to call for a constitutional amendment to overturn *Johnson*.[259] Within a week of the decision, nearly half of the members of Congress, 172 House members and 43 senators, had sponsored thirty-nine resolutions calling for a constitutional amendment.[260] Opinion surveys showed that approximately 70 percent of the public supported a constitutional amendment excluding flag burning from constitutional protection. Given this state of public opinion and congressional outrage, such an amendment proposal most likely would have passed in an immediate floor vote in Congress.[261]

Not wanting to appear unpatriotic, but uneasy about tinkering with the Constitution's guarantee of freedom of expression, the Democratic leadership in Congress proposed a statutory response to the *Johnson* decision—the Flag Protection Act. The proposed federal legislation provided for a one-year prison sentence and a $1000 fine for knowingly defacing, burning, or otherwise damaging a United States flag. The self-conscious motive behind this legislation was to obviate the need for Democratic congressional members to vote on a constitutional amendment.[262] Notwithstanding general agreement that the Court likely would find this legislation unconstitutional, both the House and the Senate overwhelmingly adopted the legislation. President Bush signed it while continuing publicly to press for a constitutional amendment. A vote thereafter was taken in the Senate on a proposed flag desecration constitutional amendment but the measure failed by fifteen votes to secure the necessary two-thirds majority.[263]

There are few clearer examples in congressional politics of Article V's pivotal political role in influencing congressional action. The constitutional amendment proposals had gained traction, forcing Democrats in Congress to seek political cover that would protect them from having to vote against a constitutional amendment. So Congress postured. It enacted a manifestly unconstitutional statute and in the process bought time for the voices of moderation to gain control of the agenda once passions cooled.[264] And if (when) the Court struck down the Flag Protection Act, members of Congress could shift political blame to the Court and thus avoid responsibility. The vote to enact the Flag Protection Act represented what is termed a "politically compelling" vote—a vote where members of Congress feel pressured to align themselves with certain popular policy positions notwithstanding that the policies supported are unlikely to resolve an underlying problem.[265] By enacting the Flag Protection Act while reserving the option to reintroduce a constitutional amendment solution if necessary, Democrats in Congress crafted for themselves the politically advantageous flexibility to assert that they both defend the flag and support the constitution.[266]

Unsurprisingly, in 1990 the Court struck down the Flag Protection Act, in *United States v. Eichman*.[267] Within an hour of announcement of the *Eichman* decision, flag protection advocates, including President Bush, again called for a constitutional amendment. Unwilling to risk being viewed on the wrong side of protecting the flag, nervous politicians agreed to hold more hearings. But by 1990, public passion over the issue of flag burning had waned, the political heat had cooled. Amendment proposers, at least some, felt satisfied that they had been provided their day in court, as it were, to make their case to Congress for a constitutional amendment. The 1989 Flag Protection Act had created opportunities for reflection by thoughtful persons. The Supreme Court's *Eichman* decision had stoutly reaffirmed the principles of *Texas v. Johnson*, thereby evidencing the Court's unwavering conviction that flag burning should be viewed as constitutionally protected speech.

Both the House and the Senate voted on a flag protection constitutional amendment soon after *Eichman* was decided, and the proposal failed to secure two-thirds support in each house.[268] Subsequently, a proposed constitutional amendment banning flag desecration received the necessary two-thirds majority in the House six times between 1995 and 2005 but fell short by small margins in the Senate in 1995 (63 yes and 36 no); in 2000 (63 yes and 37 no); and in 2006 (66 yes and 34 no).[269]

Appeasing the furor over *Texas v. Johnson* when it was decided in 1989 was a formidable task. Enacting the unconstitutional Flag Protection Act of 1989 in lieu of proposing a constitutional amendment was a brilliant ploy. It provided members of Congress cover while simultaneously furnishing time for the voices of moderation to dominate the debate. This strategy was successful *only because* congressional leaders were able to assure amendment proponents that if the legislative solution failed, reversing the Court through a constitutional amendment would remain an option.

Eradication of the Poll Tax

One will not find the phrase "right to vote" in the 1787 Constitution, which contains only two references to voting. Both confer on the states near complete control over the voter qualification for both state and federal elections.[270] Nor did the Constitution of 1787 provide for federal oversight of the states' voting practices, other than to provide in Article IV, § 4 that "The United States shall guarantee to every State . . . a Republican form of government." But the Court early on held that claims brought under this so-called Guarantee Clause are non-justiciable political questions.[271] Moreover, in *Minor v. Happersett*,[272] the Court upheld a state's refusal to permit women to vote, reasoning that a woman's US citizenship status conveys no right to vote.

The Article V amendment process has eroded this palpable state-sovereignty tilt of the Constitution of 1787. In addition to the Fourteenth Amendment's guarantee of equal protection of the law, five suffrage amendments now regulate voting eligibility. These amendments have removed (or curtailed) race, gender, District of Columbia residency, poverty, and youth as bars to suffrage.[273] Left unregulated by the five suffrage amendments was the poll tax in state and local elections. Poll taxes operated as racially and class motivated state-law obstacles to ballot access. Judicial action has now banned all use of the poll tax. Largely overlooked is the contribution of the Article V amendment procedure to the democratic process that eradicated the poll tax in state and local elections.

From colonial times and into the mid-nineteenth century, a well-accepted political principle had been that a potential voter ought to be able to demonstrate a sufficient degree of financial independence in order to prove his or her political independence and thus qualification to vote.

The poll tax was a means-testing device adopted in many states and used well into the mid-nineteenth century, but it fell into disuse in most of the North. In the states of the old Confederacy, the poll tax continued to be used during the twentieth century, primarily as a way to manipulate the franchise to deny poor blacks and poor whites the equal opportunity to vote. The poll tax was a tax levied on every registered voter at every election and was to be paid whether or not one voted. Typically, the tax had to be paid months in advance, and proof of payment of the current tax, as well as payment of poll taxes for the past two years, was required to vote.[274] Voter participation often was less than 5 percent among African Americans in states with a poll tax.

By the 1930s, opposition to the poll tax had swelled. In 1937, in *Breedlove v. Suttles*, the Georgia poll tax was challenged as a violation of the Fourteenth Amendment Equal Protection Clause.[275] In *Breedlove*, the Court unanimously upheld the constitutionality of the poll tax as a reasonable state limit on eligibility for the franchise. By 1939, legislation eliminating the poll tax in federal elections was introduced annually in Congress.[276] On five occasions, beginning in the early 1940s, the US House of Representatives enacted statutory bans on use of the poll tax, but resistance in the Senate thwarted all efforts to enact a legislative solution. Some opposition to a poll tax ban was thinly disguised racism and some was concern over encroachment by the federal government on the states' prerogative to set eligibility standards for voting. By the end of World War II, both the Democratic and Republican parties' platforms supported enactment of a constitutional amendment banning the poll tax. Many such amendment proposals were introduced, but none advanced.

These failed efforts to secure either a legislative or constitutional ban on the use of the poll tax proved important in the long run, however. These failed efforts to attack the poll tax mobilized opposition and entrenched elimination of the poll tax in the agenda of Congress's liberal coalition, thereby readying poll tax opposition for use when more favorable political conditions developed.[277] Political conditions became more favorable in the early 1960s when some members of Congress from Southern states gradually changed their strategy and expressed support for a limited constitutional amendment banning the poll tax *in federal elections*. Their reasoning was that ratification of such an amendment banning the poll tax was unlikely and, in any event, limiting a poll tax ban only to federal elections would undercut the more sweeping ongoing efforts to enact legislation banning the poll tax in *both* federal and state elections.[278] Plus, banning by constitutional amendment a practice that Congress had ample power to ban legislatively could set a strong precedent for routing civil rights initiatives through the Article V amendment process rather than through the congressional legislative process.

Beginning in 1949, conservative senator Spessard Holland (D-FL) initiated a determined effort to secure a constitutional ban on poll taxes in federal elections.[279] In 1962, when only five states still required payment of a poll tax, Senator Holland finally was able to secure two-thirds support in the Senate for an anti-poll-tax constitutional amendment, limited to federal elections. Liberals objected, arguing that excluding a ban on the poll tax for state and local elections provided a mere half-loaf. Moreover, liberals complained that employing Article V to ban what Congress more easily could ban by statute would create the very precedent conservatives sought, that future civil rights progress also might require a constitutional amendment rather than simply legislative action. In the end, Senate liberals yielded to the Holland half-loaf because the Holland approach was the only politically viable option, given the hostility of the Senate Judiciary Committee to a more expansive poll-tax ban. Thus the Holland amendment proposal, which ultimately became the Twenty-Fourth Amendment, is best understood as a failed effort by liberals to secure a constitutional ban on the poll tax in both federal and state elections.

The Holland constitutional amendment proposal faced stiff opposition when it reached the House. Conservatives objected to creating a precedent permitting federal takeover of the states' prerogative to set franchise eligibility rules, and liberals protested the proposed amendment's failure to cover both state and local elections. Emanuel Celler (D-NY), who at the time was chair of the House Judiciary Committee, acknowledged and lamented the limited scope of the proposed amendment, but frankly told the House members that it was this or nothing. The House adopted the Senate version. Congressman Charles Goodell (R-NY), who strongly opposed all poll taxes, voted against the proposed amendment because it failed to ban the poll tax in both state and local elections. He acknowledged that human rights groups would condemn him for his decision, but he expressed confidence that history would vindicate him.[280]

Congressman Goodell seriously miscalculated. As it turned out, it was a mistake for a poll tax opponent to oppose the Twenty-Fourth Amendment. There is no question that the Twenty-Fourth Amendment represented a failed effort to amend the Constitution more expansively than it did. But this "failed" effort to ban all poll taxes had a salutary influence on other efforts to secure voter equality for all Americans, including ultimately influencing the Court to reverse its *Breedlove* decision and declare all poll taxes unconstitutional.

The Twenty-Fourth Amendment ban on poll taxes in federal elections was added to the Constitution on February 4, 1964. Those who campaigned to secure the states' ratification of the Twenty-Fourth Amendment amassed such a compelling case against all poll taxes that a wave of opposition to all poll taxes erupted, transforming the poll-tax-in-federal-election debate into a national controversy and referendum on the legitimacy of any poll tax.[281] By the time the Twenty-Fourth Amendment was ratified, only three states still enforced a poll tax in state and local elections. The year following ratification of the Twenty-Fourth Amendment, Congress enacted the 1965 Voting Rights Act. By attacking entrenched racial discrimination in voting, "an insidious and pervasive evil which had been perpetrated in certain parts of our country though unremitting and ingenious defiance of the Constitution,"[282] the Voting Rights Act of 1965 revolutionized Southern politics. The Voting Rights Act did not ban the poll tax in state elections, but its sections 9 and 10 contained Congress's judgment through legislative findings that the poll tax unconstitutionally abridges the right to vote and directed the Justice Department to initiate litigation challenging the constitutionality of enforcing the poll tax in either state or local elections.[283]

The Justice Department intervened in *Harper v. Virginia State Board of Elections*, a case already pending before the Supreme Court.[284] In *Harper*, the Court fell into line with the equality principles enshrined in the Twenty-Fourth Amendment and the 1965 Voting Rights Act by reversing *Breedlove v. Suttles*. The Court concluded that enforcing a poll tax in any election constitutes impermissible discrimination in violation of the Fourteenth Amendment's Equal Protection Clause.[285]

Harper is one of the best-known voting rights cases, but its back story, which documents the influence of the Article V amendment process, has been largely lost.[286] When *Harper* came to the Court, a majority of the justices were prepared summarily to uphold the constitutionality of the poll tax in a *per curium* opinion, thus reaffirming the Court's *Breedlove* precedent. Behind-the-scenes maneuvering among the justices achieved a majority vote to hear the case on the merits and to ultimately reverse *Breedlove*. The Twenty-Fourth Amendment's half-loaf ban of poll taxes only in federal elections was a decisive factor in this turnaround.

When the Court in *Harper* initially voted (6–3) in conference to summarily affirm *Breedlove*, and thereby reaffirm the constitutionality of the poll tax, Justice Arthur Goldberg wrote a strong dissent that he circulated among the other justices. The Goldberg dissent changed sufficient votes to reverse the conference vote of summary affirmance of the *Breedlove* precedent to a vote to schedule arguments on the merits in *Harper*.

In his crucial dissent from the initial conference vote, Justice Goldberg focused on the text of the Twenty-Fourth Amendment and the congressional debates over that amendment to emphasize congressional testimony demonstrating that the poll tax did not advance any legitimate state interest. The poll tax neither identified voters who had developed an informed interest in matters to be voted upon nor did it perform a revenue-raising function.[287] In its legal briefs on the merits in *Harper*, the office of the US Solicitor General also emphasized this same congressional history of the Twenty-Fourth Amendment as well as the provisions in the Voting Rights Act expressing Congress's findings that the poll tax in any form could not be justified as a constitutional method to establish voting qualifications. The political judgments upon which the Twenty-Fourth Amendment and the Voting Rights Act are grounded expressed a widely held political commitment to end exclusionary practices in voting and provided sound reasons for the Court to reevaluate its position in *Breedlove*. The Court responded to this ideological shift by reversing *Breedlove*.

The Article V amendment process thus proved pivotal in converting constitutional doctrine from the view in *Breedlove* to the constitutional meaning adopted in *Harper*.[288] The Twenty-Fourth Amendment was a failed constitutional amendment effort from the viewpoint of those desiring a ban on poll taxes in both state and federal elections. But the policy preferences animating adoption of the Twenty-Fourth Amendment, and Congress's legislative findings, provided the ideological foundation for finding all poll taxes unconstitutional.[289]

Democratic Deliberation and the Top-Down Influence of Failed Amendments on State Politics

The ERA is an excellent example of how a failed constitutional amendment effort can have a top-down effect on state law by precipitating a constitutional dialogue at the state level of government that results in modification of state statutory and constitutional law. In the case of the ERA, one result of that dialogue was the addition of equal rights amendments by many states in their state constitutions.

As of 1972, when Congress approved the ERA, only five states had provisions in their state constitutions affirming some form of equal rights for men and women. In the approximately four decades since Congress referred the ERA to the states, eighteen more states have added provisions to their state constitutions guaranteeing equal rights on the basis of gender. In addition, some of the original five states that had legal provisions securing equal rights for men and women modified their equal-rights provisions to strengthen and expand them.[290] Some of the state constitutional ERA provisions track the defeated federal ERA amendment almost verbatim.

Others add exceptions or other qualifiers. Recent scholarship has shown that these state ERA provisions are an outgrowth of the failed federal ERA effort and are now being interpreted to expand the scope of gender equality far beyond that afforded by the Fourteenth Amendment's Equal Protection Clause.[291]

The ERA was not the first failed constitutional amendment to have a top-down effect on state politics. The Blaine Amendment did also. The Blaine Amendment was named for former House speaker and unsuccessful 1884 presidential candidate James G. Blaine (R-ME). His proposed constitutional amendment effectively would have prohibited the use of any public funds for religious schools. In 1875, President Grant delivered a speech to a Civil War veterans group. Grant advocated the states' duty to provide free public education but argued for maintaining the separation of church and state by not appropriating public funds to support "sectarian schools."[292] Blaine soon thereafter introduced his proposed constitutional amendment.

Two mid-nineteenth-century controversies found expression in the Blaine Amendment: disagreement over the propriety of mandatory prayer and Bible reading in public schools and controversy over providing public funding of sectarian education. Both issues rose out of the mid-century wave of Catholic immigration, mostly from Ireland but also from Germany. More than a million immigrants from these two countries arrived in the United States between the late 1840s and 1850s. With that large influx of Catholic immigrants came increased political power and influence of the Roman Catholic Church in America. Catholics protested Bible reading in public schools because readings came from the Protestant King James version of the Bible, and Catholics argued that the public school system was essentially a Protestant school system.[293] Accordingly, Catholics advocated for public support of parochial (Catholic) schools.[294] Catholic immigrants tended to gravitate to the Democratic Party. Indeed, in some parts of the country the Democratic Party was transformed into an Irish-Catholic institution. The arrival of Irish Catholics triggered a Protestant backlash, social turmoil, and the rise of Nativist movements. Inevitably the debate turned to strife over public financial support for religious schools. President Grant's entreaty that no public funds be used for this purpose reflected one side of that nationwide debate regarding government's involvement with religious education.

Perhaps looking for a national issue on which to run for president, Representative James Blaine introduced his amendment in 1875. In 1876 the House of Representatives approved the Blaine Amendment by more than the required two-thirds vote. Though modified from Blaine's original proposal, the measure that achieved supermajority House support contained, as it always had, a bar on use of any public property or tax monies to support parochial school education. The Senate endorsed the Blaine Amendment along party lines but only by a vote of 28–16, shy of the required two-thirds vote needed to send the amendment proposal to the states for their consideration.[295]

Though the Blaine Amendment effort never succeeded in adding an amendment to the Constitution, in two different ways it nevertheless was influential. First, though the Blaine Amendment failed to achieve ratification, the campaign in support of Blaine's amendment awakened and coalesced strong Protestant opposition to taxpayer support of religious education, eventually forcing Catholics to withdraw demands for government financial assistance.[296] Second, the tracings of the Blaine Amendment movement can be found even today in many state constitutions.[297] In the immediate aftermath of Blaine's amendment effort, supporters of the amendment turned to the state legislatures, and there they achieved great success. The national attention that the Blaine Amendment effort had generated with respect to the controversy over public financing of sectarian education prompted many state legislatures to propose adoption of Blaine-type amendments in their state constitutions. Some states even named them "Blaine Amendments." Moreover, Congress required territories to adopt a Blaine-type state constitutional provision as a condition of being admitted to the Union.[298] By 1890, twenty-nine states had adopted some version of the Blaine Amendment, all having as a common feature prohibition of the use of public funds for religious schools.[299] Many of these provisions remain in state constitutions. One judicial calculation in 1999 concluded that at least thirty states have constitutions containing provisions that parallel the Blaine Amendment.[300] What began as an Article V effort to amend the federal constitution morphed into baby Blaine Amendments that continue to influence state-church relations through state constitutional provisions.

PART II

Impact of Failed Amendment Efforts on Congressional Politics

3

Prodding Congress through Use of the Article V "Application Clause"

The Article V Application Clause as an Amending Device

The Article V constitutional amendment mechanism entails a two-step process: one for proposing amendments and one for ratifying them. The proposing step provides two alternative routes: Congress can initiate amendment proposals, or amendments can be proposed by the never-yet-used national proposing convention called by Congress upon application of two-thirds of the state legislatures. At such a convention, elected delegates from each state meet to determine what, if any, amendments ought to be proposed. If the convention properly proposes amendments, Congress has two options to provide for ratification: by approval of three-quarters (thirty-eight, at present) of the state legislatures or by approval of three-quarters of specially called state conventions. The Article V provision for states to apply to Congress to hold a constitutional convention is commonly referred to as the Application Clause.

In the original Virginia Plan considered by the delegates to the first constitutional convention held in Philadelphia from May to September 1787, Congress was excluded from the constitutional amendment process. As George Mason explained, constitutional amendments ought not depend on the consent of the national legislature for "they may abuse their power, and refuse their consent on that very account."[1] Over the course of the hot summer of 1787, the constitutional convention considered several variations of Article V amendment provisions. Eventually, and relatively late in the Philadelphia convention, the delegates settled on language providing Congress its current role in proposing constitutional amendments. Responding to Mason's cautionary counsel not to make the proposing of amendments depend in all cases on Congress's consent, the Framers provided for the states to initiate constitutional change through Article V's so-called Application Clause. The Article V Application Clause was from the beginning, and still is, a hedge against abuse of power by the national government. It is a constitutional device that often has been used by the states to prod a reluctant Congress into action. States threaten to apply to Congress to call a constitutional convention unless Congress takes certain action that the states desire.

Many convention applications have been sent to Congress. From the adoption of the Constitution until 1974 there had been 356 state applications calling on Congress to convene a proposing convention.[2] By 2013, Congress had received a total of 696 such applications.[3] Although these state applications have never resulted in Congress calling a proposing convention, it would be a grave misinterpretation of constitutional history to conclude that Article V's convention-proposing mechanism has failed to contribute to the shaping of constitutional policy.

The Article V Application Clause and Securing the Bill of Rights

With ratification by New Hampshire, the ninth state to ratify, the Constitution went into effect on June 21, 1788. But when the first United States Congress convened in March 1789, the fate of the Constitution was uncertain. Rhode Island had rejected the Constitution. North Carolina had not yet ratified and had insisted on the adoption of certain amendments as a condition of joining the union. New York had ratified but simultaneously had insisted on the convening of a new constitutional convention to consider amendments designed to wrest power from the central government. As a means to achieve this goal, New York adopted the "New York Circular Letter," a letter sent to all of the states urging each to join in demanding a second constitutional convention to repair the current Constitution's defects. Virginia, agreeing with New York, also ratified but led the effort to demand a second constitutional convention.[4] At the state conventions held to ratify the Constitution, many delegates who otherwise supported the Constitution recoiled over the absence of a bill of rights and concluded that the only safe course was to hold another convention to amend the Constitution by adding a bill of rights. To gain support for the Constitution's ratification and avoid a second constitutional convention, proponents of ratification, particularly James Madison, had promised to introduce constitutional amendments providing a series of individual rights as a first order of business once the Constitution was ratified and Congress convened. As proof against deception, anti-Federalists continued their threat of a second convention as a bargaining chip to leverage the first Congress to propose a bill of rights.[5]

Demands for a second constitutional convention had a more sinister motivation than assuring that the first Congress would in fact propose a bill of rights. At the first Congress, insistence on a second convention became a rallying call for anti-Federalists who were outright enemies of the Constitution. They desired a second convention to effect radical structural changes, particularly changes with respect to the Constitution's consolidation of power in the national government and the ability of the national government to tax.[6] While anti-Federalists attempted to turn the absence of a bill of rights into a deal breaker, Federalists doubted the genuineness of anti-Federalists' desire for a bill of rights, believing instead that what the anti-Federalists really were attempting through their complaints over the absence of a bill of rights was an argument for convening a second constitutional convention that would undo the work of the first.[7]

Meanwhile, Federalists controlled the First Congress, and most of them had no interest in amending the Constitution. Indeed, they were fiercely opposed to any amendment.[8] Madison and other more pragmatic Federalists were fully aware of the second convention threat that hung over the first Congress and understood that a constitutional amendment adding a bill of rights would work political wonders. First, those who had seized on the Article V provision for convening a proposing convention as a means to achieve amendments guaranteeing individual liberties would be satisfied once Congress adopted a bill of rights and sent it to the states for their consideration and ratification. Moreover, anti-Federalists opposed to the Constitution in general and desiring systemic change to the Constitution would then lose their leverage for a second convention that would threaten the very existence of the United States. Duly prodded, Federalists in Congress voted to propose the Bill of Rights, and support for a second convention subsided.

Dueling Article V Clauses during the Quasi-War with France

America's first foreign relations crisis was the so-called "Quasi-War" with France, an undeclared naval war that lasted from 1797 to 1801.[9] That crisis produced strong anti-alien sentiments arising from widespread fear of imminent invasion from France. Arch-conservative Federalists reacted by proposing constitutional amendments that would have barred aliens from holding federal office. These amendment proposals were supported by nearly half of the states. Congress instead enacted the "milder," yet much-maligned, Alien and Sedition Acts of 1798. The Sedition Act criminalized untruthful peaceful criticism of the incumbent federal government and government officials. Although the Alien and Sedition Acts can be seen as moderate compromises when compared to the more radical proposed constitutional amendments, the legislation, especially the Sedition Act, left the Jeffersonian Republicans aghast. The Jeffersonian Republicans reacted by adopting the Kentucky and Virginia Resolutions. These were state-initiated resolutions of disapproval that were sent to the legislatures of the other states requesting support for efforts to convene a convention of the states to overturn this deplored Federalist legislation. Each side, Federalist and Republican, thus simultaneously attempted to use different clauses of Article V for their own political advantage. This story of the confluence of dueling Article V provisions illuminates an early example of not just the threat, but the use of Article V to prod Congress—albeit attempting to prod Congress to act in diametrically different ways.

The backdrop of this drama begins with France's declaration of war against Great Britain and Holland on February 1, 1793, several years following the French Revolution. King Louis XVI had just met his fate at the guillotine in January, but the profoundly disturbing massacres of September 1793, the so-called Reign of Terror, had not yet occurred. Many Americans from all walks of life welcomed the French Revolution and were elated by news of the demise of the French monarchy.[10]

In this climate of popular support for the French Revolution, in the spring of 1793 the newly declared French Republic dispatched twenty-nine-year-old Edmund Charles Genet ("Citizen Genet"), to the United States as its envoy.[11] Genet's mission was to drum up support for the French Revolution, spread the principles of the Revolution, attempt to persuade the US government to honor France's understanding of America's obligations under the French-American Alliance of 1778, arrange for the outfitting of privateers in US ports that would attack British commercial shipping, and solicit US seamen to sail these privateers. He also was directed by his superiors to attempt to secure US assistance in organizing attacks on the Spanish in Florida and Louisiana and the British in Canada.[12]

Upon his arrival in the United States, Genet received a warm welcome from the local population, especially in Philadelphia, but he received a courteous but chilly reception from the US government. Just weeks following Genet's arrival, President George Washington issued a Proclamation of Neutrality regarding the conflict between France and Great Britain. Genet blundered badly by attempting to rally people against Washington's Proclamation of Neutrality. Mob protest against the Proclamation of Neutrality in the streets of Philadelphia reinforced fear that Genet's converts would attempt to gain French control over American politics. Many Federalists viewed as subversive Genet's impulsive and cocky efforts to arouse the American public in support of the French Revolution and interpreted the public's zeal for the French Revolution as an instrument that Genet and his Republican supporters in America intended to use to overthrow the US government.[13]

This dissension that Genet spawned occurred during the summer preceding the beginning of the French Reign of Terror, which commenced in September 1793 and ended in July 1794.[14] These mass executions in France exacerbated the great anxiety regarding foreign influence in American politics created by Genet and events in Philadelphia during the summer of 1793.[15] This anxiety persisted long after the French government, at the request of the US government, recalled Citizen Genet in the fall of 1793.

There were factually grounded fears of a French invasion of North America and sedition in America. In 1796, French naval units probed the St. Lawrence River in preparation of an invasion of Lower Canada in 1797 (French-Canadian Canada centered in Quebec). Also in 1796, off the coast of Ireland a British warship intercepted an US merchant ship loaded with two dozen cannons and twenty thousand muskets and bayonets intended for anti-British Irish immigrant settlers living in Canada to promote revolution in support of an invasion of Canada by the French. The French government sent these weapons in direct support of a scheme by a Vermont citizen who intended that, after the French invaded Canada in 1797, Vermont would secede from the United States, join French-controlled Canada, and form a new republic called United Columbia.[16] In short, Genet's revolutionary zeal and intrigue over the course of his six-month US stay combined with well-documented French imperialist designs in North America laid a solid foundation for the development of intense anti-immigrant jingoism, which was manifested in part through efforts to amend the Constitution.[17]

Federalists suspected that Jeffersonian Republicans were plotting to subvert the US government, fears made more credible due to the Jeffersonian Republicans' widespread support for the French Revolution.[18] French émigrés in America were estimated to number 25,000 or more. Many were aristocrats who had fled the Reign of Terror but most were refugees from the slave uprisings on the Island of Santa Dominique. In Philadelphia, French newspapers sprouted up, as well as French restaurants and bookstores and schools. Rumors spread of a plot to burn Philadelphia, causing a city-wide exodus. Rioting broke out with street brawls between pro-French and pro-British groups. Aliens were viewed as a grave danger to civil society. Irish immigrants represented fully half of all immigrants to America in the several decades immediately following 1783.[19] Many were fresh from the Irish Rebellion of 1798, an uprising against British rule in Ireland. Many Americans thought that these Irish immigrants entered the United States with a deep hostility toward Great Britain, were ripe for recruitment to France's side in the event of a French invasion, and in fact were preparing to assist in such an invasion. More generally, it was feared that French émigrés and aliens in general who sympathized with the French Revolution would become collaborators following a French invasion.[20] Many Americans believed that civil war was on the horizon.[21]

These fears of war with France, invasion of North America by France, and internal subversion by those supporting the French Revolution seemed all the more credible when, in the spring of 1797, the newly installed administration of John Adams learned that the French Directory (the name of the current French revolutionary government) had issued decrees launching an undeclared war against United States commerce trafficking to and from Europe, the Mediterranean, and the Caribbean. By late spring of 1797, French warships had taken more than three hundred US trading vessels.[22]

It was in this convulsive and fear-filled political environment that the Federalist-dominated Congress in June and early July 1798 considered the Alien Act and the Naturalization Act (as well as the infamous Sedition Act), neither of which President Adams had advocated but nevertheless signed.[23] History's verdict is that no act of the Adams's presidency was more reprehensible, but at the time strong majorities in Congress and among the American citizenry supported this legislation.[24] The Alien Act gave the president authority to expel any alien from the country without a hearing or any justifying rationale if the president considered the person "dangerous to the peace and safety of the United States." The Naturalization Act had three key provisions: it extended the period of residence before one was eligible for citizenship from five years to fourteen years (prior to 1795 it had been two years); required aliens to register and file reports; and barred citizenship to those who were citizens of countries with which the United States was at war.[25]

As draconian as these provisions were, they were moderate compared to other proposals, including several proposed constitutional amendments introduced at this time. Massachusetts Federalist congressman Harrison Gray Otis, not the most extreme Federalist, had proposed eliminating all future immigration, thereby limiting the future population to those already here.[26] One extremist member of Congress from South Carolina proposed limiting citizenship to just those persons born in the United States. As early as when New York held its convention to ratify the US Constitution, state leaders had concluded that it was a mistake for the Constitution to permit naturalized citizens to hold senior federal political office.[27] Accordingly, New York's legislature directed its representatives in Congress to introduce a constitutional amendment limiting eligibility for the offices of president, vice-president, and membership in Congress to native-born Americans, excepting only those who were residents in the Colonies as of the date of the Declaration of Independence. Such an amendment was introduced on July 26, 1788,[28] and loomed as a backdrop when Congress considered enactment of the Alien Act and the Naturalization Act. On July 7, and again on July 9, 1798, within days of the Congress's approval of the Alien Act and the Naturalization Act, but prior to President Adams signing the bills on July 14, 1798, Massachusetts's senators and its House delegation complied with directions from their state and introduced proposed amendments almost identical to New York's still pending constitutional amendment proposal. The Massachusetts proposed amendment would have disqualified naturalized citizens from eligibility for senior federal office. By October 1798, Connecticut's congressional delegation proposed a virtually identical amendment proposal.[29] Altogether six states concurred in proposing that the Constitution be amended to bar non-native-born citizens from eligibility for election to both Congress and the presidency. With that level of endorsement, amendment supporters needed concurrence of senators from only five additional states for the amendment to clear the Congress and be sent to the states for ratification.[30] Pressure was mounting on Adams to sign the pending Alien and Naturalization legislation, which he did not advocate but was a more moderate alternative to pending proposals for constitutional change.

With the Alien Act and the Naturalization Act on the books by the summer of 1798, no other states added their support to amending the Constitution in the manner proposed by New York, Massachusetts, Connecticut, and three other states. For more moderate Federalists, the milder Naturalization Act extending eligibility for citizenship to fourteen years of residency in the United States may have seemed adequate to sooth fears that aliens would gain citizenship, take control of the government, and join France in a war against Great Britain.

The Jeffersonian Republicans viewed this legislation as anything but moderate, especially the Alien and Sedition Acts. Considering these statutes as insidious devices designed to sustain Federalist political control and move the country toward monarchy, the Republicans mounted a countermove in late 1798 to resist what they viewed as Federalist tyranny. Since Federalists controlled the national government, Southern and some Northern Republicans plotted to use the state legislatures to attack the Alien and Sedition Acts. Their vehicle of attack has become known as the Kentucky and Virginia Resolutions. These were resolutions of disapproval from the Kentucky and Virginia legislatures that declared the reserved right of either the state legislature or the people of the state to declare acts of the federal government unconstitutional and unenforceable within that state. These resolutions were sent to the legislatures of all of the other states.

Madison's *Report on the Virginia Resolutions* made explicit reference to the Article V convention clause when it explained why it was fitting for the Virginia legislature to approve the resolution. Madison argued that the Constitution sanctioned the authority of the states to oppose actions by the federal government by petitioning Congress to hold a second constitutional convention to propose amendments designed to reverse actions by the federal government. By communicating to other state legislatures this justification for Virginia's opposition to the Alien and Sedition Acts, Madison, at least implicitly, was suggesting deployment of an agenda-setting strategy that the Constitution provided states desiring to oppose federal abuse of power.[31]

The Alien and Sedition Acts lapsed by their own terms before any state formally petitioned Congress to call a second constitutional convention, so the states' challenge to those statutes dissolved.[32] But the Kentucky and Virginia Resolutions are important because their political and constitutional justifications were built on the view that these state resolutions were sanctioned by the Article V Application Clause—the first such use of the Article V Application Clause in our constitutional history.[33]

The Contested Election of 1800

The contested 1800 presidential election also generated a political crisis spawning a threat that states might combine to force Congress to convene a second constitutional convention. President John Adams's term expired on March 3, 1801. It appeared that the country might be left with no President and no way to choose an interim as of March 4, 1801, the date set for the presidential inauguration. Thomas Jefferson and Aaron Burr had each received an equal number of electoral votes, and the election was to be decided by the House of Representatives. The support of nine state delegations in the House was needed for election.[34] In the lame-duck House of Representatives in the winter of 1801, the Federalists controlled six state delegations and the Republicans controlled eight. In two states, Vermont and Maryland, the state delegations were evenly divided between Federalists and Republicans. Over the course of a week in February, and after thirty-five ballots, the House was deadlocked. As March 4 quickly approached, it was rumored that the incumbent Federalist Congress intended to enact legislation designating an interim President.[35] Rumors of military intervention and civil war abounded. Militias in Virginia and Pennsylvania were readied to prevent any statutory naming of a president and mobs gathered around the capital threatening to bar the inauguration of any president appointed by statute. Jefferson stated that in the event of the

House being unable to choose a successor to Adams by the time Adams's term expired, it would be necessary to call a constitutional convention to address the crisis. This option, Jefferson reported to Monroe in a letter, alarmed the Federalists. The very word convention gives them "horrors [for] they fear they should lose some of the favourite morsels of the constitution."[36] Jefferson well understood that a second convention could serve as a device to effect a textual change in the then-flawed method for choosing presidents but also, and perhaps more importantly, could operate as a political tool to prod Congress into action.

The Federalists blinked. Just days before the March 4 inauguration date, some Federalist delegations abstained from voting and Jefferson was elected by a vote of ten states to four with two states not voting. Was it the threat of military intervention, the mobs around the capital, the threat of a second constitutional convention that could dramatically change the constitutional order, or the desire for peace by moderates that resolved the crisis? No constitutional historian has attempted to unscramble that egg. But Jefferson certainly thought that the threat of a second constitutional convention would be an irresistible provocation for Federalists in Congress to compromise—as they did.

Collective Action by the States to Limit Congress's Power to Impose Embargos

The self-destructive Embargo Act of 1807 enacted by the Jeffersonian Republican Congress, with Jefferson's blessing, created yet another political crisis. This embargo crippled New England's economy and ultimately resulted in the threat of secession by some New England political leaders. As an alternative to secession, New England Federalists called upon all of the states harmed by the Embargo Act (especially the New England states) to meet in convention to propose a constitutional amendment solution. Within weeks of that convention call, Congress retreated: it repealed the ill-conceived Embargo Act rather than face an enraged citizenry intent on constitutional change that might impede Congress's future ability to wage commercial war by instituting embargos. This "failed" effort to amend the Constitution is one of the lesser-known episodes in US legal and constitutional history but is one of the most telling examples of how the *opportunity* for concerted action by the states, using the Article V Application Clause, can create political leverage to force Congress's hand. Most of these events occurred between the waning days of 1808 and March of 1809. But the story begins in March 1805, the day Jefferson took the oath of office for a second time.

By the time Jefferson began his second term, Napoleon Bonaparte had crowned himself Emperor, and his armies controlled most of Europe. France and Britain had resumed their war after a failed temporary peace provided by the 1801 Peace of Amiens. The United States was on cordial terms with both France and Great Britain, and trade with each was brisk. Notwithstanding the British maritime rule banning "direct" shipments to and from belligerents' ports, Britain was willing to permit US ships to carry on highly profitable trans-Atlantic freighting of goods on neutral US ships.[37] Trade between the Caribbean and Europe soared, and US ships captured most of it. US exports doubled between 1803 and 1807.[38]

This commercially profitable state of affairs began to unravel in 1805. First, grumbling increased in Great Britain over US shipping interests benefitting financially from Britain's investment of some blood and much treasure as a result of its fighting Napoleon and driving French ships from the seas. Great Britain therefore determined that forthwith US ships carrying cargo to or from a belligerent's port would be subject to seizure unless the US ships actually unloaded their goods at a US port and reloaded them for transshipment to their final destination.[39] British warships began seizing US commercial vessels and their cargoes with a devastating impact on the US economy.

Most humiliating was the claimed right by the British navy to stop US ships on the high seas, board them, and impress crew members (kidnap seamen and force them to serve on British warships).[40] The inevitable clash occurred on June 22, 1807, when the frigate *USS Chesapeake* refused a demand by the fifty-gun British warship *HMS Leopard* that *Chesapeake* voluntarily permit itself to be boarded and searched for British deserters. *Leopard* fired three broadsides at close range into *Chesapeake*, killing three and wounding many more. A party from *Leopard* boarded *Chesapeake* and impressed four sailors, three of whom, it turned out, were American citizens and not British navy deserters.

Competing French and British trade regulations added fuel to the crisis. Each country decreed that it would seize neutral ships that traded with the other, with the result that neutral countries' trade with most of Europe was rendered impossible unless shipping interests were willing to risk seizure of ship and cargo.[41] The US government was under great pressure to take action so that commercial shipping on neutral US vessels (and a return to high profitability) could safely resume.

The Jefferson administration responded with what historian Gordon Wood has characterized as "an act of self-immolation."[42] Deciding that economic retaliation, rather than war, was the best response, Republican leaders in Congress enacted trade restrictions. They were designed to apply economic pressure on the belligerents, both France and Great Britain (but especially Great Britain), to force them to yield by denying them the US market for their goods and access to US exports. After several false starts, the Jefferson Congress passed the Embargo Act of 1807—a non-exportation law barring the departure of all US merchant ships and goods from any US port to engage in international trade.

The embargo caused a calamitous economic depression, the worst since colonial times.[43] Overseas trade was the lifeblood of the New England mercantile economy, so New England sustained the greatest economic harm from the embargo, but farmers and others outside of New England also suffered miserably.[44] One wag described the Embargo Act as an effort "to cure corns by cutting off the toes."[45]

Matters were made worse when Jefferson's Secretary of the Treasury Gallatin persuaded Congress that the Treasury Department, charged with enforcing the embargo, needed extraordinary and arbitrary powers to organize a vast police effort against the nation's own citizens, many of whom would not willingly forego opportunities to trade.[46] Congress provided these powers, eventually authorizing the Treasury Department to use armed ships to apprehend those suspected violating the embargo. In addition, the federal government imposed systems for licensing of shipping, required bonds, and insisted that ships be loaded under the watchful eyes of federal revenue officers.

As the federal enforcement effort intensified, an uprising against the Embargo Act erupted. Violation of the embargo was so rampant on the New York/Canadian border that Jefferson declared this border region to be in a state of insurrection, viewed the embargo violators as rebels, and ordered the US military to crush the insurrection by armed force.[47]

Furious over what it perceived as political repression by the federal government, commercial New England roared in protest. Many other parts of the country, including New York and Maryland, also resisted and expressed hostile objection to the embargo.[48] The poor suffered the greatest privation due to soaring unemployment, rising prices, and shortage of staples such as flour.[49] Civil war was a realistic possibility in New England, especially Massachusetts.[50] Jefferson was unmoved by the flood of petitions from towns that had been devastated economically by the embargo. He was convinced the embargo was an effective coercive measure to force Great Britain and France to remove their trade restrictions.[51] Meanwhile, France and Britain suffered little from the embargo.[52]

This opposition to the Embargo Act, which became an insurrection in some parts of the country, reached a climax during the roughly one hundred days between the election of James Madison as president in November 1808 and his scheduled inauguration in March of 1809, by which time the incumbent Republican Congress had finally repealed the Embargo Act.[53] This hundred-day period witnessed momentous events.

First, the lame-duck Republican Congress gravely misjudged the mood of New England and escalated the crisis by enacting a new, even more draconian, Embargo Act. This legislation provided customs officials even broader and more arbitrary powers to capture and punish embargo violators, including the power to seize goods on the mere *suspicion* that they were intended for exportation.[54] History's verdict is that the provisions of this legislation, as enforced, were constitutionally invalid.[55]

The federal government's remorseless enforcement of the embargo was a grave political miscalculation. It stoked the fire of defiance among political leaders and the citizenry, primarily in the North. Throughout New England (other than in Vermont) Federalists had gained politically during the 1808 elections. But Congress's post-election grant of enhanced enforcement powers to the Jefferson administration resulted in an even greater defection from the Republican Party, undercut moderates, and shifted the political initiative to radicals who urged contempt for the federal government and argued for increased reliance on state government to obtain redress.[56] At local town and county meetings along the New England coast, citizens characterized embargo backers as Constitution violators, called for concerted disobedience of federal law, and formed local armed committees of safety as a means to prevent compliance with the Embargo Act.[57] Throughout New England, the embargo was flouted. Attempts to enforce the Act judicially were fruitless, because juries refused to convict embargo violators.[58] Calls for secession appeared in the press.

The public outcry against the embargo became so vehement that New England political leaders feared that the public, losing patience with moderate responses, would turn to armed insurrection. Accordingly, party leaders in Massachusetts decided to work with Connecticut Federalists to organize a general meeting of New England Federalist leaders for the purpose of proposing amendments to the Constitution that would address public concerns over the embargo and thereby dampen calls for secession and generally discourage radical protest.[59] By early January 1809, general agreement had been reached that the New England state legislatures would recommend convening a convention in the spring to amend the Constitution. An overriding concern was the tinder box of public anger and the risk that protest at such a convention could not peacefully be contained. For example, although the Massachusetts legislature had agreed to cooperate with other states wishing to meet in convention, it recently had approved a nullification resolution stating that the Embargo Act was unconstitutional and not legally binding on its citizens.[60] It was not possible to squelch rumors that the convention would propose disunion.[61]

The convention of New England states, called to propose constitutional amendments, never convened. The Republican Congress retreated early in 1809, just weeks before Madison was to assume the presidency. Shaken by these events in New England, the Republican majority in Congress reversed course by expressing support for repeal of the Embargo Act. This congressional retreat drained the momentum from the initiative to assemble the states in convention, but the call for the convention had done its work of freeing New England from the embargo. This is historian James Banner's conclusion.[62] And this also became Jefferson's conclusion, who candidly acknowledged that this "failed" effort to amend the Constitution through the calling of a convention of New England states contributed to the Embargo Act's repeal.[63] Once the Republican majority in Congress concluded that the threat of a constitutional convention controlled by radicals was credible, the forces for statutory repeal gained purchase.[64]

The Nullification Crisis

The tariff wars during the first third of the nineteenth century, which precipitated the nullification crisis, spawned the first formal applications that the states sent to Congress requesting that it convene a constitutional convention. The cotton South resented the protective tariffs of 1828 and 1832, which imposed high tariffs on imported manufactured goods. Northern manufacturers argued that they needed the protection of the tariffs to stay in business. The agrarian South, having little manufacturing industry, paid higher prices for imported manufactured goods as a result of the tariff and thus considered the protective tariff a subsidy for Northern business at their expense.[65] In 1832, South Carolina's gifted politician, John C. Calhoun, led South Carolina to declare the tariff unconstitutional and null and void within the state. South Carolina banned collection of the tariff duties within its borders until the matter could be resolved by an Article V constitutional convention of all the states. South Carolina also filed an application with Congress requesting that it call such a convention.[66] South Carolina's convention application did not generate widespread support from other states, but two states, Georgia and Alabama also filed convention applications with Congress. Moreover, Georgia proposed that all the Southern states meet to develop a concerted strategy to gain relief from the tariff.[67] Andrew Jackson and the Jacksonian Congress shrank from a fight in the face of this mobilization by the Southern states against the tariff. In late 1832, Congress approved a compromise tariff that the South found acceptable. Protective tariff proponents concluded that it was better to avoid inflamed Southern agitation by adopting tariff rates acceptable to the South.[68] Opponents of the protective tariff had achieved an important political victory, aided in part by the specter of discontented states insisting that Congress convene an Article V constitutional amendment–proposing convention.[69]

Direct Election of Senators

Supreme Court Justice Antonin Scalia once expressed the view that the decline of states' rights in the twentieth century can be traced to the "burst of progressivism in 1913" that added the Seventeenth Amendment to the Constitution and thus changed the way we select US senators.[70] The Seventeenth Amendment provides for the popular election of senators, thereby transferring political power from state legislatures to the state's voters. This power transfer to the voters did dramatically alter the system of federalism, and its 1913 addition to the Constitution did occur in the context of a rise in progressivism. However, a full account of the forces that resulted in the adoption of the Seventeenth Amendment also requires an understanding of state law developments occurring many decades prior to the dawn of the progressive era and the prodding of Congress provided by the threat of a constitutional convention.

The state legislatures' prerogative to select the state's US senators was famously part of the "great compromise" at the Philadelphia Constitutional Convention that balanced the needs of the large and small states to have adequate representation in the national legislature. The Senate was chosen as the chamber where the states themselves would be represented—the people's chamber was the House of Representatives. In the early days of the Republic, state legislatures developed an almost proprietary relationship with their two US senators, even binding them through instructions.[71] The selection of US senators by state legislatures proved unsatisfactory. First, denying voters a direct vote for US senator was contrary to a growing impulse for more direct political democracy that developed during the nineteenth century. In addition, insistence on the popular election of US senators reflected a burgeoning public hostility to government extravagance, corruption, and special favor.[72] Herman Ames, the premier chronicler of proposed constitutional amendments from 1789 to 1897, reported that selection of senators by state legislatures "leads to corruption of legislatures, and to the selection of men whose only claim to office is their great wealth or their subserviency [sic] to corporate interests."[73] Moreover, the state legislatures' elections for US senators could become three-ring circuses where state legislative business was held up for weeks due to the haggling over whom to choose to become the state's US senator. Fistfights sometimes broke out as well as riotous demonstrations. Members of the state legislature often abandoned all pretense of decorum and detached judgment in choosing a US senator. Sometimes a state legislature would not be able to agree on whom to select, and the prolonged deadlock would leave the state partially or totally unrepresented in the Senate for a period of time.[74]

Dissatisfaction with the Constitution's procedure for selecting senators became so pronounced that, after 1872, in virtually every session of Congress, one or more resolutions were offered to amend the Constitution to provide for choosing senators by popular election.[75] On five occasions prior to 1913, the House voted its approval for such a constitutional amendment, but the Senate refused to brings any of these resolutions to a vote.[76] Unsurprisingly, incumbent US senators, who owed their office to their ability to manipulate the current system, had no incentive to risk their political careers by placing the decision in the hands of the state's voters.

Checked by insurmountable Senate intransigence, reformers devised alternative approaches that did not require a two-thirds Senate vote to amend the Constitution. Every schoolboy and -girl knows that in 1858, before Abraham Lincoln was elected president, he "ran" for the Senate from Illinois and debated Stephen Douglas in the famous Lincoln-Douglas debates. Seldom considered is how that could have occurred since the direct election of senators did not begin until the 1913 adoption of the Seventeenth Amendment. The answer is found in the state-by-state lobbying that reformers initiated to change the way state legislatures selected senators. These experiments pre-tested systems for direct election of senators and smoothed the way for the eventual adoption of the Seventeenth Amendment.

One popular experiment utilized state political parties and the party convention, which nominated a slate of the party's candidates for the state legislature. These candidates for the state legislature pledged that if they were elected to the state legislature they would vote for the party's candidate for the US Senate. Normally, each party would not name its Senate candidate until the state legislature convened. But breaking precedent, the delegates to the 1858 Illinois Republican Party convention nominated Lincoln as their Senate candidate. Douglas was the Democratic incumbent US senator. So the campaign of 1858 to elect Illinois state legislators in effect became a contest to decide whether Lincoln or Douglas would represent Illinois in the US Senate.[77]

The political party convention system soon morphed into the direct primary election system. Between 1890 and 1900, state political parties began holding direct primaries to provide voters an opportunity to express their preference for US senator. These served as a substitute for the convention but, like the convention, each party's candidates for the state legislature were pledged to support the person who had won the party's Senate primary election.

A variation on this, which became known as the Oregon system, was begun in Oregon in 1904. Its popularity soon spread across the country. Under this approach, a statewide election would be conducted for US senator. State law required that each candidate for election to the state legislature was required to sign one of two statements. The candidate could sign a statement publicly pledging that, in the state legislature's election of the state's US senator, the candidate for the state legislature would vote for the person who had won the statewide election for the US Senate. Or the candidate for the state legislature could sign a second statement that he would consider the statewide Senate election as advisory but not binding. In addition, throughout the state, concerned citizens circulated petitions that committed those signing them to vote only for candidates for the state legislature who had agreed to be bound by the outcome of the statewide election for US senator. Unsurprisingly, most candidates for the state legislature agreed to be bound by the popular vote for US senator. By 1908 fifteen states had adopted the Oregon system and, altogether, twenty-eight states had some mechanism effectively electing US senators by popular mandate.[78]

There is wide agreement that this state-by-state lobbying strategy was instrumental in the adoption of the Seventeenth Amendment.[79] First, the direct-election reforms in many states created inexorable pressure on the Senate to go along and propose the Seventeenth Amendment to the states. It would be perilous for an incumbent US senator to oppose the Seventeenth Amendment if a senator represented a state whose voters had chosen a system that effectively already elected senators by direct vote (nearly half of the Senate). Indeed, as the debate over the Seventeenth Amendment reached its zenith, it was the senators from states that popularly elected senators who led the effort to support the Seventeenth Amendment. Some realized that they would not have been elected to the Senate but for popular election of senators in their home state.[80] Finally, pre-testing the direct election of senators at the state level built grassroots support that greatly facilitated the Seventeenth Amendment's ratification. Little debate was needed because most states had completed their deliberation on the question of direct election of senators many years previously.

But in the case of the Seventeenth Amendment, proponents concluded that state-by-state adoption of methods for directly providing citizen input into the election of US senators was a necessary but not sufficient strategy to secure passage of the Seventeenth Amendment. The amendment's adoption also required deploying the Article V Application Clause as a way to protest, to goad Congress (especially the US Senate) into proposing the Seventeenth Amendment to the states.[81]

Fully 20 percent of all of the convention applications received by Congress from the date of the adoption of the Constitution until 1974 dealt in one way or another with direct election of senators.[82] Convinced that the Senate never would propose an amendment providing for the popular election of senators until faced with convention applications from two-thirds of the state legislatures, Pennsylvania's legislature led the effort to recruit other states. By 1912, Congress had received convention applications from thirty-one state legislatures, just one short of the number needed to require Congress to call a convention. Commentators during this period reasoned that either the thirty-one-state show of support for a convention would prod Congress into proposing its own amendment or the holdouts in the Senate would be defeated at their next election due to the national support for the direct election of senators. In May 1912 the Senate capitulated and proposed the Seventeenth Amendment to the states.[83]

The ratification of the Seventeenth Amendment thus once again crystallizes how constitutional politics are more circular than linear. Frustrated efforts to amend the Constitution forced amendment supporters to take matters into their own hands by organizing law reform at the state level. That reform, in conjunction with grassroot applications for a second constitutional convention, was effective in prodding the Senate to capitulate and propose the Seventeenth Amendment to the states. In this, as in so many instances, each development turned upon itself until a political equilibrium emerged.[84]

Counter-Attack on the Court's Reapportionment Cases: The Dirksen Convention Application Effort

In 1961, the Supreme Court decided *Baker v. Carr*,[85] and over the next several terms the Court decided many additional so-called "reapportionment" cases, the three most influential of which were decided in 1963 and 1964.[86] Chief Justice Earl Warren described the *Baker v. Carr* decision as "the most vital decision" rendered by the Court during his tenure and the reapportionment of legislative bodies it launched as the Court's most important achievement during his term as chief justice.[87] These reapportionment decisions precipitated a second constitutional convention application effort that came within one state application of the two-thirds needed to force Congress to convene a convention.

Prior to the 1960s, many states had adopted long-entrenched voting systems that resulted in blatant inequalities favoring those living in rural portions of the state to the disadvantage of the state's urban dwellers. The discrimination resulted from substantial disparity in the populations of voting districts. For congressional districts, it would not be unusual for populations in some voting districts to be two or three times larger than in others, as was the case, for example, in *Wesberry v. Sanders*.[88] The population disparity in state legislative voting districts created huge discriminatory effects. For example, in *Reynolds v. Sims*, the Court pointed out that approximately one-quarter of the voters in the state of Alabama possessed the ability to elect a majority in both houses of the Alabama legislature. This population disparity in voting districts, in practical effect, allotted different individuals a different number of votes and in practice created rural dominance of the legislative process in many states. Beginning in 1842, federal legislation required states to provide "contiguous, equal [congressional voting] districts." That requirement ended in 1929 and in *Wood v. Broom* the Supreme Court found that Congress had intentionally abandoned the requirement that each state provide equipopulous congressional voting districts.[89]

Opponents of legislative malapportionment brought challenges to the Supreme Court. But in its 1946 decision in *Colegrove v. Green*,[90] the Court refused to consider the merits of a challenge to the apportionment of the Illinois congressional districts, concluding that apportionment of legislative voting districts was a non-justiciable "political question." *Baker v. Carr* was ground-breaking because it reversed this political question bar, holding that courts could adjudicate whether malapportioned voting districts were unconstitutional. *Baker v. Carr* thus opened the way for the Court subsequently to conclude that the Constitution requires that representation in governmental bodies must be based on voting districts that are as nearly of equal population "as is practicable" in order to give each citizen equal weight in electing representatives, or what has come to be known as the requirement of *one person, one vote*. This principle was applied first to congressional voting districts in *Wesberry v. Sanders*. Later, in *Reynolds v. Sims*, a challenge to the apportionment of the Alabama legislature, the Court specifically rejected the state's argument that, by analogy to the system of representation in the US Congress, states ought to be provided the option to choose to establish voting districts that are equipopulous in only one house of the state legislature.

The Court's one person, one vote doctrine immediately provoked passionate opposition. First, the doctrine extended the range of federal oversight into an area of governance that states had once thought was sacrosanct.[91] Moreover, the reapportionment doctrine portended a nationwide upheaval in voting rights because the Court's underlying rationale invalidated the voting districts in one or both houses in nearly every state legislature. Perhaps most distressing to many was the expectation that the one person, one vote principle would have the effect of transferring political power from small-town, rural, conservative regions of the state to the heavily populated, more liberal, urban areas.[92]

The Council of State Governments, an organization formed to promote cooperation among state officials, strongly opposed the reapportionment decisions and assumed an initial leadership role in reversing the Court's reapportionment cases by constitutional amendment. Many members of the Council were rural state legislators who could anticipate being reapportioned out of their positions as state legislators. The Council of State Governments' General Assembly approved a plan designed to amend the Constitution to eliminate federal judicial authority over the apportionment of state legislatures. The central feature of the plan was to persuade all state legislatures to file uniform applications with Congress providing that unless Congress itself acted to propose a constitutional amendment solution, Congress was to convene a constitutional convention to propose amendments. This was a self-conscious attempt to repeat the successful prodding of Congress that occurred in 1912, which had resulted in Congress proposing the Seventeenth Amendment—the direct election of US senators.[93] Within a short period of time, the legislatures of thirteen states and one house of five other state legislative bodies had endorsed the strategy to petition Congress to call a constitutional convention. Chief Justice Earl Warren sounded an alarm, warning of the dangers of a constitutional convention and urging the legal establishment to mount an opposition drive. Soon a groundswell of opposition to the convention proposal overwhelmed the Council of State Governments' convention effort.[94]

Congress soon entered the fray. In an excess of fury over the Court's reapportionment decisions, Congress reduced the pay raise for Supreme Court justices below that provided for other federal court judges.[95] In January 1965, Senator Everett Dirksen (R-IL), the Republican Minority Leader, introduced a compromise constitutional amendment proposal. It provided that only one chamber of a state legislature must be based on equal population districts; the other chamber could be elected from voting districts based on factors other than population. The Dirksen amendment twice came to a vote in the Senate, once as a rider to a resolution designating a week in the late summer of 1965 as American Legion Baseball Week.

On both occasions the Dirksen Amendment received a majority, but not a two-thirds, support. Soon thereafter, the Council of State Governments endorsed the Dirksen Amendment and sixteen state legislatures filed applications with Congress to convene a constitutional convention.

Senator Dirksen then shifted his own strategy to one centered on the Article V Application Clause. Dirksen's plan was to proceed surreptitiously to assemble the necessary state applications for a constitutional convention until the necessary number of petitions from state legislatures had been obtained, then dramatically announce that fact to the Congress, and insist that Congress comply with its Article V obligation by convening a convention. In many states during this effort to force a proposing convention, there were no public hearings on proposals to send convention applications to the Congress, or no debate, or in some cases not even a printing of the legislature's resolution approving the convention application.[96] Moreover, some state legislators misunderstood their vote, erroneously interpreting it merely as an endorsement of opposition to the reapportionment cases, not a call for a second constitutional convention.[97]

Dirksen's under-the-radar strategy might well have succeeded but for the *New York Times* reporting in March 1967 that with little knowledge of the public, or most members of Congress, thirty-two state legislatures (of the thirty-four needed) already had filed convention applications.[98] At that point, the Dirksen convention campaign attracted almost immediate nationwide opposition, including coordinated opposition both in Congress and in many state legislatures. A powerful argument raised in Congress was that most of the applications should be rejected as invalid because they came from state legislatures that themselves were malapportioned. Accepting these applications, it was argued, simply would perpetuate the power of the minority, though malapportioned legislatures, to overwhelm the will of the majority.[99] Moreover, the fear of a runaway constitutional convention permeated the arguments against convening a convention—the fear that, once convened, a second constitutional convention, like the first in the summer of 1787, could not be contained. The last thing that Dirksen and other conservatives wanted was a wide-open constitutional convention that might well backfire if controlled by liberals.

Iowa's application for a constitutional convention in 1969 brought the total of state applications to thirty-three, but at that point the convention effort stalled: Wisconsin's legislature rejected a resolution to file an application, three states rescinded their applications, and a federal court voided Utah's application due to its having been approved by a malapportioned legislature. Moreover, Republicans found that they could fare quite well in properly apportioned legislative voting districts after all, by attracting suburban voters. In addition, enough state legislatures had been reapportioned that these governing bodies had no incentive to return to the status quo ante. In addition, Senator Dirksen unexpectedly died in September 1969, which deprived the movement of its most effective leader.[100]

The efforts by Dirksen and many state leaders to prod Congress by threatening to rally around a demand that Congress convene a constitutional amendment–proposing convention illustrate again the powerful political potential of the Article V Application Clause. Proponents' actual goal often is quite different from their apparent goal. For example, Dirksen and the Council of State Governments actually feared a convention and instead deployed the convention effort as a means to goad Congress into proposing its own constitutional amendment, a tactic successfully deployed by proponents of the direct election of senators. As a *Wall Street Journal* article reported, the consensus was that Dirksen in fact *did not want a convention*. Rather, "the idea . . . is to terrorize liberal Senators with the thought of a runaway convention [and] to avoid such a calamity . . . Congress itself would propose . . . a Constitutional amendment."[101]

But there is possibly another political outcome that the Dirksen Amendment effort helped achieve: influencing the Supreme Court to loosen its requirements for mathematical precision when designing voting districts. In *Reynolds v. Sims* the Court had stated that mathematical exactness or precision was not required, but the Court did not prescribe guidelines. In fact, however, the lower courts soon imposed quantifiable standards that could be applied uniformly. By 1969, just as the Dirksen Amendment effort was heating up, the Court decided *Kirkpatrick v. Preisler*, rejecting a congressional apportionment plan where the "most populous district was 3.13 percent above the mathematical ideal, and the least populous was 2.84 percent below." The Court ruled that the Constitution imposed a duty of government to "make a good faith effort to achieve *precise mathematical equality among districts.*"[102] While *Kirkpatrick* was a congressional voting district case, the baseline for all of the justices was the Court's opinion in *Reynolds v. Sims*, a state legislative districting case, suggesting that the same degree of mathematical precision would be applied to state legislative voting districts.

That did not occur, however. The Court sounded a tactical retreat in 1973, at a time when the near-victory of the Dirksen convention effort had not yet fully subsided and it was reasonable to expect that it could be resurrected. In a series of 1973 cases, the Court distinguished state legislative districts and adopted more flexible guidelines for evaluating the constitutionality of state redistricting. In 1973 the Court upheld plus-to-minus variation of 16.4 percent when reviewing Virginia's state legislative apportionment and explicitly held that greater deviation from the goal of equipopulous voting districts would henceforth be permitted in state legislative districts. That same term the Court upheld a plus-to-minus 10 percent deviation, concluding that it was de minimis and required no justification.[103] In later cases, the Court tolerated deviations of as much as 20 percent in state voting districts.[104]

It is entirely possible that the Court might have applied these less stringent standards for evaluating the constitutionality of state legislative redistricting plans even if there never had been a Dirksen-proposed second convention effort that came within one state application of triggering the mandatory congressional obligation to call a second constitutional convention. However, a careful reading of the Court's 1969 decision in *Kirkpatrick v. Preisler* suggests the contrary. The *Kirkpatrick* opinion contains no reasoning that supports the dichotomy that emerged in 1973 between the precision required in congressional districts and the lack of precision permitted in state legislative voting districts. In *Kirkpatrick*, the Court flatly rejected Missouri's argument that "there is a fixed numerical or percentage population variance small enough to be considered *de minimis* and [thus] satisfy without question the 'as nearly as practicable' standard."[105] Yet four years later the Court accepted 10 percent as a de minimis deviation for state legislative districts without the state being required to justify it. Clearly the Court had changed its view and did so following the state legislatures' nearly successful effort to press Congress into calling a second constitutional convention that likely would have proposed constitutional amendments withdrawing, or at least modifying, the Court's state redistricting authority.[106]

4

The Impact of Article V on Federal Legislation

Article V as a Bargaining Chip to Secure Federal Legislation: The Gramm-Rudman-Hollings Deficit Reduction Act of 1985

As recently as November 2011 the House of Representatives voted 261–165 in favor of a balanced budget amendment, failing by 23 votes to secure the requisite two-thirds majority needed to submit the proposal to the states. The next month, a proposed balanced budget amendment failed to gain majority support in the Senate. The 2011 measure mirrored a 1995 constitutional amendment proposal that the House approved by a two-thirds vote but that fell one vote shy of a two-thirds majority in the Senate. These proposed balanced budget constitutional amendments provided that federal spending could not exceed revenues in any year and, except for a serious military conflict, that a three-fifths majority would be required to raise the debt ceiling or waive the balanced budget requirement in any year.[1] These are some of the more widely reported congressional efforts to regulate federal taxing and spending through constitutional amendment.[2]

As of this writing, these amendment efforts have failed, but only in the sense that they have added no new text to the Constitution. But there can be little doubt that the efforts to add a balanced budget amendment to the Constitution have influenced congressional and executive branch fiscal policies. The political impact of failed balanced budget amendment efforts is best understood when examined through the lens of their interrelationship with a wider range of issues, policies, and strategies that have been devised to control federal spending and balance the federal budget. These other strategies include the president's assertion of unilateral authority to impound funds and the so-called line-item veto, which provides the president statutory authority to cancel or postpone spending programs. These abortive attempts to restrain federal spending within existing constitutional structure, and thus avoid the need to amend the Constitution, comprise the backdrop of the political controversy surrounding efforts to adopt a balanced budget constitutional amendment.

Impoundment

Fiscally conservative Republican president Thomas Jefferson informed Congress in 1803 of his, probably unconstitutional, decision to impound (choose not to spend) a fifty-thousand-dollar congressional appropriation for gunboats. In his unilateral judgment, Jefferson had concluded that these gunboats were unnecessary following the Louisiana Purchase.[3] President U. S. Grant infuriated Congress and raised constitutional questions when he announced he would not expend certain appropriated funds in the August 14, 1875, River and Harbor Act for local projects deemed by him to have no national benefit (referred to today as "pork-barrel" projects).[4]

Presidents rarely used impoundment after President Jefferson's and President Grant's precedent of impounding appropriated funds. The practice became more prevalent following World War II when impoundment was used as a means of controlling defense spending and pork-barrel special interest spending.[5] President Lyndon Johnson's advisors provided a constitutionally suspect legal opinion that impoundment was constitutional, reasoning that an appropriation is not a legally enforceable mandate to spend. Congress benignly acquiesced and never pressed the point of the constitutionality of impoundment as long as the impoundment decisions were noncontroversial. Indeed, impoundment often served the interests of members of Congress. Members could vote to appropriate funds for their favored constituents, and the president could take the political heat when exercising discretion not to expend the funds.

President Nixon upset this cozy arrangement when he vetoed amendments to the Federal Water Pollution Control Act of 1972, and Congress overrode the veto. In response to the override of his veto, the president immediately directed the administrator of the Environmental Protection Agency to withhold spending of approximately 50 percent of the funds Congress had appropriated for federal financing of municipal sewage treatment facilities that the Water Pollution Control Act of 1972 had authorized. This type of impoundment is referred to as a "policy impoundment," a decision not to expend funds as a means to advance a political agenda. President Nixon's use of a policy impoundment with respect to the Water Pollution Control Act of 1972 changed the political calculus sufficiently that Congress at first threatened impeachment of President Nixon for impounding the funds but settled for the Congressional Budget and Impoundment Control Act of 1974, legislation designed to stifle the future ability of the president to halt disfavored congressionally authorized expenditures. This legislation is a manifestation of Congress's strongly held view that the president lacks inherent executive power to impound funds.[6]

Because this 1974 Impoundment Control Act applied only prospectively, it did not settle the constitutional issue raised by President Nixon's directive to impound funds appropriated by the amendments to the Federal Water Pollution Control Act of 1972. Thus the Supreme Court addressed President Nixon's impoundment authority in *Train v. City of New York* and rejected the president's claimed inherent executive authority to impound funds.[7] The Court decided the case on statutory construction grounds, holding that the Water Pollution Control Act mandated that the appropriated funds be expended. Inherent in this reasoning by the Court are two important principles: first, that in the face of a statutory mandate that funds be expended, the president possesses no inherent executive power to resist, and second, that the Court possesses authority to order the president to comply with the statutory mandate that funds be expended.[8] *Train* eliminated all doubt that a constitutional amendment would be required if the president was to be provided authority to halt expenditures that Congress had mandated. Congress has not considered such a proposed constitutional adjustment of presidential authority, concluding that an early form of the line-item-veto authority provided in the Congressional Budget and Impoundment Control Act of 1974 adequately would balance the needs of both Congress and the president to participate in decisions to cancel or postpone spending programs. As it turned out, this conclusion was ill founded.

Line-Item Veto

From Congress's point of view, impoundment is unacceptable because it places spending control entirely in a unitary president, leaving Congress no role in limiting spending following enactment of spending legislation. The Congressional Budget and Impoundment Control Act of 1974 was Congress's effort to fashion a compromise by providing a role for itself as well as the president. This legislation provided that if the president desires to postpone or withhold the use of authorized funds, he must submit a special message to Congress informing Congress of his reasons. The president's request to impound is denied if both Houses of Congress fail to approve the request within forty-five days or if either House adopts a resolution of disapproval.[9] This procedure is not constitutionally problematic because the president's special message is, in effect, merely a request that Congress enact legislation postponing or repealing a current spending authorization. This procedure shifts most control to Congress, however, because through inaction Congress can reject the president's suggestion that appropriated funds not be spent. For the most part, since 1974 Congress has asserted its power simply by ignoring the special messages that various presidents have sent to Congress that budget authority be rescinded, with the result that the Congressional Budget and Impoundment Control Act of 1974 has provided the president little ability to choose not to expend appropriated funds.[10]

Some in Congress concluded that a different type of line-item veto represents a better accommodation of the Executive's desire for discretion not to expend funds on the one hand with the Congress's interest in retaining meaningful control over the decision whether appropriated funds are expended on the other. The 1994 midterm elections resulted in a Republican victory built around the Republican Party's Contract with America, which contained a commitment to provide the president line-item veto power. In 1996 both the House and the Senate enacted the Line-Item Veto Act. This statute provided that if, within thirty days following notification by the president of a decision to postpone or withhold spending, Congress fails to enact a "disapproval bill" by majority vote in each chamber, the president is empowered to cancel any dollar amount of discretionary budget authority, any new direct spending, and certain "limited" (special interest) tax benefits. The president could veto any such "disapproval bill," shifting to Congress the burden of overcoming the veto by a two-thirds majority vote in each chamber. The political reality of the Line-Item Veto Act was that it provided the president virtually unlimited discretion to veto much of each year's enacted spending and certain tax benefits after they became law except in the unusual circumstance of there being sufficient votes in Congress to overcome a presidential veto.

The line-item veto failed to serve as the much-sought-after magic bullet for reining in federal spending and the granting of tax benefits to special interest groups because the Supreme Court found the scheme unconstitutional in *Clinton v. City of New York*.[11] The Court held that the cancellation authority provided by the Line-Item Veto Act invested the president with authority, in effect, to repeal legislation after it became law. The Constitution's provisions for bicameralism (legislative power residing in two legislative chambers) and presentment of enacted legislation to the president for either concurrence or veto provide a legislative role for the president *before* a bill becomes law but prohibits unilateral executive actions that either repeal or amend parts of duly enacted statutes.

In *Clinton v. City of New York*, the Court acknowledged the strong support for the line-item veto among many members of Congress and the Executive Branch from both political parties. And the Court accepted, without deciding, that the line-item veto could represent sound government policy. Yet, in a nod to the constitutional amendment process, the majority concluded, "[I]f there is to be a new procedure in which the president will play a different role in determining the final text of what may 'become a law' such change must come not by legislation but through the amendment procedures set forth in Article V of the Constitution."[12] It is quite out of the ordinary, though not unprecedented, for the Court to remind Congress of its Article V options.[13] Doing so suggests that some members of the slim six-justice majority in *Clinton v. City of New York* may have been swayed by the availability of a constitutional amendment solution that could adjust the current allocation of relative congressional and executive control over federal spending as a way to address "runaway" federal spending.[14]

Balanced Budget Amendment Proposals and the Gramm-Rudman-Hollings Deficit Reduction Act of 1985

Since the decision in *Clinton v. City of New York*, no proposed constitutional amendment authorizing the president to exercise a line-item-veto authority has gained congressional support. Congress held hearings in 2006 to consider a form of line-item-veto legislation that would be constitutional, but no legislation was forthcoming.[15] Since neither presidential impoundment nor the line-item veto is constitutional, the remedy of choice for those desiring to limit the role of the federal government by encumbering its power to finance its programs has become some form of balanced budget requirement. The advocates of a balanced budget constitutional amendment have been most persistent in achieving their goal.[16]

The idea of requiring a balanced budget is as old as the country itself. Fiscal conservative and small government apostle Thomas Jefferson proposed a constitutional amendment in 1798 withdrawing the federal power the Constitution confers in Article I, section 8 to "borrow Money on the credit of the United States."[17] Amendment proposals to limit the national debt were discussed as early as the 1870s and 1880s; however, the first balanced budget constitutional amendment was not formally proposed in Congress until 1936. Altogether hundreds of similar proposed constitutional amendments have been introduced.[18] Other than the Equal Rights Amendment, the proposed amendment to require an annually balanced federal budget has been the most persistently advocated and widely debated constitutional amendment proposal in recent times.[19]

Though never yet successful, the balanced budget amendment effort has greatly influenced the political process by fueling an ongoing conversation about the proper role of the federal government. Some advocates seek only to impose fiscal discipline and limit (and reduce) the growing federal debt. Others support the proposed amendment out of hostility to government in general and opposition to New Deal and post–World War II social reforms in particular. These advocates view a balanced budget constitutional amendment as transformative, believing that such an amendment effectively would curb the federal government's ability to fund its activities, fundamentally alter and reverse the federal government's post–New Deal dominance over state government, create a less active federal establishment, and return power to the states. For these advocates of a balanced budget amendment, budget reduction is a means for achieving permanent structural change in government.[20] Other proponents of a constitutional amendment requiring a balanced budget are motivated by none of the above goals. Their support of the balanced budget amendment is purely symbolic, a way to finesse the intractable problem of government spending without actually being required to explain how reducing the federal budget would be implemented.

Congressional support for a balanced budget constitutional amendment never approached the two-thirds tipping point until the 1980s, when the federal deficit began to soar following the Reagan administration's economic policies and after state legislatures responded by filing petitions with Congress requesting that it convene a constitutional convention to consider a balanced budget amendment. Members of Congress could not ignore this nearly successful state petition drive to force them to call a constitutional convention, a development creating the always-present apprehension that such a convention could not be contained with respect to the constitutional changes that it might propose.[21] These various political pressures to restrain federal spending, accentuated by a rising federal deficit, finally coalesced to move Congress to action. In 1985, in lieu of proposing a constitutional amendment or convening a constitutional convention, Congress devised a legislative solution to the growing federal deficit. Congress enacted the Balanced Budget and Emergency Deficit Control Act of 1985, commonly known after its senatorial sponsors as the Gramm-Rudman-Hollings Act. It was designed to balance the budget without the need for a constitutional amendment by setting annual ceilings for deficits in the federal budget until achievement of a balanced federal budget by 1991.[22] The Act is widely viewed as having been adopted as an alternative to a constitutional amendment.[23] The Gramm-Rudman-Hollings Act had the effect its sponsors sought—to weaken congressional support for a balanced budget amendment. In 1986, one year after Gramm-Rudman-Hollings was enacted, the Senate support for a proposed balanced budget constitutional amendment began to collapse. Proponents were able to generate support only from a simple majority in the Senate. This was a far different outcome from four years previously when the Senate approved such a proposed amendment by a two-thirds supermajority.[24] This constitutional history nicely uncovers the political relationship between proposals for constitutional revision and legislative reform.

The Gramm-Rudman-Hollings statutory alternative to a balanced budget constitutional amendment never performed as intended, however. In the year following its enactment, the Court declared the Gramm-Rudman-Hollings Act unconstitutional in *Bowsher v. Synar*.[25] The statute attempted to control federal deficits through a mechanism called "sequestration." When the deficit in any given year exceeded annual targets, federal funds would be withheld across the board until the statutorily prescribed spending reduction goals were achieved. Unwilling to concede to the president the unilateral authority to determine when deficit targets were not being met and what cuts to initiate, Congress placed enforcement powers in the Comptroller General, an official who headed what was then called the Government Accounting Office (GAO). The Comptroller General is considered a legislative officer because Congress can initiate removal of the incumbent from office by joint resolution of both houses of Congress. The president can veto Congress's decision to remove the Comptroller General, but Congress retains the final decision on removal since they have the option to override the president's veto by a two-thirds vote of each chamber. The Gramm-Rudman-Hollings Act provided that the Comptroller General would decide if sequestration was needed as well as the spending cuts that would be adopted to meet the deficit target for any given year. If Congress could not agree on spending cuts sufficient to meet the annual deficit target, the president was obligated to sign and implement the Comptroller General's sequestration order without any power to revise or veto the order. And therein resided the constitutional defect. The Gramm-Rudman-Hollings Act had delegated an executive function to the Comptroller General, a legislative branch official. By a vote of 7–2 the Supreme Court struck down this enforcement provision of the Act as violative of the Constitution's separation of powers doctrine. The Court reasoned that the Comptroller General's duties under the statute were executive since they entailed *applying* legal standards found in a statute and only executive officers of the government, those subject to removal control by the executive, are constitutionally empowered to perform executive functions. It was unconstitutional for Congress to reserve to itself the power to initiate the appointment process and participate in the removal decision of the Comptroller General and also assign that official executive functions.

Following the Court's 1986 decision in *Bowsher*, the balanced budget movement did not regain its pre-*Bowsher* momentum until the Republican victory in the 1994 midterm elections and the Republican Party's success in advocating the principles contained in the so-called Contract With America. With that development, the slumbering balanced budget amendment effort awoke. Indeed, as noted above, proponents of a balanced budget amendment nearly triumphed in 1995 when the amendment proposal passed in the House by the requisite two-thirds majority but failed by one vote to muster two-thirds support in the Senate. Thereafter, the Clinton administration exercised spending restraint, and the Clinton administration's subsequent budget surpluses eased pressure for an amendment. As of this writing, the balanced budget amendment initiative never has regained its 1995 level of support in either the House of Representatives or the US Senate.[26]

Victims' Rights Legislation

In 1999, a highly respected victims' rights advocate predicted that the Victims' Rights Amendment [VRA] would likely be the Constitution's next amendment.[27] In 2012 this same advocate reported that members of Congress were continuing their attempt to add the VRA to the Constitution,[28] an effort that began in 1990.[29] More than twenty years of failed efforts to add the VRA to the Constitution does not bode well for the prediction that the American people can expect the VRA sometime soon. But even if the VRA never becomes constitutional text, the effort to add it to the Constitution has been instrumental in moving the political process in directions desired by victims' rights advocates.[30]

Since the 1970s, the national victims' rights movement has given voice to the view that the criminal justice system is imbalanced in the sense that the rights of the accused are accommodated out of proportion to the interests of the victims of crime. The proposed VRA is designed to address this perceived injustice through a constitutional amendment. The VRA would extend to victims of crime various constitutional rights that are designed to integrate the victim's viewpoints into the state and federal criminal justice systems. These rights include: 1) *Notice* —victims would receive timely notice of any public proceedings involving the crime and of any escape or proposed release of the accused; 2) *Attend and be heard*—victims could not be excluded from such public proceeding and must be provided a reasonable right to be heard at release, plea, sentencing, reprieve, and pardon proceedings; and 3) *Adjudication of victims' rights*—any adjudicative decision must consider the victim's safety, interest in avoiding unreasonable delay, and claims for restitution from the offender.

The initial strategy for securing ratification of the VRA was a states-first approach—adding victims' rights amendments to state constitutions. As of 2012, that effort has resulted in thirty states protecting victims through state constitutional amendments. A state law approach results in a patchwork of protection, lacks uniformity, and does not apply to victims of federal crimes. But the goal was to use modifications in state constitutions to pave the way for acceptance of similar changes in the US Constitution. Ironically, the success of this effort at the state level to change public sentiment to a more supportive view of victims' rights may have undermined the goal of adding the VRA to the federal Constitution.

First, in *Payne v. Tennessee* the Supreme Court, apparently influenced by the movement for victims' rights, reversed two previous decisions that barred use of evidence at the penalty phase of a criminal proceeding relating to the personal characteristics of the victim and the emotional impact of the crimes on the victim's family.[31] Agreeing with a core argument of the victims' rights movement, the Court in *Payne* reasoned that "the assessment of harm caused by the defendant as a result of the crime charged has understandably been an important concern of the criminal law, both in determining the elements of the offense and in determining the appropriate punishment."[32] Accordingly, in *Payne* the Court upheld use of evidence at the penalty phase of a capital crime regarding the effect of crimes on the lives of victims. The decision in *Payne* assured that, without the need to amend the US Constitution, such testimony by victims is constitutional. *Payne* provides a rare look into the forces that influence the Court. In his concurring opinion, Justice Scalia observed that resistance to considering the interests of victims of crime "conflicts with a public sense of justice keen enough that it has found voice in a nationwide 'victims' rights' movement."[33] This is hardwired evidence of a link between a nationwide movement (that included a proposed constitutional amendment) and its impact on the Court's understanding of constitutional meaning.

Efforts to add a VRA to the US Constitution have not resulted in a constitutional amendment, but they have prodded Congress to take legislative action. Through a series of federal statutes, Congress attempted to provide in federal court much of what the VRA would have provided victims of crime by constitutional amendment. The year 2004 was pivotal in this regard. After several years of unsuccessful attempts, those in Congress proposing a constitutional amendment concluded that it was not then realistic to expect success in securing the supermajorities required in the House and the Senate for passage of the VRA. The congressional leadership was prepared to offer a trade. Professor Paul Cassell, active in the constitutional amendment effort, reports that in April of 2004, victims' rights advocates, in consultation with members of Congress, negotiated a compromise. In exchange for at least temporarily withdrawing insistence for a constitutional amendment, victims' rights proponents gained overwhelming congressional support for a victims' right statute—the Crime Victims' Rights Act (CVRA).[34]

Professor Cassell's account of the political trading that occurred in 2004 evidences how the VRA triumphed notwithstanding the failure to obtain a constitutional amendment. But the triumph may have been ephemeral. As it turned out, the victims' rights community became disillusioned with the *quid pro quo* it had negotiated with Congress. From their point of view, the statute never lived up to their expectations, and the imprimatur that Congress bestowed on victims' rights in the 2004 CVRA legislation never convinced courts to provide victims the "respect and dignity" they deserve, something that victims' advocates now believe can be achieved only through a constitutional amendment. Moreover, some lower federal courts were reluctant to give victims the full scope of rights that the federal legislation prescribes due to concerns that doing so would trammel the accused's constitutional rights. Here again, in the view of victims' advocates, only a victims' rights constitutional amendment can allay those concerns. Accordingly, in recent years the victims' rights movement has revived its effort to secure a constitutional amendment.

Putting aside whether the bargain struck with Congress in enacting the CVRA in 2004 provides victims adequate protection, the record is clear that the proposed victims' rights constitutional amendment was used successfully as a bargaining chip in achieving congressional support of the CVRA.[35] From a broader perspective, the VRA effort may one day be seen as providing its advocates an even more significant victory. The victims' rights community has argued that a core hurdle in achieving equal rights for victims is an adverse socialization within American culture and the legal system that has yet to acknowledge victims of crime as possessing a legitimate role in criminal proceedings.[36] That socialization may never change, but if it does change in favor of victims, it is reasonable to conclude that more likely than not the victims' rights advocacy efforts in support of amending the Constitution will have played a part.

Article V as a "Straw Man" in Congressional Debate

The Sixteenth Amendment—The Ploy That Backfired

The strategy of introducing a constitutional amendment as a pretext to suppress momentum for enactment of legislation can, and famously has, backfired, as occurred with the Sixteenth Amendment, the constitutional change that permitted Congress to enact federal income tax legislation. In

1895 the Supreme Court had held (5–4) in *Pollock v. Farmers' Loan and Trust Company* that an 1894 tax on private and corporate income was unconstitutional.[37] The Court seemed swayed by the oral argument of Joseph Choate, who advanced a view that appealed to class and sectional sentiments by emphasizing that since the citizens of four states would pay a great proportion of the tax (Massachusetts, New York, New Jersey, and Pennsylvania), the income tax represented an effort by the more impoverished parts of the country to oppress the wealthy parts.[38] By 1909 there was good reason to conclude that the Court might be prepared to reverse itself and uphold the constitutionality of a federal income tax.[39] Anticipating this strong potential for reversal in 1909, a coalition of Democrats and progressive Republicans proposed adding an income tax provision to a pending tariff bill then working its way through Congress. This legislation would become a vehicle to provide the Court an opportunity to reassess the constitutionality of the income tax. There was wide-ranging congressional support for re-enacting income tax legislation, in effect using it as a functional petition for reconsideration addressed to the Court.

Republican senator Nelson Aldrich, a vehement opponent of the federal income tax, sought to drive a wedge between Democrats and progressive Republicans and foil their legislative strategy by proposing a constitutional amendment as a substitute for the pending income tax legislation. The Democrats in the coalition could not vote against the constitutional amendment because their 1908 platform contained support for such an amendment. And once the constitutional amendment proposal was adopted in the Senate by a coalition of Democrats and conservative Republicans, the progressive Republicans in Congress who supported the income tax legislation either would need to withdraw their efforts to enact income tax legislation or appear to be supporting legislation that the Senate had just declared required a constitutional amendment to enact. The ploy seemed to work: the tariff bill was enacted without an income tax provision.[40]

Senator Aldrich's strategy of proposing a constitutional amendment that he fiercely opposed was a calculated gamble, but a reasonable one. Not since Congress had proposed the Fifteenth Amendment in 1869 had both houses of Congress approved and sent to the states any proposed constitutional amendment. Moreover, several previous efforts in Congress to propose an income tax constitutional amendment had failed to generate significant legislative support in Congress. One reasonably could conclude, therefore, that Aldrich shrewdly had foiled opponents' efforts to enact a federal income tax: support for a constitutional amendment in lieu of legislation would derail the legislation, and the constitutional amendment proposal would fall by the wayside somewhere in its long travel along the formidable gauntlet Article V creates for ratification of amendments to the Constitution.

The Aldrich ploy boomeranged. By 1909 the Court was under widespread and relentless attack for its unprecedented use of judicial power to promote the interests of corporations and monied interests in general and its decision declaring the 1894 income tax unconstitutional in particular. Public confidence in the Court was the lowest it had been since the end of the Civil War.[41] For this reason, President Taft decided to support the proposed constitutional amendment as a way to avoid enacting income tax legislation. Taft's reasoning was that enacting income tax legislation and putting the income tax issue again before the court would force the justices to face an unwelcome choice. The Court could reverse itself and concede that its *Pollock* decision had been wrongly decided, but that would humiliate the Court and further undermine public respect. Or the Court could stand its ground by not reversing *Pollock*, but that would further increase an angry populace's contempt for the Court.[42] Of course, the rest is history. The Senate approved the Sixteenth Amendment unanimously (77–0), the House voted 318–14 to approve it, and by February 1913, the requisite three-fourths of the state legislatures had ratified the Sixteenth Amendment. The Aldrich gambit, sound in principle, had failed in execution.

Philippine Independence
In July 1930, Senator Royal Copeland (D-NY) introduced a resolution proposing a constitutional amendment providing for the independence of the Philippines, then a US possession. In 1934, in the Tydings-McDuffe Act, Congress legislatively provided for Philippine independence by 1946.[43] Senator Copeland proposed his constitutional amendment as a political maneuver designed to defeat the Tydings-McDuffe Act and the Philippine independence it provided. His goal was not to amend the Constitution but rather to make the political point that Congress should not (could not) provide for Philippine independence by statute—such a political action required constitutional amendment. In other words, Article V became a straw man in the congressional debate over Philippine independence.[44]

Following the Spanish-American War, the Philippine Islands were acquired from Spain, and the United States annexed the islands in 1899. At first, Congress established a military government there, followed in 1901 by a civil government under United States control. This was a tumultuous and violent time during which the United States fought an insurgency that cost over four thousand American lives between 1898 and 1902. By 1902 an anti-imperialism movement had taken root in the Philippines and Congress enacted the Philippine Organic Act of 1902 (the Cooper Act), which began the long road toward eventual Philippine independence. The Organic Act provided for a bicameral legislature, the first in Asia, that shared legislative responsibilities.[45] Members of the lower House, the Philippine Assembly, were elected by popular election. The US president appointed members of the upper House, called the Philippine Commission, and the civilian governor. The Jones Act of 1916 was the next major step toward independence. It gave Filipinos the right to elect both houses of their legislature. That statute's preamble stated the intent of the US government to grant the Philippines independence. The United States continued to control the executive branch of the Philippine government through the US president's appointment of the governor.[46]

In the early 1930s, Congress considered legislation that would set a date for Philippine independence. It was at this time that Senator Copeland introduced his proposed constitutional amendment providing Congress constitutional authority to grant independence to the Philippines. Senator Copeland actually opposed the amendment and Philippine independence, but proposed the amendment as a strategy to gain attention during the legislative debate in his effort to defeat the legislation. During the three days of debate in the Senate, Copeland argued that without a constitutional amendment to permit Congress to sell, give away, or award independence to any part of the United States or any of its territories, doing so would alienate the nation's sovereignty, a political act that is contrary to the Constitution.[47] Congress rejected Senator Copeland's view that it lacked constitutional authority to grant Philippine independence, adopting the contrary view that the Constitution's treaty-making power authorized Congress and the president to award independence to a territory. Congress legislated Philippine independence in the Tydings-McDuffe Act of 1934.

The Philippine independence constitutional amendment was hardly a failed effort if it was never intended to gain the support of two-thirds of each house in Congress in the first place. Because it was intended as a tool to advance a viewpoint opposing Philippine independence, the proposed amendment served Senator Copeland quite well.[48]

Proposed Right-to-Work Amendments

Labor unions are the exclusive bargaining representatives for all employees in the collective bargaining unit where a union holds bargaining rights. Unions are legally obligated to represent fairly all of the employees whom it represents, whether or not they are union members. When a union negotiates a collective bargaining contract benefit for workers, that benefit applies to union members and nonmembers alike. Because of this, unions have argued successfully to the Congress and the courts that all represented employees who benefit from union representation should be required to pay their fair share of the cost of representation—there ought to be no "free riders."[49] Adopting this principle, the nation's labor laws, beginning with the 1935 Wagner Act (National Labor Relations Act), have permitted unions and employers to enter into voluntary agreements called union security agreements. In the private sector, these agreements may lawfully provide for what is called the union shop. After a probationary period of thirty days, all represented employees (including those who are not union members), as a condition of continued employment, must become "members."[50] But member in this context means only that the worker who is not an actual member of the union must pay a certain amount of money to the union each month to contribute a "fair share" to the cost of collective representation. Unions may insist only that nonmembers pay that portion of the regular union dues paid by members that the union uses to finance employee representation activities.[51]

Anti-union groups, during and immediately after World War II, considered it essential that states retain authority to ban union security agreements through so-called state right-to-work laws. These groups had mobilized an aggressive but unsuccessful campaign to oppose the Wagner Act in general and its provision permitting union security agreements in particular. With that defeat, the centerpiece of the anti-union strategy became persuading state legislatures to enact right-to-work laws banning union security agreements within the state. By 1947, fourteen states had done so.[52] These right-to-work groups were well aware that unions were gearing up to mount preemption attacks on state right-to-work laws, that is, constitutional challenges asserting that the state right-to-work laws are contrary to federal labor policy as expressed in the Wagner Act and thus violate the Constitution's Supremacy Clause.[53]

The Wagner Act's legislative history is inconclusive with respect to whether Congress intended the Wagner Act to preempt state right-to-work laws.[54] During World War II, the War Labor Board's position was that "in view of the practical desirability of . . . settling wartime disputes . . . union security . . . clauses [ought to be enforced] despite inconsistent State law."[55] During the years immediately following World War II, proponents of state right-to-work laws feared the courts would follow the War Labor Board's precedent and find that state right-to-work laws are preempted by the Wagner Act.[56]

This concern motivated anti-union groups to campaign for the addition of an "open-shop" constitutional amendment banning all union security agreements. For example, an editorial on Labor Day 1941 in the *Dallas Morning News* called upon Congress to pass and send to the states for ratification a constitutional amendment barring all union security agreements.[57] The Christian American Association was at the center of the right-to-work movement and the effort to secure a constitutional amendment.[58] In its campaign against unions, the Christian American Association formed a lasting alliance with Texas governor Wilbert "Pappy" O'Daniel. When O'Daniel became a US senator following a special election in 1941 (in which he defeated Representative Lyndon Johnson), he introduced a resolution proposing a constitutional amendment "to prohibit denial of the right to work and forbid collection of dues from union members."[59]

The O'Daniel right-to-work constitutional amendment proposal was a straw man designed to advance arguments for the adoption of federal legislation explicitly permitting state right-to-work laws, thus protecting state right-to-work laws from preemption challenges. This proved to be a successful political strategy. In 1947, Congress added section 14(b) to the Taft-Hartley Act Amendments to the Wagner Act. A non-preemption provision, this section states that nothing in the statute shall be construed to authorize union security agreements in states that prohibit them. As of January 2016, twenty-five states had enacted right-to-work statutes.[60]

The effort of the Christian American Association, Senator O'Daniel, and others to secure a right-to-work constitutional amendment was so intertwined with other efforts in state legislatures to enact right-to-work laws and efforts in Congress to add non-preemption language to the Taft-Hartley Act that is it impossible to unravel all the strands to determine which were most instrumental in securing the addition of section 14(b) to the 1947 Taft-Hartley Act. In retrospect, there is no reason to believe that the O'Daniel amendment ever had a realistic chance of achieving two-thirds support in the Senate in 1947 or that Senator O'Daniel could have reasonably believed otherwise.[61] His amendment proposal thus was designed to achieve other political goals. One way of understanding the O'Daniel amendment strategy is that it provided political cover to members of Congress who voted in support of section 14(b). Senator O'Daniel's proposed constitutional amendment would have banned *all* union security agreements, but section 14(b) preserves the right of unions to negotiate union security agreements except in states that ban them through the adoption of state right-to-work laws. Thus, the O'Daniel ploy provided cover to members of Congress, who could argue that they supported the less anti-union section 14(b) as a means to head off the more draconian O'Daniel amendment proposal. Perhaps there were other political motives such as using the proposed right-to-work constitutional amendment as a bully pulpit to express opposition to union security agreements. Since O'Daniel and his supporters surely understood that their amendment had no realistic chance of supermajority support in Congress and support from three-quarters of the state legislatures, the amendment proponents' motive had to have been achievement of some ancillary political benefit to advance their quest to gain congressional support for the addition of section 14(b) to the Taft-Hartley Act.

The Legislative Veto: The "dog that did not bark"

The 1980s balanced budget amendment saga discussed earlier is a good example of how efforts to amend the Constitution can gain traction and influence the larger political process by creating political pressure on Congress to enact legislation. Sometimes the reverse occurs: political arrangements evolve in the absence of proposals to amend thus obviating any need for, and intentionally or unintentionally discouraging, proposals to amend the Constitution. The legislative veto demonstrates this variation of the role of the amendment process in congressional politics.

The legislative veto has been a mainstay of national politics since 1929 when Congress negotiated an arrangement with the Hoover administration. As a cost-saving and efficiency measure, President Hoover desired authority to reorganize the executive branch subject to review by a joint committee of Congress. Congress acceded to this request but with the caveat that Hoover agree to a one-House veto arrangement whereby either house of Congress would be empowered to override any changes made by the president. Hoover agreed and the legislative veto was born as a device for Congress to control the delegation of legislative authority to the executive branch. For example, a federal statute that delegates rule making or adjudicatory authority to an administrative agency may include a legislative veto provision that gives Congress the option to disapprove (reverse) a particular administrative rule or adjudication. Sometimes Congress reserves veto authority through the vote of a joint congressional committee. More often, the legislative veto is exercised either by what is referred to as a one-house veto or a two-house veto. Under the one-house veto system, either congressional chamber (the House or the Senate) can reverse executive agency action by a vote of just that chamber through what is called a "simple resolution." Sometimes legislation provides for the legislative veto through a "concurrent resolution," requiring a majority vote in each chamber of Congress (a two-house veto). Another variation provides for a legislative veto by the vote of a single legislative committee in either the House of Representatives or the Senate. In any case, once Congress exercises the legislative veto the matter ends: Congress's resolution of disapproval reverses the executive action, and it is not presented to the president for concurrence or veto.

During the post–World War II period, the legislative veto became increasingly prevalent. Congressional leaders accepted presidential arguments that in order for the executive branch to manage its affairs efficiently, executive branch agencies required delegation from Congress of certain discretionary authority. In return, presidents accepted the reality that Congress would be willing to delegate such authority only on condition that legislation provide a mechanism for Congress to control the exercise of that delegation through the legislative veto.[62] Although the legislative veto is an elegant political accommodation that made practical sense, more so as governing became more administratively complex following the New Deal and World War II, the device has always been constitutionally suspect. When exercised by just one house of Congress, the arrangement bypasses the Constitution's bicameralism provision, the requirement that congressional action be the product of input from both houses of Congress. But even when operating as a two-house legislative veto, this method of retained congressional control over executive action compromises the Constitution's Presentment Clause, the provision requiring Congress to share legislative authority with the executive branch of government by presenting enacted legislation to the president for concurrence or veto.

Following World War II, the legislative veto increasingly morphed into a system of legislative committee veto. Legislation might, for example, authorize the executive branch to enter into contracts for public works projects or to acquire or dispose of public property but only after "coming into agreement" with the legislative committee responsible for oversight of the executive agency exercising the delegated authority. Presidents have balked at this reserved legislative control over executive discretion but acquiesced because the alternative was for Congress to withhold delegation and require, for example, that before a public works contract or lease could be finalized Congress would first need to be informed and enact authorizing legislation. Such a system would be unworkable. Accordingly, as long as presidents required delegation and as long as Congress was unwilling to delegate without the legislative veto, both ignored the constitutional issues that the legislative veto created. The legislative veto became a standard provision in legislation delegating power to the executive agencies, and presidents accepted delegation with strings attached.[63]

This uneasy accommodation came to a crashing halt in *INS v. Chadha*, or so it appeared.[64] In *Chadha*, federal legislation provided for a one-house veto of the Attorney General's delegated authority to suspend deportation of an otherwise deportable alien. In its decision in *Chadha*, the Supreme Court held that this one-house-veto limitation on delegated authority to the Attorney General constituted an unconstitutional form of congressional control over the executive branch. The Court reasoned that the act of deciding whether to disapprove the Attorney General's decision to suspend deportation constitutes an exercise of legislative power because it "had the purpose and effect of altering the legal rights, duties and relations of persons"—here the Attorney General and Chadha, the deportee. The Constitution requires that Congress perform its legislative functions in conformance with the Constitution's requirements of bicameralism and the Constitution's Presentment Clause. The one-house legislative veto at issue in *Chadha* violated both principles. But even if the legislative veto device had been deployed as a two-house veto, the legislation would still have been unconstitutional because it would have violated the Presentment Clause. When *Chadha* was decided, nearly two hundred federal statutes contained some provision for a legislative veto. *Chadha* rendered each such law unconstitutional and in the process "str[uck] down in one fell swoop provisions in more laws enacted by Congress than the Court ha[d] cumulatively invalidated in its history."[65]

Following *Chadha*, Congress amended some federal statutes to substitute the legislative veto with a "joint resolution" of disapproval—indistinguishable from normal legislation in the sense that an agency action would become effective unless both houses of Congress concur in disapproving it and, after presentment to the president, the president agrees (an unlikely occurrence) or Congress overrides a presidential veto by a two-thirds vote in each chamber of Congress. Congress considers this alternative unsatisfactory. It provides Congress inadequate control over congressional delegation to the executive branch since the burden is on Congress to assemble disapproval support in both houses and most likely the need to muster two-thirds support for disapproval to overcome an anticipated presidential veto.

Congress has replaced the legislative veto in other statutes with a process referred to as a joint resolution of approval. Requiring prior joint congressional approval and presidential concurrence *before* the executive branch may take certain action, this device in effect provides Congress a negative one-house veto—any one house can block executive action by failing to enact a resolution of approval. The president understandably considers this approach onerous, highly inefficient, and unacceptable. In short, neither the joint resolution of approval nor the joint resolution of disapproval is a satisfactory alternative to the legislative veto, which the political branches prefer but *Chadha* bars as unconstitutional.

The solution has been essentially to disregard *Chadha*. Since the *Chadha* decision, Congress has added a legislative veto provision to more than one thousand enacted statutes, and presidents have continued to sign into law legislation containing a legislative veto. Most of these are federal statutes that delegate authority to administrative agencies, such as the right to exceed certain appropriation ceilings, but require an administrative agency to obtain approval from a specified congressional committee before acting on the discretion granted—no bicameralism and no Presentment is provided for and thus clearly this legislation violates *Chadha*.[66] Post-*Chadha* presidential signing statements often assert that the president will not consider these committee pre-approval provisions binding, but the agencies that must work with their supervising congressional committees in fact do comply. Thus, the legislative veto thrives today.[67]

The political branches' defiance of the Supreme Court's holding in *Chadha* has more recently moved underground. Instead of public laws openly providing for legislative committee veto, an increasingly prevalent legislative model entails legislative committees and administrative agencies entering into informal "handshake deals." Legislation provides an administrative agency no-strings-attached discretion to initiate certain programs and engage in certain actions, such as exceeding an annual appropriation. But an informal side agreement provides that the agency will not exercise that discretion without (sometimes informal) legislative committee approval. The incentive for the administrative agency to honor its part of the bargain is clear knowledge that a deviation from this unwritten system of congressional control could result in retaliation from the legislative committee that annually approves the agency's programs and budget.[68]

Thus today, through various formal and informal arrangements, the political branches of government have agreed that congressional committees may exercise control over administrative agencies in exchange for delegating authority to those agencies, and all of this is accomplished as if *Chadha* had never been decided—much of it "off the books." Constitutional law with respect to the legislative veto thus is determined less by Supreme Court–announced doctrine than by the elected branches' pragmatic arrangements.[69]

With such broad-based support for the legislative veto among members of Congress, it is reasonable to conclude that proponents of a constitutional amendment to reverse *Chadha* most likely could muster two-thirds support for such an amendment if they so chose. But no amendment to reverse *Chadha* has been advanced. Such a *nonevent* provides a useful clue to understanding post-*Chadha* congressional and executive politics—no less instructive than Sir Arthur Conan Doyle's "dog that did not bark."[70] A constitutional amendment to reverse *Chadha* might have been expected if Congress deemed it efficacious. The absence of such a proposed amendment is evidence that Congress and the president have concluded that the seemingly endless variety of methods developed to outfox *Chadha* provide the political process a highly desirable, and preferable, level of flexibility for asserting committee control over administrative agencies that no single constitutional amendment likely could provide without dangerously tinkering with the constitutional fundamentals of bicameralism and the Presentment Clause—something few would consider desirable. That understanding of post-*Chadha* developments provides insight into how Article V has influenced institutional arrangements that preserve the legislative veto. Because Congress and the president have concluded that Article V's amendment process cannot resolve the dilemma *Chadha* has created, it has been necessary for Congress and administrative agencies to become creative by developing innovative ways to circumvent *Chadha*. The Article V amendment provisions, or more precisely the limitations built into the Article V amendment option, therefore, may best explain why Congress and the executive branch have spawned creative alternatives to *Chadha*.

PART III

Impact of Failed Amendment Efforts on Federal Executive Policy

5

Failed Amendment Efforts and the President's War-Making and Foreign Relations Powers

The Great Secession Winter of 1860–1861

Following the election of Abraham Lincoln and the beginning of Southern secession in 1861, the constitutional amending process was used for the political purpose of attempting to defuse the national crisis by diverting discussion away from secession and toward conciliation. Secession began during the "Great Secession Winter of 1860–61"—the four-month interval between Lincoln's November 1860 election and March 1861 inauguration.[1] President Buchanan remained in office during this lame-duck period. The Congress elected in 1860 with Lincoln was not scheduled to meet in regular session until December 1861.[2] President Buchanan desired that no coercion be asserted against the seven deep-South states that had seceded as of February 1861. Instead, he adopted a position of "watchful waiting"—offering no major concessions while simultaneously avoiding provocation. This strategy was founded on the hope that unionist sentiment in the South would prevail over arguments for disunion and the seceding states would rejoin the Union.[3] Buchanan called for a constitutional convention and also proposed three constitutional amendments during this lame-duck period. None of Buchanan's proposed amendments had any realistic chance of achieving even majority support in Congress, but Buchanan proposed them in an attempt to defuse the crisis by focusing the discussion from secession to accommodation.[4]

During the Secession Winter, Congress received fifty-seven constitutional amendment proposals, many from Democratic Party leaders.[5] Most proposals, like Buchanan's, shared the common feature of requiring Republicans and others opposed to slavery to make the bulk of the concessions. This was an unrealistic basis for resolving the crisis since the Republicans had just prevailed in the recent 1860 elections. Many Republicans considered it nothing short of surrender on their part to agree to any of the amendment proposals. There never was any consensus in Congress to offer significant new compromises to the South. In any event, no compromise could have ended secession, for when the seven seceding states met in Montgomery, Alabama, on February 4, 1861, to organize a new provisional government, no one was in a mood to pay serious attention to compromise efforts in Washington.[6]

The proposed constitutional amendments nevertheless were considered in Congress, and this bought valuable time for those attempting to retain within the Union the critically important eight upper-South states that had not yet seceded as of February 1861. The decision by the upper-South states not to secede immediately was dependent on the North abstaining from any act of coercion toward the Confederate states.[7] The amendment proposals introduced in the Senate suggested the North's willingness to exercise that forbearance. These amendment proposals were considered by a Senate "Committee of Thirteen." John J. Crittenden, a leader among the committee members, drew up a package of six constitutional amendments designed as a compromise, but Crittenden was unable to obtain majority support among members of the committee. Crittenden reported his package to the full Senate, which also rejected them.

Thereafter, in early February 1861, the so-called Washington Peace Convention met. After much deliberation over a three-week period, the convention recommended a package of amendments similar to the Crittenden package. When presented to Congress, these amendments too were considered but soundly rejected. Many politicians were desperate to avoid war, but the quest for a political solution to maintain the union through constitutional amendment proved impossible.[8]

Nonetheless, Congress never retreated from the goal of attempting to find a compromise. Finally, Congress did adopt and send to the states for their consideration the Corwin constitutional amendment proposal. The Corwin Amendment originated in the House of Representatives and was passed by two-thirds of each congressional chamber, the Senate's approval coming in the twilight hours on the morning of Lincoln's inauguration. The amendment provided an unamenable guarantee protecting slavery in the states where it existed against any future interference by the federal government.

In his inaugural address on March 4, 1861, Lincoln endorsed the idea of a constitutional convention as preferable to amendments coming from Congress but expressed no objection to ratification of the Corwin Amendment.[9] Too little, too late, Corwin's proposed amendment was ratified by only three states, and the Civil War overtook any future prospect that it could become an instrument of peace. Ironically, the Corwin Amendment, which would have entrenched slavery in the Constitution, would have become the Thirteenth Amendment. Instead, the current Thirteenth Amendment outlaws slavery.

It has been argued by well-respected historians that none of the Secession Winter constitutional amendment efforts warrant being taken seriously. First, none had any realistic chance of achieving ratification from three-quarters of the states remaining in the Union. Moreover, the North's best offer, an ironclad assurance of a perpetual ban on congressional interference with slavery within the existing slaveholding states, failed to meet the slaveholding states' minimum demand of the right of territorial expansion for the slaveholding system and protection of the domestic interstate slave trade.[10]

Peremptorily dismissing the constitutional amendment efforts during the Secession Winter of 1860–1861 as a nonevent is a grave mistake. These efforts were instrumental in assisting the executive branch of government in achieving important goals.

The most important immediate goal was keeping the upper-South states in the Union, at least for a time. By eroding loyalty for the deep South among the citizenry in the border states, these conciliation efforts helped keep the eight non-seceding upper-South border states in the Union until April and May of 1861.[11] Ultimately, Virginia, Arkansas, North Carolina, and Tennessee did secede, but Kentucky, Maryland, and Delaware remained in the union, as did Missouri, even though a pro-Southern government in exile enacted an ordinance of secession and Missouri was admitted into the Confederacy.[12] Unionist support in the border states remained strong. For example, nearly 75 percent of the white male combatants in Missouri fought on the Union side.[13] The upper South contributed 235,000 white soldiers and 85,000 black soldiers to the Union army. Unionist support in the upper South enabled the North to control strategic rivers, railroads, and mountain passes. Failed constitutional amendment efforts thus contributed substantially to the ability of the president, in the role of commander-in-chief, to prepare for the defense of the Union.

In addition, conciliation efforts toward the South had a more subtle, longer-term goal, one that most American historians have overlooked. Offers of compromise were not made to cancel secession and avert civil war. That was impossible. The long-term issue during the Secession Winter of 1861 was who would be blamed if conciliation efforts failed—the secessionists or the Republicans in Congress? The answer to that question would affect the ultimate allegiance of moderates in the border states, would impact how they would react when forced to take sides in the war, and also would influence strategies for determining how the impending American Civil War might have to be waged. A more or less unspoken goal of the constitutional amendment movement, therefore, was to make it appear that the other side was responsible for preventing reconciliation.[14]

Emergence from Isolationism: The Struggle for Control of Foreign Policy

The administration of foreign policy covers a vast spectrum. It includes activities as varied as making war; imposing economic sanctions; intelligence gathering; fostering trade relationships; protecting human rights; settling claims; joining international bodies such as NATO, the United Nations, the World Bank, and the International Monetary Fund; and negotiating or terminating treaties and executive agreements.

Control of foreign affairs is the domain of the federal government. The president, as "the sole organ of the federal government in the field of foreign affairs . . . alone has the authority to speak or listen as representative of the nation."[15] But Congress retains an important constitutional role in managing the nation's foreign policy. The Framers allotted to the Senate an "advice and consent" role in the making of treaties and appointing ambassadors. The full Congress retains the important power to regulate foreign commerce, declare war, and carry out a variety of other foreign relations–associated powers such as authorizing appropriations to implement the foreign policy of the United States.

Because the Constitution blurs the boundaries that define the allocation of foreign relations decision-making authority, inter-branch conflicts between the president and the Congress periodically flare up. But historically, few such conflicts arise, mainly because Congress has demonstrated much restraint in exercising its broad foreign relations authority.[16] This restraint is the product of a tradition, begun soon after the Constitution's ratification, of Congress and the president slowly negotiating understandings that shape the allocation of authority to regulate foreign affairs. That process is ongoing. At significant times, proposed constitutional amendments have been introduced providing for the reallocation of the national foreign affairs power. None has resulted in a change in constitutional text. Three in particular have influenced the outcome of important inter-branch negotiations that have shifted the respective authority of Congress and the president to initiate and effectuate the nation's foreign policy. These three are: 1) the Ludlow Amendment effort to limit the national government's authority to declare war; 2) the Bricker Amendment's effort to limit the domestic effects of treaties and presidential executive agreements; and

3) an effort to amend the Constitution's Treaty Clause, which influenced the rise of the congressional-executive agreement as an alternative to formal treaties that require two-thirds Senate consent. Each amendment proposal arose during different periods of US foreign relations history, but all developed in the caldron of conflict over shifting attitudes regarding this country's appropriate level of engagement in world affairs.[17]

The Ludlow Amendment: An Attempt to Limit the War Power

As the disillusionment with the US involvement in World War I grew, so did the electorate's support for international isolationism and/or pacifism. A strong preference developed that the United States remain neutral and distance itself politically and diplomatically from "foreign entanglements" arising from bilateral alliances and multiparty international arrangements. As the instrument of these inchoate emotions among the electorate, Congress began a twenty-year experiment to restrain presidential authority in the conduct of foreign affairs and substitute it with congressional control of important aspects of foreign policy.[18]

Most famously, the Republican Party controlled the US Senate following the 1918 congressional elections, and Republican senator Henry Cabot Lodge became chair of the Senate Foreign Relations Committee. He and the sixteen "Irreconcilables" led a successful effort to reject ratification of the Treaty of Versailles and US membership in both the League of Nations and the World Court.[19]

Many Americans supported isolationist views out of concern that the United States again would be drawn into a European war. It was in this atmosphere that some began to question whether *either* the Congress or the president could be trusted with the war-making power. Support thus developed for what has become known as the "war referendum," the proposal that a national referendum should be required as a precondition for the declaration of war. The idea was not new. Following the Spanish-American War and again in 1914, prior to the United States entry into World War I, proposals were advanced to democratize the war-making power by putting the question of going to war to a national referendum prior to any participation in a foreign war. By the 1924 presidential election, both the Democratic and Progressive Party platforms contained endorsement for a national referendum on any declaration of war except in the case of invasion or other attack.[20] Both progressives and conservatives viewed war as threatening American values and liberties. For progressives, war was viewed as an occasion for the aggrandizement of executive authority and the loss of individual liberty, such as the freedom of speech. For conservatives, war became a pretext for diminishing states' rights due to the expansion of the federal bureaucracy and increased intervention by the federal government in the economy.[21] By the 1920s, as isolationism and pacifism became ever more deeply rooted, constitutional amendment proposals for a war referendum averaged about two per year.[22]

The 1928 Kellogg-Briand Pact, officially known as the "General Treaty for Renunciation of War as an Instrument of National Policy," initially eased demands for a war referendum constitutional amendment. Signed by Germany, France, and the United States and soon thereafter by most other countries, Kellogg-Briand provided for no penalties or enforcement mechanism and, of course, did not achieve its aim of ending war. But the pact provided international isolationists in Congress another platform to voice their view of the need to distance the United States from other countries' conflicts.[23]

During this twenty-year experiment with isolationism, Congress's most aggressive move to advance an isolationist foreign policy was congressional enactment of the 1935 Neutrality Act, which was designed to preclude American involvement in another European war. The Nye Committee (the Senate's Special Committee Investigating the Munitions Industry), headed by Senator Gerald Nye (R-ND), had uncovered facts making a plausible (but never proven) case of both excessive war profiteering in the munitions industry during World War I and the United States having been tricked into entering World War I by the combined efforts of arms merchants ("merchants of death"), bankers, and foreign influences. The 1935 Neutrality Act was the first of several similar laws specifically designed to insulate the United States from the wars brewing across the globe.[24] This legislation banned the sale of arms and war materials to belligerents upon the president's proclamation that a state of war existed between two countries. In subsequent neutrality acts, Congress did not ban the sale of strategic commodities such as oil and copper to belligerents but adopted the policy of "cash and carry." A belligerent nation could purchase strategic commodities, but only if it paid cash and carried the goods from US ports in non-US merchant ships.[25] In short, Congress had seized from the president control of an important aspect of foreign relations policy and incorporated isolationism as a core aspect of our foreign policy.

It was in this cycle of increasing international and economic isolationism and ongoing efforts in Congress to undermine presidential foreign affairs autonomy that Representative Louis Ludlow (D-IN) ramped up his efforts to secure a constitutional amendment banning the declaration of war without prior approval from a national referendum. Public support for such an amendment was robust. A Gallup Poll in September 1935 showed that 75 percent of Americans supported such a constitutional amendment.

Polls showed similar levels of support in 1936 and 1937. In 1938, when the matter finally came to Congress for a vote, 68 percent of Americans supported the measure—a two-to-one margin. Even in the military, many senior officers were antiwar isolationists. One of the most isolationism-minded was General Stanley Embick, a former Army deputy chief of staff and head of the Army's War Plans Department. Believing that the country should arm itself only for defense, Embick circulated among his colleagues literature advocating support for the Ludlow Amendment.[26]

In 1935, Congress scheduled a hearing on Ludlow's war referendum amendment proposal. Congress took no action in 1935, but, moved by the conviction that the United States had been duped into entering World War I, Ludlow persisted. Ludlow's constitutional amendment proposals remained bottled up in the House Judiciary Committee until the *Panay* affair in December 1937.

On December 12, 1937, Japanese warplanes bombed the *USS Panay* during daylight. The *Panay* was an American gunboat anchored in the Yangtze River near Nanjing, China, during the undeclared war between Japan and China. When bombed, the *Panay* was displaying two eighteen-foot-by-fourteen-foot American flags. Film showed Japanese planes strafing escaping survivors. Public outrage against Japan was immediate and Japan eventually apologized and paid $2 million in reparations. Surpassing outrage against Japan, however, was the *increase* in pacifism and isolationism caused by the *Panay* affair. The Roosevelt administration's forceful response to Japan over the bombing of the *Panay* reinforced fears that just as the sinking of the battleship *Maine* in 1898 and the ocean liner *Lusitania* in 1915 had led to war, so also would the sinking of the *Panay* draw the United States into war with Japan. There were outcries over the fact that the president had permitted one of our warships to be stationed in a war zone in the first place. The sinking of the *Panay* produced calls for US withdrawal from China, especially after it was rumored that the *Panay* was on station in China to protect the interests of an US oil company. Isolationists had a field day arguing that we ought to mind our own business.[27]

Due to the isolationist reaction to the bombing of the *Panay*, Ludlow was able to obtain sufficient congressional support to force a vote on a discharge petition to bring his war referendum constitutional amendment proposal from committee to the House for debate and vote on the merits. In early January 1938, Roosevelt sent Congress a message strongly urging rejection of the Ludlow Amendment, arguing that it was impracticable and contrary to our representative form of government, would cripple the president, and would encourage other countries to believe they could violate American sovereignty with impunity. The House rejected the discharge petition by the slim margin of 209–188 and thus returned the bill to committee where it remained.[28]

From one perspective, 188 votes in support of the Ludlow Amendment proposal, while a sizeable number, is hardly a convincing turnout since it is far short of the 290 votes Ludlow would have needed to obtain a two-thirds vote in the House to send his amendment to the states for consideration. But Ludlow's failed effort to amend produced other results that conventional constitutional history tends to neglect.

First, the debate on the discharge petition provided international isolationists a worldwide bully pulpit to denounce internationalism and warn against the United States becoming entangled in other countries' conflicts. In addition, the Gallup poll's finding of the electorate's two-to-one support for the Ludlow Amendment affirmed the presence of mass isolationist sentiment in the country that the Roosevelt administration could not lightly dismiss. Nor could Roosevelt simply disregard the fact that 188 members of Congress had supported an amendment to the Constitution that Roosevelt had argued would have crippled the president's ability to conduct foreign affairs. In short, Roosevelt could not, and did not, take lightly this evidence, illuminated by the Ludlow Amendment effort, that verified strong public resistance to the United States becoming ensnared in the increasingly hostile international environment during the waning days prior to the outbreak of World War II.

There is reason to conclude that the Ludlow Amendment in fact caused Roosevelt to take a more cautious approach to mobilizing US support for those countries fighting against the Axis powers.[29] In his October 5, 1937, "quarantine speech" in Chicago, delivered just months before the *Panay* incident and the vote on the Ludlow Amendment, the president warned against isolationism and urged that the world community should "quarantine" aggressor nations, suggesting the need to restrain them through strategies such as trade embargos. Roosevelt never followed up on this proposal. He instead retreated from his criticism of isolationism and neutrality following the defeat of the Ludlow Amendment proposal.[30] For example, not until the summer of 1940 did Roosevelt sufficiently regain the political initiative to be able to challenge isolationists in Congress and assist Great Britain in its fight against the Axis powers. It was only then that Roosevelt bypassed Congress and negotiated the famous "destroyers-for-bases" agreement based on his executive authority. But even then Roosevelt worried that isolationist criticism in Congress might result in his being impeached for making the transfer.[31]

The Ludlow Amendment effort influenced presidential constitutional politics in yet another way, with a longer-lasting effect. In his epic account of the modern presidency, Arthur Schlesinger Jr. observes that, in defeating the Ludlow Amendment, Congress successfully defended its own prerogative to declare war. But through its neutrality legislation Congress undermined the established presidential prerogative to control foreign affairs and, in the process, placed the president in a straitjacket during the crucial years prior to the outbreak of war in 1939. Schlesinger concedes, as he must, that Congress acted as the instrument of strong public isolationist sentiment but contends that, having done so, Congress could not escape responsibility for the result. The verdict of history, he argues, is that Congress's isolationist foreign relations policies, manifested in the neutrality acts and substantial support for the Ludlow Amendment, enfeebled US foreign policy, were a complete failure, and came home to roost. One consequence of Congress's mismanagement of foreign policy during the years preceding World War II is that the American public thereafter refused to entrust Congress with basic foreign policy decisions. This revived presidential prerogative and power in the design and effectuation of American foreign policy.[32] If one accepts Schlesinger's account of the postwar ramifications of Congress's appropriation of important aspects of US foreign policy in the pre–World War II years, including broad support among isolationists for the Ludlow Amendment, then it follows that the Ludlow Amendment proposal became one of many forces contributing to the "Imperial Presidency" that has been dominant through much of the post–World War II period.

The Bricker Amendment: An Effort to Alter the Constitutional Treaty System

In some respects the Ludlow Amendment masked its intent to erode presidential foreign relations power because it deprived *both the president and the Congress* of their constitutional authority to join together to make war. There was no such disguising in the so-called Bricker Amendment.

The president's renewed power to control foreign policy following the end of World War II and the beginning of the Cold War became a burr under the saddle of congressional conservatives. By the mid-1950s, the Bricker Amendment was chosen as their preferred means to rein in presidential control over foreign policy. The Bricker Amendment is a collective name for a series of proposed constitutional amendments submitted in various forms beginning in 1951 and is so-named because the chief advocate was Senator John Bricker (R-OH), the Republican Party's 1944 vice-presidential candidate before winning a Senate seat in the 1946 Republican landslide. The Bricker Amendment had several aims. A primary goal was to make treaties, as well as presidential-executive agreements, non-self-executing, that is, unenforceable as domestic law unless implemented by congressional legislation. This assured that no international compact negotiated by the president (with Advice and Consent of the Senate or on the president's own executive authority) could have any effect as domestic law unless both houses of Congress concurred.

The best-known version of the Bricker Amendment provided, "A treaty shall become effective as internal law in the United States only through legislation which would be valid in the absence of a treaty."[33] To the casual observer, this language might seem innocuous. Yet a contemporary concluded that Bricker's proposed amendment was the most radical constitutional change to gain serious attention since the effort to enact the Ludlow Amendment. The question the Bricker Amendment posed was fundamental. Which branch of the federal government, executive or legislative, would formulate US foreign policy?[34] The late Louis Henkin, considered one of the most influential contemporary scholars of international law and US foreign policy, concluded that at stake in the Bricker Amendment controversy was nothing less than the integrity of the Constitution's treaty-making process.[35] Although Senator Bricker's amendment effort failed in the sense that it added no new language to the Constitution, it had a profound influence on the course of US foreign policy for nearly three decades. Even today, in defeat, Bricker's proposed amendment has taken root in contemporary US treaty ratification policy.

Postwar congressional conservatives supported the Bricker Amendment as a means to reverse what they viewed as three particularly vexing developments in foreign relations law—all of which had taken root in the 1920s and continued into the 1950s when Senator Bricker mounted his amendment drive. These developments were: 1) the Supreme Court's decision in *Missouri v. Holland* holding that federalism principles, which limited the scope of congressional domestic legislative authority, do not limit the scope of federal authority to enter into treaties and enact implementing legislation; 2) the concern that the Constitution's Treaty Power provided the federal government authority to incur treaty obligations that would otherwise violate constitutionally protected individual rights; and 3) presidential encroachment on Congress's legislative authority by implementing foreign policy through so-called presidential-executive agreements that completely bypassed Congress.

THE BRICKER AMENDMENT'S ATTEMPT TO REVERSE *MISSOURI V. HOLLAND*

In 1920, the Supreme Court decided the landmark case *Missouri v. Holland*.[36] There the state of Missouri sought to enjoin a United States game warden from enforcing federal regulations implementing a federal statute providing for protection of migratory birds. Relying on its Commerce Power, Congress had enacted an earlier statute protecting migratory birds. Lower courts had held the statute unconstitutional as violative of the Tenth Amendment, reasoning that the birds are owned by the states in their sovereign capacity and thus are immune from federal regulation of interstate commerce. This was a predictable result because at the time the Tenth Amendment posed formidable limits on the scope of Congress's Commerce Power. The difference in *Missouri v. Holland* was that the Federal Bird Act, the federal statute whose regulations the federal game warden was enforcing, had been enacted by Congress to implement a treaty with Great Britain to protect migratory birds. The Court upheld the constitutionality of the federal statute because it was a "necessary and proper" means to comply with treaty obligations that the US government had validly undertaken pursuant to the federal government's Treaty Power. Since the treaty was valid, the Supremacy Clause of the Constitution provided that the treaty and federal legislation implementing it superseded conflicting state law.

Missouri v. Holland immediately became the object of strong conservative criticism. Some viewed the decision as, in effect, amending the Constitution to create a new federal domestic legislative power that was bootstrapped onto the Treaty Power. The *Holland* case generated apprehension that an expansive application would have the effect of eviscerating the Constitution's distinction between what is properly a federal concern and what is to be left to the states to regulate exclusively. The *Missouri v. Holland* principle seemed restrained only by limits on the substantive reach of the Treaty Power (what might properly be the subject of treaties). But it was well accepted that the Treaty Power "covers all subjects that properly pertain to our foreign relations."[37] As the Court had made clear decades before the *Holland* case was decided, "it is not perceived that there is any limit to the questions which can be adjusted touching any matter which is properly the subject of negotiations with a foreign country."[38]

The legal doctrine of self-executing treaties exacerbated states' rights advocates' conviction that the decision in *Missouri v. Holland* had struck a fatal blow to state sovereignty. In *Missouri v. Holland*, opponents had challenged a treaty's implementing legislation. But the Supremacy Clause of the Constitution (Article VI) provides that "Treaties made . . . under the Authority of the United States, shall be the supreme Law of the Land; and the Judges in every State shall be bound thereby, any Thing in the Constitution or Law of any State to the Contrary notwithstanding." In other words, treaties and federal legislation are coequal in terms of superseding conflicting state law.[39] A treaty may be self-executing, meaning that it "operates of itself, without the aid of any legislative provision."[40] As with federal legislation, provisions contained in a self-executing treaty supersede conflicting state law and alone may create a private right of action enforceable judicially by private parties.[41]

But a treaty might be non-self-executing and thus require implementing congressional legislation before it can operate as domestic law that creates judicially enforceable rights by private parties. A paradigmatic example of a non-self-executing treaty might be a treaty reducing a country's stock of nuclear arms. But, generally speaking, when treaties address how private persons are to be treated or regulate the activities or interests of private persons, courts are more likely to interpret the treaty as self-executing, thus creating rights that a court will enforce at the behest of a litigant, without the need for implementing legislation.[42]

Accordingly, the reasoning in *Missouri v. Holland* paved the way for treaties themselves, without any implementing legislation, to supersede conflicting state law and provide enforceable private rights with respect to matters of traditional local concern. For example, four years after its decision in *Missouri v. Holland*, the Court decided *Asakura v. City of Seattle*.[43] There the Court invalidated a Seattle ordinance that excluded Japanese nationals from operating pawnshops, concluding that the ordinance was contrary to a US–Japan treaty. *Asakura* left no doubt that self-executing treaties could operate domestically like a federal civil rights statute. It was alarming to states'-rights adherents that the federal government possessed a power to arm private litigants with recourse in the federal courts for invasion of human rights that are governed by a treaty.

This all came to a head in the aftermath of World War II and the emergence of a variety of human rights treaties.[44] The United States ratified the UN Charter in 1945. Then came the Convention on the Prevention and Punishment of the Crime of Genocide, followed by the Universal Declaration of Human Rights in 1948.[45] These treaties, and particularly the genocide treaty, generated apprehension among conservatives that the treaties would operate as domestic law that banned racial discrimination.[46] The United States signed the genocide treaty in 1948, but the Senate had not ratified it by the early 1950s when Senator Bricker launched his constitutional amendment effort. Conservatives' anxieties escalated, however, when four Supreme Court justices and a lower California state court in 1950 concluded that the human rights provisions in the Senate-ratified UN Charter are self-executing and require invalidation of California's Alien Land Law. It appeared that the US courts were poised to find that provisions in ratified international human rights treaties are self-executing and thus constitute judicially enforceable US domestic law.[47]

The Bricker Amendment was elegantly designed to make it impossible for the United States to enforce commitments made in human rights treaties. The amendment made these treaties non-self-enforcing, and congressional conservatives could delay, and perhaps completely bottle up, legislation designed to implement human rights treaties. But even if such legislation were enacted, conservatives rationally calculated that the Supreme Court would conclude that, without the analytical assist provided by *Missouri v. Holland*, which the Bricker Amendment reversed, Congress lacked legislative authority to enact a civil rights legislation implementing a human rights treaty.[48] It is useful to remember that the Supreme Court did not decide *Brown v. Board of Education* until May 17, 1954 (after the Bricker Amendment had been defeated in the Senate). So de jure racial segregation seemed beyond constitutional restraint in the aftermath of World War II when these human rights treaties were being negotiated at the United Nations and Senator Bricker was pushing his amendment proposal in Congress. And, in any event, it was not until 1964 that the Supreme Court made clear that Congress possessed power under the Constitution's Commerce Clause to ban racial discrimination by private businesses.[49] Strong evidence substantiates Louis Henkin's view that states'-rights proponents who were opposed to federal civil rights statutes seemed to be motivated to support the Bricker Amendment as a means to prevent the federal government from using international treaties to end racial discrimination and segregation.[50] Subsequent scholars have described support for the Bricker Amendment in even starker terms, as a transparent attempt to forestall employing international human rights agreements as a means to eradicate racial segregation in America.[51]

THE BRICKER AMENDMENT'S ATTEMPT TO BAN TREATY OBLIGATIONS VIOLATING INDIVIDUAL RIGHTS

The Bricker Amendment's proponents were motivated by a second goal—to ban treaty obligations that violated individual rights. Article VI of the Constitution is worded in a way that provides a rhetorical argument that treaties might not be bounded by the Constitution's individual rights restraints on government. Article VI provides that laws of the United States qualify as the "supreme law of the land" only when "made in Pursuance of the Constitution." However, Article VI provides that treaties are the supreme law of the land, and trump conflicting state law, if "made . . . under the Authority of the United States." The Court's decision in *Missouri v. Holland* seemed to substantiate the fear that this language could permit the federal government to act without constitutional restraint when entering into treaties. If those treaties operated as domestic law, then the Treaty

Power gave the federal government carte blanche to invade the Constitution's individual rights guarantees. The Bricker Amendment's language assuaged these fears by providing that a treaty would have no effect as domestic law until implemented by congressional legislation (that it would not be constitutional unless made "in pursuance of the Constitution").[52]

THE BRICKER AMENDMENT'S ATTEMPT TO CURB EMPLOYMENT OF PRESIDENTIAL-EXECUTIVE AGREEMENTS

The third development forming the backdrop to the Bricker Amendment is the penchant of presidents to implement foreign policy by presidential-executive agreement. Unlike treaties, these are agreements with other countries that are effective when signed by the president, without congressional participation. The Constitution makes no reference to this source of presidential authority to conduct foreign affairs, but presidential-executive agreements have been deployed by presidents from the beginning of the Republic. For example, they were used in 1799 to settle claims against Holland arising out of damage to a ship owned by a US company. Presidential-executive agreements initially were noncontroversial since early practice limited their use to relatively minor, technical, or routine matters.[53]

Use of the presidential-executive agreement to conduct US foreign policy began to provoke strong political resistance when President Roosevelt increasingly used the device to address matters of great national concern. For example, unable to obtain congressional authorization to transfer naval destroyers to Great Britain in the summer of 1940, when it appeared that Germany would invade Britain, Roosevelt concluded he could use the presidential-executive agreement. On executive authority alone, and bypassing Congress altogether, Roosevelt agreed to transfer fifty US Navy destroyers to Great Britain in exchange for two naval bases (in Newfoundland and Bermuda) and ninety-nine year leases on several bases in the British West Indies. Contemporary critics claimed that Roosevelt's destroyers-for-bases agreement was the most arbitrary and dictatorial in the history of the US presidency.[54]

During World War II, Roosevelt, and then Truman, continued to make major foreign policy commitments by presidential-executive agreement, including the postwar settlements agreed to at Yalta and Potsdam. President Eisenhower followed the lead of his predecessors' use of the presidential-executive agreement when his administration entered into a defense pact with Spain in 1953 that included military bases, concluded a cease-fire agreement with North Korea, and negotiated presidential-executive agreements for establishment of military bases around the world.[55]

The presidential-executive agreement can provoke resistance not only because it represents unchecked expansion of executive foreign relations authority but also because it can have significant legal consequences for individuals by operating as domestic law that overrides conflicting state law. For example, in 1933 Roosevelt granted diplomatic recognition to the Soviet Union through a presidential-executive agreement, known as the Litvinov Agreement. This agreement provided that the Soviet Union would assign to the United States its interest in assets in the United States (and vice versa) and the US government would use those assets to settle claims that it and others had against the Soviet Union. In *United States v. Belmont*, a banker refused to transfer to the United States certain funds deposited in his bank by a Russian company prior to the Russian Revolution, arguing that title to the funds was to be determined by state law.[56] The Supreme Court in *Belmont* upheld the Litvinov Agreement as a valid international compact that superseded state law, reasoning that not all international compacts require Senate approval.

Subsequently, the United States government brought an action in the New York state courts to recover assets of the New York branch of a Russian insurance company that the Soviet Union had nationalized in 1918 and 1919, assets that the Litvinov Agreement had assigned to the United States. The New York courts rebuffed the United States, this time on the ground that under New York law the Soviet Union had no interest in the insurance company that it could assign to the United States. Moreover, New York courts were not bound by anything the Litvinov Agreement might provide to the contrary because the Senate had never ratified that agreement. The Supreme Court disagreed in *United States v. Pink*.[57] The Court again upheld the presidential-executive agreement's preemptive effect on conflicting state law, reasoning that "all constitutional acts of power, whether in the executive or in the judicial department, have as much legal validity and obligation as if they proceeded from the legislature." Accordingly, although the agreement giving the US government priority over other claimants to the assets of the insurance company was a presidential-executive agreement and not a "treaty" requiring Senate approval, and even though the agreement had never otherwise been ratified by Congress, it had the legal effect of domestic legislation that prevails over conflicting state law. For just as a treaty is the law of the land that preempts conflicting state law, so also, "such international compacts and agreements as the Litvinov Assignment had a similar dignity."[58]

Given the expansive use of presidential-executive agreements discussed above, and the Court's reasoning in *Pink* and *Belmont*, many in Congress understandably concluded that the presidential-executive agreement posed a genuine threat of eclipsing Congress's role in framing foreign relations policy as well as important aspects of domestic policy. The reasoning in *Pink* and *Belmont* positioned presidents to transform themselves into unchecked domestic lawmakers through the use of the presidential-executive agreement. The only check seemed to be that the presidential-executive agreement could not violate the Constitution or override any pre-existing *federal* statute.[59] In an effort to counter executive lawmaking through use of the presidential-executive agreement, one of the Bricker Amendment variations provided that "executive agreements shall not be made in lieu of treaties."[60] The intent of this provision was to channel all international agreements into the Treaty Clause's Senate-controlled ratification process.

DEFEAT OF THE BRICKER AMENDMENT

Senator Bricker introduced a revised version of his amendment proposal in 1951 and reintroduced the amendment in 1952, the latter effort with fifty-eight cosponsors.[61] The newly installed Eisenhower administration mobilized political opposition against what it viewed as Bricker's proposed attempt to subvert the Constitution's Treaty Power. Many other Republican politicians, and many scholars, also voiced strong opposition to the amendment. No action was taken until the 83rd Congress (1953–1954), the first time since the New Deal that Republicans had captured both the presidency and the Congress. Bricker then introduced a revised amendment proposal, now with sixty-two cosponsors.[62] With Senator Bricker's vote, this totaled nearly the sixty-four votes required for two-thirds Senate approval if the entire Senate were to vote on the resolution. Through persistent effort, and working with Democrats in the Senate, the Eisenhower administration was able to erode support for Bricker's amendment. The Senate voted on February 26, 1954, and rejected the Bricker Amendment by a vote of 42–50. The Senate agreed to permit a vote on a milder substitute constitutional amendment proposal offered by conservative Georgia senator Walter George. It would have made all presidential-executive agreements, but not treaties, non-self-executing, that is, requiring congressional approval before having any domestic legal effect. The vote on the George substitute was 60–31, one vote shy of the required two-thirds of those voting that was needed to send the constitutional amendment proposal to the states for consideration.[63]

CONTINUING IMPACT OF THE BRICKER AMENDMENT

Of the thousands of failed efforts to amend the Constitution, none can more strongly lay claim to triumph in the face of defeat than can the Bricker Amendment. The victory over the Bricker Amendment came with a huge price tag for the human rights movement.[64] The cost for defeating the Bricker Amendment has two components.

First, to help defeat the Bricker Amendment, the Eisenhower administration, through Secretary of State John Foster Dulles, found it necessary to appear before the Senate Judiciary Committee in April 1953 and pledge that the administration would adopt as State Department policy most of what Bricker had sought to achieve through his amendment proposal: the administration would not become a party to any additional human rights covenants or conventions nor seek ratification of the UN Genocide treaty, which had been before the senate since 1948; and it agreed to exercise the treaty-making power within "traditional limits" and prevent the use of treaties to effect internal changes with respect to "matters of domestic concern."[65] The year following the 1954 defeat of the Bricker Amendment, Senator Bricker once again introduced his amendment for Senate consideration, and Secretary Dulles countered by publically reaffirming that "the United States will not sign or become a party to the covenants on human rights, the convention on the political rights of women, and certain other proposed multilateral agreements."[66] Then, in 1956, when Senator Bricker once again introduced his amendment proposal, the State Department responded by publishing a circular stating that "treaties are not to be used as a device for the purpose of effecting internal social changes or to circumvent the constitutional procedures established in relation to what are essentially matters of domestic concern."[67]

Though his proposed constitutional amendment was defeated, Senator Bricker won a stunning victory insulating US domestic law from the prescriptions and proscriptions of international human rights treaties. Moreover, Bricker had used the Article V amending process to obtain a commitment that the president would not use the *Missouri v. Holland* principle to reach matters of traditional local concern. Indeed, for several subsequent decades after the "defeat" of the Bricker Amendment, the executive branch of the federal government did not submit any major human rights treaties to the Senate, and ratification of the 1948 genocide treaty was shelved until 1988.[68] Not until the 1970s and the Carter administration did presidents resume sending significant human rights treaties to the Senate for ratification. Secretary Dulles's 1953 pledge not to become party to any human rights treaties, deemed necessary to counter the Bricker Amendment, stood as US foreign policy for twenty years following the Bricker Amendment's defeat.

But the high price paid by the human rights community to defeat the Bricker Amendment was not limited to retarding for twenty years the development of international human rights law in the United States. The price for defeating Bricker had a second, longer-lasting, element that continues to the present. The Senate has adopted treaty ratification policies providing for conditional ratification of human rights treaties.[69] These ratification policies accommodate domestic concerns in much the same way that Bricker had advanced through his proposed amendment and accomplish many of the goals of the Bricker Amendment.

The conditions the United States routinely adds to its human rights treaty ratifications are referred to as RUDs—reservations, understandings, and declarations. A RUD, for example, may exempt from the Senate's ratification certain substantive provisions in a human rights convention. Often the Senate's RUD declares that the treaty is non-self-executing—exactly what Senator Bricker proposed for all treaties, assuring that the treaty will have no domestic legal consequences unless Congress enacts implementing legislation. Finally, a RUD may provide that state and local governments, rather than the federal government, are to implement certain treaty provisions.[70] The Senate regularly uses RUDs as a strategy to assert or reassert its legislative authority to participate in the formation of foreign policy.[71] The Bricker Amendment has left its tracings on US foreign policy through these RUDs. Most of what Bricker's amendment sought to achieve is provided now through the Senate's standard treaty ratification policies.[72]

The Court's decision in *Medellin v. Texas*, represents yet another step toward adoption of principles that the Bricker Amendment championed.[73] This case goes a long way toward adopting the portion of the Bricker Amendment rendering all treaties non-self-executing. In *Medellin*, the Court held that a treaty obligation to comply with a decision of the International Court of Justice was non-self-executing. The majority subscribed to the familiar tenet that the Senate's intent when ratifying a treaty is key for determining whether a treaty is self-executing, and intent is to be ascertained by examination of both the language and structure of the treaty. Yet it has been suggested that in practical effect the Court has created a rule of construction for treaties that is consistent with a presumption against self-execution, rebuttable but only by clear language to the contrary.[74] One study has shown that most lower courts have interpreted *Medellin* as creating such a presumption against self-execution, even with respect to treaties that were widely presumed to be self-executing prior to the Court's decision in *Medellin*.[75] If, in operation, *Medellin* has created such a presumption of non-self-execution, then as a practical matter most treaties will operate as non-self-executing treaties, except in the unusual case where the treaty or its ratification history contains clear evidence rebutting the presumption of non-self-execution. If *Medellin* indeed has that effect, US treaty law will have moved almost exactly to where the Bricker Amendment would have taken it with respect to rendering all treaties non-self-executing.

An additional contemporary impact of the Bricker Amendment effort can be found in presidents' reduced reliance on presidential-executive agreements. One of Bricker's complaints was the propensity of presidents to implement foreign policy by presidential-executive agreement, a practice that entails no consultation with Congress. One noted scholar has concluded that the Bricker Amendment had the effort of alerting the nation to the objections to the presidential-executive agreement and the need to recruit opposition against it.[76] So alerted, and recognizing the concerns of Bricker's supporters, the Eisenhower administration diffused these complaints by refusing to act on his own executive authority (i.e., without congressional approval) with respect to providing France aid in Vietnam in the spring of 1954 and providing aid to Formosa the following year.[77] Moreover, when President Eisenhower was asked at a press conference on September 11, 1956, if the United States would support Britain and France if they resorted to force in connection with Egypt's nationalization of the Suez Canal, the president responded, "This country will not go to war ever while I am occupying my present post unless Congress is called into session, and Congress declares war."[78] Thus, at least for several years, Bricker could fairly claim that his amendment effort had reformed executive use of presidential-executive agreements to implement foreign policy.

And it was not only President Eisenhower who changed policy in order to signal that there was no need for the Bricker Amendment. So did the judiciary. One of the main concerns of Bricker's supporters was that *Missouri v. Holland* authorized the federal government to abrogate individual constitutional rights of its citizens by entering into a treaty. Whether the *Missouri v. Holland* decision had that effect came before the Court in 1957, even as Senator Bricker continued his efforts to add his amendment to the Constitution. In *Reid v. Covert*, the Court set aside the court-marshal convictions of two military wives, each of whom had killed her husband while accompanying her husband overseas.[79] The military had asserted courts-marshal jurisdiction over the wives pursuant to status-of-forces executive agreements with the two countries where the deceased husbands had been stationed. These agreements provided for exclusive jurisdiction in US military courts over offenses committed by civilian dependents. Each of the two wives was convicted of murder and sentenced to life in prison, and each objected to trial by court-marshal since these trials do not provide criminal defendants the same safeguards as provided by the Constitution's Bill of Rights.

Overruling two cases that it had decided by majority decision *just one year previously*,[80] and bitterly divided, the Court struck down the treaty to the extent that it permitted trial of military dependents in military courts without the guarantees of the Fifth and Sixth Amendments. The four-person plurality made plain in *Reid v. Covert* that "it would be manifestly contrary to the . . . Constitution . . . to construe Article VI as permitting the United States to exercise power under an international agreement without observing constitutional prohibitions."[81] Some historians have advanced a compelling account of *Reid v. Covert* demonstrating that Justice Black's plurality opinion in that case deliberately reached out to address the claims of Senator Bricker and his supporters that *Missouri v. Holland* authorized the federal government to violate individual constitutional rights by means of treaties.[82] Moreover, it also has been argued that *Reid v. Covert* may have reduced support for the Bricker Amendment by placating many of the fears aroused during the debate on the failed Bricker Amendment.[83]

Senator Bricker died on March 22, 1986, at the age of ninety-two. The 1948 genocide convention, whose ratification he had helped stall, would not be ratified for another two years. No doubt, the senator was well aware that his failed amendment efforts had virtually shut down US adoption of human rights conventions for decades; had enormously influenced the Senate's adoption of the policy to use RUDs to condition treaty ratifications once the United States again began considering human rights treaties; had altered presidential-congressional relations through President Eisenhower's decision to consult Congress before making significant foreign relations commitments; and had contributed to the Supreme Court's conclusion in *Reid v. Covert* to reverse two of its very recent decisions and limit the scope of its holding in *Missouri v. Holland*. Measured by its influence on the course of foreign relations law and practice, Senator Bricker's decision to use the Article V amendment process must be rated as one of the most inspired in the history of the Constitution.

The Rise of the Congressional-Executive Agreement

The traditional vehicle for obtaining congressional ratification of an international agreement is to view the agreement as constituting a "treaty," which requires a two-thirds Senate approval vote for ratification. But that is not the president's only option. Presidents can gain congressional approval of the international agreements that the executive negotiates without confronting the often daunting task of assembling support from two-thirds of the Senate. Presidents can characterize an international agreement as a "congressional-executive agreement" rather than a "treaty." The advantage is that congressional adoption of a congressional-executive agreement requires only a simple majority of both houses of Congress. In the decades following World War II, to gain enhanced flexibility and power, presidents increasingly submitted their international agreements to Congress as congressional-executive agreements. The inconvenient truth, however, is that the Constitution makes no textual provision for congressional-executive agreements. This absence of any textual foundation for avoiding the less flexible provisions of the Constitution's Treaty Clause by the simple device of characterizing an international agreement as a congressional-executive agreement has spawned a not-yet-fully-resolved question of whether the congressional-executive agreement is constitutionally permitted. No member of Congress has yet attempted to resolve the issue by proposing a clarifying constitutional amendment. However, the rise of the congressional-executive agreement for managing foreign relations could not have occurred as it did without the aid of the Article V constitutional amendment process.

The short story is that in May 1945 two-thirds of the House of Representatives voted to adopt a constitutional amendment that would permit the House to share in approving treaties. That amendment proposal would have substituted the Constitution's current provision of requiring a two-thirds Senate vote to ratify a treaty with language providing for treaty ratification by an absolute majority vote of both the House and the Senate. Predictably, the Senate balked over ceding its treaty-ratification monopoly. The president and the House of Representatives used this proposed constitutional amendment to leverage the Senate into giving informal assent to a strategic compromise that strikingly has adjusted the balance of foreign affairs power. The compromise provided that the Constitution's Treaty Clause would remain unchanged. But for some, though not all, foreign relations commitments, the president could bypass the formal treaty ratification process (and its two-thirds Senate approval requirement) and instead act upon the majority vote of both houses of Congress through congressional-executive agreements. Thereafter, the use of treaties dramatically declined as presidents far more often deployed the congressional-executive agreement for committing the nation to critically important international obligations such as the North American Free Trade Agreement (NAFTA) and the World Trade Organization (WTO). The normal sequence currently, in what is referred to as ex post congressional review, is that the president negotiates the terms of the agreement with a foreign government without any preexisting congressional statutory grant of authority and submits the agreement to both houses of Congress for approval by majority vote, usually either by congressional enactment of implementing legislation or by joint resolution.[84]

In 1995, Bruce Ackerman and David Golove wrote a seminal article illuminating how the failed 1945 constitutional amendment proposal to include the House in ratifying treaties contributed to a political climate that compelled the Senate to accept a compromise validating use of the congressional-executive agreement as a substitute for the formal treaty.[85] That same year Laurence Tribe published a masterful and spirited response.[86] Those publications tell the story eloquently and in engrossing detail. What remains is to locate the failed 1945 amendment effort within the larger narrative of how failed constitutional amendment proposals throughout our history have influenced the evolution of political arrangements and our understanding of what is constitutional.

Throughout most of the Philadelphia constitutional convention, it was the Framers' intent that the Senate would be elected proportionally, and it was assumed that the appointment power (of ambassadors and others) and the conduct of foreign affairs would be lodged in the Senate. Once each state gained equal representation in the Senate as a result of the Great Compromise, nationalists became alarmed and no longer wanted the aristocratic, state-dominated Senate to possess exclusive control over appointments and foreign affairs. Thus, the decision was made that the president and the Senate should share these powers with each acting as a check on the other.[87]

This sharing arrangement had two primary weaknesses: it incorporated an anti-democratic bias into the treaty ratification process, and it proved to be flawed in practice. First, it excluded the House of Representatives, the Congress's most representative body, from any direct role in treaty ratification. With each state equally represented in the Senate, thirty-four of the Senate's one hundred senators, perhaps from states with relatively small populations harboring parochial and/or isolationist attitudes, could thwart the will of the president and a majority in each house of Congress by voting against a proposed treaty.[88] Moreover, because the House often needs to adopt treaty-implementing legislation and appropriate funds to effectuate a treaty, it seemed to some that it made no sense to exclude the House from participating at the treaty policy formation stage. In addition, in practice the Article II Treaty Clause method of making international commitments, particularly with respect to trade, proved too slow and cumbersome to provide the flexible, decisive, and rapid action required for the nation to benefit from economic opportunities and address the economic challenges in a modern age.[89]

Dissatisfaction with the Treaty Clause is hardly a new phenomenon. From the beginning of the Republic, members of Congress have proposed constitutional amendments to alter the Treaty Clause, either to end the Senate's monopoly on treaty ratification by providing for participation by the House of Representatives or to provide for treaty ratification by majority vote in the Senate rather than a two-thirds vote.[90] The Senate's forty-nine to thirty-five vote to ratify the Treaty of Versailles provided majority support for the treaty but fell seven votes short of the two-thirds needed to ratify the Treaty. The rejection of the Treaty of Versailles produced renewed efforts to amend the Treaty Clause between 1919 and 1925—again by proposing ratification by either majority vote of the Senate or majority vote of both the House and the Senate. One proposal even contemplated treaty ratification by national referendum.

None of these amendment proposals gained traction. Yet the congressional-executive agreement, requiring majority vote by both houses of Congress, has largely replaced the formal treaty system requiring two-thirds Senate approval. Various theories have been advanced to explain why the congressional-executive agreement gained recognition as a legitimate alternative to the formal treaty.

One view is that over the course of about sixty years, precedent built upon precedent until the congressional-executive agreement developed an unassailable pedigree as a legitimate alternative to the treaty. This is referred to as the continuity theory. One persuasive recent rendition is that, beginning with the McKinley Tariff Act of 1890 and through subsequent trade legislation enacted and re-enacted for more half a century thereafter, Congress essentially gave the president treaty-making authority to negotiate reciprocal trade agreements without returning to Congress to obtain treaty ratification.[91] This legislation survived constitutional challenge in the landmark case of *Field v. Clark* based in large part on a long history of Congress delegating power to the president with reference to trade and commerce.[92] *Field v. Clark* and subsequent decisions became the legal foundation for the legitimacy of Congress gradually replacing the treaty with the congressional-executive agreement in the area of international trade. By the mid-1930s, President Roosevelt, acting on the authority of the 1934 Reciprocal Trade Agreement Act, routinely negotiated trade agreements with other countries providing for tariff reductions of up to 50 percent. None of these agreements required Senate ratification. This wide-ranging presidential authority over tariffs transformed US international trade by equipping the president with the power to act decisively and promptly to make internationally binding trade agreements that took advantage of trade opportunities. No longer was the president handicapped during trade negotiations by uncertainty as to ultimate Senate ratification nor required to return to the Senate where an international agreement could easily sink into the quagmire of delay, congressional logrolling, horse trading, and the need to satisfy demands of local constituents. But in the process, continuity theorists argue, Congress more generally abandoned the original intent of the Treaty Clause and transformed international lawmaking by increasingly delegating control to the executive branch in many diverse areas of international relations.[93]

The historical detective work by Ackerman and Golove has attracted attention because it locates the rise of the congressional-executive agreement quite differently from those who subscribe to the continuity theory. Ackerman and Golove refer to the continuity argument as simply a myth and show that the New Deal continuity theorists' argument that the congressional-executive agreement is merely an extension of earlier precedents is unsupportable because pre–New Deal precedents were materially distinguishable. The modern congressional-executive agreement, which has virtually replaced the Article II treaty, is an ex post arrangement that was virtually unknown prior to the New Deal. The ex post congressional-executive agreement is different from Congress merely authorizing the president to enter into negotiations and commit the United States in some future international agreement. An ex post arrangement entails both houses of Congress displacing the Senate's advice and consent regarding agreements the president unilaterally enters into on his own initiative without first seeking congressional authorization to do so. To this degree, they are indistinguishable from treaties: Congress approves an agreement that the president already has negotiated without any *prior* congressional authorization.[94] This type of agreement, Ackerman and Golove argue, is largely a New Deal creation whose constitutional legitimacy cannot be explained by the accumulation of pre-existing precedent. Ackerman and Golove locate the rise of the ex post congressional executive agreement as an outgrowth of an institutional struggle between Congress and the president that reached its apex during the 1944–1948 Roosevelt-Truman administration.[95] Of particular significance was the attempt to amend the Constitution in 1945 to provide for treaty ratification by a majority vote of both houses of Congress.

The Senate's rejection of the Versailles Treaty became the poster child for what many concluded was wrong with the Constitution's Treaty Clause. Particularly with the rise of Nazism and the resumption of worldwide hostilities, the rejection of the Versailles Treaty became the symbol of isolationists' irresponsibility in the conduct of foreign affairs, and many blamed the Constitution's Treaty Clause.[96] Then, with Pearl Harbor and the carnage of World War II, isolationism lost its appeal for most people, and the American public became determined that the Senate ought not be permitted to again use the Treaty Clause's two-thirds provision, this time to block ratification of the UN Charter or prevent US participation in other international organizations designed to build the peace. Most Americans preferred substituting the two-thirds Senate treaty ratification vote with a system of congressional approval that entails the majority vote of both houses of Congress. Soon calls for a constitutional amendment became standard fare among newspaper editorial writers and politicians. In May 1945 the House of Representatives approved a constitutional amendment proposal by a vote of 288–88. It provided for treaty ratification by an absolute majority of both houses of Congress.[97]

The democratic justification and functional superiority of the two-house solution to treaty ratification was clear, but, predictably, the Senate was unwilling to surrender its traditional prerogative. Attempts to force the Senate to submit risked fracturing the fragile bipartisan coalition the Roosevelt-Truman administration depended on for forging a new internationalist foreign policy and particularly for securing ratification of the UN Charter.[98] Ackerman and Golove argue that to avoid a bitter struggle in the Senate over ratification of the constitutional amendment proposal passed by the House, the administration designed an elegant compromise bottomed on informal adoption: the Senate would retain its Treaty Power monopoly, but the Senate would not object to the president choosing to bypass the Treaty Clause provisions on some occasions by securing congressional approval of international obligations through majority votes in both houses of the Congress.

The Senate ultimately accepted the compromise. The 1944 election had witnessed the departure or defeat of nine leading isolationist senators. Ackerman and Golove argue that Senate leaders began taking the constitutional amendment proposal seriously once they sensed the profound change in public sentiment and understood the 1944 election as a mandate to continue advocating for a constitutional amendment that would address the Senate's monopoly on treaty ratification. Rather than launch an all-out struggle to resist the proposed constitutional amendment, fighting to the bitter end in full view of the US electorate, inviting perhaps even greater demands for constitutional change, and risking a further backlash from the electorate in the next election, Senate leaders chose a half-measure settlement.[99]

Moreover, by accepting the compromise, not only would the Senate avoid a fight it might lose, but the arrangement provided an increased measure of congressional monitoring of presidential foreign relations authority. In the face of the Senate's obstructionism during the treaty-ratification process, presidents had resorted to managing foreign policy through unilateral executive agreements that excluded Congress altogether. The new arrangement did not ban executive agreements but encouraged the president to include Congress by characterizing an international agreement as a congressional-executive agreement. The president then is required to come before Congress, defend the agreement's terms, and obtain approval by majority vote in both the Senate and the House. In other words, the proposal to amend the Constitution's Treaty Clause influenced foreign relations in two ways. It convinced the Senate to surrender its monopoly in ratifying international agreements and share that responsibility with the House, but it also helped forge a compromise that enhanced Congress's ability overall to monitor and restrain the president in the conduct of foreign affairs.

The first application of this compromise was the decision to submit the UN Charter to the Senate for ratification as a treaty and to submit the Bretton Woods Agreements, which established the World Bank and the International Monetary Fund, to both houses of Congress for approval as congressional-executive agreements. The Senate went along with this arrangement and subsequently even approved a congressional-executive agreement regarding the building the St. Lawrence Seaway, even though previously the Senate had defeated the same proposal when presented to the Senate as a treaty.[100] There no longer was a need for a constitutional amendment, for the Senate had executed a strategic retreat just in time.

The congressional-executive agreement has now eclipsed the treaty mechanism for securing congressional approval of international agreements. The Trade Act of 1974 has restructured the modern congressional-executive agreement by formalizing a dynamic framework providing for inter-branch consultation and fast-track congressional consideration. In addition to NAFTA and the World Trade Organization agreements, several rounds of the General Agreement on Tariffs and Trade (GATT) followed the congressional-executive agreement/fast-track process. Unresolved is the constitutionality of using the congressional-executive agreement interchangeably with the treaty. The Restatement (Third) of the Foreign Relations Law of the United States concludes that the prevailing view is that the congressional-executive agreement can be used as an alternative to the treaty method in every instance.[101] The academic community is split on that question but is in accord that the proposed constitutional amendment approved by the House in 1945 was instrumental in changing the course of international law in the United States.[102] The courts have not resolved the constitutionality of excluding the Senate from its role under the Treaty Clause by submitting international agreements to both houses of Congress. The issue may never be judicially resolved if the Court deems it a political question for the president and the Congress to resolve.

Conclusion

In a 2003 interview, retired Arkansas senator Dale Bumpers stated that he wanted to be remembered most for having cast votes in the Senate opposing thirty-eight proposed constitutional amendments. He said, "Constitutional amendments are palpable nonsense, because they are all crafted for political advantage."[1] Senator Bumpers's years of political experience provided him the keen insight that is the thesis of this book: that constitutional amendments are indeed crafted for political advantage. However, the evidence assembled in these pages disputes that amendment proposing therefore is "palpable nonsense." Just the opposite is true. The political changes that amendment efforts have sought to influence were inextricably bound up with some of the most contentious controversies of their time. For example, soon after the Constitution's ratification, political disputes arose over adding a bill of rights to the Constitution. Later, the quasi-war with France during the Adams administration generated intense feelings of xenophobia and an intractable conflict over the Alien and Sedition Acts. There was, in addition, the contested election of 1800 followed by the bitter controversy over the self-destructive embargo of 1807 and later the nullification crisis of 1832 and, of course, the fight over slavery. The Article V amendment process was in the middle of all of these bitter controversies as amendment proponents used it as a tool to secure diverse forms of political leverage. Over the past seventy-five years, some of the most vigorously contested political disputes have included gender equality, abortion, prayer and Bible reading in public schools, flag burning, reapportionment of voting districts, the balanced budget, rights of victims of crime, and the relative power of the president and Congress with respect to the negotiation and ratification of international agreements. Advocates deployed the Article V amendment process in each of these political battles in order to influence the outcome, and amendment proposals in fact were instrumental in influencing the outcomes.

Members of Congress think and act strategically; at least, those who get reelected do. It makes sense that members of Congress, and others, must find political utility in proposing constitutional amendments that they know have virtually no chance of becoming ratified. Otherwise, why do so? The challenge is understanding how amendment proposing fits into the strategic thinking of individuals and groups. There seldom are contemporaneous statements explaining the strategic role of a proposed amendment because political actors are not in the habit of disclosing their strategic thinking, even post hoc.

This is not to say that compelling evidence cannot be found upon which to ground an inference of motive and impact. What the case studies in this book have shown is that there is no one-size-fits-all political explanation for why amendments are proposed.

Movement building can be an important ancillary political benefit achieved through amendment proposing. This occurred during the ERA ratification effort, which helped build and sustain both the modern feminist movement and a conservative counter movement. Movement building also occurred as a byproduct (or perhaps the intended purpose) of the efforts to eliminate the constitution's Three-Fifths Clause through constitutional amendment and John Quincy Adams's amendment proposals to eliminate slavery, all of which not only helped build the abolition movement but also contributed to the evolution of what became the Republican Party. Constitutional amendment efforts establishing Prohibition, and later repealing it, also operated as resources for movement building.

Resource for expressing dissent and promoting deliberation: The ERA helped build the modern feminist movement, but it also is a paradigmatic example of how proposing a constitutional amendment can influence constitutional meaning through the interrelationship of the backlash amendment proposing can generate and the democratic deliberation that takes place as a result. The dialectic over what gender discrimination ought to mean resulting from the ERA ratification effort and its backlash greatly influenced the current understanding of constitutionally proscribed sex discrimination. Many other constitutional amendment proposals similarly have provided opportunities for democratic deliberation resulting in a mediated understanding of constitutional meaning. This occurred mostly when amendment proposals were deployed as a means to express opposition to a disfavored Supreme Court decision. For example, the 1937 Wheeler-Bone constitutional amendment proposal generated a national conversation about the deference the judiciary owes the political branches in the formation of the nation's economic policy and is a far more convincing candidate for explaining the Court's New Deal–era "switch in time" than Roosevelt's Court-packing scheme. The pro-life attack on *Roe v. Wade* was launched with a barrage of proposed constitutional amendments that helped the pro-life movement sustain itself during lean times and was the background for a national discussion on abortion that resulted in a constitutional settlement in *Planned Parenthood of Southeastern Pennsylvania v. Casey.*

Engel v. Vitale, the school prayer case, precipitated a flood of amendment proposals to reverse the case. These proposals to amend the Constitution in turn motivated the Court to initiate a dialogue with the American people the next year in *School District of Abington Township v. Schempp*, the Bible reading case. Thereafter the school prayer and school Bible reading proposed constitutional amendments created the need for congressional hearings. These hearings facilitated democratic dialogue and a cooling off period needed for many persons (those who possessed a sufficiently open mind) to reassess their views regarding the desirability of government-required school prayer and Bible reading in public school.

The widespread public and congressional support for a flag burning amendment following the Court's decision in *Texas v. Johnson* provided Democrats in Congress with both a crisis and an irresistible opportunity for "position taking" and "credit claiming," which they took advantage of by enacting the Flag Protection Act of 1989 in lieu of endorsing one of the many proposed constitutional amendments related to flag burning. Congressional Democrats thereby reaped the political advantage of being able to claim that they both defend the flag and support the Constitution. This strategy of enacting legislation in lieu of supporting a proposed constitutional amendment succeeded only because amendment proponents knew that they could renew their amendment efforts if the Flag Protection Act were declared unconstitutional—as it was. This political maneuvering bought time that permitted, and invited, deliberation, provided a cooling of emotions regarding flag burning, and subsequently positioned moderates to be able to assert decisive influence on the debate.

The history leading to the Court's eventual conclusion that poll taxes are unconstitutional is another elegant example of the catalytic potential of amendment efforts for influencing constitutional meaning through the process of democratic debate. In *Harper v. Virginia State Board of Elections*, the Court initially voted to uphold the precedent in *Breedlove v. Suttles*, which had held that poll taxes are constitutional. But the Court changed its view in *Harper* due to arguments advanced by Justice Goldberg that were developed during the congressional consideration of the Twenty-Fourth Amendment and the Constitution's suffrage amendments.

Top-down influence on state politics is another political impact of the failed ERA. Following the failed ERA ratification effort, ERA advocates were successful in adding ERA provisions to many state constitutions. There was precedent for this top-down impact from failed efforts to amend the Constitution. After the Civil War, the Blaine Amendment also failed, but Blaine Amendment supporters transferred their advocacy to state politics, persuading many states to add Blaine-type amendments to their state constitutions, provisions that remain today.

Prodding Congress through use of the Article V Application Clause is a time-honored use of Article V. A second convention threat may not have been needed to secure Congress's passage of the Bill of Rights, or to secure repeal of the Alien and Sedition Acts, or, perhaps, to resolve the disputed election of 1800. Yet history shows that in each of these three periods of political turmoil, political actors advanced a second constitutional convention threat as leverage to prod Congress into action.

History has provided evidence of a direct link between a convention threat and congressional response by enacting legislation. President Jefferson and the lame-duck Congress decided in the spring of 1809 to repeal the much-maligned Embargo Act of 1807 because of the New England states' threat to meet in convention to propose constitutional amendments.

In addition, during the nullification crisis of 1832, protective tariff proponents in Congress retreated in the face of Southern agitation that was built upon and intensified by demands for a second constitutional convention to resolve the crisis, though at least one historian has concluded that it was Calhoun who backed down once he realized that President Jackson was not bluffing when he threatened to use military force if necessary to enforce federal law. What is uncontested is that calling for an Article V constitutional convention was integral to South Carolina's strategy for pushing back against the 1832 protective tariff.

There also is a consensus that proponents of the direct election of senators successfully prodded Congress to propose the Sixteenth Amendment in part by their threat to organize state legislatures to request that Congress convene a constitutional convention if Congress did not itself enact and send to the states an amendment resolution providing for direct election of senators. This is one of the most celebrated uses of the Article V Application Clause to prod Congress.

The Dirksen counter-attack on the Court's reapportionment cases also was built around a strategy of attempting to organize the states to petition Congress to convene a constitutional convention. Two related events strongly suggest a nexus between Dirksen's second convention effort and the Court's partial retreat on reapportionment. The first is that Dirksen was nearly successful in soliciting the required two-thirds of the state legislatures to request that Congress convene a convention to propose amendments relating to legislative apportionment. The second is that soon after the nearly successful second convention effort, the Supreme Court modified its reapportionment doctrine, retreating with respect to the degree of voting equality required in the re-apportionment of state legislatures.

The impact of proposed amendments on securing federal legislation has a rich history. Proposed balanced budget amendments gained such robust traction in Congress that Representatives were motivated to enact the Gramm-Rudman-Hollings Deficit Reduction Act of 1985 as an alternative to enacting a resolution sending a balanced budget constitutional amendment proposal to the states. Efforts to add a Victims' Rights Amendment to the Constitution also resulted in Congress opting instead for a legislative solution. This nexus is substantiated by contemporaneous statements by members of Congress and by the leading proponents of the Victims' Rights Amendment effort demonstrating that efforts to amend the Constitution were self-consciously withdrawn in return for Congress agreeing to enact victims' rights legislation.

Deploying Article V as a straw man is one of the more interesting political uses of Article V in congressional legislative politics. This use has had several variations. One is proposing an amendment that the proponent actually opposes in an effort to defeat federal legislation. This occurred when Senator Nelson Aldrich, as a ploy to derail congressional income tax legislation then under consideration in Congress, supported a constitutional amendment permitting the federal government to enact income tax legislation. Aldrich gambled that his scheme would derail the pending income tax legislation and that the amendment would never pass and become the Sixteenth Amendment. This is the ploy that failed.

At a time when he could not have entertained a rational belief that Congress would support his amendment proposal, and when he had no desire that his proposed amendment should prevail, Senator Royal Copeland used his Philippine independence amendment proposal as a ploy to gain his colleagues' attention and structure his arguments in opposition to the Tydings-McDuffe Act granting the Philippines its independence. And when Senator Wilbert "Pappy" O'Daniel proposed a right-to-work constitutional amendment during the 1947 congressional legislative debate over adding section 14(b) to the Taft-Hartley Act, it did not matter that congressional passage of the amendment was unrealistic because that was never the intent for proposing the amendment. The amendment proposal was a useful strategy to secure the necessary votes to enact section 14(b).

The impact of failed efforts to amend the Constitution on federal executive policy also has a rich pedigree. During the Great Secession Winter of 1860–1861, United States policy was to resolve the secession controversy if possible, or at least to discourage secession of the eight upper-South states. The strategy entailed defusing the crisis by refocusing the discussion from secession to accommodation, in part by attempting to find a constitutional amendment solution that might save the union by constitutionally protecting the institution of slavery. These efforts failed to find amendment language that met the needs of all parties, though Congress did approve the Corwin Amendment, which three states ratified. This failed amendment strategy succeeded in delaying secession among the eight border states, in persuading some to remain in the union, in buying time that provided the Union important military advantages later in the war, and in convincing moderates in the border states that the North had made a good faith effort at reconciliation and was not, therefore, culpable in causing the political rupture that resulted in the Civil War.

But it may be in the realm of foreign policy that the interrelationship of the Article V amendment process and the impact on federal executive policy has been most profound. The strong popular and congressional support for the Ludlow Amendment restrained the Roosevelt administration's push-back against isolationism prior to the attack at Pearl Harbor. The Bricker Amendment greatly influenced the negotiation of international treaties for many years after it was defeated, and its influence continues even to the present. And the 1945 amendment effort to modify the Article II Treaty Clause by giving the House of Representatives a role in the ratification of international agreements was the moving force in persuading the Senate to accept widespread use of congressional-executive agreements, which are now used routinely instead of formal treaties that depend on Senate ratification by a two-thirds vote.

In short, Article V may be a "road to nowhere" when assessed merely as a means for modifying government structure and constitutional norms by adding new text to the Constitution. For the past seventy-five years, *those* changes have occurred primarily off-text. But it is a mistake to evaluate Article V entirely by the number and quality of amendments it has added to the Constitution. The focus needs to be the political opportunities created by *the option to propose amendments* that Article V provides. Surely it is this political dimension of Article V that accounts primarily for the robust ongoing interest in proposing constitutional amendments when the odds of success are so meager.

Cases Cited

Adkins v. Children's Hospital, 261 US 525 (1923)
Agostini v. Felton, 521 US 203(1997)
Algoma Plywood & Veneer Co. v. Wisconsin Employment Relations Board, 336 US 301 (1949)
American Federation of Labor v. Watson, 327 US 582 (1946)
Asakura v. City of Seattle, 265 US 332 (1924)
Baker v. Carr, 369 US 186 (1962)
Bowsher v. Synar, 478 US 714 (1986)
Bradwell v. Illinois, 83 US (16 Wall.) 130, 141 (1873)
Breedlove v. Suttles, 302 US 277 (1937)
Brown v. Board of Education, 347 US 483 (1954)
Carter v. Carter Coal Company, 298 US 238 (1936)
Chamberlin v. Dade County Board of Public Instruction, 377 US 402 (1964)
Citizens United v. Federal Election Commission, 558 US 310 (2010)
City of New Haven, Connecticut v. United States, 809 F.2d 900 (DC Cir. 1987)
City of Akron v. Akron Center for Reproductive Health, Inc., 462 US 416 (1983)
Clinton v. City of New York, 524 US 417 (1998)
Colegrove v. Green, 328 US 549 (1946)

Communication Workers v. Beck, 487 US 735 (1988)
Cook v. Gralike, 531 US 510 (2001)
Cooper v. Aaron, 358 US 1 (1958)
Engel v. Vitale, 370 US 421 (1962)
Field v. Clark, 143 US 649 (1892)
Foster v. Neilson, 27 US (2 Pet.) 253 (1829)
Frontiero v. Richardson, 411 US 677 (1973)
Geofroy v. Riggs, 133 US 258, 267 (1890)
Gray v. Sanders, 372 US 368 (1963)
Hadley v. Junior College District of Metropolitan Kansas City, Missouri, 397 US 50 (1970)
Harper v. Virginia State Board of Elections, 383 US 663 (1966)
Harris v. McCrea, 448 US 297 (1980)
Hawke v. Smith (I), 253 US 221 (1920)
Hawke v. Smith (II), 253 US 231 (1920)
Heart of Atlanta Hotel v. United States, 379 US 241 (1964)
Hylton v. United States, 3 US (3 Dall.) 171 (1796)
INS v. Chadha, 462 US 919 (1983)
Katzenbach v. McClung ("Ollie's Barbecue"), 379 US 294 (1964)
Kendall v. United States *ex rel*. Stokes, 37 US (12 Pet.) 524 (1838)
Kimble v. Swackhamer, 439 US 1385 (1978)
Kinsella v. Krueger, 351 US 470 (1956)

Kirkpatrick v. Preisler, 394 US 526 (1969)
Kotterman v. Killian, 193 Arizona 273, 972 P.2d 606 (1999)
Kramer v. Union Free School District, 395 US 621 (1969)
Lee v. Weisman, 505 US 577 (1992)
Luther v. Borden, 48 US (7 How.) 1 (1849)
Maher v. Roe, 432 US 464 (1977)
Marbury v. Madison, 5 US (1 Cranch) 137 (1803)
McCollum v. Board of Education, 333 US 203 (1948)
Medellin v. Texas, 552 US 491 (2008)
Minor v. Happersett, 88 US (21 Wall.) 162 (1875)
Missouri v. Holland, 252 US 416 (1920)
Mitchell v. Helms, 530 US 793 (2000)
Morehead v. Tipaldo, 298 US 587 (1936)
Mueller v. Allen, 463 US 388 (1983)
NLRB v. General Motors Corp., 373 US 734 (1963)
NLRB v. Jones and Laughlin Corporation, 301 US 1 (1937)
Oyama v. California, 332 US 633 (1948)
Payne v. Tennessee, 501 US 808 (1991)
Planned Parenthood of Southeastern Pennsylvania v. Casey, 505 US 833 (1992)
Pollack v. Farmers' Loan & Trust Co., 157 US 429 (1895) (Pollack I)
Pollack v. Farmers' Loan & Trust Co., 158 US 601 (1895) (Pollack II)
Reed v. Reed, 404 US 71 (1971)
Reid v. Covert, 354 US 1 (1957), *on rehearing*, 351 US 487 (1956)
Reynolds v. Sims, 377 US 533 (1964)
Rosenfeld v. Southern Pacific Company, 444 F.2d 1219 (9th Cir. 1971)
Santa Fe Independent School District v. Doe, 530 US 290 (2000)

Santovincenzo v. Egan, 284 US 30, 40 (1931)
Schechter Poultry Corporation v. United States, 295 US 495 (1935)
School District of Abington Township v. Schempp, 374 US 203 (1963)
Sei Fujii v. State, 217 P.2d 481 (Cal. App 2d Dist. 1950), *vacated* Sei Fujii v. State, 38 Cal. 2d 718 (Cal. 1952)
South Carolina v. Katzenbach, 383 US 301 (1966)
Springer v. United States, 102 US 586 (1881)
Texas v. Johnson, 491 US 397 (1989)
Train v. City of New York, 420 US 35 (1975)
US Term Limits, Inc. v. Thorton, 514 US 779 (1995)
United States v. Eichman, 496 US 310 (1990)
United States v. Pink, 315 US 203 (1942)
United States v. Curtis-Wright Export Corp., 299 US 304 (1936)
United States v. Belmont, 301 US 324 (1937)
United States v. The Libellants and Claimants of the Schooner Amistad, 40 US (15 Pet.) 518 (1841)
United States v. Guy W. Capps, Inc., 204 F.2d 655 (4th Cir. 1953)
United States v. Butler, 297 US 1 (1936)
Wallace v. Jaffe, 472 US 38 (1985)
Wesberry v. Sanders, 376 US 1 (1964)
West Coast Hotel v. Parrish, 300 US 379 (1937)
Westside Community Schools v. Mergens, 496 US 226 (1990)
Whitney v. Robertson, 124 US 190 (1888)
Wood v. Broom, 287 US 1 (1932)

Notes

Introduction

1. See discussion at Richard B. Bernstein with Jerome Agel, *Amending America: If We Love the Constitution So Much, Why Do We Keep Trying to Change It?* (Lawrence: University Press of Kansas, 1993), 221, 270.
2. The ten amendments that deal with suffrage and elections are: the Twelfth (amends electoral college procedures); Fourteenth (establishes United States citizenship and penalizes states that abridge suffrage of male citizens); Fifteenth (bans suffrage discrimination based on race); Seventeenth (requires direct election of senators); Nineteenth (bans suffrage discrimination based on gender); Twentieth (sets the dates of the terms of office for members of Congress, the president, and the vice president); Twenty-Second (sets term limits for the president); Twenty-Third (provides suffrage for DC residents in presidential elections); Twenty-Fourth (bans the poll tax in federal elections); and the Twenty-Sixth (provides suffrage for eighteen year olds).
3. Professor John Vile's excellent *Encyclopedia of Constitutional Amendments, Proposed Amendments*, 2d ed. (Santa Barbara: ABC-CLIO, 2003), 563–96, provides the best single-source bibliography of work on the theory and practice of constitutional amending. Vile's conclusions regarding the most important scholarly contributions in the field of constitutional revision through the formal amendment process can be found at pp. xix–xxii. Most informed specialists likely would agree that the following are among the most acclaimed and comprehensive studies of the constitutional amendment process: David E. Kyvig, *Unintended Consequences of Constitutional Amendment* (Athens: University of Georgia Press, 2000); David E. Kyvig, *Explicit and Authentic Acts: Amending the US Constitution, 1776–1995* (Lawrence: University Press of Kansas, 1996) (recipient of the 1997 Bancroft and Henry Adams Prizes); Sanford Levinson, ed., *Responding to Imperfection: The Theory and Practice of Constitutional Amendment* (Princeton: Princeton University Press, 1995); Bernstein and Agel, *Amending America*; Russell Caplan, *Constitutional Brinksmanship: Amending the Constitution by National Convention* (New York: Oxford University Press, 1988) (surveying efforts to amend by use of the Article V Application Clause providing a mechanism for the states to apply to Congress to convene a constitutional convention); Michael Kammen, *The Machine That Would Go of Itself: The Constitution in American Culture* (New York: Alfred A. Knopf, 1987); Alan P. Grimes, *Democracy and the Amendments to the Constitution*

(Lanham, MD: University Press of America, 1978). For a lucidly written call for democratic reform of the Constitution and its amendment process, see Sanford Levinson, *Our Undemocratic Constitution: Where the Constitution Goes Wrong (And How We the People Can Correct It)* (New York: Oxford University Press, 2008). For a comprehensive assessment of proposals to rewrite the Constitution, see John R. Vile, *170 Eccentric, Visionary, and Patriotic Proposals to Rewrite the US Constitution* (Santa Barbara: ABC-CLIO, 2014).

4. As of 2003, the number of proposed amendments had reached 11,500. Vile, *Encyclopedia of Constitutional Amendments*, 38. A search of THOMAS (a database of federal legislative information, now retired) on October 1, 2011, reveals that an additional approximately 350 proposed amendments had been introduced since 2003, in the 107th to the 111th Congresses. On the difficulty of calculating an exact count of proposals for constitutional amendment see Richard A. Davis, *Proposed Amendments to the Constitution of the United States of America Introduced in Congress from the 91st Congress, 1st Session, through the 98th Congress, 2nd Session, January 1969—December 1984* (Washington, DC: Congressional Research Service *Report No. 85–36*, Feb. 1, 1985), 267–68.

5. Thomas E. Brennan, *The Article V Amendatory Constitutional Convention* (Lanham, MD: Lexington Books, 2014), 8.

6. See Kathleen M. Sullivan, "Constitutional Constancy: Why Congress Should Cure Itself of Amendment Fever," 17 *Cardozo Law Review* 691, 691 (1996); David E. Kyvig, "Introduction," in David E. Kyvig, ed., *Unintended Consequences of Constitutional Amendment*, 8 (noting that the frequency of constitutional amendment proposing in the current era is unprecedented). See Erwin Chemerinsky, "Amending the Constitution," 96 *University of Michigan Law Review* 1561, 1572 (1998) (calling for restraint in proposing constitutional amendments and listing guidelines).

7. See John Paul Stevens, *Six Amendments: How and Why We Should Change the Constitution* (New York: Little, Brown, 2014).

8. See Reid McConnell "Joust Over Campaign Law," *Washington Post*, June 3, 2014, accessed August 15, 2016, *www.washingtonpost.com/news/post-politics/wp/2014/06/03/reid-mcconnell-joust-over-campaign-law*.

9. Erwin Chemerinsky, *The Case Against the Supreme Court* (New York: Viking, 2014). See Robert Barnes, "Supreme Court Fails Frequently, Professor Writes," *Washington Post*, Sept. 29, 2014, accessed Aug. 15, 2016, *www.highbeam.com/doc/1P237227619.html* (reporting that a constitutional amendment providing term limits for Supreme Court justices is supported by other academics and at least one conservative politician, Texas governor Rick Perry).

10. See Katie Zezima, "Cruz No Longer Such a Friend of the Court," *Washington Post*, July 7, 2015, accessed Aug. 15, 2016, *www.pressreader.com/usa/thewashingtonpost1047/20150707/281706908348408/TextView*.

11. Brennan, *The Article V Amendatory Constitutional Convention*, 166 (urging states to convene a constitutional amending convention).

12. See Bernstein and Agel, *Amending America*, 169.

13. Bernstein and Agel, *Amending America*, 169.

14. Although this has never happened, a small number of voters in small states representing less than 5 percent of the population could block constitutional

change favored by an overwhelming majority of Americans. See Daniel Okrent, *Last Call: The Rise and Fall of Prohibition* (New York: Scribner, 2010), 234, 329.
15. See, e.g., Sanford Levinson, *Our Undemocratic Constitution: Where the Constitution Goes Wrong*, 7, 21–22 (identifying the difficulty of amending and the undemocratic operation of the amendment process as weaknesses in the Constitution that need to be addressed).
16. See Ira Katznelson, *Fear Itself: The New Deal and the Origins of Our Time* (New York: W. W. Norton, 2013), 421, 439, 477 (describing the contours of the permanent a national security state developed since the New Deal); Stephen M. Griffin, "Constitutionalism in the United States: From Theory to Politics," in Sanford Levinson, ed., *Responding to Imperfection: The Theory and Practice of Constitutional Amendment* (Princeton, NJ: Princeton University Press, 1995), 49–50; Bruce Ackerman, "Higher Lawmaking," in Levinson, ed., *Responding to Imperfection*, 67 (concluding that no serious observer has difficulty recognizing the monumental differences between the present Constitution and the eighteenth century version). For a discussion of the expansion of congressional power at the close of the nineteenth century in response to pressures arising from a successful national economy, see David M. O'Brien, *Constitutional Law and Politics: Struggles for Power and Government Accountability*, vol. 1 (8th ed.) (New York, W. W. Norton and Co. 2011), 574–75 [*Constitutional Law and Politics I*]. See also O'Brien, *Constitutional Law and Politics*, 590–95 (discussion of the expanded administrative state following the New Deal). The escalating role of the federal government began with the New Deal, and change occurred quickly. Joshua B. Freeman, *American Empire, 1945–2000* (New York: Viking (Penguin Group), 2012), 28 (discussing the escalating size of the federal government from 1930 to 1940).
17. See discussion at Bruce Ackerman, *We the People, Vol. 2: Transformations* (Cambridge, MA: Belknap Press, 1998), 7–8. The Four Horsemen was the moniker given by the press to four conservative members of the United States Supreme Court during the terms of the Court spanning the years 1932–1937 who opposed the New Deal agenda. They were Justices Pierce Butler, James Clark McReynolds, George Sutherland, and Willis Van Devanter.
18. See discussion at Alan P. Grimes, *Democracy and the Amendments to the Constitution* (Lanham, MD: University Press of America, 1978), 2.
19. See Griffin, *Constitutionalism in the United States*, 51. See also Sanford Levinson, "How Many Times Has the United States Constitution Been Amended? (A) <26; (B) 26; (C) 27; (D) > 27: Accounting for Constitutional Change," in Levinson, ed., *Responding to Imperfection*, 26 (concluding that truly understanding American constitutionalism requires remaining mindful of the frequency that the Constitution has been amended through political inventiveness rather than by adding new text).
20. Excluded is the anomalous 1992 addition of the Twenty-Seventh Amendment, which limits Congress's authority to adjust its own salary. In 1789, Congress proposed this amendment to the states along with amendments that became the Bill of Rights. This proposed amendment likely would have remained dormant but for it being unearthed by a twenty-year-old college student who began a ten-year campaign to persuade enough additional state legislatures to ratify the amendment to bring the total ratifications to the required thirty-eight needed for adoption. It

was a "sleeper" because few Americans even realized that the amendment had been ratified and added to the Constitution. See Richard B. Bernstein, "The Sleeper Wakes: The History and Legacy of the Twenty-Seventh Amendment," 61 *Fordham Law Review* 497, 536–542 (1992).

21. Many divergent forces have converged to encourage "off-text" methods for changing constitutional meaning, but four stand out: the *indeterminateness* of the language chosen for crucial constitutional provisions; the *difficulty* of the constitutional amendment process; a *national reverence for the Constitution's existing text*, which inspires enormous resistance to any textual change; and the *pragmatic demands* of day-to-day governing. See discussions at Gordon S. Wood, *Empire of Liberty: A History of the Early Republic, 1789–1815* (New York: Oxford University Press, 2009), 368–71; Kammen, *The Machine That Would Go of Itself*, 22, 60; Thomas Fleming, *The Louisiana Purchase* (Hoboken: Thomas Wiley and Sons, 2003), 144; Donald S. Lutz, "Toward a Theory of Constitutional Amendment," 88 *American Political Science Review* 355, 357 (1994).

22. David A. Strauss, "The Irrelevance of Constitutional Amendments," 114 *Harvard Law Review* 1457, 1476–77 (2001).

23. Robert G. Dixon Jr., "Article V: The Comatose Article of Our Living Constitution," 66 *University of Michigan Law Review* 931 (1968).

24. See Stephen M. Griffin, "The Nominee Is . . . Article V," in William N. Eskridge Jr., and Sanford Levinson, eds. *Constitutional Stupidities, Constitutional Tragedies* (New York: New York University Press, 1998), 51–53.

25. Levinson, *Our Undemocratic Constitution*, 165, 167, 170. See also Sanford Levinson, *Framed: America's 51 Constitutions and the Crisis of Governance* (New York: Oxford University Press, 2012) (arguing that Article V's dysfunctional amendment procedures, in part, account for a dysfunctional federal government).

26. See, e.g., Gilbert Y. Steiner, *Constitutional Inequality: The Political Fortunes of the Equal Rights Amendment* (Washington, DC: Brookings Institution, 1985), 29 (reasoning that requiring ratification by both houses in 75 percent of the state legislatures to adopt a single constitutional amendment is excessive when the Founders themselves required only nine of the thirteen states (70 percent) to dissolve the Articles of Confederation and form *a completely new* system of government).

27. Bruce Ackerman, "Canonizing the Civil Rights Revolution: The People and the Poll Tax," 13 *Northwestern University Law Review* 63, 130 (2009). Ackerman has argued that while professing faith in our written constitution, sophisticated reformers no longer seriously attempt to modify constitutional text but instead advocate landmark statutes and appointment of Supreme Court justices whose background and prior decisions forecast Supreme Court opinions that solidify a shift in constitutional values. Bruce Ackerman, "The Living Constitution," 120 *Harvard Law Review* 1737, 1741–42 (2007).

28. See, e.g., Darren Patrick Guerra, *Perfecting the Constitution: The Case for the Article V Amendment Process* (Lanham, MD: Lexington Books, 2015). See also Laurence H. Tribe, "Taking Text and Structure Seriously: Reflections on Free-Form Method in Constitutional Interpretation," 108 *Harvard Law Review* 1221 (1995).

29. See Mark Tushnet, *Why the Constitution Matters* (New Haven, CT: Yale University Press, 2010), 150.

Chapter 1

1. For some of the best work on the role of political agitation in shaping changes in constitutional norms and the forces that encourage or inhibit civic participation, see Bruce Ackerman, "Constitutional Politics/Constitutional Law," 99 *Yale Law Journal* 453, 484–86 (1989); Bruce Ackerman, "The Storrs Lectures: Discovering the Constitution," 93 *Yale Law Journal* 1013, 1022–23 (1984) (describing the shift from "normal politics" to more vibrant political involvement during time of constitutional change). See generally, Bruce Ackerman, *We the People, Vol. 1: Foundations* (Cambridge, MA: Belknap Press, 1991), 230–65. See also James Gray Pope, "Republican Moments: The Role of Direct Popular Power in The American Constitutional Order," 139 *University of Pennsylvania Law Review* 287, 304–13 (1990) (summarizing causes of the vacillation of American politics between relative apathy and ferment).

2. See Stuart A. Scheingold, preface to *Politics of Rights: Lawyers, Public Policy, and Political Change* (2d ed.) (Ann Arbor: University of Michigan Press, 2004), xxxii (explaining that collective mobilization research establishes the unlikelihood of collective mobilization absent initiatives from a cadre of movement activists). Accord Michael W. McCann, *Rights at Work: Pay Equity Reform and the Politics of Legal Mobilization* (Chicago: University of Chicago Press, 1994), 279–80 (cadre of movement organizers needed to build the pay equity for women movement). Sometimes, public protest spontaneously erupts, when, for example, opposition explodes over a Supreme Court decision accompanied with a demand a constitutional amendment to reverse the decision. Excellent examples are the immediate hostile public reaction to the Court's school prayer decision in *Engel v. Vitale*, 370 US 421 (1962) and public reaction to the Court's decision in *Texas v. Johnson*, 491 US 397 (1989), finding flag burning is a form of protected speech.

3. Stuart A. Scheingold, *Politics of Rights: Lawyers, Public Policy, and Political Change* (New Haven, CT: Yale University Press, 1974), 131, 148. Scheingold published a second edition in 2004 (Ann Arbor: University of Michigan Press). The two editions of *Politics of Rights* have identical text and pagination and differ in substance only by the extensive "Preface to the Second Edition" added by Professor Scheingold.

4. Scheingold, *Politics of Rights*, 21, 203. A compelling example for Scheingold of this gap between law and reality was the continuation of school segregation many years following the Court's ruling in *Brown v. Board of Education*, 347 US 483, 495 (1954) that "separate educational facilities are inherently unequal and thus unconstitutional." (100–104). Scheingold also was struck by the persistence of government-mandated school prayer throughout parts of the United States many years after the Court ruled that practice unconstitutional in *Engel v. Vitale*. 370 US 421 (1962). See discussion at 119–21.

5. Scheingold, *Politics of Rights*, 2nd ed., xxi. See Gerald N. Rosenberg, *The Hollow Hope: Can Courts Bring About Social Change?* (2d ed.) (Chicago: University of Chicago Press, 2008), 15–16, 21, 431 (demonstrating that judicial victories fail to yield direct benefits of social reform because for various reasons courts are powerless to create such reform); Michael McCann, *Rights at Work*, 278–79 (judicial victories providing women the right to pay equity did not translate over

time into changes in pay equity for women); Joel F. Handler, *Social Movements and the Legal System: A Theory of Law Reform and Social Change* (New York: Academic Press, 1979). For a thorough review of judicial impact scholarship demonstrating that courts are either unwilling or unable to implement meaningful social reform, see Douglas NeJaime, "Winning Through Losing," 96 *Iowa Law Review* 941, 948–50 and nn. 20–33 (2011).

6. Scheingold, *Politics of Rights*, at 131, 148. For excellent summation of "Politics of Rights" see McCann, *Rights at Work*, 88.

7. Scheingold, *Politics of Rights*, 131, 134. This principle has famously been summarized as "law is . . . mobilized when desire or want is translated into a demand as an assertion of rights." Frances Kahn Zemans, "Legal Mobilization: The Neglected Role of the Law in the Political System," 77 *American Political Science Review* 690, 700 (1983).

8. See Frances Fox Piven and Richard A. Cloward, *Poor People's Movements: Why They Succeed, How They Fail* (New York: Vintage Press, 1979), 12

9. See Joel F. Handler, "'Constructing the Political Spectacle': The Interpretation of Entitlements, Legalization, and Obligations in Social Welfare History," 56 *Brooklyn Law Review* 899, 972 (1990) (explaining how rights talk can lead to mobilization when people come to believe that change is both justified and possible).

10. Scheingold, *Politics of Rights*, 136–37 (explaining that even if the outcome of litigation is unfavorable, the act of *seeking official redress* redefines the problem as one that is recognized officially rather than languishing merely as a private matter). Accord McCann, *Rights at Work*, 88–89.

11. See, e.g., Martin Dupuis, *Same-Sex Marriage, Legal Mobilization, and the Politics of Rights* (New York: Peter Lang, 2002), 21 (concluding that judicial victory is unnecessary because political leveraging can occur through the process of subjecting a targeted party with significant pressure indirectly). Irrespective of outcome, disability rights litigation has been found to constitute a resource promoting movement building by framing claims (naming) and generating publicity. See Susan M. Olson, "The Political Evolution of Interest Group Litigation," in Richard A. L. Gambitta, Marlynn L. May, and James C. Foster, eds. *Governing Through Courts* (Thousand Oaks, CA: SAGE Publications, 1981), 227.

12. Michael McCann's research of litigation asserting pay equity for women found that the claim of a woman's right to pay equity was exploited successfully as a resource to build a social movement notwithstanding that proponents of pay equity never won appellate court endorsement of the movement's comparable worth theory. McCann, *Rights at Work*, 58.

13. For example, the evocation of rights by attorneys or community leaders can be sufficient to change expectations, which is a critical step in successful mobilization. Scheingold, *Politics of Rights*, 147–48. Accord McCann, *Rights at Work*, 89 (concluding that gaining support from institutional allies is useful in movement building because it raises members' expectations that injustices might realistically be challenged). See Scott Barclay and Shauna Fisher, "Cause Lawyers in the First Wave of Same Sex Marriage Litigation," in Austin Sarat and Stuart A. Scheingold, eds., *Cause Lawyers and Social Movements* (Redwood City, CA: Stanford University Press, 2006), 91 (showing that even when unsuccessful, the *process* of seeking

legal redress to secure the right to same-sex marriage moved the idea of same-sex marriage from the absurd notion to the achievable).
14. See discussion in McCann, *Rights at Work*, 89.
15. See, e.g., Thomas M. Keck, "From Bakke to Grutter: The Rise of Rights-Based Conservatism," in Ronald Kahn and Ken I. Kersch, eds., *The Supreme Court and American Political Development* (Lawrence: University Press of Kansas, 2006), 414–42 (discussing the role of the ideological framework of eliminating all race-conscious policies in shifting white racial consciousness to the view that affirmative action renders whites as the injured parties deserving redress).
16. For a discussion of the utility of naming rights by placing demands for redress of discontents within legally derived categories in order to demarcate "them" from "us" see Samuel Bowles and Herbert Gintis, *Democracy and Capitalism: Property, Community, and the Contradictions of Modern Social Thought* (New York: Basic Books, 1986).
17. See Charles R. Epp, "Law as an Instrument of Social Reform," in Keith E. Whittington, R. Daniel Kelemen, and Gregory A. Caldeira, eds., *The Oxford Handbook of Law and Politics* (New York: Oxford University Press, 2008), 595, 608 (explaining that to initiate social change, advocacy groups must successfully move their claims to the forefront of the public agenda and this generally requires securing the endorsement from key governing institutions); Epp, "Law as an Instrument of Social Reform," 608 (explaining that social reform effort success is associated with advocacy groups securing financial and organizational resources and allies among the administrative professions). See also Joyce Gelb and Marian Lief Palley, "Women and Interest Group Politics: A Comparative Analysis of Federal Decision-Making," 41 *Journal of Politics* 362, 377–380 (1979) (explaining how, during the ERA controversy, anti-ERA activists strengthened their social movement through overlapping memberships in anti-abortion groups).
18. McCann, *Rights at Work*, 62.
19. Michael McCann and Helena Silverstein, "Rethinking Law's 'Allurements': A Relational Analysis of Social Movement Lawyers in the United States," in Austin Sarat, ed., *Cause Lawyering: Political Commitments and Professional Responsibilities* (New York: Oxford University Press, 1997), 268. Accord Paul R. Brewer, *Value War: Public Opinion and the Politics of Gay Rights* (Lanham, MD: Rowman and Littlefield Publishers, 2008), 35 (showing that seeking legal redress to eradicate racial segregation in the 1950s, and later litigation to advance gay rights, significantly increased the national prominence of the civil rights debate).
20. See, e.g., James R. Carroll, "Public Sours on Mother's Milk—Money," *Courier-Journal* (Louisville, Ky.), June 8, 2014, accessed August 15, 2016, available at Westlaw 2014 WLNR 15546966 (reporting on the campaign finance debate that occurred during Senate hearings and reporting on poll data showing the public's impression that the political contributions have distorted the political system to benefit the rich); Dana Milbank, "This Is No Way to Fix the Problem of Billionaires Buying Elections," *Washington Post*, June 3, 2014, accessed August 15, 2016, *www.washingtonpost.com/opinions/dana-milbank-this-is-no-way-to-fix-the-problem-of-billionaires-buying-elections/2014/06/03/f6e8228e-eb62-11e3-93d2-edd4be1f5d9e_story.html* (reporting on the amendment hearings conducted by the Senate Judiciary Committee and the opposition by influential Senate

conservatives). See also "Hearing of the Senate Judiciary Committee Subject: 'Examining a Constitutional Amendment to Restore Democracy to the American People,'" *Federal New Service Transcripts*, June 3, 2014, accessed June 15, 2014, available at Westlaw 2014 WLNR 15116740 (providing eighty-six page transcript of testimony presented at the Senate hearing).
21. See Robert Barnes, "Supreme Court Fails Frequently, Professor Writes," *Washington Post*, September 29, 2014, accessed August 15, 2016, www.highbeam.com/doc/1P237227619.html (interviewing Erwin Chemerinsky, a law school dean and eminent constitutional scholar, regarding his then recently published book calling for a constitutional amendment providing term limits for Supreme Court justices).
22. Political education of targeted audiences through periodicals, pamphlets, flyers, newsletters, films, workshops, and internet blogs also assists in movement building. See Stephen Mezias and Rikki Abzug, "The Fragmented State and Organizational Governance: The Case of Comparable Worth" (unpublished paper) (The Stern School, New York University, 1993) 23, cited at McCann, *Rights at Work*, 63 and n. 12. Efforts to amend the Constitution can provide movement activists similar, and probably greater, opportunities to communicate a seriousness of purpose to targeted audiences.
23. See Handler, *Social Movements and Legal Systems*, 216 (assembling evidence that a rights-based legal strategy to secure legal redress of grievances can benefit a movement's fund-raising efforts).
24. See McCann, *Rights at Work*, 281–82.
25. See Rosenberg, *The Hollow Hope*, 257.
26. See Jo Freeman, "Social Revolution and the Equal Rights Amendment," 3 *Sociological Forum* 145, 147 (1988) (concluding that by the mid-1960s' birth of the modern feminist movement, the ERA was not a prominent issue); Jo Freeman, "The Origins of the Women's Liberation Movement," 78 *American Journal of Sociology* 792, 803 (1973) (concluding that as late as 1969, the ERA was unknown to most feminists).
27. Michael A. Musmano, *Proposed Amendments to the Constitution* (Washington, DC: US Government Printing Office, 1929), reprinted (Westport, CT: Greenwood Press, 1976), 253. None of these proposed ERA resolutions ever came to the floor for debate.
28. See Jane J. Mansbridge, *Why We Lost the ERA* (Chicago: University of Chicago Press, 1986), 8–14.
29. See Cary Franklin, "Inventing the 'Traditional Concept' of Sex Discrimination," 125 *Harvard Law Review* 1307, 1326–27 (2012).
30. Mansbridge, *Why We Lost the ERA*, 9–10 (emphasis added).
31. Carl M. Brauer, "Women Activists, Southern Conservatives, and the Prohibition of Sex Discrimination in Title VII of the 1964 Civil Rights Act," 49 *Journal of Southern History* 37, 41 (1983) (emphasis added). Accord David S. Meyer and Deana A. Rohlinger, "Big Books and Social Movements: A Myth of Ideas and Social Change," 59 *Social Problems* 136, 144 (2012) (concluding that Kennedy created the Presidential Commission on the Status of Women in part to undermine the effort to enact an ERA); Cynthia E. Harrison, "A 'New Frontier' for Women: Public Policy for the Kennedy Administration," 67 *Journal of American History* 630, 632, 638 (1980) (documenting that Kennedy proposed the commis-

sion in large part in response to Esther Peterson's argument that the ERA would have a negative impact and the Commission was a preferable substitute for the current "troublesome and futile agitation" over adoption of the ERA).
32. See discussion at Mansbridge, *Why We Lost the ERA*, 10.
33. See Freeman, "The Origins of the Women's Liberation Movement," 797.
34. As Jo Freeman has concluded, while feminists by the late 1960s may not have heard of the NWP or the ERA, they and the emerging women's movement owed much to the pre-1970 struggle over the ERA. Freeman, "Social Revolution and the Equal Rights Amendment," 147.
35. See discussion in Serena Mayeri, "Constitutional Choices: Legal Feminism and the Historical Dynamics of Change," 92 *University of California Law Review* 755, 764 (2004). Accord Brauer, "Women Activists, Southern Conservatives," 40 (concluding that the pro-ERA NWP's overwhelmingly and perhaps exclusively white membership evinced little concern for racial or economic equality; that more of its members appeared to be politically conservative or reactionary than liberal or radical; and that their associations with Southern politicians proved politically beneficial in their efforts to oppose the 1964 Civil Rights Act). See also Mary J. Farmer and Donald C. Nieman, "Race, Class, Gender, and the Unintended Consequences of the Fifteenth Amendment," in Kyvig, ed., *Unintended Consequences of Constitutional Amendment*, 154 (tracing the history of racist appeals by some in the early women's movement to 1869, when many feminists severed their ties with the abolition movement over the Fifteenth Amendment's extension of the franchise to black men but not to women).
36. Brauer, "Women Activists, Southern Conservatives," 43 (reporting that some NWP members concluded that adding the sex amendment to Title VII was part of a strategy to undermine enactment of *any* Civil Rights Bill).
37. See Franklin, "Inventing the 'Traditional Concept' of Sex Discrimination," n. 36.
38. Brauer, "Women Activists, Southern Conservatives," 42 (showing that many in the NWP supported addition of the sex amendment in order undermine efforts to enact any Civil Rights legislation and thus add pressure to enact the ERA). A second motivation was that if Title VII was going to be enacted, which it appeared it would be, then white women wanted to be included within its protections. Franklin, "Inventing the 'Traditional Concept' of Sex discrimination," 1318 and n. 36.
39. See Mayeri, "Constitutional Choices," 770–72. Rep. Smith proposed the sex amendment to Title VII as a strategy to undermine passage of the 1964 Civil Rights Act, to which he was strongly opposed. Smith also was motivated by a desire to advance the cause of the ERA, which he supported solely as a means of advancing his anti-union ideology (the ERA undercut efforts by organized labor to enact protective labor legislation). Brauer, "Women Activists, Southern Conservatives," 43–45.
40. See discussion at Mayeri, "Constitutional Choices," 773.
41. Barry Friedman, *The Will of the People* (New York: Farrar, Strauss and Giroux, 2009), 292. See, e.g., Rosenfeld v. Southern Pac. Co., 444 F.2d 1219, 1225–27 (9th Cir. 1971) (invalidating California's maximum hour law and weight-lifting legislation as violative of Title VII); Mayeri, "Constitutional Choices," 769.

42. Franklin, "Inventing the 'Traditional Concept' of Sex Discrimination," 1335 and n. 131.
43. See Gerald N. Rosenberg, "The 1964 Civil Rights Act: The Crucial Role of Social Movements in the Enactment and Implementation of Anti-Discrimination Law," 49 *Saint Louis University Law Journal* 1147, 1152 (2005).
44. See discussion at Franklin, "Inventing the 'Traditional Concept' of Sex Discrimination," 1333–42. Franklin explains that some high level Washington officials in the mid-1960s considered amending Title VII to eliminate the sex discrimination provisions from the statute (1338–39) and not until 1969 did the EEOC revise its guidelines to provide that sex-segregated employment advertisements violated Title VII (1345).
45. Mayeri, "Constitutional Choices," 775. See also Rosenberg, *The Hollow Hope*, 253 (concluding that the EEOC's inaction in enforcing the sex discrimination provisions of the 1964 Civil Rights Act vexed many women activists).
46. Freeman, "The Origins of the Women's Liberation Movement," 798. On the importance of being taken seriously, see Jo Freeman, *The Politics of Women's Liberation* (New York: David Mackay, 1975), 79 (relating that the President's Commission on the Status of Women was told by a Justice Department official that the reason the Justice Department did not file its first sex discrimination suit until 1970 was that the Department responds to social agitation and the failure of women to generate public protest and turmoil over sex discrimination suggests that women are not genuinely concerned about employment discrimination).
47. Freeman, "The Origins of the Women's Liberation Movement," 799.
48. Rosenberg, *The Hollow Hope*, 253.
49. See Verta Taylor, "Review of *Sex, Gender, and the Politics of ERA: A State and the Nation*, by Donald G. Matthews and Jane Sherron DeHart," 21 *Contemporary Sociology* 37, 38 (1992). Accord Sarah A. Soule and Susan Olzak, "When Do Movements Matter? The Politics of Contingency and the Equal Rights Amendment," 69 *American Sociological Review* 473, 474 (2004) (stating that social movements and political parties deployed the ERA as a resource to mobilize support).
50. Taylor, "Review of *Sex, Gender, and the Politics of ERA*" (summarizing the findings of historians Donald G. Mathews and Jane S. De Hart); Serena Mayeri advances a convincing case that the ERA amendment effort's effect on consciousness raising was enhanced by the decision to pursue a "dual strategy" of pressing both for the ERA and for bringing gender discrimination within the proscriptions of the Equal Protection Clause of the Fourteenth Amendment. Mayeri, "Constitutional Choices," 759, 802. (concluding that the dual strategy reinvigorated the women's movement's ideals and goals and forced women to articulate why the Constitution ought to ban gender discrimination).
51. Mayeri, "Constitutional Choices," 805.
52. Meyer and Rohlinger, "Big Books and Social Movements," 144. Other groups such as the Women's Equity Action League (WEAL) and ERAmerica, an umbrella group representing one hundred pro-ERA organizations, also used the ERA to mobilize membership support. Donald T. Critchlow and Cynthia L. Stachecki, "The

Equal Rights Amendment Reconsidered: Politics, Policy, and Social Mobilization in a Democracy," 20 *Journal of Policy History* 157, 159 (2008).

53. See Maryann Barasko, "Civic Engagement and Voluntary Associations: Reconsidering the Role of the Governance Structures of Advocacy Groups," 37 *Polity* 315, 323 (2005); Freeman, "The Origins of the Women's Liberation Movement," 803–08. See also Freeman, "Social Revolution and the Equal Rights Amendment," 147 (explaining how pre-and early-1970s consciousness-raising efforts by women's groups generated new interest in the ERA).
54. Rosenberg, *The Hollow Hope*, 243 and table 8.3.
55. See Joyce Gelb and Marian Lief Palley, *Women and Public Policies* (Princeton: Princeton University Press, 1982), 29. Accord Rosenberg, *The Hollow Hope*, 244.
56. See Jo Reger and Suzanne Staggenborg, "Patterns of Mobilization in Local Movement Organizations: Leadership and Strategy in Four National Organization for Women Chapters," 49 *Sociological Perspectives* 297, 318 (2006) (finding that the ERA ratification effort provided unique mobilization and organizing opportunities for NOW and many local NOW chapters). Roger and Staggenborg state in the 1970s, at the Chicago NOW chapter, the ERA campaign became the focus of the chapter's organizing and mobilization efforts and conclude that as NOW chapters around the United States increasingly focused on the ERA ratification in the late 1970s, these chapters experienced an increase in membership (306–8, 319).
57. James G. Ennuis and Richard Schreuer, "Mobilizing Weak Support for Social Movements: The Role of Grievance, Efficacy, and Cost," 66 *Social Forces* 390, 395 (1987).
58. Mansbridge, *Why We Lost the ERA*, 121.
59. Of course, the political opportunity structure (POS)—the political environment in which the women's movement interacted during the ERA controversy—also was a critical factor in successfully building the women's movement. The political opportunity structure accounts for things such as the political establishment's openness to advocacy for change, the current political preferences of powerful political actors, the extent that movements may already have negotiated alliances with political elites, and the likelihood that government will initiate repressive measures against a movement. NeJaime, "Winning Through Losing," 899. Soule and Olzak explain how POS affects the likelihood that collective mobilization will influence policy and in particular how POS has an important gender component: the relationship of outcomes favorable to women and the number of women active in the public sphere (e.g., politics and business), which causes political actors to alter their view of women's societal role and provides women greater political opportunities). Soule and Olzak, "When Do Movements Matter?," 474 and 478. For very good summary of the leading POS scholarship see Critchlow and Stachecki, "The Equal Rights Amendment Reconsidered," n. 3.
60. Quoted in Mayeri, "Constitutional Choices," 795 (emphasis added).
61. Freeman, "Social Revolution and the Equal Rights Amendment," 148; Freeman, *The Origins of the Women's Liberation Movement*, 799 (discussing NOW's facility at gaining publicity).
62. See Rosenberg, *The Hollow Hope*, 264–65. See Mayeri, "Constitutional Choices,"

795 (concluding that the increased publicity associated with the ERA ratification effort facilitated feminist activism and political mobilization).
63. See Karen Oppenheim Mason, John L. Czajka, and Sara Arber, "Change in US Women's Sex-Role Attitudes, 1964–1974," 41 *American Sociological Review* 573, 575 n. 4 (1976) (showing that women nationally increasingly were aware of the women's movement during the 1970s, the same time that ERA also was gaining national attention). In addition, these authors uncovered evidence linking changing women's sex-role attitudes and the women's movement's growing popularity and rapid development (589, 593).
64. For a chronology of the ERA's consideration by Congress between 1970 and 1972 see Mansbridge, *Why We Lost the ERA*, 10–12; Rosenberg, *The Hollow Hope*, 257–58.
65. Rosenberg, *The Hollow Hope*, 229–30 and table 8.2A and 8.2B at 233–34.
66. Rosenberg, *The Hollow Hope*, 229.
67. Rosenberg, *The Hollow Hope*, 233–34, tables 8.2A and 8.2B (the only exception was one measure, the *NYT* index that had higher media coverage of these issues during the period 1940–1945).
68. In 1970, 40 percent of women favored efforts to strengthen women's societal status. The next year showed an 8-point (20 percent) increase in the percentage of women supporting such efforts for change. That change in attitude persisted over the next several years when women were asked the same question. Similarly high increases occurred the year Congress passed the ERA and the years thereafter among males favoring efforts to increase women's societal status. See discussion at Rosenberg, *The Hollow Hope*, 239.
69. See Soule and Olzak, "When Do Movements Matter?," 480 (showing benefits that the ERA gained from support from powerful allies).
70. Rosenberg, *The Hollow Hope*, 258.
71. See Louis Bolce, Gerald De Maio, and Douglas Muzzio, "The Equal Rights Amendment, Public Opinion and American Constitutionalism," 19 *Polity* 552, 552 (1987).
72. Mayeri, "Constitutional Choices," 785–86.
73. See Mansbridge, *Why We Lost the ERA*, 179–80.
74. Most of NOW's increase in revenue was from membership increases resulting from the mobilization of women and the concomitant recruitment of NOW members during the early ERA ratification period. Rosenberg, *The Hollow Hope*, 244 (citing Maren Lockwood Carden, *Feminism in the Mid-1970s* (New York: Ford Foundation, 1977), 19–20).
75. During the entire three-year period of 1971–1974 foundation grants to women's rights organizations totaled about $2 million, and within one year after (in 1975) that total had more than doubled to $4.2 million. Rosenberg, *The Hollow Hope*, 244.
76. Rosenberg, *The Hollow Hope*, 244 (citing Carden, *Feminism in the Mid-1970s*, 125).
77. From its inception, one of NOW's central tenets was grassroots membership-based mobilization through consciousness raising. See Maryann Barasko, "Civic Engagement and Voluntary Associations: Reconsidering the Role of the Governance Structures of Advocacy Groups," 37 *Polity* 315, 323 (2005). Other, more

radical feminist groups also contributed significantly to raising women's collective consciousness by organizing consciousness-raising opportunities for women throughout the United States, in small groups, in workshops, and through film, book stores, etc. See Voichita Nachescu, "Radical Feminism and the Nation," 3 *Journal for the Study Radicalism* 29, 31 (2008) (showing that "consciousness-raising" contributed enormously to the growth of the women's movement). For a discussion of "second wave" feminism, see Freeman, *The Origins of the Women's Liberation Movement*, 796–803.

78. See Barasko, "Civic Engagement and Voluntary Associations," 317. See also Ann Costain, "Representing Women: The Transition from Social Movement to Interest Group," in Ellen Boneparth, ed., *Women, Power and Policy* (New York: Pergamon Press, 1982), 19–37.

79. For example, NOW has a political action committee (NOW/PAC) that endorses candidates for political office who have been approved by local NOW chapters. NOW attempts to balance this focus with its historic commitment to grassroots mobilization and consciousness raising. Barasko, "Civic Engagement and Voluntary Associations," 317, 323.

80. See Gelb and Palley, "Women and Interest Group Politics," 362, 378, 389 (1979).

81. See *now.org/issues/constitutionalequality*, accessed August 15, 2016.

82. See Kyvig, *Explicit and Authentic Acts*, 395.

83. See Critchlow and Stachecki, "The Equal Rights Amendment Reconsidered," 171–72.

84. See, e.g., Critchlow and Stachecki, "The Equal Rights Amendment Reconsidered," 171–72 (describing how the anti-ERA forces mobilized public opinion against ERA and arguing that the ERA battle is best understood as diverse groups successfully mobilizing for political action); Gelb and Palley, "Women and Interest Group Politics," 377–80 (pointing out that anti-ERA activists often had overlapping memberships in anti-abortion groups); Soule and Olzak, "When Do Movements Matter?," 476 (discussing issue-framing by the anti-ERA organizations).

85. See Critchlow and Stachecki, "The Equal Rights Amendment Reconsidered," 165–66 (discussing Phyllis Schlafly and the Stop ERA movement in energizing a counter mobilization effort opposing the ERA).

86. See, e.g., Critchlow and Stachecki, "The Equal Rights Amendment Reconsidered," 165.

87. Joel F. Handler, "'Constructing the Political Spectacle': The Interpretation of Entitlements, Legalization, and Obligations in Social Welfare History," 56 *Brooklyn Law Review* 899, 972 (1990). See Soule and Olzak, "When Do Movements Matter?," 492 (referring to the interplay as a "double-edged sword"); Critchlow and Stachecki, "The Equal Rights Amendment Reconsidered," 161 (concluding that competition between pro- and anti-ERA forces encouraged mobilization and counter mobilization by each).

88. Floyd McKissick, *Three-Fifths of a Man* (New York: Macmillan Company, 1969).

89. On the political impact of the Three-Fifths Clause, see Daniel Walker Howe, *What Hath God Wrought: The Transformation of America, 1815–1848* (New York: Oxford University Press, 2007), 150 (concluding that the Three-Fifths Clause so inflated the voting power of the slaveholding states that it largely accounts for the perpetuation of the Virginia dynasty of presidents during thirty-two of the country's

first thirty-six years). See also Albert F. Simpson, "The Political Significance of Slave Representation, 1787–1821," 7 *Journal of Southern History* 315, 315–42 (1941).
90. Louis Ruchames, *The Abolitionists* (New York: Capricorn Books, 1963), 23.
91. Garry Wills, *Negro President: Jefferson and the Slave Power* (Boston: Houghton Mifflin, 2003), 9, 122–25; Gordon S. Wood, *Empire of Liberty: A History of the Early Republic, 1789–1815* (New York: Oxford University Press, 2009), 532–33 and n. 57.
92. Herman V. Ames, *The Proposed Amendments to the Constitution of the United States During the First Century of Its History*, Annual Report, American Historical Association (1896) (Breinigsville, PA: Kessinger Legacy Reprints, 2011), 45 and n. 5.
93. Ames, *The Proposed Amendments*, 46.
94. Ames, *The Proposed Amendments*, 46; Wood, *Empire of Liberty*, 696.
95. Ames, *The Proposed Amendments*, 47–49. The final chapter regarding the Three-Fifths Clause was an effort to amend the Constitution in the winter of 1860–61 to insulate the clause from Article V's amendment procedures. Ames explains that this amendment was proposed in an attempt to appease the South and avert Civil War, but the momentum of secession outran these amendment efforts and the emancipation provided by the Thirteenth Amendment swept away any further need to repeal the Three-Fifths Clause (49).
96. See David M. Potter, *The Impending Crisis: 1848–1861* (completed and edited by Don E. Fehrenbacher) (New York: Harper Collins Publishing, 1976).
97. See William H. Riker, *The Art of Political Manipulation* (New Haven, CT: Yale University Press, 1986), 2 (excluded from the calculation is Lincoln's 1864 election because Lincoln was elected by a coalition with War Democrats).
98. Riker, *The Art of Political Manipulation*, 3. See discussion at Bruce Ackerman, *We the People, Vol. 3: The Civil Rights Revolution* (Cambridge, MA: Belknap Press, 2014), 37.
99. For example, in 1835, when antislavery pamphlets were discovered on a mail boat, the Charleston, South Carolina, postmaster refused to permit their delivery. Unknown citizens broke into the post office, seized the pamphlets, and destroyed them by nighttime bonfires, to the hoots of an excited crowd. A citizens' committee thereafter rifled through incoming mail addressed to white citizens to intercept delivery of antislavery literature. Wills, *Negro President*, 197–98, 200–20; Ruchames, *The Abolitionists*, 121, 126 (pointing out that in addition to imposing a prior restraint on speech by barring what could be placed in the mail, Southern states banned schoolbooks and works of fiction for inconsequential references to slavery, and slave owners were warned against permitting slaves to attend Fourth of July celebrations for fear that they might hear the text of the Declaration of Independence). On the significance of postal censorship to the South, see Clement Eaton, "Censorship of the Southern Mails," 48 *American Historical Review* 266, 266–80 (1943).
100. See Lucas A. Powe Jr., *The Supreme Court and the American Elite, 1789–2008* (Cambridge: Harvard University Press, 2009) 95 (explaining that the gag rule was extended in 1840 to preclude the House from even *receiving* any antislavery petitions).
101. Ames, *The Proposed Amendments*, 193. See discussion at William Lee Miller, *Arguing*

about Slavery: John Quincy Adams and the Great Battle in The United States Congress (New York: Alfred A. Knopf, 1996), 354 (providing the text of the proposed constitutional amendment).

    Soon thereafter, January 1841, the seventy-four-year-old former president agreed to represent the Africans in the famous case arising out of the June 1839 mutiny on the slave-trade vessel *Amistad*. See *United States v. The Libellants and Claimants of the Schooner Amistad*, 40 US (15 Peters) 518 (1841). See discussion of this case at Howe, *What Hath God Wrought*, 520–24; Don Fehrenbacher, *The Slaveholding Republic: An Account of the United States Government's Relations to Slavery* (New York: Oxford University Press, 2001), 193–95 and nn. 112–14.

102. Wills, *Negro President*, 198, 221. That Adams presented 693 petitions in the 1838–39 session is found at Wills at 203.
103. See William W. Freehling, *The Road to Disunion: Secessionists at Bay, 1776–1854* (New York: Oxford University Press, 1990), 343.
104. Kyvig, *Explicit and Authentic Acts*, 144.
105. See Howe, *What Hath God Wrought*, 514 (describing the detailed press coverage of the ongoing debate over the gag rule in the nation's newspapers, including the full-text reporting of congressional speeches).
106. Howe, *What Hath God Wrought*, 611. Ronald Kahn's explication of the social construction of law (including constitutional law) provides the theoretical foundation for understanding the dynamics explaining how Adams's failed antislavery amendment efforts could shape public opposition to slavery. As Kahn explains, through a national dialectic the public develops a growing understanding of the meaning of liberty. The advocacy associated with constitutional amendments opposing slavery (or any other view of the contours of liberty) positions amendment proponents to influence this emerging appreciation of the contours of liberty. See Ronald Kahn, "Social Constructions, Supreme Court Reversals, and American Political Development: Lochner, Plessy, Bowers, but Not Roe," in Ronald Kahn and Ken I. Kersch, eds., *The Supreme Court and American Political Development* (Lawrence: University Press of Kansas, 2006), 83–85.
107. See James M. McPherson, "The Fights Against the Gag Rule: Joshua Leavitt and Antislavery Insurgency in the Whig Party," 48 *Journal of Negro History* 177, 178 (1963).
108. McPherson, "The Fights Against the Gag Rule," 190. See Potter, *The Impending Crisis*, 227 (explaining that once the question of slavery developed as a public issue, the major political parties attempted to keep the slavery issue out of politics as much as possible due to the fear of its divisive potential).
109. See Miller, *Arguing About Slavery*, 356–60 (describing the years that John Quincy Adams spent defying the deeply entrenched "gag rule" in Congress that banned any discussion or consideration of antislavery petitions).
110. See Ruchames, *The Abolitionists*, 11, 14.
111. Potter, *The Impending Crisis*, 35–40, 476–77. On the ambivalence of John Quincy Adams with respect to the Congress's power to intervene as an effective arbiter of the sectional dispute over slavery, see Miller, *Arguing About Slavery*, 354.
112. Potter, *The Impending Crisis*, 476.
113. On the shift from slavery being regarded as respectable behavior that must at most

be contained to a barbaric practice that must be excised see discussion at Potter, *The Impending Crisis*, 476–77.
114. Quoted in Jack M. Balkin, *Constitutional Redemption* (Cambridge: Harvard University Press, 2011), 5, 46–48.
115. Balkin, *Constitutional Redemption*, 5, 46–48.
116. See discussion at McPherson, "The Fights Against the Gag Rule," 177, 194.
117. Quoted in Riker, *The Art of Political Manipulation*, 4.
118. Those forces include the impulse toward a clear-cut antislavery party that had manifested itself as early as 1840 with the Liberty Party and 1848 with the Free Soil Party. Other contributing developments were the admission of Texas as a slave state; the Compromise of 1850, which amended and strengthened the Fugitive Slave Act; the 1854 Kansas-Nebraska Act, which abrogated the Missouri Compromise of 1820 and threatened to extend slavery into the territories; the rise of nativism and the Know Nothing Party in the 1850s; the 1857 Dredd Scott decision; and adoption of the Lecompton Constitution for the Kansas Territory, which placed a taint on the principle of popular sovereignty to decide whether a territory would permit slavery. These events, in combination, contributed to a national schism over slavery, an increase in antislavery consciousness in the North, and the rise of the antislavery Republican Party. See Potter, *The Impending Crisis*; Fehrenbacher, *The Slaveholding Republic*.
119. Howe, *What Hath God Wrought*, 514.
120. Scheingold, *Politics of Rights* (2d ed.), 224, 339.
121. Scheingold, *Politics of Rights* (2d ed.), 134.
122. Kyvig, *Explicit and Authentic Acts*, 395.
123. See Steve Neal, *Happy Days Are Here Again: The 1932 Democratic Convention, the Emergence of FDR—and How America Was Changed Forever* (New York: Harper Collins, 2004), 236
124. The state Prohibition laws enacted prior to adoption of the Eighteenth Amendment undercut, to some degree, the necessity for national regulation as well as the propriety of federal regulation. The many state Prohibition laws, it was argued, conclusively demonstrated that a Prohibition constitutional amendment movement was unnecessary and an untoward attempt to invade the reserved right of local self-government. Alan P. Grimes, *Democracy and the Amendments to the Constitution* (Lanham, MD: University Press of America, 1987), 88.
125. See Daniel Okrent, *Last Call: The Rise and Fall of Prohibition* (New York, Scribner, 2010), 3.
126. See, e.g., Gelb and Palley, "Women and Interest Group Politics," 389.
127. Orkent, *Last Call*, 224, 239.
128. By 1932 the country had turned against Prohibition and the political parties could not ignore public opinion. Therefore the 1932 party platforms of both political the Republican and Democratic parties supported opponents of Prohibition. Neal, *Happy Days Are Here Again*, 240–49.
129. Orkent, *Last Call*, 336.
130. Orkent, *Last Call*, 363–64.
131. The factual background discussed in this section can be found in Clement E. Vose, *Constitutional Change* (Lexington, MA: Lexington Books, 1972), 245–47 (Twentieth Century Fund study) and Richard F. Hamm, "Short Euphorias

Followed by Long Hangovers: Unintended Consequences of the Eighteenth and Twenty-First Amendments," in Kyvig, ed., *Unintended Consequence of Constitutional Amendment*, 183–84.

132. This change would have reversed *Hawke v. Smith (I and II)*, 253 US 221 (1920) and 253 US 231 (1920) (declaring unconstitutional a state constitutional provision providing for a referendum vote on a state legislature's ratification of a proposed constitutional amendment). Compare *Kimble v. Swackhamer*, 439 US 1385 (1978) (voter referenda of constitutional amendments lawful as long as not binding) with *Cook v. Gralike*, 531 US 510 (2001) (state law providing for binding instructions to the state's congressional representatives to advocate for and support a constitutional amendment unconstitutional).

133. Vose, *Constitutional Change*, 246.

134. See discussion in Grimes, *Democracy and the Amendments to the Constitution*, 109–13.

Chapter 2

1. Citizens United v. Fed. Election Commission, 558 US 310 (2010).
2. See. e.g., Susanna Kim Ripken, "Corporate First Amendment Rights after Citizens United: An Analysis of the Popular Movement to End the Constitutional Personhood of Corporations," 14 *University of Pennsylvania Journal of Business Law* 209 (2011); Nancy S. Lind and Erik T. Rankin, *First Amendment Rights: An Encyclopedia* (Santa Barbara: ABC-CLIO/Greenwood, 2012), 269 (explaining that the corporate abolitionists' call to abandon legal personhood of corporations is rooted in the reality that law contributes to the formation of values and understandings and calling a corporation a person makes it so in our minds and changes the way we perceive the world; this perception is what the movement seeks to reverse). For text of the proposed amendment, see *movetoamend.org*, accessed August 15, 2016.
3. Seven successful amendment efforts overturned or effectively nullified a Supreme Court decision. These are amendments Eleven (suit against states in federal court), Thirteen (slavery), Fourteen (definition of United States citizenship), Sixteen (income tax), Nineteen (women's suffrage), Twenty-Four (poll tax), and Twenty-Six (age eligibility to vote).
4. Among the more important failed efforts to amend the Constitution to reverse a Supreme Court decision have been movements to permit child labor legislation and efforts to reinstate school prayer, permit the banning of abortion, eliminate busing, permit one house of state legislatures to be apportioned on a basis other than population, and banning flag desecration. See discussion at William G. Ross, "The Resilience of *Marbury v. Madison*: Why Judicial Review Has Survived So Many Attacks," 38 *Wake Forest Law Review* 733, 749–50 and 776 (2003).
5. Ripken, "Corporate First Amendment Rights," 255.
6. See Barry Friedman, *The Will of the People* (New York: Farrar, Strauss and Giroux, 2009), 362 (concluding that mobilization against Supreme Court decisions represents one of the greatest forces actuating constitutional change).
7. Ripken, "Corporate First Amendment Rights," 255.
8. Ripken, "Corporate First Amendment Rights," 256.
9. Ripken, "Corporate First Amendment Rights," n. 212 (citing Sanford Levinson, *Constitutional Faith* (Princeton: Princeton University Press, 1988)).

10. Ripken, "Corporate First Amendment Rights," 256.
11. See Lucas A. Powe, "Are 'the People' Missing in Action (and Should Anyone Care)," review of Larry D. Kramer, *The People Themselves: Popular Constitutionalism and Judicial Review*, 83 *University of Texas Law Review* 855, 889–95 (2005).
12. Ripken, "Corporate First Amendment Rights," 258.
13. C. Herman Pritchett, "Judicial Supremacy from Marshall to Burger," in M. Judd Harmon, ed., *Essays on the Constitution of the United States* (Port Washington, NY: Kennikat Press, 1978), 99, 108.
14. See Benjamin I. Page and Robert Y. Shapiro, "Effects of Public Opinion on Policy," 77 *American Political Science Review* 175, 175–90 (1983). Also important is the nature of the public that holds the opinion because the correlation between opinion and policy is greatest when the public holding the opinion is politically informed and involved. Donald Devine, *The Attentive Public: Polyarchical Democracy* (Chicago: Rand McNally, 1970), 91–92. See also Louis Bolce, Gerald De Maio, and Douglas Muzzio, "The Equal Rights Amendment, Public Opinion and American Constitutionalism," 19 *Polity* 551, 555 and n. 7, 562 (1987) (discussing the importance of the quality of the public opinion in assessing opinion polls, in particular the importance of the issue to those holding the opinion, as well as the political attentiveness of opinion holders).
15. Thomas R. Marshall, *Public Opinion and the Supreme Court* (Boston: Unwin Hyman, 1989); K. T. McGuire and L. A. Stimson, "The Least Dangerous Branch Revisited: New Evidence on Supreme Court Responsiveness to Public Preferences," 66 *Journal of Politics* 1018, 1018–35 (2004). Research also establishes that success of arguments before the Court supported by the president are correlated with presidential popularity. See J. Yates, *Popular Justice* (Albany: State University of New York Press, 2002).
16. See discussion at William Mishler and Reginald S. Sheehan, "Public Opinion, the Attitudinal Model and Supreme Court Decision Making: A Micro-Analytic Perspective," 58 *Journal of Politics* 169, 198 (1996).
17. Friedman, *The Will of the People*, 221 (explaining how Chief Justice Taft promoted speech-protective decisions to demonstrate the Court's commitment to the protection of individual rights). See Ross, "The Resilience of *Marbury v. Madison*," 772 (same).
18. Benjamin N. Cardozo, *The Nature of the Judicial Process* (New Haven, CT: Yale University Press, 1921), 168.
19. Richard Posner, "Pragmatism Versus Purposivism in First Amendment Analysis," 54 *Stanford Law Review* 737, 739 (2002).
20. Quoted in Jeffrey Rosen, "Rehnquist the Great? Even Liberals May Come to Regard William Rehnquist as One of the Most Successful Chief Justices of the Century," *Atlantic Monthly*, April 2005, 84–86, reprinted in Friedman, *Will of the People*, 371. Justice Sandra Day O'Connor has explained that because the court has no independent enforcement capability, it depends on the confidence and support of the citizenry. That is why the justices must always be aware of public preferences and why the Court must attempt to maintain the public trust. Sandra Day O'Connor, "Public Trust as a Dimension of Equal Justice: Some Suggestions to Increase Public Trust," 36 *Court Review (Journal of the American Judges Association)* 10, 13 (1999). Most scholars agree that public support for the

Court wanes when its decisions consistently run counter to clear trends in public attitudes. Georg Vanberg, "Establishing and Maintaining Judicial Independence," in Keith E. Whittington, R. Daniel Kelemen, and Gregory A. Caldeira, eds., *The Oxford Handbook of Law and Politics* (New York: Oxford University Press, 2008), 113–15 (citing authority).

21. Robert McCloskey, *The American Supreme Court* (Chicago: University of Chicago Press, 1960), 225.
22. Robert A. Dahl, "Decision-Making in a Democracy: The Supreme Court as a National Policy-Maker," 6 *Journal of Public Law* 279, 285 (1957).
23. Friedman, *The Will of the People*, 364 and n. 411. Freeman cites numerous contemporary commentators across the political spectrum who agree that the Court follows public attitudes and changes decisional course when necessary to keep in sync with dominant public opinion (364–65).
24. Keith E. Whittington, *Political Foundations of Judicial Supremacy: The Presidency, the Supreme Court, and Constitutional Leadership in US History* (Princeton: Princeton University Press, 2007), 102–3. Whittington collects authority at 102–3 nn. 70–75.
25. Lee Epstein, "The US Supreme Court," in Whittington, Kelemen, and Caldeira, *The Oxford Handbook of Law and Politics*, 487, 496–97.
26. See Erwin Chemerinsky, "The Vanishing Constitution," 103 *Harvard Law Review* 44 (1989) (discussing the receptivity of the Court to majoritarian politics). Robert Dahl, the Sterling Professor emeritus of political science at Yale University, has insightfully observed that most Americans are unwilling to acknowledge the political nature of the Court nor quite able to deny it and thus simultaneously espouse both positions. Ordinary Americans thus are able to "retain the best of both worlds." Dahl, "Decision-Making in a Democracy," 279.
27. See Dahl, "Decision-Making in a Democracy," 293. Accord Friedman, *The Will of the People*; Whittington, *Political Foundations of Judicial Supremacy*. Most justices, prior to appointment, had been politically involved as loyal party activists. See John MacGregor Burns, *Packing the Court: The Rise of Judicial Power and the Coming Crisis of the Supreme Court* (New York: Penguin, 2009), 3. Accord Curator, United States Supreme Court, "Trivia and Traditions of the Court," in Kermit L. Hall, ed., *The Oxford Companion to the Supreme Court of the United States* (2d ed.) (New York: Oxford University Press, 2005), 1152 (stating that files maintained in the Supreme Court's Curator's Office show that among the 108 justices on the Supreme Court between 1790 and 2005, 91 had previous state or federal political experience).
28. The Court enjoys some discretion to render decisions periodically that run counter to public attitudes or preferences of public officials in specific cases, but this is a limited option that must be exercised with restraint. See Georg Vanberg, "Establishing and Maintaining Judicial Independence," 115. Segal and Spaeth suggest a spectrum, where political forces constrain the Court more in some contexts than in others. Jeffrey A. Segal and Harold J. Spaeth, *The Supreme Court and the Attitudinal Model Revisited* (New York: Cambridge University Press, 2002), 349–50.
29. Whittington, *Political Foundations of Judicial Supremacy*, 9, 12, 28–73. See also Robert Dahl, "The Supreme Court and Judicial Review Performance," in Theodore

L. Becker and Malcolm M. Feeley. eds., *The Impact of Supreme Court Decisions* (2d ed.) (New York: Oxford University Press, 1973), 50 (concluding that overwhelming evidence shows that in confrontations over major policy issues with the executive or legislative branches of the federal government the Court rarely prevails; the Court occasionally wins a skirmish but never an ongoing encounter).
30. Dahl, "The Supreme Court and Judicial Review Performance," 61. Dahl concludes that what is most critical in a struggle over constitutional meaning is whether dominant political actors accept the president's viewpoint (65 n. 147).

    Court-curbing efforts by the political branches designed to "discipline" the Court have sometimes, though not often, been necessary and tend to come in cycles. Perhaps lasting several years (even a decade or more), high frequencies of Court-curbing efforts subside once the Court sounds retreat, hopefully a graceful retreat, either by declining to hear cases presenting provocative issues or by reversing or modifying policy. *Stuart S. Nagel*, "Court-Curbing Periods in American History," in Theodore L. Becker and Malcolm M. Feeley, eds., *The Impact of Supreme Court Decisions* (2d ed.) (New York: Oxford University Presas, 1973), 10–12 (presenting statistical evidence of seven periods of a high frequency of Court-curbing efforts—curbing efforts that account for 87 percent of the total—and the relative success of the efforts in each period). Nagel states that in 1937, twenty-five joint congressional resolutions were proposed and from 1935–1937 thirty-three constitutional amendment proposals introduced, all designed to reduce the power of the Court (10).
31. See discussion at Whittington, *Political Foundations of Judicial Supremacy*, 45.
32. See Edward S. Corwin, *Court over Constitution: A Study of Judicial Review as an Instrument of Popular Government* (Princeton: Princeton University Press, 1938), 7.
33. Myers McDougal, "Law as a Process of Decision: A Policy-Oriented Approach to Legal Study," 1 *National Law Forum* 53, 63 (1956).
34. David M. O'Brien, *Constitutional Law and Politics: Struggles for Power and Government Accountability* (vol. 1) (8th ed.) (New York: W. W. Norton, 2011), 35 (*Constitutional Law and Politics I*)
35. Quoted in Louis Fisher, *Constitutional Dialogues: Interpretation as Political Process* (Princeton, NJ: Princeton University Press, 1988), 3.
36. Louis Fisher and Neal Devins, *Political Dynamics of Constitutional Law* (5th ed.) (St. Paul, MN: West Group, 2011), 1.
37. Ruth Bader Ginsburg, "Speaking in a Judicial Voice," 67 *New York University Law Review* 1185, 1198 (1992).
38. Ronald Kahn wisely cautions that while constitutional meaning closely follows public opinion, judicial actors do not understand their function as simply mimicking majority will. Public opinion rather insinuates itself implicitly into judicial decision-making because the justices apply legal concepts by considering the "lived lives" of those who inhabit the world beyond the courtroom. Kahn, "Social Constructions," 86–89.
39. See, e.g., Lucas A. Powe Jr., *The Warren Court in American Politics* (Cambridge, MA: Belknap Press, 2000), 214–15 (demonstrating that the Warren Court's magisterial civil rights and civil liberties decisions represented the product of

a harmonious partnership with the political branches to effectuate dominant constitutional values widely shared by national elites at that time).
40. Reed v. Reed, 404 US 71 (1971) (invalidating law preferring males to females for selecting administrators of intestate estates).
41. For a discussion of these five cases and a concise legal history of gender discrimination, see Erwin Chemerinsky, *Constitutional Law: Principles and Policies* (4th ed.) (New York: Wolters Kluwer, 2011), 769–75.
42. Bradwell v. Ill., 83 US (16 Wall.) 130, 141 (1873) (Bradley J. concurring).
43. See David A. Strauss, "The Irrelevance of Constitutional Amendments," 114 *Harvard Law Review* 1457, 1476–77 (2001). Justice Ruth Bader Ginsburg has concluded that in practical effect, there is no difference between what the ERA would have provided and Fourteenth Amendment doctrine as it has evolved since the ERA's ratification failure. See discussion at Martha Craig Doughtrey, "Women and the Constitution: Where We Are at the End of the Century," 75 *New York University Law Review* 1, 22 (2000).
44. See discussion in Michel C. Dorf, "Equal Protection Incorporation," 88 *University of Virginia Law Review* 951, 985 (2002); William N. Eskridge Jr., "Channeling: Identity-Based Social Movements and Public Law," 150 *University of Pennsylvania Law Review* 419, 502 (2001). A compelling demonstration of the ERA's role in the evolution of the Court's Equal Protection jurisprudence can be found in Reva Siegel, "Constitutional Culture, Social Movement Conflict and National Change: The Case of the De Facto ERA," 94 *University of California Law Review* 1323, 1334 and n. 30 (2006).
45. Fourteenth Amendment Equal Protection doctrine now provides that the burden of justification for a gender classification rests with the government, which must "demonstrate an exceedingly persuasive justification" for official sex discrimination. This standard of review is one that the government can rarely satisfy.
46. See Mayeri, *Constitutional Choices*, 755, 766, 785–94 (2004) (providing the most detailed account demonstrating that as early as 1962 certain members of the women's movement supported such a dual strategy).
47. See discussion at Mayeri, *Constitutional Choices*, 795, 803–5, 823.
48. Frontiero v. Richardson, 411 US 677 (1973).
49. This meant that from this point forward gender classifications would be treated as virtually *per se* unconstitutional because government would seldom be able to survive "strict judicial scrutiny," that is, the government would be unable to demonstrate a compelling state interest that cannot be accomplished through any less drastic alternative.
50. See *Frontiero*, 411 US at 687–88. As Justice Brennan noted, "Congress itself has concluded that classifications based on sex are inherently invidious [and] this conclusion of a coequal branch of Government is not without significance to the question presently under consideration." *Frontiero*, 411 US at 687–88. In his *Frontiero* decision, Justice Brennan returned to the significance of the political support for the ERA in a memorandum to Justice Powell, arguing that the Court needs to recognize that Congress and the legislatures of a majority of the states have concluded that gender classifications are inherently suspect. See discussion in Mayeri, *Constitutional Choices*, 818.

51. See *Frontiero*, 411 US at 686 and n. 16. See also Friedman, *The Will of the People*, 293 (concluding that the four justices who joined the *Frontiero* opinion may have been responding to the criticism of the Court in the pro-ERA literature).
52. See discussion of this and other internal correspondence among the justices at Mayeri, *Constitutional Choices*, 827.
53. See Serena Mayeri, *"When the Trouble Started": The Story of Frontiero v. Richardson*, in Elizabeth Schneider and Stephanie M. Wildman, eds., *Women and the Law Stories* (New York: Foundation Press, 2011), 57–99.
54. Justice Blackmun joined the Powell concurring opinion, rejecting the advice of his law clerk, a former aide to Senator James O. Eastland of Mississippi, who had urged that Justice Blackmun support finding gender is a suspect classification *as a means of derailing the ERA*—undermining it by providing judicially what the ERA sought to secure for women. See Mayeri, *"When the Trouble Started,"* 57–99. In a memorandum, Justice Blackmun expressed the view that finding sex discrimination a suspect classification was ill-advised as that would have the effect of the Court insinuating itself in the political process of the ERA's ratification. Mayeri, *Constitutional Choices*, n 311.
55. Bob Woodward and Scott Armstrong, *The Brethren: Inside the Supreme Court* (New York: Simon and Schuster, 1979), 255.
56. See, e.g., Robert C. Post, "The Supreme Court, 2002 Term—Foreword: Fashioning the Legal Constitution: Culture, Courts, and Law," 117 *Harvard Law Review* 4, 25–26 (2003) (concluding that the Brennan plurality opinion and subsequent development of Equal Protection jurisprudence are rooted in Congress's acknowledgment of a national shift in how the citizenry understand sex discrimination).
57. See Mayeri, *Constitutional Choices*, 785–87 (discussing a proposal that instead of the ERA, feminists ought to champion a more far-reaching constitutional amendment banning all government-sponsored sex discrimination to include a ban on expenditure of public funds to any person or entity that engages in sex discrimination (as well as discrimination based on race, color, national origin, or ancestry) and guaranteeing woman's right to terminate a pregnancy under medical supervision).
58. See Siegel, *Constitutional Culture*, 1324–25.
59. Siegel, *Constitutional Culture*, 1324–419. Similar arguments are advanced by Jack Balkin, *Constitutional Redemption* (Cambridge: Harvard University Press, 2011).
60. Except where otherwise noted, the following summary is substantiated by the closely reasoned arguments at Siegel, *Constitutional Culture, Social Movement Conflict and National Change* at 1330–31 and the supporting historical evidence at 1370–403.
61. See Suzanne M. Marilley, "The Unintended Consequences of the Nineteenth Amendment: Why So Few?," in Kyvig, ed., *Unintended Consequences of Constitutional Amendment*, 211–12.
62. See Balkin, *Constitutional Redemption*, 104, 119, 235 (arguing that constitutional meaning is contested through argument over the Constitution's enduring principles and values and how best to redeem them). Accord Siegel, *Constitutional Culture*, 1357.
63. Siegel, *Constitutional Culture*, 1331. See Friedman, *The Will of the People*, 294

(concluding that ERA opponents conceded the importance of women's equality as a necessary strategy for winning over moderates to their stop ERA campaign).
64. Siegel, *Constitutional Culture*, 1331.
65. In previous work, Reva Siegel demonstrated how social movement conflict also shaped contemporary understandings of the contours of race discrimination. See Reva B. Siegel, "Equality Talk: Antisubordination and Anticlassification Values in Constitutional Struggles over Brown," 117 *Harvard Law Review* 1470 (2004).
66. Siegel, *Constitutional Culture*, 1335.
67. See Siegel, *Constitutional Culture*, 1341–42. Siegel collects authority at n. 54.
68. Douglas NeJaime, "Constitutional Change, Courts, and Social Movements," 111 *University of Michigan Law Review* 877, 881 (2013).
69. See, e.g., Balkin, *Constitutional Redemption*. For a concise summary of Balkin's views, see discussion at NeJaime, "Constitutional Change, Courts, and Social Movements," 877.
70. Balkin, *Constitutional Redemption*, 180, 182.
71. Balkin, *Constitutional Redemption*, 13 (emphasis in the original).
72. Balkin, *Constitutional Redemption*, 11, 70, 98.
73. Balkin, *Constitutional Redemption*, 70, 100, 246.
74. See Siegel, *Constitutional Culture*, 1339.
75. See, e.g., Barry Cushman, *Rethinking the New Deal Court: The Structure of a Constitutional Revolution* (New York: Oxford University Press, 1998) (arguing that the Court's switch in 1937 ending its resistance to New Deal reforms is best understood as the Court's internally driven abandonment of laissez-faire constitutionalism).
76. See, e.g., Bruce Ackerman, *We the People, Vol. 2: Transformations* (Cambridge, MA: Belknap Press, 1998), 332–42; David M. Kennedy, *Freedom From Fear: The American People in Depression and War, 1929–1945* (New York: Oxford University Press, 1999), 335. For a debate over whether the 1937 switch was one animated by principle or by political considerations, compare Michael Ariens, "A Thrice-Told Tale, or Felix the Cat," 107 *Harvard Law Review* 620 (1994) with Richard D. Friedman, "A Reaffirmation: The Authenticity of the Roberts Memorandum, or Felix the non-Forger," 142 *University of Pennsylvania Law Review* 1985 (1994).
77. See, e.g., Cushman, *Rethinking the New Deal Court*, 1063 (stating that historians who advance externalist accounts of the "switch in time" focus on the court responding to Roosevelt's court-packing plan and shifts in public opinion).
78. See, e.g., Jeff Shesol, *Supreme Power: Franklin Roosevelt vs. The Supreme Court* (New York: W. W. Norton, 2010); Ackerman, *We the People, Vol. 2: Transformations*, 279–312; Cushman, *Rethinking the New Deal Court*; William E. Leuchtenburg, *The Supreme Court Reborn: The Constitutional Revolution in the Age of Roosevelt* (New York: Oxford University Press, 1995); Friedman, *A Reaffirmation*; William E. Leuchtenburg, "The Origins of Franklin D. Roosevelt's 'Court Packing' Plan," 1966 *Supreme Court Review*, 347–400.
79. For a summary of the Court's invalidation of New Deal legislation during the 1934 and the 1935 Court terms, see Ackerman, *We the People, Vol. 2: Transformations*, 293–307.
80. Most non-specialists in constitutional law, as well as many specialists, are unaware

that Congress has been packing and unpacking the Court throughout our history as a means of political manipulation. See Charles Warren, *The Supreme Court in United States History*, Vol. II (Boston: Little, Brown, 1922), 39, 380, 422–23, 446–47. The last change was in 1869 when the number of justices comprising the Court stabilized at the current total of nine justices. See John MacGregor Burns, *Packing the Court: The Rise of Judicial Power and the Coming Crisis of the Supreme Court* (New York: Penguin, 2009) (assembling the Court-packing history).

81. For a concise summary of this conventional understanding of the switch-in-time story see Cushman, *Rethinking the New Deal Court*, 3 (rejecting the conventional story and referring to it as a "morality play" that has endured over time).
82. Some amendment proposals would have expanded federal regulatory authority. Some provided for mandatory retirement or other mechanisms to neutralize the voting impact of older justices. Others provided Congress a mechanism to override Supreme Court decisions that invalidate federal legislation. See, e.g., Ackerman, *We the People, Vol. 2: Transformations*, 279–312; David E. Kyvig, "The Road Not Taken: FDR, the Supreme Court, and Constitutional Amendment," 104 *Political Science Quarterly* 463, 463–81 (1989).
83. Schechter Poultry Corp. v. United States, 295 US 495 (1935).
84. Ackerman, *We the People, Vol. 2: Transformations*, 298.
85. See discussion at Shesol, *Supreme Power*, 3, 134–153.
86. Shesol, *Supreme Power*, 145. Shesol explains that one concern was that the process of ratifying a constitutional amendment would take too long. But, more importantly, Southern congressional leaders were concerned that a constitutional amendment expanding the scope of the Commerce Power, for example, would strengthen the federal government and concomitantly weaken state sovereignty (145).
87. Quoted at Shesol, *Supreme Power*, 150–51. See also Lyle Denniston, "*Schechter Poultry Corp. v. United States* and *United States v. Butler*," in Melvin I. Urofsky, ed., *The Public Debate over Controversial Supreme Court Decisions* (Thousand Oaks, CA.: CQ Press, 2006), 137.
88. Shesol, *Supreme Power*, 251.
89. See discussion in Ackerman, *We the People, Vol. 2: Transformations*, 298–300.
90. See discussion at Shesol, *Supreme Power*, 97, 121, 151–52.
91. For a discussion of Roosevelt's several trial balloons and the conservative response, see Shesol, *Supreme Power*, 155–64.
92. United States v. Butler, 297 US 1 (1936).
93. Carter v. Carter Coal Co., 298 US 238 (1936).
94. See Denniston, "*Schechter Poultry v. US* and *US v. Butler*," 135, 140–41.
95. Morehead v. Tipaldo, 298 US 587 (1936).
96. Denniston, "*Schechter Poultry v. US* and *US v. Butler*," 142.
97. See Shesol, *Supreme Power*, 222.
98. Shesol, *Supreme Power*, 185–88, 195–96.
99. Shesol, *Supreme Power*, 196.
100. See Ackerman, *We the People, Vol. 2: Transformations*, 313; Shesol, *Supreme Power*, 239.
101. Kyvig, "The Road Not Taken," 470–78 (explaining that the constitutional amendment solutions considered but rejected by FDR included a requirement of

a two-thirds vote rather than a simple majority of justices to reverse congressional legislation, provide Congress authority to enact legislation for the general welfare where states individually could not effectively do so, empower Congress to vote to override a judicial determination that congressional legislation is unconstitutional, and provide for mandatory retirement of justices at age seventy).

102. The president's own vice-president, Nance Garner, held his nose and brandished a thumbs-down in the Senate corridor when the Court-packing bill was introduced in Congress. Garner soon left town for a previously unscheduled extended Texas vacation, depriving FDR of crucial leadership in Congress in support of his Court-packing plan. See Friedman, *The Will of the People*, 223. For a comprehensive summary of the scope of the opposition to FDR's Court-packing proposal, see Cushman, *Rethinking the New Deal Court*, 13–15.
103. See discussion at Kennedy, *Freedom from Fear*, 331.
104. The *New York Times* announced Robinson's support of an amendment in a front-page story. After examining all of the options, Robinson concluded that the constitutional amendment option held the greatest promise for reining in the Court. See Ackerman, *We the People, Vol. 2: Transformations*, 316 (also reporting that Bankhead stated his hope to avoid an amendment but, absent a change in direction by the Court, that he saw no alternative to one).
105. Shesol, *Supreme Power*, 270. Accord Friedman, *The Will of the People*, 224 (concluding that at this time there was substantial support in Congress for constitutional amendments that either clarified Congress's constitutional powers or limited the constitutional authority of the Court).
106. Steve Neal, *Happy Days Are Here Again*, 177–79, 302.
107. Wheeler's opposition to Court-packing may not have been entirely based on principle. In 1932, Wheeler "desperately" wanted to be chosen by Roosevelt as Roosevelt's vice-presidential running mate. Roosevelt's choice of John Nance Garner as his 1932 running mate reportedly soured Wheeler on Roosevelt, and Roosevelt insiders concluded that Wheeler never thereafter wholeheartedly supported Roosevelt even though he supported most New Deal measures and campaigned for Roosevelt in 1936. Neal, *Happy Days Are Here Again*, 177, 302, 322. See also Lynne Olson, *Those Angry Days: Roosevelt, Lindbergh and America's Fight over World War II, 1939–1941* (New York: Random House, 2013), 65, 185, 276 (noting Wheeler's presidential ambitions and arguing that Wheeler developed an intense dislike of the president based on his view that Roosevelt's appetite for power was insatiable).
108. Neal, *Happy Days Are Here Again*, 320–32 (expressing the view that without Wheeler's opposition Roosevelt would have achieved enactment of the Court-packing legislation).
109. West Coast Hotel v. Parrish, 300 US 379 (1937).
110. Morehead v. Tipaldo, 298 US 587 (1936). In *Parrish*, the Court also reversed *Adkins v. Children's Hospital*, 261 US 525 (1923), a case finding unconstitutional a federal law providing minimum wage for women in the District of Columbia.
111. Quoted in Kennedy, *Freedom from Fear*, 335. The other three cases decided the same day as *Parrish* was announced also upheld reform legislation by reversing precedent. See John MacGregor Burns, *Packing the Court*, 149.
112. Burns, *Packing the Court*, 149.

113. See discussion at Ackerman, *We the People, Vol. 2: Transformations*, 343 (concluding that the Court's motivation for unequivocally accepting the constitutional legitimacy of the New Deal legislation was to remove the threat posed by a proposed institutionally perilous constitutional amendment).
114. NLRB v. Jones and Laughlin Corporation, 301 US 1 (1937).
115. The overwhelming scholarly view is that external forces operated on the Court to influence its change of direction. See Cushman, *Rethinking the New Deal Court*, 4, 8 (surveying the literature and concluding that immediately in the wake of the Court's switch, and through the postwar period, the accounts have given the constitutional revolution an externalist interpretation).
116. See, e.g., Rayman L. Solomon, "Black Monday," in Hall, ed., *The Oxford Companion to the Supreme Court of the United States*, 88. Accord William M. Beaney and Edward N. Beiser, *Presidential Reactions to the Supreme Court: Altering Personnel and Power* in Theodore L. Becker and Malcolm M. Feeley, eds., *The Impact of Supreme Court Decisions* (2d ed.) (New York: Oxford University Press, 1973), 38 (concluding that the controversy over passage of the Court-packing legislation is widely understood as influencing the views of at least two justices); Leuchtenburg, *The Supreme Court Reborn*, 132–62 (same).
117. See Gregory A. Caldeira, "Public Opinion and the US Supreme Court: FDR's Court-Packing Plan," 81 *American Political Science Review* 1139, 1147 (figure 3) (1987), cited in Ackerman, *We the People, Vol. 2: Transformations*, 333. See also Shesol, *Supreme Power*, 372 (reporting that on March 1, approximately one month prior to the *Parrish* decision, Gallup poll data showed that 48 percent of those polled opposed Court-packing and 41 percent supported it).
118. Professor Bruce Ackerman has argued that if the Court had continued its resistance, Court-packing would have been the most practical solution to the problem. Ackerman, *We the People, Vol. 2: Transformations*, 335. Ackerman points out that by June 1937, after the Court's switch, Roosevelt had accepted a compromise Court-packing plan providing for a new appointment when a non-retiring justice turns seventy-five, rather than seventy, and no more than one such appointment per year. When the compromise reached the Senate floor for a vote, the majority leader, Joseph Robinson, was confident that it would pass and Capitol Hill correspondents had concluded that Robinson had enough votes to secure passage of the compromise measure. When Robinson died suddenly of a heart attack, after just a few days of debate on the compromise, all hope of passage of the compromise expired (335–36).
119. See Edward G. White, *The Constitution and the New Deal* (Cambridge, MA: Harvard University Press, 2000), 305.
120. Cushman, *Rethinking the New Deal Court*, 18–20. The December vote was 4-4. Justice Stone was absent from the conference due to poor health but Chief Justice Hughes was certain that Stone would vote with the liberals to uphold the statute. Stone finally returned to the Court and cast his vote with the liberals in early February and the *Parrish* decision was announced at the end of February. Cushman, *Rethinking the New Deal Court*, 18–20.
121. James MacGregor Burns plausibly has argued that in the spring of 1937, the Court-packing bill, as initially proposed by Roosevelt, had no realistic chance of being enacted. The bill did not command a majority in the Senate. And in

the House, the House Committee on the Judiciary opposed the Court-packing bill and it was unlikely to overcome either the "unyielding" resistance of Hatton Sumners, the powerful chair of the House Judiciary Committee, or the House Rules Committee, which could delay legislation for weeks. See James MacGregor Burns, *Roosevelt: The Lion and the Fox* (New York: Harcourt, Brace, and World, 1956), 314.

122. Cushman, for example, dismisses the impact of the Court-packing plan on the 1937 constitutional revolution, arguing that the justices could reasonably conclude that the Court-packing plan lacked sufficient public and congressional support to threaten the Court institutionally. Cushman, *Rethinking the New Deal Court*, 23.

123. See Burns, *Packing the Court*, 148–49; Charles A. Leonard, *A Search for the Judicial Philosophy: Mr. Justice Roberts and the Constitutional Revolution of 1937* (Ann Arbor, MI: Kennikat Press, 1971).

124. See Donald Bruce Johnson and Kirk Harold Porter, *National Party Platforms, 1840–1972* (Urbana: University of Illinois Press, 1973), 362.

125. See discussion at Kyvig, "The Road Not Taken," 475–76 (stating that many party activists had concluded that now Roosevelt too would support an amendment effort).

126. Later in life, Justice Roberts claimed that he never switched and that his *Tipaldo* and *Parrish* votes were consistent. Roberts claimed that he had come to the view that *Adkins v. Children's Hospital*, 261 US 525 (1923) should be reversed. When the issue of reversing *Adkins* was before the Court in *Parrish*, he voted to reverse *Adkins*. But Roberts stated that he did not vote to reverse *Adkins* in *Tipaldo* because counsel in *Tipaldo* never sought a reversal of *Adkins*. See discussion at Shesol, *Supreme Power*, 414; Felix Frankfurter, "Mr. Justice Roberts," 104 *University of Pennsylvania Law Review* 311, 314–15 (1955). Robert's self-serving defense against the accusation of a political vote in *Parrish* has been both challenged and defended. Compare Ariens, "A Thrice-Told Tale, or Felix the Cat" (challenging Robert's rendition) with Friedman, "A Reaffirmation" (defending Roberts's claim). See also Ackerman, *We the People, Vol. 2: Transformations*, 363–64 (stating that Roberts did change his position in *Parrish* but acknowledging that his motivation for doing so has become the subject of endless disagreement).

127. See Shesol, *Supreme Power*, 415, 521 (agreeing that avoiding institutional harm to the Court as a result of the various Court-curbing proposals pending before the Congress greatly concerned Hughes and Roberts and influenced their decision to align the Court doctrinally with the New Deal vision of activist government).

128. On March 9, 1937, about three weeks before announcement of the Court's decision in the *Jones and Laughlin* case, Roosevelt gave a nationally broadcasted "fireside chat" in which he acknowledged his awareness that the idea of a constitutional amendment had gained momentum. A recent Gallup poll had shown a thirteen-point jump since December, to 58 percent, in public support for a constitutional amendment solution to the crisis of judicial nullification of federal New Deal legislation. By then Roosevelt was committed to Court-packing and distrusted the efficacy of the constitutional amendment process, as he told his listeners during the fireside chat. Shesol, *Supreme Power*, 381–82.

129. David Garrow, "Mental Decrepitude on the US Supreme Court: The Historical Case for a 28th Amendment," 67 *University of Chicago Law Review* 995, 1023

(2000) (pointing out that it is inexplicable that the leading accounts of the Court-packing confrontation have ignored the role of proposed constitutional amendments). A notable exception is the work of Bruce Ackerman. See Ackerman, *We the People, Vol. 2: Transformations*, 323, 325, 332 (inviting consideration of the Wheeler-Bone amendment proposal as a change agent during the constitutional crisis of 1937).
130. Accord Ackerman, *We the People, Vol. 2: Transformations*, 337.
131. Garrow, "Mental Decrepitude on the US Supreme Court," 1024 (discussing an amendment fixing the tenure of the justices by requiring them to retire at a specified age).
132. Garrow, "Mental Decrepitude on the US Supreme Court," 1025.
133. Marbury v. Madison, 5 US (1 Cranch) 137 (1803).
134. Cooper v. Aaron, 358 US 1, 18 (1958).
135. See Rafael Gely and Pablo Spiller, "The Political Economy of Supreme Court Constitutional Decisions: The Case of Roosevelt's Court Packing Plan," 12 *International Review of Law and Economics* 45, 47 (1992).
136. See discussion at Ackerman, *We the People, Vol. 2: Transformations*, 341.
137. See Gely and Spiller, *The Political Economy of Supreme Court Constitutional Decisions*, 45, 63 (Table 5), cited at Ackerman, *We the People, Vol. 2: Transformations*, 341 and n. 77.
138. See Shesol, *Supreme Power*, 520 (quoting Stanley High, a Roosevelt aide).
139. Owen J. Roberts, *The Court and the Constitution: The Oliver Wendell Holmes Lectures* (Cambridge: Harvard University Press, 1951), 61; Shesol, *Supreme Power*, 522.
140. Ackerman, *We the People, Vol. 2: Transformations*, 325. Ackerman reports that even former President Herbert Hoover gave a radio address committing support for the constitutional amendment proposals being advanced by eminent Republican senators (325).
141. See William G. Ross, "The Resilience of *Marbury v. Madison*," 772 (concluding that whether any justice deliberately revised his vote during the 1937 constitutional crisis continues as one of constitutional history's most disputed issues).
142. For an argument that the Court switched in response to a consensus that, following the New Deal economic crisis, it no longer seemed satisfactory that government should be precluded from adopting policies aimed at promoting economic development, see Tushnet, *The New Deal Constitutional Revolution*, 1064–65. See also Planned Parenthood of Southeastern Pennsylvania v. Casey, 505 US 833, 861–62 (1992) (stating that to most people by 1937 the unmistakable lesson was "that the interpretation of contractual freedom of contract . . . rested on fundamentally false factual assumptions about the capacity of a relatively unregulated market to satisfy minimal levels of human welfare").
143. Roe v. Wade, 410 US 113 (1973). See Chemerinsky, *Constitutional Law: Principles and Policies*, 839 (concluding that the Court's abortion decisions are among the Court's most controversial); Lucas A. Powe, *The Supreme Court and the American Elite*, 277 (describing *Roe v. Wade* as the twentieth century's "most controversial" Supreme Court ruling).
144. Roe v. Wade, 410 US at 153 (concluding that the "right of privacy . . . is broad

enough to encompass a woman's decision whether or not to terminate her pregnancy").
145. See Richard H. Pildes, "Is the Supreme Court a 'Majoritarian' Institution?," 2010 *Supreme Court Review* 103, 151 (2010).
146. Planned Parenthood of Southeastern Pennsylvania v. Casey, 505 US 833 (1992).
147. Robert Post and Reva Siegel, "Roe Rage: Democratic Constitutionalism and Backlash," 42 *Harvard Civil Rights-Civil Liberties Law Review* 373 (2007).
148. Lee Epstein and Joseph F. Kobylka, *The Supreme Court and Legal Change: Abortion and the Death Penalty* (Chapel Hill: University of North Carolina Press, 1992), 207.
149. Epstein and Kobylka, *The Supreme Court and Legal Change*, 207.
150. Friedman, *The Will of the People*, 305.
151. Epstein and F. Kobylka, *The Supreme Court and Legal Change*, 207 (quoting a *New Republic* article written twelve years after *Roe*).
152. Jack Balkin has argued that the pro-life movement's contestation and political agitation kept their point of view before the public as a "reasonable" point of view that deserved respect, or at least acknowledgment, by fair-minded people. Balkin, *Constitutional Redemption*, 69. Give and take among contesting parties during the New Deal also had a moderating influence. See Ackerman, *We the People, Vol. 2: Transformations*, 385.
153. See Ross, "The Resilience of *Marbury v. Madison*," 747. One explanation for why amendment proposals have remained such an attractive means for reversing judicial decisions is that an amendment proposal is a dramatic gesture attracting public attention, an amendment focuses attention directly on the issues, and amending the Constitution is merely an expression of the popular will that connotes no disrespect to the Court. See William Lasser, *The Limits of Judicial Power: The Supreme Court in American Politics* (Chapel Hill: University of North Carolina Press, 1988), 236.
154. Powe, *The Supreme Court and the American Elite*, 300 (listing state legislation requiring spousal notification and consent, requiring parental notification and consent for minors, denying public funding, and denying use of public facilities as methods used to undermine *Roe*).
155. See, e.g., Rosenberg, *The Hollow Hope*, 176–77 (summarizing post-*Roe* abortion legislation representing defiance to *Roe* in the form of legislative provisions openly hostile to *Roe*'s core holding); Pildes, *Is the Supreme Court a Majoritarian Institution?*, 151–52 (stating that thirty-two states enacted new abortion restrictions within ten months after *Roe*, much of it designed to thwart women's ability to choose to end a pregnancy by making it difficult for a woman to obtain an abortion and otherwise cabin *Roe*). Whittington argues that much of this early state legislative response to *Roe* were merely symbolic—merely politicians gaining the advantage of position-taking opportunities—since so much of this legislation was plainly unconstitutional after *Roe* and state elected officials could depend on the courts to invalidate it. Whittington, *Political Foundations of Judicial Supremacy*, 137.
156. Epstein and Kobylka, *The Supreme Court and Legal Change*, 205. Resistance by public hospitals to providing abortions became so widespread that between 1973

194 Notes to Pages 61–62

and 1985 80 percent or more of all public hospitals did not provide abortions. Overall most hospitals (private or public) never performed abortions. See Rosenberg, *The Hollow Hope*, 190 and Table 6–2.

157. Rosenberg, *The Hollow Hope*, 183–85. Initially expressing anti-abortion views, Nixon backed off the issue in an effort to present a neutral image during the 1972 presidential election. Epstein and Kobylka, *The Supreme Court and Legal Change*, 187. The abortion issue polarized Democrats, and the Carter administration faced a "frayed party coalition." Carter, therefore, tried to de-politicize the abortion issue, arguing that the president was powerless to take action as he was duty bound to defer to the Court. Whittington, *Political Foundations of Judicial Supremacy*, 66.

158. Maher v. Roe, 432 US 464 (1977).

159. Harris v. McCrea, 448 US 297 (1980). For a summary of anti-choice legislators' use of funding restrictions as a strategy to limit the availability of abortion services, see Cynthia Soohoo, "Hyde-Care For All: The Expansion of Abortion-Funding Restrictions under Health Care Reform," 15 *CUNY Law Review* 391, 401–9 (2012).

160. Edward Keynes with Randall K. Miller, *The Court vs. Congress: Prayer, Busing, and Abortion* (Durham, NC: Duke University Press, 1989), 285–87 (discussing the divisions and competing objectives and interests within the pro-life movement).

161. Epstein and Kobylka, *The Supreme Court and Legal Change*, 209–11 (explaining the consensus within the pro-life movement that their focus of attention ought to be a constitutional amendment strategy and describing the bitter fights over wording of such an amendment).

162. Epstein and Kobylka, *The Supreme Court and Legal Change*, 210, n. 8 (detailing three approaches to amending the Constitution to quash *Roe*). Gerald Rosenberg reports "in toto" sixty-eight anti-*Roe* constitutional amendments as reported by one source, and forty-eight from another source. See Rosenberg, *The Hollow Hope*, 185 and n. 15. Altogether, during the first three decades following *Roe*, members of Congress introduced 331 proposed constitutional amendments designed *in various ways* to counter *Roe*. See National Committee for a Human Life Amendment, "Human Life Amendments: 1973–2003," accessed August 16, 2016, *www.nchla.org/datasource/idocuments/HLAlst7303.pdf*.

163. Epstein and Kobylka, *The Supreme Court and Legal Change*, 210, n. 8 (pointing out that one amendment proposal reached the floor of the Senate in 1975 but lacked adequate support). Over fifty amendment proposals were introduced in the Ninety-Fourth Congress (1975–1977). None came to a vote. Rosenberg, *The Hollow Hope*, 186.

164. Epstein and Kobylka, *The Supreme Court and Legal Change*, 210, n. 9.

165. The New Right had ascended to power by the 1980 election. The Republican Party's platform opposed the ERA and supported a constitutional amendment permitting a ban on abortions. See Friedman, *The Will of the People*, 305.

166. Kyvig, *Explicit and Authentic Acts*, 447.

167. Whittington, *Political Foundations of Judicial Supremacy*, 67.

168. Laurence H. Tribe, *Abortion: The Clash of Absolutes* (revised edition) (New York: W. W. Norton, 1992), 150–59.

169. See National Committee for a Human Life Amendment, "Human Life Amend-

ment Highlights: United States Congress (1973–2003)," accessed August 16, 2016, *www.nchla.org/datasource/idocuments/HLAhghlts.pdf.*

170. See On the Issues, "Republican Party on Abortion: Party Platform," *www.ontheissues.org/celeb/Republican_Party_Abortion.htm.*

171. Gerald Rosenberg states that by the end of the Ninety-Fourth Congress (1975–1977) it became clear to most sophisticated members of Congress that the constitutional amendment strategy lacked efficacy. Rosenberg, *The Hollow Hope*, 186.

172. Epstein and Kobylka, *The Supreme Court and Legal Change*, 210, n. 9; Kyvig, *Explicit and Authentic Acts*, 450–51.

173. Overall, between 1973 and 1982, Congress enacted thirty statutes restricting access to abortion in different ways. Rosenberg, *The Hollow Hope*, 186, n. 17 (reporting conclusions from the Congressional Research Service).

174. See Charles Epp, *Law as an Instrument of Social Reform*, 608. See also Epstein and Kobylka, *The Supreme Court and Legal Change*, 53 (explaining that those who led the campaign opposing the death penalty understood the need to take stock of the political environment, maintain momentum, and advance an aspirational reform agenda centered on "threat of crisis" that provides an immediate political impact).

175. Deploying an agenda built around constitutional rights as a means of mobilization is a well-worn strategy that has been used in other mobilization efforts. See, e.g., Carol Nackenoff, "Constitutionalizing Terms of Inclusion: Friends of the Indian and Citizenship for Native Americans, 1880–1930s," in Ronald Kahn and Ken I. Kersch, eds., *The Supreme Court and American Political Development* (Lawrence: University Press of Kansas, 2006), 397 (strategy used by Native American activists in the 1920s).

176. See discussion at Gelb and Palley, "Women and Interest Group Politics," 379. It is well-established that members of Congress tend to vote the wishes of well-organized and committed groups such as the organized opposition to *Roe*—single-issue groups composed of constituents who are aware of specific issues and strongly desire certain outcomes. See R. Douglas Arnold, *The Logic of Congressional Action* (New Haven, CT: Yale University Press, 1990), 66–83; John Kingdon, *Congressmen's Voting Decisions* (New York: Harper and Row, 1973), 41 (demonstrating the tendency of members of Congress to vote with constituents who are perceived as intense and having high salience).

177. Powe, *The Supreme Court and the American Elite*, 300. Ten years after *Roe* was decided, the Court majority in *City of Akron v. Akron Center for Reproductive Health, Inc.* considered it necessary to acknowledge the success of the *Roe* opposition in politicizing the abortion issue and thus felt that it must attempt to distance itself from the view that *Roe* was merely a political decision subject to a politically driven reevaluation. See City of Akron v. Akron Center for Reproductive Health, Inc., 462 US 416, 420 and n. 1 (1983).

178. See Whittington, *Political Foundations of Judicial Supremacy*, 67 (explaining that once the Republicans became committed to the reversal of *Roe*, there existed many options for politicizing the abortion issue, among them support for constitutional amendments).

179. Epstein and Kobylka, *The Supreme Court and Legal Change*, 210, n. 9. Suzanne

Marilley has explained that sustaining pressure in behalf of a cause is important for a movement's growth because it helps sustain belief that improvement is possible. Suzanne M. Marilley, *The Unintended Consequences of the Nineteenth Amendment*, 226.

180. Thomas M. Keck, "From Bakke to Grutter: The Rise of Rights-Based Conservatism," in Ronald Kahn and Ken I. Kersch, eds., *The Supreme Court and American Political Development* (Lawrence: University Press of Kansas, 2006), 414. Accord Keith E. Whittington, *Constitutional Construction: Divided Powers and Constitutional Meaning* (Cambridge: Harvard University Press, 1999), 226 (concluding that historically, citizen debate over competing visions of constitutional meaning has strongly influenced development of the Constitution's construction).

181. See Whittington, *Political Foundations of Judicial Supremacy*, 65 n. 147.

182. For example, Ellen McCormick ran for president in 1976 on a right-to-life platform. The Human Life constitutional amendment effort, in conjunction with the anti-ERA effort, attracted sophisticated, educated women whose activism was motivated by traditional social and religious values. Gelb and Palley, "Women and Interest Group Politics," 377–78.

183. It is clear that by the second Reagan term, the pro-life movement had shifted from a constitutional amendment–centric strategy when that strategy proved inefficacious and better options presented themselves through the elite support of President Reagan and a supportive Congress. The pro-life movement nevertheless benefitted from the experience of unsuccessfully advancing constitutional amendments to reverse *Roe*. This failure was essential for *Roe*'s opponents to accept that there was no national consensus in opposition to *Roe* and, therefore, the movement would need to concentrate its efforts on more efficacious options such as a strategy to restrict abortion through legislation. See Ross, "The Resilience of *Marbury v. Madison*," 750–51.

184. See Julie Novkov, "Law and Political Ideologies," in Whittington, Kelemen, and Caldeira, eds., *The Oxford Handbook of Law and Politics*, 638 (explaining how transformations in constitutional law developed from framing legal issues around a coherent ideological framework that changes the public discourse, and how development of a coherent conservative constitutional vision at the Court's explains the success of conservative judicial activism).

185. For an argument that group conflict centered on a coherent legal claim can create a dialectic that expands the "scope, intensity, and visibility" of a particular controversy so that it comes to command the public attention and in turn elevates controversy to priority on the governmental agenda, see Epstein and Kobylka, *The Supreme Court and Legal Change*, 29.

186. See Novkov, "Law and Political Ideologies," 640 (arguing that it is not ideology that directly drives judicial outcomes; ideology plays a more nuanced role by providing decision makers a political stake in the outcomes).

187. See, e.g., Friedman, *The Will of the People*, 315–20 (detailing the Bork appointment fight and the role of abortion contestation in that dispute); Epstein and Kobylka, *The Supreme Court and Legal Change*, 261–65 (same).

188. See discussion of the varied roots of the *Roe* backlash at Post and Siegel, *Roe Rage*, 409–22.

189. Planned Parenthood of Southeastern Pennsylvania v. Casey, 505 US 833, 866 (1992) (emphasis added).
190. In *Lawrence v Texas*, 539 US 558, 590 (2003), Justice Kennedy explicitly acknowledged the importance of the "emerging awareness" among citizens of the meaning of liberty when stating that there is "an *emerging awareness* that liberty gives substantial protection to adult persons in deciding how to conduct their private lives in matters pertaining to sex" (emphases added).
191. Kahn, "Social Constructions," 85.
192. Friedman, *The Will of the People*, 354, 382.
193. Engel v. Vitale, 370 US 421, 436 (1962). The text of the prayer was: "Almighty God, we acknowledge our dependence upon Thee, and we beg Thy blessings upon us, our parents, our teachers, and our Country." Quoted in Phillip Kurland, "The Regents' Prayer Case: Full of Sound and Fury, Signifying. . . . ," 1962 *Supreme Court Review* 1, 4.
194. Keynes, *The Court vs. Congress*, 174, 191.
195. See Philip Kurland, Forward, "Equal in Origin and Equal in Title to the Legislative and Executive Branches of the United States Government," 78 *Harvard Law Review* 143, 176 (1964) (referring to proponents of school prayer as "religious zealots").
196. Bruce J. Dierenfield, "*Engel v. Vitale*," in Urofsky, ed., *The Public Debate over Controversial Supreme Court Decisions*, 215 (estimating that by the mid-twentieth century, roughly half of the 35,000 American public school districts continued to sanction various types of religious exercises in public schools, including King James Bible reading and oral recitation of prayer).
197. Noah Feldman, "Non-Sectarianism Reconsidered," 18 *Journal of Law and Politics* 65, 112–14 (2002).
198. See generally Powe, *The Warren Court and American Politics*, 186.
199. Engel v. Vitale, 370 US 421 (1062).
200. The Court was down by two when the case issued: Justice Frankfurter had suffered a stroke soon following oral argument in *Engel* and Justice White had been nominated but not yet confirmed to fill the seat of retired Justice Whittaker. See Susan D. Gold, *Engle v. Vitale: Prayer in the Schools* (Supreme Court Milestones Series) (Tarrytown, NY: Marshall Cavendish, 2006), 81.
201. See Dierenfield, "*Engel v. Vitale*," 220; Powe, "Are 'the People' Missing in Action," 875 (concluding that the quantity of mail was exceeded only by the amount the Court received following its decision in *Roe v. Wade*).
202. William M. Beaney and Edward N. Beiser, "Prayer and Politics: The Impact of *Engel* and *Schempp* on the Political Process," in Theodore L. Becker and Malcolm M. Feeley, eds., *The Impact of Supreme Court Decisions: Empirical Studies* (2d ed.) (New York: Oxford University Press, 1973), 23–24, 28.
203. Beaney and Beiser, "Prayer and Politics," 24–25.
204. *New York Herald Tribune*, July 5, 1962, quoted in Kurland, "The Regents' Prayer," n. 4.
205. *Wall Street Journal*, June 27, 1962, quoted in Powe, *The Warren Court and American Politics*, 187–88.
206. *Washington Evening Star*, June 18, 1963, quoted in Terry Eastland, ed., *Religious*

Liberty in the Supreme Court (Washington, DC: Ethics and Public Policy Center, 1993), 166.

207. See Corinna Barrrett Lain, "God, Civic Virtue, and the American Way: Reconstructing *Engel*," 67 *Stanford Law Review* 479, 502–14, 523–25 (2015).
208. Two justices wrote minority opinions—Justices Stewart and Douglas. Dissenting, Justice Stewart wrote of the many practices in American culture that recognize religion and God, inferring that this part of our culture might now be at risk. Concurring, Justice Douglas argued for a ban on any commingling of religion and government. The Douglas opinion received wide media coverage, almost as if it were the majority opinion, thus feeding the public hysteria over *Engel*. See discussion at Lain, "God, Civic Virtue, and the American Way," 500–506.
209. See Lain, "God, Civic Virtue, and the American Way," 498–525.
210. Lain, "God, Civic Virtue, and the American Way," 550. The following discussion of Article V's instrumental role in facilitating democratic deliberation following *Engel* has benefitted greatly from the excellent scholarship found in Lain, "God, Civic Virtue, and the American Way."
211. Dierenfield, "*Engel v. Vitale*," 217.
212. Kurland, "The Regents' Prayer Case," 3; Alexander Burnham, "Court's Decision Stirs Conflicts," *New York Times*, June 27, 1962.
213. Keynes, *The Court vs. Congress*, 192–93 (reporting fifty-six amendment proposals); Dierenfield, "*Engel v. Vitale*," 217 (discussing the impeach Earl Warren effort).
214. School District of Abington Township v. Schempp, 374 US 203 (1963).
215. Parents could request that their children be excused in both cases.
216. Powe, *The Warren Court and American Politics*, 378.
217. See Lain, "God, Civic Virtue, and the American Way," 520–21.
218. Lain, "God, Civic Virtue, and the American Way," 550.
219. Lain, "God, Civic Virtue, and the American Way," 533.
220. Powe, *The Warren Court and American Politics*, 360–61.
221. See Lain, "God, Civic Virtue, and the American Way," 533–34.
222. Keynes, *The Court vs. Congress*, 193.
223. See Beaney and Beiser, "Prayer and Politics," 24–26.
224. Beaney and Beiser, "Prayer and Politics," 34.
225. See Lain, "God, Civic Virtue, and the American Way," 523 and n. 275.
226. See Joseph A. Fisher, "The Becker Amendment: A Constitutional Trojan Horse," 11 *Journal of Church and State* 427, 439 (1969).
227. Fisher, "The Becker Amendment," 528.
228. The legal department of the National Catholic Welfare Conference circulated an advisory to all dioceses cautioning Roman Catholics to be wary about supporting any of the proposed school prayer and Bible reading constitutional amendments, warning against the risks of "tampering" with First Amendment freedoms. See "Catholics Urged to be Wary of Backing School Prayers," *New York Times*, June 23, 1964, accessed December 19, 2016, *www.nytimes.com/1964/06/23/catholics-urged-to-be-wary-of-backing-school-prayers.html*.
229. Lain, "God, Civic Virtue, and the American Way," 525.
230. Quoted at Robert Sikorski, *Prayer in Public Schools and the Constitution, 1961–1992: Government-Sponsored Religious Activities in Public Schools and the*

Constitution (Controversies in Constitutional Law) (New York: Routledge, 1993), 439.
231. In subsequent years, hearings on school prayer amendments were held in either the House or the Senate and proposals reached the floor of the Senate, none generating the required two-thirds support. See Keynes, *The Court vs. Congress*, 191–95.
232. See Kammen, *The Machine That Would Go of Itself*, 327 (concluding that a core dynamic of American constitutionalism is the readiness of government officials—administrative, judicial, and legislative—to defy the Supreme Court by willfully circumventing objectionable Supreme Court decision).
233. See Friedman, *The Will of the People*, 262 (discussing the disregard of the Court's school prayer decision and explaining the difficulty of enforcing judicial decrees, such as the school prayer ban, that mandate that many people in diffuse parts of the country do something that is strongly opposed or abstain from doing something). The Court's earlier decision in *McCollum v. Board of Education*, 333 US 203 (1948), which invalidated practices that released students for religious instruction on public school property, also was ignored by some school districts. See Kammen, *The Machine That Would Go of Itself*, 327.
234. Only one Tennessee school district had complied with *Schempp* by entirely eliminating devotional Bible reading from its schools. Seventy had made no change at all and continued to follow the pre-*Schempp* requirements of state law that required daily Bible reading. The remaining fifty school districts made student participation in daily Bible reading voluntary and delegated to each teacher the decision whether to conduct a classroom devotional exercise. This resulted in little change in fact. Robert H. Birkby, "The Supreme Court and the Bible Belt: Tennessee Reaction to the *Schempp* Decision," in Theodore L. Becker and Malcolm M. Feeley, eds., *The Impact of Supreme Court Decisions* (2d ed.) (New York: Oxford University Press, 1973), 110–14.
235. See Kenneth M. Dolbeare and Phillip E. Hammond, *The School Prayer Decisions: From Court Policy to Local Practice* (Chicago: University of Chicago Press, 1971). See also Dierenfield, "*Engel v. Vitale*," 223 (stating that leaders in almost half of the states circumvented the Court's mandate in *Engel*).
236. Chamberlin v. Dade County Board of Public Instruction, 377 US 402 (1964).
237. Wallace v. Jaffe, 472 US 38 (1985).
238. Lee v. Weisman, 505 US 577 (1992).
239. Santa Fe Independent School District v. Doe, 530 US 290 (2000).
240. See Powe, "Are 'the People' Missing in Action," 877.
241. Quoted in Powe, "Are 'the People' Missing in Action," 876–77 (citing the 1980 Republican Party platform). Polls conducted in the early 1980s showed consistent majority support for school prayer and for a constitutional amendment allowing it. Friedman, *The Will of the People*, 327 and n. 39 (reporting polling data showing that in 1980, and again in 1984, roughly 70 percent of Americans believed schools should start the day with a prayer, and a 1983 Gallup poll that found among the "aware public" 81 percent favored a constitutional amendment allowing voluntary school prayer).
242. Another Mayhew-coined phrase is "credit claiming"—acting in ways that erroneously lead constituents to believe one has influenced government in ways

desired by constituents. For a discussion of position taking and credit claiming, see David R. Mayhew, *Congress: The Electoral Connection* (2d ed.) (New Haven, CT: Yale University Press, 2004), 52–53, 61.
243. See discussion in Robert McClosky, "Principles, Powers, and Values," in Donald A. Gianella, ed., *1964 Religion and Public Order* (Chicago: University of Chicago Press, 1965), 3, 28.
244. See Powe, *The Warren Court and American Politics*, 362 (referring to support for school prayer amendments during the Warren Court years after school prayer amendments had lost their political currency).
245. The Reagan-administration-supported school prayer amendment came to a vote in the Senate in 1984, but the 56 to 44 favorable vote fell far short of the required two-thirds support. See Vile, *Encyclopedia of Constitutional Amendments*, 352–53.
246. See James T. Patterson, *Restless Giant* (New York: Oxford University Press, 2005), 177 (discussing National Day of Prayer and the Reagan administration's support for a school prayer constitutional amendment as a means of mollifying social conservatives who grew restive and frustrated by the Reagan administration's inattention to the issue of school prayer). See also discussion at Kyvig, *Explicit and Authentic Acts*, 452.
247. See, e.g., Mueller v. Allen, 463 US 388 (1983) (upholding a program of tax credits for expenses incurred in educating children, including parochial school tuition); Agostini v. Felton, 521 US 203(1997) (upholding use of public school teachers to teach remedial classes in secular subjects on the premises of religious schools); Mitchell v. Helms, 530 US 793 (2000) (providing instructional materials to religious schools).
248. See discussion at Ira C. Lupu, "Statutes Revolving in Constitutional Law Orbits," 79 *University of Virginia Law Review* 1, 30 (1993). The Court upheld the Equal Access Act, 8–1, in *Westside Community Schools v. Mergens*, 496 US 226 (1990).
249. See discussion of the tactical and strategic use of school prayer amendments at Keynes, *The Court vs. Congress*, 196–97. Keynes argues that to keep the school prayer issue alive, Senate conservatives held hearings on a school prayer amendment as late as 1982 and 1985, when there was no realistic chance of securing a school prayer amendment, and that this strategy struck a "responsive chord" in the American electorate at a time when Congress was considering enactment of the Equal Access Act (202).
250. H.R. Rep No. 98–710, at 13 (1984).
251. Davidson, "The Lawmaking Congress," 56 *Law and Contemporary Problems* 99, 116 (1993).
252. Davidson, "The Lawmaking Congress," 116.
253. See John R. Vile, *Constitutional Change in the United States: A Comparative Study of the Role of Constitutional Amendment, Judicial Interpretations, and Legislative and Executive Actions* (Westport, CT: Praeger, 1994), 39.
254. See Dierenfield, "*Engel v. Vitale*," 224.
255. It was pointed out earlier in this chapter that opponents of *Roe v. Wade* similarly were forced to confront the reality of the need to change strategies once it became clear that efforts to reverse *Roe* by constitutional amendment were not feasible.
256. Texas v. Johnson, 491 US 397 (1989).

257. Quoted in Robert Justin Goldstein, "*Texas v. Johnson*," in Urofsky, ed., *The Public Debate over Controversial Supreme Court Decisions*, 330.
258. Goldstein, "*Texas v. Johnson*," 332.
259. Powe, *The Supreme Court and the American Elite*, 288.
260. Goldstein, "*Texas v. Johnson*," 332.
261. Whittington, *Political Foundations of Judicial Supremacy*, 140–41.
262. Whittington, *Political Foundations of Judicial Supremacy*, 141.
263. Kyvig, *Explicit and Authentic Acts*, 456–57.
264. See Whittington, *Political Foundations of Judicial Supremacy*, 141.
265. R. Douglas Arnold, *The Logic of Congressional Action* (New Haven, CT: Yale University Press, 1990), 77–78.
266. See discussion at authorities cited at Whittington, *Political Foundations of Judicial Supremacy*, 141, n. 232.
267. United States v. Eichman, 496 US 310 (1990). In an unusual addition to its decision in *Eichman*, the Court served notice on Congress that it would strike down any legislation proscribing flag desecration since all such legislation is inescapably addressed at the government's disapproval of the content of the message conveyed by the act of flag desecration.
268. Kyvig, *Explicit and Authentic Acts*, 458.
269. See David M. O'Brien, *Constitutional Law and Politics: Struggles for Power and Government Accountability* (vol. 2) (8th ed.) (New York, W. W. Norton, 2011), 675–76 (Constitutional Law and Politics II) (reporting the 2006 Senate vote); Robert Justin Goldstein, *Flag Burning and Free Speech: The Case of* Texas v. Johnson (Lawrence: University Press of Kansas, 2000), 258 (summarizing all of the votes between 1995 and 2005); Goldstein, *Flag Burning and Free Speech*, 340 (concluding that public passions had cooled by 1995).
270. Article II, § 1 provides for the election of the president and vice-president by the Electoral College but leaves to the states the decision of how these electors are to be chosen. And, more important for present purposes, Article I, § 2 provides that whomever a state permits to vote for the most numerous chamber in the state legislature is entitled to vote for the United States House of Representatives. Each state's legislature originally chose senators, but the 1913 Seventeenth Amendment now provides for direct election of senators using the same voter eligibility rules used for eligibility to vote for members of the House of Representatives.
271. Luther v. Borden, 48 US (7 How.) 1 (1849).
272. Minor v. Happersett, 88 US (21 Wall.) 162 (1875).
273. These are the Fifteenth (1870), Nineteenth (1920), Twenty-Third (1961), Twenty-Fourth (1964), and Twenty-Sixth (1971) Amendments.
274. See Alan P. Grimes, *Democracy and the Amendments to the Constitution* (Lanham, MD: University Press of America, 1978), 134. The account of the history of the poll tax and the ratification of the Twenty-Fourth Amendment draws on Grimes, *Democracy and the Amendments*, 130–36 and Kyvig, *Explicit and Authentic Acts*, 351–57.
275. Breedlove v. Suttles, 302 US 277 (1937).
276. Peter M. Shane, "Voting Rights and the 'Statutory Constitution,'" 56 *Law and Contemporary Problems* 243, 254–55 (1993).

277. See Bruce Ackerman, "Canonizing the Civil Rights Revolution: The People and The Poll Tax," 13 *Northwestern University Law Review* 63, 88 (2009).
278. Ackerman, "Canonizing the Civil Rights Revolution," 67, 70–79, 85–86 (also explaining that Southern Democrats desired to eliminate the poll tax in federal elections in order to enfranchise poor whites who would support Democratic candidates for federal office, confident that African American voters could continue to be disenfranchised through other devices such as the literacy test).
279. See Michael R. Belknap, "Twenty-Fourth Amendment," in Hall, ed., *The Oxford Companion to the Supreme Court of the United States*, 817, 1031–32.
280. See Grimes, *Democracy and the Amendments to the Constitution*, 135. Congress's recommending the Twenty-Fourth Amendment to the states was a "godsend" for the Kennedy administration. The administration could support the amendment and thereby support an initiative by a conservative Southern senator and, at the same time, claim credit in the North for supporting an important civil rights program. See discussion at Ackerman, *We the People, Vol. 3: The Civil Rights Revolution*, 89.
281. Ackerman, *We the People, Vol. 3: The Civil Rights Revolution*, 283.
282. South Carolina v. Katzenbach, 383 US 301, 309 (1966).
283. In the Voting Rights Act, Congress found that 1) the poll tax as a precondition for voting imposed an unreasonable burden on persons of limited means, 2) it bore no reasonable relationship to any legitimate state interest, and (3) it was being used to deny persons the right to vote because of race or color. Relying on these findings, Congress declared that the poll tax constituted an unconstitutional abridgement of the right to vote. Voting Rights Act § 10, 42 USC. § 1973h(a) (2000).
284. Harper v. Virginia State Board of Elections, 383 US 663 (1966).
285. Harper v. Virginia, 383 US at 666 (concluding that "a state violates the Equal Protection Clause . . . whenever it makes the affluence of the voter or payment of any fee an electoral standard. Voter qualifications have no relation to wealth nor to paying or not paying this or any other tax").
286. This back story of *Harper* was first documented and described in Ackerman, "Canonizing The Civil Rights Revolution," 103–33.
287. See Bernard Schwartz, "More Unpublished Warren Court Opinions," 1986 *Supreme Court Review* 317, 321–27.
288. Ackerman, "Canonizing the Civil Rights Revolution," 110–13 (noting that Justice Goldberg's dissenting opinion urging the Court to hear the *Harper* case on the merits, had emphasized the role of the 1960s' constitutional accomplishments in undercutting the *Breedlove*'s doctrinal foundations and showing that this radical change in the legal landscape had caused members of the Court to question constitutional assumptions that previously had been considered unquestionable). Even the dissent in *Harper* paid homage to the role of Article V in undermining support for poll taxes in state and local elections. Justice Harlan's dissenting opinion, joined by Justice Stewart, admitted that arguments for any poll tax as a qualification for voting "ring hollow on most contemporary ears" due to the "cognate fact that Congress and three-quarters of the States quickly ratified the Twenty-Fourth Amendment." Harper v. Virginia State Board of Elections, 383 US 663, 685–86 (1965) (Harlan, J., dissenting).

Notes to Pages 82–84   203

289. Three years later, in 1969, a state law requiring property ownership as a prerequisite for eligibility to vote also fell, in *Kramer v. Union Free School District*, 395 US 621 (1969). In *Kramer*, the Court relied on *Harper*'s doctrinal predicate that wealth may not constitutionally be used as a determinant for voting eligibility.
290. See Linda J. Wharton, "State Equal Rights Amendments Revisited: Evaluating Their Effectiveness in Advancing Protection Against Sex Discrimination," 36 *Rutgers Law Journal* 1201, 1288–93 (2005) (containing an appendix of citations to the constitutions of twenty-two states: Alaska, California, Colorado, Connecticut, Florida, Hawaii, Illinois, Iowa, Louisiana, Maryland, Massachusetts, Montana, New Hampshire, New Jersey, New Mexico, Pennsylvania, Rhode Island, Texas, Utah, Virginia, Washington, and Wyoming).

   For a periodic update of state ERA adoptions, see "The Equal Rights Amendment: Unfinished Business for the Constitution," *www.equalrightsamendment.org/faq.htm#q7*.
291. Wharton, "State Equal Rights Amendments Revisited," 1227–68.
292. Richard G. Bacon, "Rum, Romanism, and Romer: Equal Protection and the Blaine Amendment in State Constitutions," 6 *Delaware Law Review* 1 (2003). Except where otherwise indicated, the factual background relating to the Blaine Amendment is drawn from Bacon's excellent research regarding the Blaine Amendment.
293. See Paul G. Kauper, *Civil Liberties and the Constitution* (Ann Arbor: University of Michigan Press, 1962), 4.
294. Bacon, "Rum, Romanism, and Romer," n. 5 (citing Steven E. Green, "The Blaine Amendment Reconsidered," 36 *American Journal of Legal History* 38, 72 (1992)).
295. See Joseph P. Viteritti, "Choosing Equality: Religious Freedom and Educational Opportunity Under Constitutional Federalism," 15 *Yale Law and Policy Review* 113, 144 (1996).
296. Ian Bartrum, "The Constitutional Structure of Disestablishment," 2 *New York University Journal of Law and Liberty* 311, 358 (2007); Noah Feldman, "Non-Sectarianism Reconsidered," 18 *Journal of Law and Politics* 65, 68, 111 (2002) (concluding that the non-sectarianism advocated by proponents of the Blaine Amendment has largely triumphed).
297. See Meir Katz, "The State of Blaine: A Closer Look at the Blaine Amendments and their Modern Application," 12 *Engage* 111, 112 (2011) (summarizing the Blaine Amendment's "lasting legacy" in state constitutions).
298. Feldman, "Non-Sectarianism Reconsidered," 111 and n. 181 (citing the admission of North and South Dakota, Washington, and Montana).
299. Twenty-nine is the most widely cited number. See, e.g., Feldman, "Non-Sectarianism Reconsidered," 68. But see Katz, "State of Blaine," 112 (stating that between 1870 and 1900 forty-one states adopted Blaine Amendments); Charles J. Russo and Ralph D. Mawdsley, "The United States Supreme Court and Aid to Students Who Attend Religiously-Affiliated Institutions of Higher Education," 14 *Education Law Journal* 301, 308–9 (2005) (stating that Washington state is among the thirty-seven states containing state constitutional amendments adopted following the failed Blaine Amendment).
300. Kotterman v. Killian, 193 Arizona 273, 972 P.2d 606 (1999).

Chapter 3

1. Quoted in David E. Kyvig, "Arranging for Amendment: Unintended Outcomes of Constitutional Design," in Kyvig, ed., *Unintended Consequences of Constitutional Amendment*, 22.
2. Frank J. Sorauf, "The Political Potential of an Amending Convention," in Kermit L. Hall, Harold M. Hyman, and Leon V. Sigal, *The Constitutional Convention as an Amending Device* (Washington, DC: The American Historical Association and The American Political Science Association, 1981), 114.
3. See Friends of the Article V Convention, "Images of Article V Applications," accessed August 16, 2016, *www.article-5.org/file.php/1/Amendments/index.htm* (listing 746 known state Article V convention applications, but the calculation of 696 represents a reduction of 50 applications requesting that a state's application be rescinded). See also Thomas E. Brennan, *The Article V Amendatory Constitutional Convention* (Lanham, MD: Lexington Books, 2014), 10 (listing the number as of 2014 as 746).
4. See discussion at Chris DeRose, *Founding Rivals: Madison and Monroe, the Bill of Rights and the Election That Saved a Nation* (Washington, DC: Regnery Publishing, 2011), 200–208, 223, 248, 258.
5. Sorauf, "The Political Potential of an Amending Convention," 39–40.
6. Chris DeRose, *Founding Rivals*, 152, 233–34.
7. Powe, *The Supreme Court and the American Elite*, 14. See also DeRose, *Founding Rivals*, 161 (detailing James Madison's view that opponents of the union would be chosen as delegates to a second convention who would advance demands unacceptable to other states with the "express purpose" of causing the convention to break down and the union collapse).
8. DeRose, *Founding Rivals*, 220–21, 256–57, 263.
9. See Alexander DeConde, *The Quasi-War: The Politics and Diplomacy of the Undeclared War with France 1797–1801* (New York: Charles Scribner's and Sons, 1966).
10. Stanley Elkins and Eric McKitrick, *The Age of Federalism* (New York: Oxford University Press, 1993), 309–11.
11. The factual materials for this section draw on Gordon S. Wood, *Empire of Liberty: A History of the Early Republic, 1789–1815* (New York: Oxford University Press, 2009), 185–275; David McCullough, *John Adams* (New York: Simon and Schuster, 2001), 443–522; and Elkins and McKitrick, *The Age of Federalism*, 303–43, 529–662.
12. After his arrival in the United States, Genet helped form Republican-Democratic Societies in America (pro-French secret political societies), issued letters of marque, and paid out large sums of money to outfit several privateers to attack British commercial shipping.
13. President Washington's Secretary of the Treasury, Alexander Hamilton, an arch Federalist, was a leading advocate of this subversion theory. He argued that most Republicans who supported Genet's work in the summer of 1793 were enemies of the current American government and intended to subvert the government. See Elkins and McKitrick, *The Age of Federalism*, 360.
14. More than sixteen thousand people were executed by guillotine, with nearly three thousand in Paris alone, including the execution in Paris of the widowed Queen

Marie Antoinette by guillotine at Place de la Concorde on October 16, 1793. See Donald Greer, *The Incidence of Terror during the French Revolution: A Statistical Interpretation* (Harvard Historical Monographs, No. 8) (Cambridge, MA: Harvard University Press, 1935).

15. As John Adams recalled late in his life, Genet created a frenzied atmosphere of terrorism that spread throughout Philadelphia, creating the real risk, in Adams's view, of the people "threaten[ing] to drag Washington out of his House and effect a Revolution in the Government, or compel it to declare War in favor of the French Revolution, and against England." Adams in a letter to Jefferson, quoted in Wood, *Empire of Liberty*, 185–86.

16. Alan Taylor, *The Civil War of 1812* (New York: Vintage Books, 2011), 77–79.

17. The Genet affair had an ironic ending. After the United States sought Genet's recall, and France agreed, Genet was accused by French authorities of complicity with England in a plot harmful to France. Concluding that he would face the guillotine if he returned to France, Genet sought, and was granted, asylum in the United States. He married the daughter of New York governor George Clinton and lived out the rest of his life in the United States as a gentleman farmer and amateur scientist. See George C. Herring, *From Colony to Superpower: US Foreign Relations since 1776* (New York: Oxford University Press, 2008), 72.

18. There was evidence that France had used native collaborators to subvert governments of other countries and set up puppet regimes in the Netherlands and Switzerland. Wood, *Empire of Liberty*, 246.

19. Taylor, *The Civil War of 1812*, 81.

20. The depth of the Federalists' concern that Jeffersonian Republicans intended to align with aliens to restructure the Constitution and in effect make America a French province can be seen in Alexander Hamilton's May 1798 letter to George Washington and Washington's general agreement with that assessment. See Wood, *Empire of Liberty*, 266.

21. The United States had no fleet in the 1790s. Accordingly, private US citizens filled the void by soliciting subscriptions to build warships to be used by the United States government to defend the country from privateers menacing American merchant vessels. Merchants from Newburyport, Massachusetts, initiated this by building a twenty-gun warship in ninety days. Money obtained from thousands of subscribers financed construction of nine subscription warships from eight cities (Baltimore built two). Even before the first ship was completed, Congress enacted legislation to purchase the ships in exchange for 6 percent stock certificates. See Frederick C. Leiner, *Millions for Defense: The Subscription Warships of 1798* (Annapolis: US Naval Institute Press, 1999); Theodore J. Crackel, Review of *Millions for Defense: The Subscription Warships of 1798*, by Frederick C. Leiner, H-SHEAR, H-Net Reviews. November 2000, accessed August 16, 2016, *www.h-net.org/reviews/showrev.php?id=4687*.

22. DeConde, *The Quasi-War*, 9 (reports arrived that in one year the French had captured 316 American ships). This war-like action by France was taken in response to the United States entering into the Jay treaty with Great Britain. The Jay Treaty resolved issues arising from British policies resulting Britain's seizure of more than 250 American ships during 1794 because the ships were trading with the French West Indies during Britain's war with France. France inaccurately interpreted

the Jay Treaty as an alliance between the United States and Great Britain and began these war-like activities directed at American commerce. DeConde, *The Quasi-War*, 9.
23. Powe, *The Supreme Court and the American Elite*, 32. See generally John C. Miller, *Crisis In Freedom: The Alien and Sedition Acts* (Boston: Little, Brown, 1951).
24. McCullough, *John Adams*, 504–05.
25. See John C. Miller, *The Federalist Era: 1789–1801* (New York: Harper, 1960), 230.
26. Miller, *The Federalist Era*, 230. Otis also proposed excluding all foreign-born who were not then citizens from all offices of honor, trust, or profit in the national government. This proposal was defeated in the House. Miller, *Crisis in Freedom*, 48.
27. The Constitution already limited eligibility for election to the office of president to natural-born citizens and those who were residents when the Constitution was adopted and had been a resident within the United States for fourteen years. US Const. art. II, § 1.
28. Ames, *The Proposed Amendments*, 30, 73–75, 308–9.
29. Miller, *Crisis in Freedom*, 48; Ames, *The Proposed Amendments*, 30, 73–75, 322–23.
30. Miller, *The Federalist Era*, 230. By1798, sixteen states had been admitted to the union. Thus, to obtain two-thirds support, amendment supporters would have needed support of senators from eleven states.
31. See Gaillard Hunt, ed., *The Writings of James Madison, Comprising His Public Papers And His Private Correspondence, Including His Numerous Letters and Documents Now for the First Time Printed*, Vol. 6 (New York: G. P. Putnam's Sons, 1900) 403–4, available at *files.libertyfund.org/files/1941/1356.06_Bk.pdf*. For a discussion of Madison's view of the role of the convention to redress abuse of power by the national government, see Wood, *Empire of Liberty*, 269–71; Nick Dranius, "Introducing 'Article V 2.0': The Compact for a Balanced Budget," 15 *Engage* (August 22, 2014) n. 54 and accompanying text, available at *www.fedsoc.org/publications/detail/introducingarticlev20thecompactforabalancedbudget* (arguing that in his "Report on the Virginia Resolutions," Madison cited the Article V Application Clause as a reminder to the other states that the Constitution assured the states a way to set the agenda for a proposing convention to redress the federal government's abuse of power through constitutional amendments).
32. Moreover, Horatio Nelson's defeat of the French fleet in the historic Battle of the Nile in August 1798 eliminated all realistic possibility of a French invasion of either Great Britain or the United States. In addition, within months of the introduction of these proposed constitutional amendments, the Adams administration appointed a peace mission to travel to France to negotiate peace, and the Treaty of Mortefontaine, signed on October 3, 1800, restored peaceful relations between France and the United States. See Wood, *Empire of Liberty*, 271–75; Powe, *The Supreme Court and the American Elite*, 39.
33. The Kentucky and Virginia Resolutions failed miserably. They called on the other states to join in renouncing the Alien and Sedition Acts as unconstitutional but none of the other state legislatures did so. Nine Northern states rejected the Kentucky and Virginia resolutions explicitly and four Southern states took no action. Wood, *Empire of Liberty*, 270. The Federalists' amendment proposals thus have been understood as more a symbolic "gesture" than a serious attempt to amend

the Constitution since the composition of the Congress in the late-1790s made adoption of a meaningful amendment highly problematic. See Kyvig, *Explicit and Authentic Acts*, 119.
34. The factual account here can be substantiated at Wood, *Empire of Liberty*, 283–85.
35. Powe, *The Supreme Court and the American Elite*, 40 (concluding that among the Federalists' options was adopting a procedure for choosing an interim president pending a new election).
36. Quoted at George Tucker, *The Life of Thomas Jefferson* (Philadelphia: Carey, Lea and Blanchard, 1837), 83 (digitized November 27, 2014). Accord Wood, *Empire of Liberty*, 285; Russell L. Caplan, *Constitutional Brinkmanship: Amending the Constitution by National Convention* (New York: Oxford University Press, 1988), 42–45.
37. Britain initially accepted the legal fiction that making a stopover in a United States port when transporting goods from the French West Indies to Europe constituted a "broken voyage" not "direct" shipment.
38. Donald R. Hickey, *The War of 1812: The Forgotten Conflict* (Urbana: University of Illinois Press, 1989), 7–10.
39. Wood, *Empire of Liberty*, 640. 649.
40. Wood, *Empire of Liberty*, 641; Hickey, *The War of 1812*, 11. Great Britain impressed approximately 10,000 who claimed American citizenship, either by birth or naturalization. Some were released, but an estimated 6,000 American citizens were forced into service in the Royal Navy. Hickey, *The War of 1812*, 11.
41. During the four years following expansion of the commercial war between France and Britain, nine hundred American ships were seized by France or Britain or their allies. Hickey, *The War of 1812*, 17–19.
42. Wood, *Empire of Liberty*, 647.
43. Exports valued at $108,000,000 in 1807 plunged to $22,000,000 within one year. It would take the United States a quarter century to recover fully from the economic devastation caused by the embargo. Wills, *Negro President*, 184.
44. Wood, *Empire of Liberty*, 649–52.
45. Quoted in Hickey, *The War of 1812*, 20.
46. Wills, *Negro President*, 149.
47. Wood, *Empire of Liberty*, 653–54.
48. By one estimate, the South suffered more than the North because the Southern states lacked merchant ships that could be used to evade the embargo and smuggle goods in or out. In addition, the South lacked the industrial capacity to produce locally the now-unavailable British manufactured goods. Wills, *Negro President*, 156.
49. Wills, *Negro President*, 150, 157.
50. Wood, *Empire of Liberty*, 656.
51. Wills, *Negro President*, 158.
52. Wood, *Empire of Liberty*, 654–55; Wills, *Negro President*, 157 (concluding that by the end of 1808 the embargo had harmed the United States far more than any other country).
53. The repealed embargo was substituted with a non-intercourse act that barred trade with France and Great Britain until either lifted its trade restrictions, which Britain did within a month. Within three years, however, the United States was at war

with Britain, the War of 1812. See Hickey, *The War of 1812*, 21–22; Wood, *Empire of Liberty*, 658.

54. James M. Banner, *To the Hartford Convention: The Federalists and the Origins of Party Politics in Massachusetts, 1789–1815* (New York: Alfred A. Knopf, 1970), 299; Powe, *The Supreme Court and the American Elite*, 54 (explaining that the new legislation provided for seizure of cargo on mere suspicion that it was intended for export).

55. See, e.g., Jerry L. Mashaw, "Reluctant Nationalists: Federal Administration and Administrative Law in the Republican Era, 1801–1809," 116 *Yale Law Journal* 1636, 1655 (2007) (concluding that the enactment and enforcement of the embargo offended most of the Jeffersonian Republicans' bedrock constitutional principles such as limited executive authority and militarily backed duress based on rumor and unsubstantiated accusation).

56. Banner, *To the Hartford Convention*, 300.

57. See Merrill D. Peterson, *Thomas Jefferson and the New Nation* (New York: Oxford University Press, 1970), 913.

58. Banner, *To the Hartford Convention*, 301.

59. Banner, *To the Hartford Convention*, 302–4.

60. One wonders if Jefferson and Madison saw the irony in this nullification resolution by Massachusetts legislature since it was they, the authors of the Kentucky and Virginia Resolutions of 1798–99, who first made the claim that the states retained the power to challenge or even override national legislation. See Eric Foner, *The Fiery Trial: Abraham Lincoln and American Slavery* (New York: W. W. Norton, 2010), 134.

61. Banner, *To the Hartford Convention*, 305 and n. 1, 304–5.

62. Banner, *To the Hartford Convention*, 306.

63. Banner, *To the Hartford Convention*, 306, n. 3.

64. Herring, *From Colony to Superpower*, 121 (concluding that although Jefferson and Madison had hoped to maintain the embargo until summer and then repeal it if it were unsuccessful, a panicked Congress was moved to repeal the embargo in March due to the apprehension over the specter of a rebellious New England).

65. See Howe, *What Hath God Wrought*, 272–75, 395–410.

66. Howe, *What Hath God Wrought*, 396–401.

67. Caplan, *Constitutional Brinksmanship*, 50.

68. Howe, *What Hath God Wrought*, 401.

69. Historian Lucas Powe interprets the nullification controversy differently. Powe argues that it was Calhoun who backed down in the face of threats from President Andrew Jackson that he would use military force if necessary to enforce federal law. Powe. *The Supreme Court and the American Elite*, 81.

70. Quoted in Robert Barnes, "Amend While the Iron is Hot?," *Washington Post*, November 29, 2010, accessed August 16, 2016, *www.washingtonpost.com/wpdyn/content/article/2010/11/28/AR2010112803865.html* (quoting Justice Scalia's remarks at Texas Tech University).

71. See discussion at Richard B. Bernstein and Jerome Agel, *Amending America: If We Love the Constitution so Much, Why Do We Keep Trying to Change It?* (Lawrence: University Press of Kansas, 1993), 122–23.

72. On the increasing popular pressure for more direct democracy and popular

hostility to the active bureaucratic state during the nineteenth century, see Morton Keller, "The Politics of State Constitutional Revision: 1820–1930," in Hall, Hyman and Sigal, *The Constitutional Convention as an Amending Device*, 70–76.

73. Ames, *The Proposed Amendments*, 62–63.
74. Herman Ames cites six such examples of state legislative paralysis leading to a state not having one or both of its senators serving in the Senate. In 1893, three states found themselves in this predicament. Ames, *The Proposed Amendments*, 63 and n. 1.
75. Ames, *The Proposed Amendments*, 61. See also Michael A. Musmano, *Proposed Amendments to the Constitution* (Washington, DC: US Government Printing Office, 1929), reprinted (Westport, Connecticut: Greenwood Press, 1976), 219 (showing that in all, 198 resolutions to amend the Constitution to provide for popular election of senators were introduced in Congress, one or more almost every year between 1872 and 1911).
76. Kris W. Kobach, "Rethinking Article V: Term Limits and the Seventeenth and Nineteenth Amendments," 103 *Yale Law Journal* 1971, 1977 (1994) (citing George H. Haynes, *The Senate of the United States: Its History and Practice* (Boston, Houghton Mifflin Co., 1938), 92 n. 1).
77. See discussion at Foner, *The Fiery Trial*, 99.
78. Kobach, "Rethinking Article V," 1978–79. See also Bernstein and Agel, *Amending America*, 126 and n. 34 (stating that by 1910, nearly a majority of senators were chosen by popular vote); Michael A. Musmano, *Proposed Amendments to the Constitution*, 217 (reporting that by 1911 at least thirty-one states had expressed support for the direct-election principle).
79. See, e.g., Musmano, *Proposed Amendments to the Constitution*, 217; Bernstein and Agel, *Amending America*, 125–27; Carlos E. Gonzalez, "Popular Sovereign Generated Versus Government Institution Generated Constitutional Norms: When Does a Constitutional Amendment Not Amend the Constitution?," 80 *Washington University Law Quarterly* 127, 203, n. 216 (2002).
80. Kobach, "Rethinking Article V: Term Limits," 1979 and n. 35.
81. See Sorauf, "The Political Potential of an Amending Convention," 115 (concluding that the prevailing academic view is that the states' petitions for a constitutional convention finally motivated the Senate to propose the Seventeenth Amendment to the states).
82. Sorauf, "The Political Potential of an Amending Convention," 114.
83. There is general agreement that the states' threat to request that Congress convene a constitutional convention if Congress did not itself pass an amendment resolution providing for direct election of senators prodded Congress to propose the Seventeenth Amendment (direct election of senators). Kyvig, "Arranging for Amendment," 36–37.
84. Similar bottom-up influences of state law also facilitated the ratification of both the Eighteenth Amendment (Prohibition) and the Nineteenth Amendment (women's suffrage). See discussion Kyvig, "Arranging for Amendment," 88 (Prohibition) and Bernstein and Agel, *Amending America*, 132 (Nineteenth Amendment); Musmano, *Proposed Amendments to the Constitution*, 244–46 (presenting data showing that by the time that the Nineteenth Amendment was ratified, twenty-nine of the then forty-eight states had already fully or partially enfranchised women).

85. Baker v. Carr, 369 US 186 (1962).
86. Gray v. Sanders, 372 US 368 (1963); Wesberry v. Sanders, 376 US 1 (1964); Reynolds v. Sims, 377 US 533 (1964).
87. Quoted in J. W. Peltason, "*Baker v. Carr*," in Hall, ed., *The Oxford Companion to the Supreme Court of the United States*, 67–68.
88. Wesberry v. Sanders, 376 US 1 (1964).
89. Wood v. Broom, 287 US 1 (1932).
90. Colegrove v. Green, 328 US 549 (1946).
91. In 1970 the Court extended the principle of one person, one vote to virtually every local election. Hadley v. Junior College District of Metropolitan Kansas City, Missouri, 397 US 50 (1970).
92. See Caplan, *Constitutional Brinksmanship*, 73.
93. Caplan, *Constitutional Brinksmanship*, 73–74 (explaining that the reapportionment amendment proposal was one of three so-called states' rights proposed constitutional amendments, the other two providing for transferring amendment proposal authority directly with the state legislatures and for creating a Court of the Union to review Supreme Court decisions affecting federal-state relations). See also Charles L. Black Jr., "The Proposed Amendment of Article V: A Threatened Disaster," 72 *Yale Law Journal* 957, 958 (1963) (critically evaluating amendments to permit the state legislatures to propose constitutional amendments); William G. Ross, "Attacks on the Warren Court by State Officials: A Case Study of Why Court-Curbing Movements Fail," 50 *University of Buffalo Law Review* 483, 529–85 (2002) (analysis of the three states rights amendments). Additional detail of these developments can be found in Kyvig, *Explicit and Authentic Acts*, 370–79.
94. Caplan, *Constitutional Brinksmanship*, 74.
95. Barry Friedman, *The Will of the People* (New York: Farrar, Strauss and Giroux, 2009), 269.
96. See Kyvig, *Explicit and Authentic Acts*, 376–77.
97. Caplan, *Constitutional Brinksmanship*, 74–75.
98. But see Kyvig, *Explicit and Authentic Acts*, 376 (explaining that as many as seven of these applications may have been invalid, because two had never been forwarded to Congress and five sought an amendment different from the Dirksen Amendment).
99. Caplan, *Constitutional Brinksmanship*, 75; Kyvig, *Explicit and Authentic Acts*, 375, 377.
100. See discussion in Gerard N. Magliocca "State Calls for an Article Five Convention: Mobilization and Interpretation," 2009 *Cardozo Law Review* 74, 82 and n. 40.
101. Arlen J. Large, "Dirksen's Crusade," *Wall Street Journal*, June 2, 1969, at 1 (quoted at Maglioocca, "State Calls for an Article V Convention," 82–83 and n. 40). It will be recalled that this also was Jefferson's ploy when threatening a constitutional convention during the contested election crisis of 1800.
102. Kirkpatrick v. Preisler, 394 US 526, 528–31 (1969) (emphasis added).
103. Kirkpatrick v. Preisler, 394 US at 528–31
104. See J. W. Peltason, "*Westbury v. Sanders*," in Hall, ed., *The Oxford Companion to the Supreme Court of the United States*, 1082.
105. Kirkpatrick v. Preisler, 394 US 526, 530 (1969).
106. There also was a nearly successful state effort to force Congress to call a constitu-

tional convention to propose a balanced budget amendment. That story is deferred to the next chapter discussing the impact of failed amendment efforts on federal legislation because these second convention efforts were inextricably intertwined with the larger story of congressional attempts to pass a balanced budget constitutional amendment, efforts that morphed into a legislative solution (The Gramm-Rudman-Hollings Deficit Reduction Act of 1985).

Chapter 4

1. See Stephanie Condon, "Obama, Dems Slam Balanced Budget Amendment," CBS News, Political Hotsheet, Nov. 18, 2011, accessed, August 16, 2016 *www.cbsnews.com/8301503544_16257326895503544/obamademsslambalancedbudgetamendment* (explaining that in an effort to attract support for the proposed constitutional amendment the House managers excised provisions limiting Congress's power to tax as a means of balancing the budget).
2. For recent efforts to enact a balanced budget amendment, see Mark Udall, "Moderate Democratic Senators Introduce Common-Sense Balanced Budget Amendment to US Constitution," accessed August 16, 2016, *www.markudall.senate.gov/?p=press_release&id=3562* (reporting that in July 2013 six Democratic United States senators introduced a balanced budget amendment).
3. See discussion at Louis Fisher, *Presidential Spending Power* (Princeton: Princeton University Press, 1975), 150–51.
4. See "The Democrats Checkmated," *New York Times*, August 15, 1876, accessed August 16, 2016, *query.nytimes.com/gst/abstract.html?res=9D06EED91F3FE73BBC4D52DFBE66838D669FDE*.
5. See Diane-Michele Krasnow, "The Imbalance of Power and the Presidential Veto: A Case for the Item Veto," 14 *Harvard Journal of Law and Public Policy* 583, 602 and n. 124 (1991) (concluding that, after Jefferson and until the Nixon administration, presidential impoundments were generally limited to pork-barrel appropriations).
6. See Fisher, *Presidential Spending Power*, 150–51; 169–70.
7. Train v. City of New York, 420 US 35 (1975).
8. Both of these conclusions were reaffirmations of the Court's previously expressed view of relative congressional and executive spending power. In 1838 the Court had concluded that the president must comply with a congressional *directive* to spend certain funds, reasoning that "to contend that the obligation imposed on the President to see the laws faithfully executed, implies a power to forbid their execution, is a novel construction of the constitution, and entirely inadmissible." Kendall v. United States *ex rel*. Stokes, 37 US (12 Pet.) 524, 611 (1838).
9. See discussion at Train v. City of New York, 420 US 35, 41 n. 8 (1975).
10. The Impoundment Control Act also provided unilateral authority for the president to *delay* expenditures of appropriated funds unless either the House of Representatives or the Senate passes a resolution mandating their immediate expenditure. This prevision was found to be unconstitutional in *City of New Haven, Conn. v. United States*, 809 F.2d 900 (DC Cir. 1987). The government did not seek Supreme Court review in light of the Court's decision in *INS v. Chadha*, 462 US 919 (1983) finding this type of one house veto unconstitutional. See discussion of *INS v. Chadha infra* in this chapter.

11. Clinton v. City of New York, 524 US 417 (1998).
12. Clinton v. City of New York, 524 US at 449.
13. See, e.g., US Term Limits, Inc. v. Thornton, 514 US 779 (1995) (invalidating an Arkansas state law restricting persons from serving in the House of Representatives for more than three terms or in the United States Senate for more than two terms and suggesting reliance on Article V if a different result was desired); Pollock v. Farmers' Loan and Trust Co., 158 US 601 (1895) (suggesting a constitutional amendment needed to authorize Congress to enact income tax legislation).
14. The Court's suggestion of a constitutional amendment in *Clinton v. City of New York* also could have been criticism directed at Congress, implicitly suggesting the need for more thoughtful consideration of the question of whether to provide the president line-item-veto authority. In *Pollock v. Farmers' Loan and Trust Co.*, 158 US 601, 635 (1895) the Court found federal income tax legislation unconstitutional and suggested a constitutional amendment to allow time for "the sober second thought of every part of the country." Historian Lucas Powe has interpreted this as the Court's strong criticism of Democrats and Populists who supported federal income tax legislation in the late nineteenth century, not too subtlety suggesting that they had failed to exercise such a sober second thought. Powe, *The Supreme Court and the American Elite*, 156–57.
15. See Louis Fisher and Neal Devins, *Political Dynamics of Constitutional Law* (5th ed.) (St. Paul: West Group, 2011), 137.
16. See discussion in Kammen, *The Machine That Would Go of Itself*, 390.
17. See Vile, *Encyclopedia of Constitutional Amendments*, 32 (pointing out the irony of Jefferson's need, as president, to borrow $15 million to finance the Louisiana Purchase).
18. Vile, *Encyclopedia of Constitutional Amendments*, 32; David E. Kyvig, "Refining or Resisting Modern Government? The Balanced Budget Amendment to the US Constitution," 28 *Akron Law Review* 97, 102–3 (1995).
19. Kyvig, "Refining or Resisting Modern Government?," 99 (comparing the balanced budget amendment efforts to the Energizer bunny because in the face of Congress's persistent rejections, the effort to amend "just keeps going, and going, and going").
20. Kyvig, "Refining or Resisting Modern Government?," 98, 100, 104–6.
21. These state petitions varied widely with respect to the constitutional amendment sought. Some provided for limiting federal spending to a percentage of the gross domestic product. Some sought to prevent expenditures from exceeding revenues and of these, some provided exceptions to permit expenditures required to respond to national emergencies such as a natural disaster or a declaration of war. Others required a supermajority to raise taxes or raise the federal debt. See Vile, *Encyclopedia of Constitutional Amendments*, 33 (detailing the various proposals from state legislatures); Kyvig, "Refining or Resisting Modern Government?," 108–9 (same). The goal of all of these petitions was the same, however: to sway Congress to propose a balanced budget constitutional amendment itself, or otherwise enact legislation to restrain growth in the federal deficit, rather than risk a mandate from the states requiring that Congress call a constitutional convention.
22. See Russell L. Caplan, *Constitutional Brinksmanship* (New York: Oxford University Press, 1988), 84.
23. See, e.g., Caplan, *Constitutional Brinksmanship*, 84–89; John R. Vile, *Constitu-*

tional Change in the United States: A Comparative Study of the Role of Constitutional Amendment, Judicial Interpretations, and Legislative and Executive Actions (Westport, CT: Praeger, 1994), 63.

In 1992, Congress also enacted legislation designed to derail a pending constitutional amendment that regulated federal spending, but this effort failed to halt the amendment's ratification. In 1789, Congress had approved, and sent to the states for ratification, the congressional pay raise limitation amendment. Lacking ratification from enough state legislatures to become part of the Constitution, it languished for two hundred years. The amendment ratification effort resurfaced in 1982 and states began adding their ratification to a growing list. Resentment against Congress and government spending fueled interest in this amendment. By 1989, thirty-three states had ratified, five shy of the thirty-eight needed to add the provision to the Constitution. Congress reacted, finally, by adopting legislation prohibiting same-term salary increases for members of Congress. This legislation was contrived to eliminate the need for the constitutional amendment. See Kyvig, *Explicit and Authentic Acts*, 466–67. The ploy failed, many more states ratified the amendment, and it entered the Constitution as the Twenty-Seventh Amendment in 1992.

24. See Kyvig, "Refining or Resisting Modern Government?," 118 (concluding that defeat of the balanced budget amendment in 1986 appeared to be explained by the recent enactment of the Gramm-Rudman-Hollings Act).
25. Bowsher v. Synar, 478 US 714 (1986).
26. See Vile, *Encyclopedia of Constitutional Amendments*, 33 (summarizing the congressional votes on balanced budget amendment proposals during the 1990s).
27. Paul G. Cassell, "Barbarians at the Gates: A Reply to the Critics of the Victims' Rights Amendment," 1999 *University of Utah Law Review* 479, 479 (referring to a then-pending proposed constitutional amendment establishing rights for crime victims).
28. Paul G. Cassell, "The Victims' Rights Amendment: A Sympathetic, Clause-By-Clause Analysis," 5 *University of Phoenix Law Review* 301, 301–2 (2012). The 2012 effort was House Joint Resolution 106, introduced on March 26, 2012. The House Judiciary Committee's Subcommittee on the Constitution held a hearing on the proposed amendment on April 26, 2012. See *www.nvcap.org/legis.html* (last visited July 7, 2012).
29. See Vile, *Encyclopedia of Constitutional Amendments*, 496. The amendment effort did not begin in earnest until 1995. Cassell, "The Victims' Rights Amendment," 306. See also Laurence H. Tribe and Paul G. Cassell, "Embed the Rights of Victims in the Constitution," *Los Angeles Times*, July 6, 1998, accessed August 16, 2016, *articles.latimes.com/1998/jul/06/local/me-1150*.
30. The factual portion of this section can be substantiated at Cassell, "The Victims' Rights Amendment," 302–12.
31. Payne v. Tennessee, 501 US 808 (1991).
32. Payne v. Tennessee, 501 US at 819.
33. Payne v. Tennessee, 501 US at 834 (Scalia J., concurring).
34. Cassell, "The Victims' Rights Amendment," 308 (emphasis added) (describing how agreeing to suspend the effort to amend the constitution by adding a Victims'

Rights Amendment was instrumental in Congress's decision to enact Pub. L. No. 108–405, 118 Stat 2260 (2004)).

35. For an additional example of how the constitutional political process circles back upon itself, it is useful to recognize that the current version of the proposed Victim's Rights Amendment is a modification of the original, incorporating many lessons learned from the years of judicial administration of the 2004 federal legislation. Cassell, "The Victims' Rights Amendment," 338.

36. Cassell, "The Victims' Rights Amendment," 338.

37. Pollock v. Farmers' Loan and Trust Co., 157 US 429 (1895) (Pollock I) and Pollock v. Farmers' Loan and Trust Co., 158 US 601 (1895) (Pollock II). In *Springer v. US*, 102 US 586 (1881) the Court unanimously had *upheld* the constitutionality of an 1862 income tax used to help finance the Civil War, concluding that the Constitution's requirement that direct taxes be apportioned according to the population of the states applied only to taxes on real property and head taxes (e.g., taxes on slaves). The Court in *Springer* pointed out that in 1796 it had upheld unanimously a federal tax on carriages in *Hylton v. United States*, 3 US (3 Dall.) 171 (1796), rejecting the argument that it was a "direct tax" that the Constitution required to be apportioned. Pollock's lawyers had urged the Court to void the income tax in order to halt the "communistic march" and reverse "a century of error" regarding the meaning of direct taxes. Robert McCloskey, *The American Supreme Court* (Chicago: University of Chicago Press, 1960).

38. See Nathaniel Wright Stephenson, *Nelson W. Aldrich: A Leader in American Politics* (New York: Charles Scribner's Sons, 1930), 126–27. The tax was a 2 percent tax on income exceeding $4000. It thus was class legislation since it exempted 99 percent of the population and functionally was sectional legislation since it impacted only four states. See Powe, *The Supreme Court and the American Elite*, 156.

39. Loren P. Beth, "*Pollock v. Farmers' Loan and Trust Co.*," in Hall, ed., *The Oxford Guide to United States Supreme Court Decisions*, 279 (concluding that *Pollock* was negated by the Sixteenth Amendment. But even before that amendment's ratification, the Court was poised to reverse its *Pollock* decision as evidenced by the Court's decision in *Flint v Stone Tracy Co.*, 220 US 107 (1911) upholding the constitutionality of a corporate income tax).

40. See Stephenson, *Nelson W. Aldrich*, at 349–56 and n. 29.

41. See Kammen, *The Machine That Would Go of Itself*, 190–92.

42. For an incisive account of the failed Aldrich Ploy and President Taft's concern that again putting the income tax issue to the court would seriously undermine respect for the Court, see Sidney Ratner, *American Taxation* (New York: W. W. Norton, 1942), 270–310.

43. See Vile, *Encyclopedia of Constitutional Amendments*, 345–46.

44. When the United States first took control of the Philippines (and Cuba and Puerto Rico) following the Spanish-American War, it was uncertain whether it would require a constitutional amendment for the federal government to acquire these territories and *not* grant them independence but rather hold them as permanent overseas possessions It became necessary for the Supreme Court, in what are known as the *Insular Cases*, to clarify the constitutional question and rule that territorial acquisition is an inherent attribute of sovereignty. Therefore, Congress

could do with these territories what it wished, including holding them as permanent overseas possessions. See Bartholomew H. Sparrow, *The Insular Cases and Emergence of American Empire* (Lawrence: University Press of Kansas, 2006). The *Insular Cases* led to "Mr. Dooley" famously concluding that "no matter whether th' constitution follows th' flag or not, th' Supreme Court follows th' iliction returns." See quotation reprinted in Powe, *The Supreme Court and the American Elite*, 162 (quoting Finley Peter Dunne's newspaper column featuring the satiric observations of the fictional Irish saloonkeeeper, Mr. Dooley).

45. Evan Thomas, *The War Lovers* (New York: Little, Brown, 2010), 12, 387–89.
46. Federal Research Division, Library of Congress, Library of Congress Country Studies, "Philippines: The First Phase of United States Rule, 1898–1935," accessed August 16, 2016, *workmall.com/wfb2001/philippines/philippines_history_the_first_phase_of_united_states_rule_1898_1935.html*; Federal Research Division, Library of Congress, Library of Congress Country Studies, "Philippines: The Jones Act," accessed August 16, 2016, *countrystudies.us/philippines/18.htm*.
47. See "Philippine Independence Comes Up before Senate," *Florence Morning News*, December 9, 1932, accessed August 16, 2016, *newspaperarchive.com/us/south-carolina/florence/florence-morning-news/1932/12-09* (describing Copeland's constitutional challenge to congressional authority to grant Philippine independence without a constitutional amendment). See also "Suit Disputes Freedom Deed," *Daily Capital News* (Jefferson City, Mo), October 19, 1938, accessed August 16, 2016, *newspaperarchive.com/dailycapitalnews/19381019/page10* (discussing declaratory judgment action challenging constitutionality of the grant of Philippine independence in the Tydings-McDuffe Act and the view of Senator Copeland that independence grant was unconstitutional).
48. In June 1964, Barry Goldwater similarly deployed Article V as a straw man during his effort to denounce the Civil Rights Act of 1964, then pending in Congress. At a time when the Civil Rights Act was moving to final passage, Goldwater condemned it as an attempt to regulate private enterprise through unconstitutional civil rights legislation. While Goldwater never would have supported a constitutional amendment to permit Congress to enact legislation such as the 1964 Civil Rights Act, he argued for rejection of the pending legislation because, without authority from a formal Article V amendment ratified by the states, Congress lacked legislative power to enact the pending legislation. See Bruce Ackerman, *We the People, Vol. 3: The Civil Rights Revolution* (Cambridge, MA: Belknap Press, 2014), 68.
49. *Cf.* Friedrichs v. California Teachers Association, 136 S. Ct. 1083 (No. 14–915) (2016), addressing the question of whether it is unconstitutional for state agencies to negotiate labor agreements providing that public employees must pay a "fair share" of the costs of negotiating for better wages and benefits and affirming, by an equally divided court, the judgment below (2014 WL 10076847 (9th Cir. 2014)) that it is constitutional for state agencies to enter into such agreements.
50. Agreements requiring post-hire union "membership" are called union shop agreements. The 1935 Wagner Act (National Labor Relations Act) permitted unions to lawfully negotiate closed shop agreements (requiring all workers to be union members as a condition for being hired) but these have been unlawful since the

1947 Taft-Hartley Act (Labor Management Relations Act). See Florian Bartosic and Roger Hartley, *Labor Relations Law in the Private Sector* (2d ed.) (Philadelphia: ALI-ABA, 1986), 419–60.

51. See NLRB v. General Motors Corp., 373 US 734, 739 (1963) ("membership" obligation means only that a worker pay the periodic union dues and initiation fee). See also Communication Workers v. Beck, 487 US 735 (1988) (holding that non-member objectors may only be charged that portion of the regular union dues paid by members that represents the percentage used for representational purposes).
52. See Marc Dixon, "Limiting Labor: Business Political Mobilization and Union Setback in the States," 19 *Journal of Policy History* 313, 318–19 (2007).
53. See, e.g., American Federation of Labor v. Watson, 327 US 582 (1946) (preemption challenge by unions to Florida right-to-work law did not reach the merits of the preemption argument because case remanded to district court for clarification of Florida's intended scope of enforcement).
54. See Charles W. Baird, "Right to Work Before and After 14(b)." 19 *Journal of Labor Research* 471 (1998) (citing legislative history supporting the view that sponsors of the Wagner Act in both the Senate and the House expressed the opinion that the legislation would not preclude states from enacting legislation banning the *closed* shop—but no such reference as to the *union* shop).
55. Algoma Plywood and Veneer Co. v. Wisconsin Employment Relations Board, 336 US 301, 311 (1949) (explaining in dicta that during World War II the Constitution's War Power Clause authorized the federal government to override state right-to-work laws but the legislative history of Wagner Act manifests a congressional intent to leave unimpaired the states' authority to regulate union security agreements, and this legislative intent is controlling once the nation is no longer at war).
56. See Dixon, "Limiting Labor," 316–17 (expressing doubt regarding the constitutionality of state laws regulating union activities in conflict with the Wagner Act). It turned out that the fear of federal preemption was misplaced, because the Supreme Court concluded that the Wagner Act permitted states to enact right-to-work statutes, but did not so decide until 1949. See Algoma Plywood and Veneer Co. v. Wisconsin Employment Relations Bd., 336 US 301, 311 (1949).
57. See Dixon, "Limiting Labor," 321.
58. Maurice Winger, "Restrictive Wartime Labor Measures in Congress," 9 *Law and Contemporary Problems* 502 (1942); Walter Davenport, "Savior from Texas," *Collier's Weekly*, August 18, 1945, 79 (reporting that the objective of the Christian American Association was amending the Constitution by adding an open-shop provision and stating that United States senator Wilbert Lee O'Daniel (D-TX) intended to guide the proposed amendment through Congress). A popular weekly news magazine reported in 1945 that a Christian American Association leader stated that the organization was funded by "citizens whose opinions about labor unions, communism, Negroes, Jews, Franklin D. Roosevelt, Mrs. Roosevelt, and similar 'un-American influences' coincides with those of the leadership of the Christian American Association." Davenport, "Savior from Texas," 79.
59. Proposed amendment language quoted in Vile, *Encyclopedia of Constitutional Amendments*, 38; Baird, "Right to Work," n. 8; Dixon, "Limiting Labor," 323–24.

See discussion at Andrew E. Kersten and Kriste Lindenmeyer, eds., *Politics and Progress: American Society and the State Since 1865* (Westport, CT: Praeger, 2001), 73–80.

60. See Zev J. Elgen, "A Moral/Contractual Approach to Labor Law Reform," 63 *Hastings Law Journal* 695, n. 94 (2012) (citing twenty-three states, but subsequent to publication of this law review article Wisconsin and Michigan enacted a RTW law). State legislatures continue to consider and enact right-to-work legislation. See, e.g., Lydia DePillus, "West Virginia House Passes Right to Work Bill after Harsh Debate," *Washington Post*, February 4, 2016, accessed August 16, 2016, *www.washingtonpost.com/news/wonk/wp/2016/02/04/amidrancourousdebatewest virginiasetsrighttoworkbillonpathtonearcertainpassage* (reporting that by February 2016, both houses of the West Virginia legislature had enacted a RTW statute). For the most current status of right-to-work legislation throughout the United States, see *www.nrtw.org/b/rtw_faq.htm*.

61. It is useful to note that there was strong congressional support for some right-to-work provisions in 1947. President Truman vetoed the Taft-Hartley Act and it was enacted over his veto, an achievement that required a two-thirds supermajority in each House of Congress. Nevertheless, enactment of O'Daniel's proposed amendment could not have been a realistic goal. A majority vote from thirty-six state legislatures was required for a constitutional amendment's ratification in 1947. Thus a single chamber in any of thirteen state legislatures could thwart an amendment's ratification. In 1946, Democrats controlled seventeen state legislatures, Republicans controlled twenty-five, and in four no political party controlled the entire legislature. In 1948 the state-by-state breakdown of party control rose to twenty state legislatures controlled by Democrats, sixteen by Republicans, and in ten no party controlled. See Michael J. Dubin, *Party Affiliations in State Legislatures: A Year By Year Summary 1796–2006* (Jefferson, NC: McFarland Publishing, 2007), 9. The above total is forty-six, rather than forty-eight, because in 1946 both Nebraska and Minnesota had nonpartisan legislative elections. See Morris P. Fiorina, "Divided Government in the American States: A Byproduct of Legislative Professionalism?," 88 *American Political Science Review* 304, 314, n. 2 (1994). Given the overt anti-union animus inspiring the right-to-work constitutional amendment drive and the traditional alignment of the Democratic party and the labor union movement (except in the South), it is clear that in 1948 such an amendment could not have been ratified. Even in 1947, a member of Congress could not have reasonably expected support by both chambers of thirty-six state legislatures, given the above-noted 1946 state-by-state breakdown of party control of state legislatures. In addition, in 1947, there were nearly fifteen million union members (25 percent of the workforce) whose political power could have been brought to bear to oppose ratification of such a constitutional amendment. See Sylvester Petro, "Union Power and Government Aid," *The Freeman*, 26–39 (July 1960), accessed August 16, 2016, *fee.org/articles/union-power-and-government-aid* (listing union membership by year).

62. See discussion in Fisher and Devins, *Political Dynamics of Constitutional Law*, 110–23.

63. Fisher and Devins, *Political Dynamics of Constitutional Law*, 122–23.

64. INS v. Chadha, 462 US 919 (1983).

218 Notes to Pages 126–32

65. INS v. Chadha, 462 US at 1002 (White J., dissenting).
66. See Fisher and Devins, *Political Dynamics of Constitutional Law*, 125.
67. See Louis Fisher, "The Legislative Veto: Invalidated, It Survives," 50 *Law and Contemporary Problems* 273, 288–89 (1993).
68. Fisher, "The Legislative Veto," 288–90.
69. See Fisher, "The Legislative Veto," 273.
70. "The dog that didn't bark" is an expression from the Sherlock Holmes mystery "Silver Blaze," one of the fifty-six Sherlock Holmes short stories written by British author Sir Arthur Conan Doyle. A killer entered and left the estate grounds one night but without the guard dog barking an alarm at the intruder's presence as expected. From this non-event, Holmes reasoned that the dog must have known the killer, and that was an important clue that led to identifying the criminal.

Chapter 5

1. See Henry Adams, "The Great Secession Winter of 1860–61," in George E. Hochfield, ed., *The Great Secession Winter of 1860–61 and Other Essays* (New York: Sagamore Press, 1958).
2. The single best overview of the Great Secession Winter is found in James M. McPherson, *Battle Cry of Freedom: The Civil War Era* (New York: Oxford University Press, 1988), 246–307.
3. McPherson, *Battle Cry of Freedom*, 249. As secession began, both Republicans and Democrats viewed the crisis with differing levels of seriousness. Many, such as Lincoln, concluded that it was not credible to view secession as a mass movement, rather preferring to view it as the conspiratorial work of a slaveholding minority that eventually would be overtaken by a surge of support for the Union. Others wrote off the secession that occurred during February 1861 as mostly a calculated effort to bleed concessions from the North. While devotion to the Union continued in the South following Lincoln's election, especially in the upper-South border states, Northerners tended to underestimate the seriousness of crisis and overestimated the moderating influence Southern Unionists could or would provide. David M. Potter, *The Impending Crisis: 1848–1861* (completed and edited by Don E. Fehrenbacher) (New York: Harper Collins, 1976), 472, 517, 525, 558.
4. Potter, *The Impending Crisis*, 519; Kyvig, *Explicit and Authentic Acts*, 146–47.
5. Ames, *The Proposed Amendments*, 194. One member of Congress proposed seventeen amendments, "protecting slavery from every conceivable interference." Eric Foner, *The Fiery Trial: Abraham Lincoln and American Slavery* (New York: W. W. Norton, 2010), 147–48.
6. McPherson, *Battle Cry of Freedom*, 254.
7. McPherson, *Battle Cry of Freedom*, 255; Potter, *The Impending Crisis*, 511 (explaining that while there was significant division in the South regarding secession, Southerners shared a united view that Southern states had certain rights that the North must observe and that no Southern state would tolerate assertion of federal force against a sister Southern state).
8. Foner, *The Fiery Trial*, 157 (concluding that once it became clear that the seven states that already had seceded would maintain their resolve to withdraw from the Union, war seemed inevitable).
9. See Potter, *The Impending Crisis*, 565. Lincoln's inaugural address stated: "This

country . . . belongs to the people who inhabit it. Whenever they shall grow weary of the existing Government, they can exercise their *constitutional* right of amending it. . . . Many worthy and patriotic citizens are desirous of having the National Constitution amended. . . . Under existing circumstances, [I] favor rather than oppose a fair opportunity being afforded the people to act upon it. I will venture to add that to me the convention mode seems preferable. . . . I understand a proposed amendment to the Constitution . . . has passed Congress, to the effect that the Federal Government shall never interfere with the domestic institutions of the States, including that of persons held to service. . . . Such a provision [is] now . . . implied constitutional law, [but] I have no objection to its being made express and irrevocable." The Avalon Project, "First Inaugural Address of Abraham Lincoln," accessed August 16, 2016, *avalon.law.yale.edu/19th_century/lincoln1.asp*.

10. See Don E. Fehrenbacher, *The Dred Scott Case: Its Significance in American Law and Politics* (New York: Oxford University Press, 1978), 547–50 (arguing the improbability of the North ever ratifying a constitutional amendment protecting slavery); Arthur Bestor, "The American Civil War as a Constitutional Crisis," 69 *American Historical Review* 327, 334, 341 (1964) (explaining that the South demanded the right of territorial expansion of the slaveholding system and protection from state or federal interference with the domestic slave trade).

11. See, e.g., Potter, *The Impending Crisis*, 529–30. Potter explains that Virginia rejected secession on February 4, 1861, in order to give reconciliation efforts a fair chance of succeeding, but support for Unionism in Virginia faded as the hope of compromise dwindled. Secessionists in the border states faced powerful forces that impeded secession. These included the border states' stronger economic ties to the North compared to the Southern states abutting the Gulf of Mexico, a long and strong tradition of Unionism in the upper-South states, and strong Unionist leaders in the border states. But, the most potent force keeping the border states in the Union was optimism of a political solution grounded on the willingness of the North to offer the South concessions. Potter, *The Impending Crisis*, 506–8 and n. 47.

12. See McPherson, *Battle Cry of Freedom*, 292–93. Kentucky continued to send representatives to Congress even as the Confederate Congress admitted Kentucky into the Confederacy as the thirteenth state following receipt of an ordinance of secession from a provisional government formed at a convention of two hundred delegates. McPherson, *Battle Cry of Freedom*, 296–97.

13. McPherson, *Battle Cry of Freedom*, 293, 306–7.

14. See discussion at Potter, *The Impending Crisis*, 529–30.

15. United States v. Curtis-Wright Export Corp., 299 US 304, 319–20 (1936).

16. See Phillip R. Trimble, *International Law: United States Foreign Relations Law* (New York: Foundation Press, 2002), 80.

17. For a discussion of the three periods of US foreign-relations history between the end of the First World War until the end of the Second World War, see Martin Folly and Niall Palmer, *Historical Dictionary of US Diplomacy from World War I through World War II* (Lanham, MD: Rowman and Littlefield, 2010), xxxv–lxxxiii.

18. See Arthur Schlesinger Jr., *The Imperial Presidency* (Boston: Houghton Mifflin, Harcourt, 2004), 98.

19. The 16 Irreconcilables were United States senators who opposed to the United

States joining the League of Nations. Their inability to compromise with Wilson kept the United States out of that international organization. See John Milton Cooper Jr., *Breaking the Heart of the World: Woodrow Wilson and the Fight Over the League of Nations* (Reprint Edition) (New York: Cambridge University Press, 2010); Ralph Stone, *The Irreconcilables: The Fight against the League of Nations* (New York: W. W. Norton and Co., 1973).

20. Stone, *The Irreconcilables*, 97–98.
21. See Michael J. Gerhart, *The Forgotten Presidents: Their Untold Constitutional Legacy* (New York: Oxford University Press. 2013), 214; Folly and Palmer, *Historical Dictionary of US Diplomacy*, xlvi.
22. Kyvig, *Explicit and Authentic Acts*, 317.
23. See Folly and Palmer, *Historical Dictionary of US Diplomacy*, xliii.
24. Kennedy, *Freedom from Fear*, 400–401; Olson, *Those Angry Days*, 28 (noting that according to a 1937 Gallup poll, 70 percent of Americans believed that the county's entry into World War I had been a mistake).
25. See Folly and Palmer, *Historical Dictionary of US Diplomacy*, lvi.
26. Ronald Schaffer, "General Stanley D. Embick: Military Dissenter," 37 *Military Affairs* 89, 92 (1973). On the pre-World War II isolationism among high-ranking United States military officers see Olson, *Those Angry Days*, 298–300.
27. Kennedy, *Freedom from Fear*, 402.
28. See Ronald Powaski, *Toward an Entangling Alliance: American Isolationism, Internationalism, and Europe, 1901–1950* (Westport, CT: Greenwood Publishing Group, 1991), 74.
29. See, e.g., Kyvig, *Explicit and Authentic Acts*, 323.
30. See Powaski, *Toward an Entangling Alliance*, 73.
31. See discussion at Kennedy, *Freedom From Fear*, 460–61.
32. Schlesinger, *The Imperial Presidency*, 97–99.
33. The proposed version of the Bricker Amendment reported by the Senate Foreign Relations Committee in 1953 is quoted in David M. Golove, "Treaty-Making and the Nation: The Historical Foundations of the Nationalist Conception of the Treaty Power," 98 *University of Michigan Law Review* 1075, 1275 and n. 680 (2000). The proposed amendment also would have empowered Congress to regulate presidential-executive agreements, as is discussed below.
34. Glendon A. Schubert, "Politics and the Constitution: The Becker Amendment during 1953," 16 *Journal of Politics* 257, 258 (1954).
35. Louis Henkin, "US Ratification of Human Rights Conventions: The Ghost of Senator Bricker," 89 *American Journal of International Law* 341, 348 (1995).
36. Missouri v. Holland, 252 US 416 (1920).
37. Santovincenzo v. Egan, 284 US 30, 40 (1931).
38. De Geofroy v. Riggs, 133 US 258, 267 (1890).
39. See Whitney v. Robertson, 124 US 190 (1888) (also holding that a treaty supersedes conflicting federal legislation enacted prior in time).
40. Foster v. Neilson, 27 US (2 Pet.) 253, 314 (1829).
41. See discussion in Trimble, *International Law*, 152–53.
42. Trimble, *International Law*, 153–54 (citing the UN Convention on the International Sale of Goods, which operates like the Uniform Commercial Code (UCC), and the Warsaw Convention, which provides a cause of action for

43. Asakura v. City of Seattle, 265 US 332, 343 (1924).
44. Oona A. Hathaway, et al., "The Treaty Power: Its History, Scope, and Limits," 98 *Cornell Law Review* 239, 260 (2013).
45. See discussion at Curtis A. Bradley and Jack L. Goldsmith, "Treaties, Human Rights, and Conditional Consent," 149 *University of Pennsylvania Law Review* 399, 410–11 (2000).
46. Duane Tananbaum, *The Bricker Amendment Controversy: A Test of Eisenhower's Political Leadership* (Ithaca, NY: Cornell University Press, 1988), 6, 27, 54, 93.
47. By 1948, four members of the Supreme Court had concluded that California's Alien Land Law violated the UN Charter. See Oyama v. California, 332 US 633, 647, 650 (1948) (concurring opinions by Black J. with Douglas J. joining and by Murphy J. with Rutledge J. joining). In *Sei Fujii v. State*, 217 P.2d 481 (Cal. App 2d Dist. 1950) a California intermediate court of appeals had concluded that the human rights provisions of the Charter are self-executing and invalidated the California Alien Land Law. The California Supreme Court concluded that the Charter's provisions were *not* self-executing but struck down the California statute based on the Fourteenth Amendment's Equal Protection Clause. Sei Fujii v. State, 38 Cal. 2d 718 (Cal. 1952).
48. The Bricker Amendment would have reversed *Holland* through its famous "which clause," a clause that provided that a treaty would become effective domestically "only through legislation *which would be valid in the absence of a treaty*" (emphasis added).
49. See Heart of Atlanta Hotel v. United States, 379 US 241 (1964) (first case upholding Congress's Commerce Clause Power to ban private racial discrimination in public accommodations). See also Katzenbach v. McClung ("Ollie's Barbecue"), 379 US 294 (1964) (same with respect to a small, essentially intrastate, restaurant).
50. Henkin, "The Ghost of Senator Bricker," 348.
51. Oona A. Hathaway, "Treaties End: The Past, Present, and Future of International Lawmaking in the United States," 117 *Yale Law Journal* 1236, 1302 (2008). Hathaway summarizes views of ABA president Frank Holman and reports in *Time* magazine expressing fear that human rights treaties would end racial segregation, either by empowering the federal government to enact civil rights legislation or by finding that racial segregation in the United States constitutes the international crime of "genocide" (1303 and n. 200). See also Golove, "Treaty-Making and the Nation," 1274 (concluding that conservative members of Congress and racist Southern politicians supported the Bricker Amendment due to their anxiety that human rights treaties could and would be used to attack racial segregation).
52. The Supreme Court's 1957 decision in *Reid v. Covert* held that the Treaty Power *is limited* by the Constitution's individual rights constraints. Reid v. Covert, 354 US 1, 16 (1957) But *Reid v. Covert* had not yet been decided when the Bricker Amendment was first proposed in Congress.
53. See Trimble, *International Law*, 132–34.
54. See Kennedy, *Freedom from Fear*, 460–61.
55. See Trimble, *International Law*, 133.
56. United States v. Belmont, 301 US 324 (1937).

57. United States v. Pink, 315 US 203 (1942).
58. United States v. Pink, 315 US at 230.
59. See United States v. Guy W. Capps, Inc., 204 F.2d 655 (4th Cir. 1953) (presidential-executive agreement not to export certain products to the United States unlawful when use of presidential-executive agreement for this purpose contravenes preexisting procedures Congress had provided for restricting imports).
60. See Tananbaum, *The Bricker Amendment Controversy*, 221.
61. See Richard W. Leopold, *The Growth of American Foreign Policy* (New York: Alfred A. Knopf, 1962), 555.
62. Leopold, *The Growth of American Foreign Policy*, 716–17.
63. Leopold, *The Growth of American Foreign Policy*, 716–17; Joshua B. Freeman, *American Empire, 1945–2000* (New York: Viking, 2012), 105 (stating that the Senate rejected the Bricker Amendment only with the assistance of Minority leader Lyndon B. Johnson, who concluded that an alliance with Republicans was in the Democrats' best interests).
64. Henkin, "The Ghost of Senator Bricker," 348–49. Accord Oona A. Hathaway, "Treaties End," 1303.
65. See Statement by Secretary of State Dulles, in Treaties and Executive Agreements: Hearings Before a Subcomm. of the Senate Comm. on the Judiciary, 83d Cong., 825 (1953).
66. Quoted in Bradley and Goldsmith, "Treaties, Human Rights, and Conditional Consent," 410–11. See Curtis A. Bradley, "The Treaty Power and American Federalism, Part II," 99 *University of Michigan Law Review* 98, 123–24 (2000) (quoting in detail Secretary Dulles's commitments on behalf of the Eisenhower administration in 1953 and 1955). Accord Bruno V. Bitker, "The United States and International Codification of Human Rights: A Case of Split Personality," in Natalie Kaufman Hevener, ed., *The Dynamics of Human Rights in United States Foreign Policy* (New Brunswick, NJ: Transaction Publishers, 1981), 90 (concluding that the price imposed for defeating the Bricker Amendment was a several year cessation of congressional consideration of human rights treaties).
67. Quoted at Bitker, "The United States and International Codification of Human Rights," 90.
68. Bitker, "The United States and International Codification of Human Rights," 90.
69. Henkin, "The Ghost of Senator Bricker," 341–50.
70. Trimble, *International Law*, 117–19; 166–77 (summarizing types of RUDs that have been attached to consent to ratification of treaties).
71. Trimble, *International Law*, 119.
72. For a vigorous defense of the Senate's use of RUDs in human rights treaties see Bradley and Goldsmith, "Treaties, Human Rights, and Conditional Consent," 402–68. For a denunciation of the use of RUDS and the claim that they jeopardize much of the post–World War II success in according international human rights standards the status of international law, see Henkin, "The Ghost of Senator Bricker," 341–50. See also Ackerman and Golove, "Is NAFTA Constitutional?," 108 *Harvard Law Review* 799, 905 (1995) (objecting that RUDS encourage political obfuscation and political irresponsibility by permitting senators to camouflage opposition to a treaty by coupling a vote to ratify with a crippling reservation).

Notes to Pages 148–55   223

73. Medellin v. Texas, 552 US 491 (2008).
74. See, e.g., Rebecca M. Kysar, "On the Constitutionality of Tax Treaties," 38 *Yale Journal of International Law* 1, 18 (2013).
75. See Oona A. Hathaway, Sabria McElroy, and Sara Aronchik Solow, "International Law at Home: Enforcing Treaties in US Courts," 37 *Yale Journal of International Law* 51, 71–76 (2012).
76. Kammen, *The Machine That Would Go of Itself*, 321.
77. Kyvig, *Explicit and Authentic Acts*, 346.
78. Quoted in David A. Nichols, *Eisenhower 1956: The President's Year of Crisis—Suez and the Brink of War* (New York: Simon and Schuster, 2012), 167. See generally Tananbaum, "The Bricker Amendment Controversy," 218–19 (expressing the view that one fallout of the Bricker controversy was alerting Eisenhower to consult with Congress on foreign policy matters).
79. Reid v. Covert, 354 US 1 (1957).
80. Kinsella v. Krueger, 351 US 470 (1956); Reid v. Covert, 351 US 487 (1956).
81. Reid v. Covert, 354 US at 17.
82. See, e.g., Tananbaum, "The Bricker Amendment Controversy," 213. Accord Golove, "Treaty-Making and the Nation," 277 (finding in Justice Black's opinion a deliberate effort to respond to apprehension inflamed by Bricker Amendment supporters).
83. Vile, *Encyclopedia of Constitutional Amendments*, 376.
84. The Restatement of Foreign Relations Law provides that congressional-executive agreements operate domestically as treaties: they supersede inconsistent state law and prior federal law and treaties. See American Law Institute, *Restatement (Third) of Foreign Relations Law* § 111(1) cmt. d and rptr note 2; § 115 cmt. C; § 303 cmt. C.
85. See Ackerman and Golove, "Is NAFTA Constitutional?"
86. Laurence H. Tribe, "Taking Text and Structure Seriously: Reflections on Free-Form Method in Constitutional Interpretation," 108 *Harvard Law Review* 1221 (1995).
87. See Gordon S. Wood, *Empire of Liberty: A History of the Early Republic, 1789–1815* (New York: Oxford University Press, 2009), 32.
88. See Ackerman and Golove, "Is NAFTA Constitutional?," 870–71 and n. 324
89. Ackerman and Golove, "Is NAFTA Constitutional?," 848–49.
90. The historical summary of early amendment efforts to alter the Treaty Clause is drawn from Vile, *Encyclopedia of Constitutional Amendments*, 460–61.
91. See discussion at Hathaway, "Treaties End," 1293–99. Hathaway explains that the trade agreements this legislation authorized the president to negotiate with foreign powers frequently were referred to as "treaties," but in fact were international agreements that the executive branch never submitted to Congress (1295).
92. See Field v. Clark, 143 US (649 1892).
93. Hathaway, "Treaties End," 1298.
94. Ackerman and Golove, "Is NAFTA Constitutional?," 814, 827.
95. Ackerman and Golove, "Is NAFTA Constitutional?," 873.
96. Ackerman and Golove, "Is NAFTA Constitutional?," 861–62.
97. Ackerman and Golove, "Is NAFTA Constitutional?," 862–66, 889–90, and nn. 287–90, 296. Ackerman and Golove report that in an October 1943 Gallup Poll, 54 percent preferred treaty ratification by a majority in both houses of

Congress over the traditional two-thirds Senate vote requirement. By May 1944 that preference for eliminating the Senate's monopoly on treaty ratification rose to 60 percent (863).

98. Ackerman and Golove, "Is NAFTA Constitutional?," 866, 889.
99. Ackerman and Golove, "Is NAFTA Constitutional?," 873, 881–85, 912.
100. Ackerman and Golove, "Is NAFTA Constitutional?," 891–93.
101. American Law Institute, *Restatement (Third) of the Foreign Relations Law of the United States*, § 303 cmt. e (1986).
102. Compare Ackerman and Golove, "Is NAFTA Constitutional?," 924 (arguing that the demand for constitutional amendment and the mandate manifested in the 1944 election generated a wave of popular opinion that effected a transformative constitutional change without the need to complete the Article V amendment process) with Tribe, "Taking Text and Structure Seriously," 1285 (arguing that the Senate's acceptance of the compromise did not signal a constitutional change as much as the Senate's defensive response to the real risk that a constitutional amendment might pass that would terminate the Senate's eminent role in the treaty-approval process).

Conclusion

1. Adam Clymer, "Dale Bumpers, Liberal Stalwart of Arkansas Politics, Dies at 90," *New York Times*, January 2, 2016, accessed August 16, 2016, *www.nytimes.com/2016/01/03/us/dalebumpersliberalstalwartofarkansaspoliticsdiesat90.html?_r=0*.

Bibliography

Ackerman, Bruce. "Higher Lawmaking," in Sanford Levinson, ed., *Responding to Imperfection: The Theory and Practice of Constitutional Amendment*. Princeton, NJ: Princeton University Press, 1995.

———. "The Living Constitution." 120 *Harvard Law Review* 1737 (2007).

———. *We the People, Vol. 1: Foundations*. Cambridge, MA: Belknap Press, 1991.

———. *We the People, Vol. 2: Transformations*. Cambridge, MA: Belknap Press, 1998.

———. *We the People, Vol. 3: The Civil Rights Revolution*. Cambridge, MA: Belknap Press, 2014.

———. "Constitutional Politics/Constitutional Law." 99 *Yale Law Journal* 453 (1989).

———. "The Storrs Lectures: Discovering the Constitution." 93 *Yale Law Journal* 1013 (1984).

Ackerman, Bruce, and David Golove. "Is NAFTA Constitutional?" 108 *Harvard Law Review* 799 (1995).

Ackerman, Bruce, and Jennifer Nou. "Canonizing the Civil Rights Revolution: The People and the Poll Tax." 13 *Northwestern University Law Review* 63 (2009).

Adams, Henry. "The Great Secession Winter of 1860–61," in George E. Hochfield, ed., *The Great Secession Winter of 1860–61 and Other Essays*. New York: Sagamore Press, 1958.

American Law Institute. *Restatement (Third) of Foreign Relations Law*.

Ames, Herman V. *The Proposed Amendments to the Constitution of the United States During the First Century of Its History*. Annual Report, American Historical Association (1896). Breinigsville, PA: Kessinger Legacy Reprints, 2011.

Ariens, Michael. "A Thrice-Told Tale, or Felix the Cat." 107 *Harvard Law Review* 620 (1994).

Arnold, R. Douglas. *The Logic of Congressional Action*. New Haven, CT: Yale University Press, 1990.

Bacon, Richard G. "Rum, Romanism, and Romer: Equal Protection and the Blaine Amendment in State Constitutions." 6 *Delaware Law Review* 1 (2003).

Baird, Charles W. "Right to Work Before and After 14(b)." 19 *Journal of Labor Research* 471 (1998).

Balkin, Jack M. *Constitutional Redemption: Political Faith in an Unjust World*. Cambridge, MA: Harvard University Press, 2011.

Banner, James M. *To the Hartford Convention: The Federalists and the Origins of Party Politics in Massachusetts, 1789–1815*. New York: Alfred A. Knopf, 1970.

Barasko, Maryann. "Civic Engagement and Voluntary Associations: Reconsidering the Role of the Governance Structures of Advocacy Groups." 37 *Polity* 315 (2005).

Barclay, Scott, and Shauna Fisher. "Cause Lawyers in the First Wave of Same Sex Marriage Litigation," in Austin Sarat and Stuart A. Scheingold, eds., *Cause Lawyers and Social Movements*. Redwood City, CA: Stanford University Press, 2006.

Barnes, Robert. "Supreme Court Fails Frequently, Professor Writes." *Washington Post*, A15, September 29, 2014.

Barnett, Randy E. "The Original Meaning of the Necessary and Proper Clause." 6 *University of Pennsylvania Journal of Constitutional Law* 183 (2003).

Bartosic, Florian, and Roger Hartley. *Labor Relations Law in the Private Sector* (2d ed.). Philadelphia: ALI-ABA, 1986.

Bartrum, Ian. "The Constitutional Structure of Disestablishment." 2 *New York University Journal of Law and Liberty* 311 (2007).

Beaney, William M., and Edward N. Beiser. "Presidential Reactions to the Supreme Court: Altering Personnel and Power," in Theodore L. Becker and Malcolm M. Feeley, eds., *The Impact of Supreme Court Decisions* (2d ed.). New York: Oxford University Press, 1973.

———. "Prayer and Politics: The Impact of *Engel* and *Schempp* on the Political Process," in Theodore L. Becker and Malcolm M. Feeley, eds., *The Impact of Supreme Court Decisions: Empirical Studies* (2d ed.). New York: Oxford University Press, 197.

Belknap, Michael R. "Twenty-Fourth Amendment," in Hall, ed., *The Oxford Companion to the Supreme Court of the United States* (2d ed.). New York: Oxford University Press, 2005.

Bernstein, Richard B. "The Sleeper Wakes: The History and Legacy of the Twenty-Seventh Amendment." 61 *Fordham Law Review* 497 (1992).

Bernstein, Richard B., with Jerome Agel. *Amending America: If We Love the Constitution So Much, Why Do We Keep Trying to Change It?* Lawrence: University Press of Kansas, 1993

Berry, Mary Francis. *Why ERA Failed: Politics, Women's Rights, and the Amending Process of the Constitution*. Bloomington: Indiana University Press, 1986.

Bestor, Arthur. "The American Civil War as a Constitutional Crisis." 69 *American Historical Review* 327 (1964).

Beth, Loren P. "*Pollock v. Farmers' Loan and Trust Co.*," in Kermit L. Hall, ed., *The Oxford Guide to United States Supreme Court Decisions* (2d ed.). New York: Oxford University Press 2009.

Birkby, Robert H. "The Supreme Court and the Bible Belt: Tennessee Reaction to the *Schempp* Decision," in Theodore L. Becker and Malcolm M. Feeley, eds., *The Impact of Supreme Court Decisions* (2d ed.). New York: Oxford University Press, 1973.

Bitker, Bruno V. "The United States and International Codification of Human Rights: A Case of Split Personality," in Natalie Kaufman Hevener, ed., *The Dynamics of Human Rights in United States Foreign Policy*. New Brunswick, NJ: Transaction Publishers, 1981.

Black, Charles L. "The Proposed Amendment of Article V: A Threatened Disaster." 72 *Yale Law Journal* 957 (1963).

Blaustein, Albert P., and Clarence C. Ferguson. "Avoidance, Evasion and Delay," in

Theodore L. Becker and Malcolm M. Feeley, eds., *The Impact of Supreme Court Decisions: Empirical Studies* (2d ed.). New York: Oxford University Press, 1973.

Bodenhamer, David J. "Lost Vision: The Bill of Rights and Criminal Procedure in American History," in David E. Kyvig, ed., *Unintended Consequences of Constitutional Amendment.* Athens: University of Georgia Press, 2000.

Bolce, Louis, Gerald Maio, and Douglas Muzzio. "The Equal Rights Amendment, Public Opinion and American Constitutionalism." 19 *Polity* 551 (1987).

Bowles, Samuel, and Herbert Gintis. *Democracy and Capitalism: Property, Community, and the Contradictions of Modern Social Thought.* New York: Basic Books, 1986.

Bradley, Curtis A. "The Treaty Power and American Federalism, Part II." 99 *University of Michigan Law Review* 98 (2000).

Bradley Curtis A., and Jack L. Goldsmith. "Treaties, Human Rights, and Conditional Consent." 149 *University of Pennsylvania Law Review* 399 (2000).

Brands, H. W. *American Colossus: The Triumph of Capitalism 1865–1900.* New York: Doubleday, 2010.

Brauer, Carl M. "Women Activists, Southern Conservatives, and the Prohibition of Sex Discrimination in Title VII of the 1964 Civil Rights Act." 49 *Journal of Southern History* 37 (1983).

Brennan, Thomas E. *The Article V Amendatory Constitutional Convention.* Lanham, MD: Lexington Books, 2014.

Brewer, Paul R. *Value War: Public Opinion and the Politics of Gay Rights.* Lanham, MD: Rowman and Littlefield, 2008.

Burns, John MacGregor. *Packing the Court: The Rise of Judicial Power and the Coming Crisis of the Supreme Court.* New York: Penguin, 2009.

———. *Roosevelt: The Lion and the Fox.* New York: Harcourt, Brace, and World, 1956.

Caldeira, Gregory A. "Public Opinion and the US Supreme Court: FDR's Court-Packing Plan." 81 *American Political Science Review* 1139 (1987).

Caplan, Russell. *Constitutional Brinkmanship: Amending the Constitution by National Convention.* New York: Oxford University Press, 1988.

Cardozo, Benjamin N. *The Nature of the Judicial Process.* New Haven, CT: Yale University Press, 1921.

Cassell, Paul G. "Barbarians at the Gates: A Reply to the Critics of the Victims' Rights Amendment." 1999 *University of Utah Law Review* 479.

Chemerinsky, Erwin. "The Vanishing Constitution." 103 *Harvard Law Review* 44 (1989).

———. *The Case Against the Supreme Court.* New York: Viking, 2014.

———. *Constitutional Law: Principles and Policies* (4th ed.). New York: Wolters Kluwer, 2011.

———. "Amending the Constitution." 96 *University of Michigan Law Review* 1561, (1998).

Congressional Record. *Index to the Proceedings and Debates of the Forty-Sixth Congress, First Session (Volume IX).* Washington: Government Printing Office, 1879.

Cook, Brian J. *Bureaucracy and Self-Government: Reconsidering the Role of Public Administration in American Politics* (2d ed.). Baltimore: Johns Hopkins University Press, 2014.

Cooper, John Milton. *Breaking the Heart of the World: Woodrow Wilson and the Fight*

Over the League of Nations. New York: Cambridge University Press, 2010. (Reprint Edition).

Corwin, Edward S. *Court over Constitution: A Study of Judicial Review as an Instrument of Popular Government*. Princeton, CT: Princeton University Press, 1938.

Costain, Ann. "Representing Women: The Transition from Social Movement to Interest Group," in Ellen Boneparth, ed., *Women, Power and Policy*. New York: Pergamon Press, 1982.

Crackel, Theodore J. "Review of Frederick C. Leiner, *Millions for Defense: The Subscription Warships of 1798*." H-SHEAR, H-Net Reviews. November 2000, available at *www.h-net.org/reviews/showrev.php?id=4687*.

Craig Doughtrey, Martha. "Women and the Constitution: Where We Are at the End of the Century." 75 *New York University Law Review* 1 (2000).

Critchlow, Donald T., and Cynthia L. Stachecki. "The Equal Rights Amendment Reconsidered: Politics, Policy, and Social Mobilization in a Democracy." 20 *Journal of Policy History* 157 (2008).

Curator, United States Supreme Court. "Trivia and Traditions of the Court," in Kermit L. Hall, ed., *The Oxford Companion to the Supreme Court of the United States* (2d ed.). New York: Oxford University Press, 2005.

Cushman, Barry. *Rethinking the New Deal Court: The Structure of a Constitutional Revolution*. New York: Oxford University Press, 1998.

Dahl, Robert A. "Decision-Making in a Democracy: The Supreme Court as a National Policy-Maker." 6 *Journal of Public Law* 279 (1957).

———. "The Supreme Court and Judicial Review Performance," in Theodore L. Becker and Malcolm M. Feeley, eds., *The Impact of Supreme Court Decisions* (2d ed.). New York: Oxford University Press, 1973.

Davidson, Roger H. "The Lawmaking Congress." 56 *Law and Contemporary Problems* 99 (1993).

Davis, Richard A. *Proposed Amendments to the Constitution of the United States of America Introduced in Congress from the 91st Congress, 1st Session, Through the 98th Congress, 2nd Session, January 1969–December 1984*. Washington, DC: Congressional Research Service, *Report No. 85–36*, Feb. 1, 1985.

DeConde, Alexander. *The Quasi-War: The Politics and Diplomacy of the Undeclared War with France 1797–1801*. New York: Charles Scribner's Sons, 1966.

Denniston, Lyle. "*Schechter Poultry Corp. v. United States* and *United States v. Butler*," in Melvin I. Urofsky, ed., *The Public Debate over Controversial Supreme Court Decisions*. Thousand Oaks, CA: CQ Press, 2006.

DeRose, Chris. *Founding Rivals: Madison and Monroe, the Bill of Rights and the Election That Saved a Nation*. Washington, DC: Regnery Publishing, 2011.

Devine, Donald. *The Attentive Public: Polyarchical Democracy*. Chicago: Rand McNally, 1970.

Diamond, Martin. *The Founding of the Democratic Republic*. Ithaca, IL: F. E. Peacock, 1981.

Dierenfield, Bruce J. "*Engel v. Vitale*," in Melvin Urofsky, ed., *The Public Debate over Controversial Supreme Court Decisions*. Thousand Oaks, CA: CQ Press, 2006.

Dixon, Marc. "Limiting Labor: Business Political Mobilization and Union Setback in the States." 19 *Journal of Policy History* 313 (2007).

Dixon, Robert G. "Article V: The Comatose Article of Our Living Constitution." 66 *University of Michigan Law Review* 931 (1968).
Dolbeare, Kenneth M., and Phillip E. Hammond. *The School Prayer Decisions: From Court Policy to Local Practice*. Chicago: University of Chicago Press, 1971.
Dorf, Michel C. "Equal Protection Incorporation." 88 *University of Virginia Law Review* 951 (2002).
Dow, David R. "The Plain Meaning of Article V," in Sanford Levinson, ed., *Responding to Imperfection: The Theory and Practice of Constitutional Change*. Princeton, CT: Princeton University Press, 1995.
Dranius, Nick. "Introducing 'Article V 2.0': The Compact for a Balanced Budget." 15 *Engage* (August 22, 2014), available at *www.fedsoc.org/publications/detail/introducingarticlev20compactforabalancedbudget*.
Driver, Justin. "Supremacies and the Southern Manifesto." 92 *University of Texas Law Review* 1053 (2014).
Dubin, Michael J. *Party Affiliations in State Legislatures: A Year By Year Summary 1796–2006*. Jefferson, NC: McFarland Publishing, 2007.
Dupuis, Martin. *Same-Sex Marriage, Legal Mobilization, and the Politics of Rights*. New York: Peter Lang, 2002.
Eaton, Clement. "Censorship of the Southern Mails." 48 *American Historical Review* 266 (1943).
Elgen, Zev J. "A Moral/Contractual Approach to Labor Law Reform." 63 *Hastings Law Journal* 695 (2012).
Elkins, Stanley, and Eric McKitrick. *The Age of Federalism*. New York: Oxford University Press, 1993.
Ennuis, James G., and Richard Schreuer. "Mobilizing Weak Support for Social Movements: The Role of Grievance, Efficacy, and Cost." 66 *Social Forces* 390 (1987).
Epp, Charles R. "Law as an Instrument of Social Reform," in Keith E. Whittington, R. Daniel Kelemen, and Gregory A. Caldeira, eds., *The Oxford Handbook of Law and Politics*. New York: Oxford University Press, 2008.
Epstein, Lee. "The US Supreme Court," in Keith E. Whittington, R. Daniel Kelemen, and Gregory A. Caldeira, eds., *The Oxford Handbook of Law and Politics*. New York: Oxford University Press, 2008.
Epstein, Lee, and Joseph F. Kobylka. *The Supreme Court and Legal Change: Abortion and the Death Penalty*. Chapel Hill: University of North Carolina Press, 1992.
Eskridge, William N. "Channeling: Identity-Based Social Movements and Public Law." 150 *University Of Pennsylvania Law Review* 419 (2001).
Farmer, Mary J., and Donald C. Nieman. "Race, Class, Gender, and the Unintended Consequences of the Fifteenth Amendment," in David E. Kyvig, ed., *Unintended Consequences of Constitutional Amendment*. Athens: University of Georgia Press, 2000.
Federal Research Division, Library of Congress, Library of Congress Country Studies. "Philippines: The Jones Act," available at *countrystudies.us/philippines/18.htm*.
Feeley, Malcolm M. "Power, Impact, and the Supreme Court," in Theodore L. Becker and Malcolm M. Feeley, eds., *The Impact of Supreme Court Decisions* (2d ed.). New York: Oxford University Press, 1973.
Feeley, Malcolm M., and Stuart A. Scheingold. *Politics of Rights: Lawyers, Public Policy, and Political Change* (2d ed.). Ann Arbor: University of Michigan Press, 2004.

Fehrenbacher, Don E. *The Dred Scott Case: Its Significance in American Law and Politics*. New York: Oxford University Press, 1978.

———. *The Slaveholding Republic: An Account of the United States Government's Relations to Slavery*. New York: Oxford University Press, 2001.

Feldman, Noah. "Non-Sectarianism Reconsidered." 18 *Journal of Law and Politics* 65 (2002).

Fiorina, Morris P. "Divided Government in the American States: A Byproduct of Legislative Professionalism?" 88 *American Political Science Review* 304 (1994).

Fischer, David Hackett. *Historical Fallacies: Toward a Logic of Historical Thought*. New York: Harper and Row, 1970.

Fisher, Joseph A. "The Becker Amendment: A Constitutional Trojan Horse." 11 *Journal of Church and State* 427 (1969).

Fisher, Louis. *Presidential Spending Power*. Princeton: Princeton University Press, 1975.

———. *Constitutional Dialogues: Interpretation as Political Process*. Princeton, NJ: Princeton University Press, 1988

———. "The Legislative Veto: Invalidated, It Survives." 50 *Law and Contemporary Problems* 273 (1993).

Fisher, Louis, and Neal Devins. *Political Dynamics of Constitutional Law* (5th ed.). St. Paul, MN: West Publishing, 2011.

Fleming, Thomas. *The Louisiana Purchase*. Hoboken, NJ: Thomas Wiley and Sons, 2003.

Folly, Martin, and Niall Palmer. *Historical Dictionary of US Diplomacy from World War I through World War II*. Lanham, MD: Rowman and Littlefield, 2010.

Foner, Eric. *The Fiery Trial: Abraham Lincoln and American Slavery*. New York: W. W. Norton, 2010.

———. *A Short History of Reconstruction, 1863–1877*. New York: Harper and Row, 1984.

Frankfurter, Felix. "Mr. Justice Roberts." 104 *University of Pennsylvania Law Review* 311 (1955).

Franklin, Cary. "Inventing the 'Traditional Concept' of Sex Discrimination." 125 *Harvard Law Review* 1307 (2012).

Freehling, William W. *The Road to Disunion: Secessionists at Bay, 1776–1854*. New York: Oxford University Press, 1990.

Freeman, Jo. "Social Revolution and the Equal Rights Amendment." 3 *Sociological Forum* 145 (1988).

———. "The Origins of the Women's Liberation Movement." 78 *American Journal of Sociology* 792 (1973).

———. *The Politics of Women's Liberation*. New York: David Mackay, 1975.

Freeman, Joshua B. *American Empire, 1945–2000*. New York: Viking, 2012.

Fried, Charles. "Forward: Revolutions?" 109 *Harvard Law Review* 13 (1995).

Friedman, Barry. *The Will of the People*. New York: Farrar, Strauss and Giroux, 2009.

Friedman, Richard D. "A Reaffirmation: The Authenticity of the Roberts Memorandum, or Felix the non-Forger." 142 *University of Pennsylvania Law Review* 1985 (1994).

Garrow, David. "Mental Decrepitude on the US Supreme Court: The Historical Case for a 28th Amendment." 67 *University of Chicago Law Review* 995 (2000).

Gelb, Joyce, and Marian Lief Palley. "Women and Interest Group Politics: A Comparative Analysis of Federal Decision-Making." 41 *Journal of Politics* 362 (1979).

———. *Women and Public Policies*. Princeton, CT: Princeton University Press, 1982.

Gely, Rafael, and Pablo Spiller. "The Political Economy of Supreme Court Constitutional Decisions: The Case of Roosevelt's Court Packing Plan." 12 *International Review of Law and Economics* 45 (1992).

Gerhart, Michael J. *The Forgotten Presidents: Their Untold Constitutional Legacy*. New York: Oxford University Press, 2013.

Ginsburg, Ruth Bader. "Speaking in a Judicial Voice." 67 *New York University Law Review* 1185 (1992).

Gold, Susan D. *Engle v. Vitale: Prayer in the Schools (Supreme Court Milestones Series)*. Tarrytown, NY: Marshall Cavendish, 2006.

Goldstein, Robert Justin. *Flag Burning and Free Speech: The Case of Texas v. Johnson*. Lawrence: University Press of Kansas, 2000.

Goldstein, Robert Justin. "*Texas v. Johnson*," in Melvin Urofsky, ed., *The Public Debate over Controversial Supreme Court Decisions*. Thousand Oaks, CA: CQ Press, 2006.

Golove, David M. "Treaty-Making and the Nation: The Historical Foundations of the Nationalist Conception of the Treaty Power." 98 *University of Michigan Law Review* 1075 (2000).

Gonzalez, Carlos E. "Popular Sovereign Generated Versus Government Institution Generated Constitutional Norms: When Does a Constitutional Amendment Not Amend the Constitution?" 80 *Washington University Law Quarterly* 127 (2002).

Green, Steven E. "The Blaine Amendment Reconsidered." 36 *American Journal of Legal History* 38 (1992).

Greer, Donald. *The Incidence of Terror During the French Revolution: A Statistical Interpretation* (Harvard Historical Monographs, N. 8). Cambridge: Harvard University Press, 1935.

Griffin, Stephen M. "Constitutionalism in the United States: From Theory to Politics," in Sanford Levinson, ed., *Responding to Imperfection: The Theory and Practice of Constitutional Amendment*. Princeton, CT: Princeton University Press, 1995.

———. "The Nominee Is . . . Article V," in William N. Eskridge Jr., and Sanford Levinson, eds. *Constitutional Stupidities, Constitutional Tragedies*. New York: New York University Press, 1998.

Grimes, Alan P. *Democracy and the Amendments to the Constitution*. Lanham, MD: University Press of America, 1978.

Guerra, Darren Patrick. *Perfecting the Constitution: The Case for the Article V Amendment Process*. Lanham, MD: Lexington Books, 2015.

Hall, Kermit L. "The Amistad," in Kermit L. Hall, ed., *The Oxford Guide to United States Supreme Court Decisions* (2d ed.). New York: Oxford University Press, 2009.

Hamm, Richard F. "Short Euphorias Followed by Long Hangovers: Unintended Consequences of the Eighteenth and Twenty-First Amendments," in David E. Kyvig, ed., *Unintended Consequence of Constitutional Amendment*. Athens: University of Georgia Press, 2000.

Handler, Joel F. "'Constructing the Political Spectacle': The Interpretation of Entitlements, Legalization, and Obligations in Social Welfare History." 56 *Brooklyn Law Review* 899 (1990).

———. *Social Movements and the Legal System: A Theory of Law Reform and Social Change.* New York: Academic Press, 1979.

Harrison, Cynthia E. "A 'New Frontier' for Women: Public Policy for the Kennedy Administration." 67 *Journal of American History* 630 (1980).

Hathaway, Oona A. "Treaties End: The Past, Present, and Future of International Lawmaking in the United States." 117 *Yale Law Journal* 1236 (2008).

Hathaway, Oona A., Spencer Amdur, Celia Choy, Samir Deger-Sen, John Paredes, Sally Pei, and Haley Nix Proctor. "The Treaty Power: Its History, Scope, and Limits." 98 *Cornell Law Review* 239 (2013).

Hathaway, Oona A, Sabria McElroy, and Sara Aronchik Solow. "International Law at Home: Enforcing Treaties in US Courts." 37 *Yale Journal of International Law* 51 (2012).

Haynes, George H. *The Senate of the United States: Its History and Practice.* Boston: Houghton Mifflin, 1938.

Henkin, Louis. "US Ratification of Human Rights Conventions: The Ghost of Senator Bricker." 89 *American Journal of International Law* 341 (1995).

Herring, George C. *From Colony to Superpower: US Foreign Relations Since 1776.* New York: Oxford University Press, 2008.

Hickey, Donald R. *The War of 1812: The Forgotten Conflict.* Urbana: University of Illinois Press, 1989.

Hoogenboom, Ari. *Outlawing the Spoils: A History of the Civil Service Reform Movement 1865–1883.* Urbana: University of Illinois Press, 1961.

Howe, Daniel Walker. *What Hath God Wrought: The Transformation of America, 1815–1848.* New York: Oxford University Press, 2007.

Hunt, Gaillard, ed. *The Writings of James Madison, Comprising His Public Papers and His Private Correspondence, Including His Numerous Letters and Documents Now for the First Time Printed*, Vol. 6. (New York: G. P. Putnam's Sons, 1900) 403–4, available at *files.libertyfund.org/files/1941/1356.06_Bk.pdf.*

Hutchinson, Dennis J. "*Swann v. Charlotte-Mecklenburg Board of Education,*" in Kermit L. Hall, ed., *The Oxford Companion to the Supreme Court of the United States* (2d ed.). New York: Oxford University Press, 2005.

Johnson, Donald Bruce, and Kirk Harold Porter. *National Party Platforms, 1840–1972.* Urbana: University of Illinois Press, 1973.

Kahn, Ronald. "Social Constructions, Supreme Court Reversals, and American Political Development: *Lochner, Plessy, Bowers*, but Not *Roe*," in Ronald Kahn and Ken I. Kersch, eds., *The Supreme Court and American Political Development.* Lawrence: University Press of Kansas, 2006.

Kamisar, Yale. "Can (Did) Congress 'Overrule' *Miranda*?" 85 *Cornell Law Review* 883 (2000).

Kammen, Michael. *The Machine That Would Go of Itself: The Constitution in American Culture.* New York: Alfred A. Knopf, 1987.

Katz, Meir. "The State of Blaine: A Closer Look at the Blaine Amendments and Their Modern Application." 12 *Engage* 111 (2011).

Katznelson, Ira. *Fear Itself: The New Deal and the Origins of Our Time.* New York: W. W. Norton, 2013.

Kauper, Paul G. *Civil Liberties and the Constitution.* Ann Arbor: University of Michigan Press, 1962.

Keck, Thomas M. "From Bakke to Grutter: The Rise of Rights-Based Conservatism," in Ronald Kahn and Ken I. Kersch, eds., *The Supreme Court and American Political Development*. Lawrence: University Press of Kansas, 2006.

Keller, Morton. "The Politics of State Constitutional Revision: 1820–1930," in Kermit L. Hall, Harold M. Hyman, and Leon V. Sigal, eds., *The Constitutional Convention as an Amending Device*. Washington, DC: The American Historical Association and the American Political Science Association, 1981.

Kellogg, S. W. "The Beginnings of Civil Service Reform." 8 *Yale Law Journal* 134 (1898).

Kendall, Willmoore. "The Two Majorities." 4 *Midwest Journal of Political Science* 317 (1960).

Kendall, Willmoore, and George W. Carey. "The 'Intensity' Problem and Democratic Theory." 62 *American Political Science Review* 5 (1968).

Kennedy, David M. *Freedom from Fear: The American People in Depression and War, 1929–1945*. New York: Oxford University Press, 1999.

Kersten, Andrew E., and Kriste Lindenmeyer, eds. *Politics and Progress: American Society and the State since 1865*. Westport, CT: Praeger, 2001.

Keynes, Edward, with Randall K. Miller. *The Court vs. Congress: Prayer, Busing, and Abortion*. Durham, NC: Duke University Press, 1989.

Kingdon, John. *Congressmen's Voting Decisions*. New York: Harper and Row, 1973.

Kobach, Kris W. "Rethinking Article V: Term Limits and the Seventeenth and Nineteenth Amendments." 103 *Yale Law Journal* 1971 (1994).

Krasnow, Diane-Michele. "The Imbalance of Power and the Presidential Veto: A Case for the Item Veto." 14 *Harvard Journal of Law and Public Policy* 583 (1991).

Kurland, Phillip. "The Supreme Court, 1963 Term—Foreword: 'Equal in Origin and Equal in Title to the Legislative and Executive Branches of the United States Government.'" 78 *Harvard Law Review* 143 (1964).

———. "The Regents' Prayer Case: 'Full of Sound and Fury, Signifying. . . .'" 1962 *Supreme Court Review* 1 (1962).

Kysar, Rebecca M. "On the Constitutionality of Tax Treaties." 38 *Yale Journal of International Law* 1 (2013).

Kyvig, David E. "Arranging for Amendment: Unintended Outcomes of Constitutional Design," in David E. Kyvig, ed., *Unintended Consequences of Constitutional Amendment*. Athens: University of Georgia Press, 2000.

———. *Explicit and Authentic Acts: Amending the US Constitution, 1776–1995*. Lawrence: University Press of Kansas, 1996.

———. "Refining or Resisting Modern Government? The Balanced Budget Amendment to the US Constitution." 28 *Akron Law Review* 97 (1995).

———. "The Road Not Taken: FDR, the Supreme Court, and Constitutional Amendment." 104 *Political Science Quarterly* 463 (1989).

———, ed. *Unintended Consequences of Constitutional Amendment*. Athens: University of Georgia Press, 2000.

Lain, Corinna Barrrett. "God, Civic Virtue, and the American Way: Reconstructing *Engel*." 67 *Stanford Law Review* 479 (2015).

Lasser, William. *The Limits of Judicial Power: The Supreme Court in American Politics*. Chapel Hill: University of North Carolina Press, 1988.

Leiner, Frederick C. *Millions for Defense: The Subscription Warships of 1798*. Annapolis, MD: US Naval Institute Press, 1999.

Leonard, Charles A. *A Search for the Judicial Philosophy: Mr. Justice Roberts and the Constitutional Revolution of 1937*. Ann Arbor, MI: Kennikat Press, 1971.

Leopold, Richard W. *The Growth of American Foreign Policy*. New York: Alfred A. Knopf, 1962.

Leuchtenburg, William E. "The Origins of Franklin D. Roosevelt's 'Court Packing' Plan." 1966 *Supreme Court Review* 347.

———. *The Supreme Court Reborn: The Constitutional Revolution in the Age of Roosevelt*. New York: Oxford University Press, 1995.

Levinson, Sanford. *Framed: America's 51 Constitutions and the Crisis of Governance*. New York: Oxford University Press, 2012.

———. "How Many Times Has the United States Constitution Been Amended? (A) <26; (B) 26; (C) 27; (D) > 27: Accounting for Constitutional Change," in Sanford Levinson, ed., *Responding to Imperfection: The Theory and Practice of Constitutional Change*. Princeton: Princeton University Press, 1995.

———. *Our Undemocratic Constitution: Where the Constitution Goes Wrong (and How We the People Can Correct It)*. New York: Oxford University Press, 2008.

———, ed. *Responding to Imperfection: The Theory and Practice of Constitutional Amendment*. Princeton: Princeton University Press, 1995.

Lind, Nancy S., and Erik T. Rankin. *First Amendment Rights: An Encyclopedia*. Santa Barbara, CA: ABC-CLIO/Greenwood, 2012.

Lupu, Ira C. "Statutes Revolving in Constitutional Law Orbits." 79 *University of Virginia Law Review* 1 (1993).

Lutz, Donald S. "Toward a Theory of Constitutional Amendment." 88 *American Political Science Review* 355 (1994).

Magliocca, Gerard N. "State Calls for an Article Five Convention: Mobilization and Interpretation." 2009 *Cardozo Law Review* 74 (2009).

Mansbridge, Jane J. *Why We Lost the ERA*. Chicago: University of Chicago Press, 1986.

Marilley, M. "The Unintended Consequences of the Nineteenth Amendment: Why So Few?," in David E. Kyvig, ed., *Unintended Consequences of Constitutional Amendment*. Athens: University of Georgia Press, 2000.

Marshall, Thomas R. *Public Opinion and the Supreme Court*. Boston: Unwin Hyman, 1989.

Mashaw, Jerry L. "Reluctant Nationalists: Federal Administration and Administrative Law in the Republican Era, 1801–1809." 116 *Yale Law Journal* 1636 (2007).

Mathews, Donald G., and Jane S. De Hart. *Sex, Gender, and the Politics of the ERA: A State and the Nation*. New York: Oxford University Press, 1992.

Mayeri, Serena. "Constitutional Choices: Legal Feminism and the Historical Dynamics of Change." 92 *University of California Law Review* 755 (2004).

———. "'When the Trouble Started': The Story of *Frontiero v. Richardson*," in Elizabeth Schneider and Stephanie M. Wildman, eds., *Women and the Law: Stories*. New York: Foundation Press, 2011.

Mayhew, David R. *Congress, The Electoral Connection* (2d ed.). New Haven, CT: Yale University Press, 2004.

McCann, Michael W. *Rights at Work: Pay Equity Reform and the Politics of Legal Mobilization*. Chicago: University of Chicago Press, 1994.

McCann, Michael, and Helena Silverstein. "Rethinking Law's 'Allurements': A Relational Analysis of Social Movement Lawyers in the United States," in Austin Sarat, ed., *Cause Lawyering: Political Commitments and Professional Responsibilities.* New York: Oxford University Press, 1997.

McCloskey, Robert. *The American Supreme Court.* Chicago: University of Chicago Press, 1960.

———. "Principles, Powers, and Values," in Donald A. Gianella, ed., *1964 Religion and Public Order.* Chicago: University of Chicago Press, 1965.

McCullough, David. *John Adams.* New York: Simon and Schuster, 2001.

McDougal, Myers. "Law as a Process of Decision: A Policy-Oriented Approach to Legal Study." 1 *National Law Forum* 53 (1956).

McGuire, K. T., and L. A. Stimson. "The Least Dangerous Branch Revisited: New Evidence on Supreme Court Responsiveness to Public Preferences." 66 *Journal of Politics* 1018 (2004).

McKissick, Floyd. *Three-Fifths of a Man.* New York: Macmillan Company, 1969.

McKitrick, Eric L. *Andrew Johnson and Reconstruction.* New York: Oxford University Press, 1960.

McPherson, James M. *Battle Cry of Freedom: The Civil War Era.* New York: Oxford University Press, 1988.

———. "The Fights Against the Gag Rule: Joshua Leavitt and Antislavery Insurgency in the Whig Party." 48 *Journal of Negro History* 177 (1963).

Meese, Edwin. "The Supreme Court of the United States: Bulwark of a Limited Constitution." 27 *South Texas University Law Review* 455 (1986).

Meyer, David S., and Deana A. Rohlinger. "Big Books and Social Movements: A Myth of Ideas and Social Change." 59 *Social Problems* 136 (2012).

Mezias, Stephen, and Rikki Abzug. *The Fragmented State and Organizational Governance: The Case of Comparable Worth* (unpublished paper) (The Stern School, New York University, 1993) 23. Cited at McCann, *Rights at Work*, 63 and n. 12.

Miller, John C. *Crisis In Freedom: The Alien and Sedition Acts.* Boston: Little, Brown, 1951.

———. *The Federalist Era: 1789–1801.* New York: Harper and Row, 1960.

Miller, William Lee. *Arguing about Slavery: John Quincy Adams and the Great Battle in the United States Congress.* New York: Alfred A. Knopf, 1996.

Mishler, William, and Reginald S. Sheehan. "Public Opinion, the Attitudinal Model and Supreme Court Decision Making: A Micro-Analytic Perspective." 58 *Journal of Politics* 169 (1996).

Musmano, Michael A. *Proposed Amendments to the Constitution.* Washington, DC: US Government Printing Office, 1929; reprinted Westport, CT: Greenwood Press, 1976.

Nachescu, Voichita. "Radical Feminism and the Nation." 3 *Journal for the Study of Radicalism* 29 (2008).

Nackenoff, Carol. "Constitutionalizing Terms of Inclusion: Friends of the Indian and Citizenship for Native Americans, 1880–1930s," in Ronald Kahn and Ken I. Kersch, eds., *The Supreme Court and American Political Development.* Lawrence: University Press of Kansas, 2006.

National Committee for a Human Life Amendment. "Human Life Amendments: 1973–2003," available at *www.nchla.org/datasource/idocuments/HLAlst7303.pdf.*

———. "Human Life Amendment Highlights: United States Congress (1973–2003)," available at *www.nchla.org/datasource/idocuments/HLAhghlts.pdf*.

Nagel, Robert F. "Disagreement and Interpretation." 56 *Law and Contemporary Problems* 11 (1993).

Nagel, Stuart S. "Court-Curbing Periods in American History," in Theodore L. Becker and Malcolm M. Feeley, eds., *The Impact of Supreme Court Decisions* (2d ed.). New York: Oxford University Press, 1973.

Neal, Steve. *Happy Days Are Here Again: The 1932 Democratic Convention, the Emergence of FDR—and How America Was Changed Forever*. New York: Harper Collins, 2004.

NeJaime, Douglas. "Constitutional Change, Courts, and Social Movements." 111 *University of Michigan Law Review* 877 (2013).

———. "Winning Through Losing." 96 *Iowa Law Review* 941 (2011).

Nichols, David A. *Eisenhower 1956: The President's Year of Crisis—Suez and the Brink of War*. New York: Simon and Schuster, 2012.

Novkov, Julie. "Law and Political Ideologies," in Keith E. Whittington, R. Daniel Kelemen, and Gregory A. Caldeira, eds., *The Oxford Handbook of Law and Politics*. New York: Oxford University Press, 2008.

O'Brien, David M. *Constitutional Law and Politics: Struggles for Power and Government Accountability*, vol. 1 (8th ed.). New York: W. W. Norton, 2011.

———. *Constitutional Law and Politics: Struggles for Power and Government Accountability*, vol. 2 (8th ed.). New York: W. W. Norton, 2011.

O'Connor, Sandra Day. "Public Trust as a Dimension of Equal Justice: Some Suggestions to Increase Public Trust." 36 *Court Review (Journal of the American Judges Association)* 10 (1999).

Okrent, Daniel. *Last Call: The Rise and Fall of Prohibition*. New York: Scribner, 2010.

Olson, Lynne. *Those Angry Days: Roosevelt, Lindbergh and America's Fight over World War II, 1939–1941*. New York: Random House, 2013.

Olson, Susan M. "The Political Evolution of Interest Group Litigation," in Richard A. L. Gambitta, Marlynn L. May, and James C. Foster, eds., *Governing through Courts*. Thousand Oaks, CA: SAGE Publications, 1981.

Oppenheim, Karen Mason, John L. Czajka, and Sara Arber. "Change in US Women's Sex-Role Attitudes, 1964–1974." 41 *American Sociological Review* 573 (1976).

Orfield, David. *The Reconstruction of Southern Education*. Hoboken: John Wiley and Sons, 1969.

Page, Benjamin I., and Robert Y. Shapiro. "Effects of Public Opinion on Policy." 77 *American Political Science Review* 175 (1983).

Patterson, James T. *Restless Giant*. New York: Oxford University Press, 2005.

Peltason, J. W. "*Baker v. Carr*," in Kermit L. Hall, ed., *The Oxford Companion to the Supreme Court of the United States* (2d ed.). New York: Oxford University Press, 2005.

———. "*Westbury v. Sanders*," in Kermit L. Hall, ed., *The Oxford Companion to the Supreme Court of the United States* (2d ed.). New York: Oxford University Press, 2005.

Peterson, Merrill D. *Thomas Jefferson and the New Nation*. New York: Oxford University Press, 1970.

Petro, Sylvester. "Union Power and Government Aid," *The Freeman*, 26–39 (July 1960), available at *fee.org/articles/union-power-and-government-aid*.
Pfander, James E. "Brown II: Ordinary Remedies for Extraordinary Wrongs." 24 *Law and Inequality* 47 (2006).
Pildes, Richard H. "Is the Supreme Court a 'Majoritarian' Institution?" 2010 *Supreme Court Review* 103 (2010).
Piven, Frances, and Richard Cloward. *Poor People's Movements: Why They Succeed, How They Fail*. New York: Vintage Press, 1979.
Pope, James Gray. "Republican Moments: The Role of Direct Popular Power in the American Constitutional Order." 139 *University of Pennsylvania Law Review* 287 (1990).
Posner, Richard. "Pragmatism versus Purposivism in First Amendment Analysis." 54 *Stanford Law Review* 737 (2002).
Post, Robert C. "The Supreme Court, 2002 Term—Foreword: Fashioning the Legal Constitution: Culture, Courts, and Law." 117 *Harvard Law Review* 4 (2003).
Post, Robert, and Reva Siegel. "*Roe* Rage: Democratic Constitutionalism and Backlash." 42 *Harvard Civil Rights-Civil Liberties Law Review* 373 (2007).
Potter, David M. *The Impending Crisis: 1848–1861* (completed and edited by Don E. Fehrenbacher). New York: Harper Collins Publishing, 1976.
Powaski, Ronald. *Toward an Entangling Alliance: American Isolationism, Internationalism, and Europe, 1901–1950*. Westport, CT: Greenwood Publishing Group, 1991.
Powe, Lucas A. "Are 'the People' Missing in Action (and Should Anyone Care)," review of Larry D. Kramer, *The People Themselves: Popular Constitutionalism and Judicial Review*. 83 *University of Texas Law Review* 855 (2005).
———. *The Supreme Court and the American Elite, 1789–2008*. Cambridge, MA: Harvard University Press, 2009.
———. *The Warren Court in American Politics*. Cambridge, MA: Belknap Press, 2000.
Pritchett, C. Herman. "Judicial Supremacy from Marshall to Burger," in M. Judd Harmon, ed., *Essays on the Constitution of the United States*. Port Washington, NY: Kennikat Press, 1978.
Ratner, Sidney. *American Taxation*. New York: W. W. Norton, 1942.
Reger, Jo, and Suzanne Staggenborg. "Patterns of Mobilization in Local Movement Organizations: Leadership and Strategy in Four National Organization for Women Chapters." 49 *Sociological Perspectives* 297 (2006).
Reichley, A. James. *Conservatives in an Age of Change: The Nixon and Ford Administrations*. Washington, DC: Brookings Institution Press, 1981.
Riker, William H. *The Art of Political Manipulation*. New Haven, CT: Yale University Press, 1986.
Ripken, Susanna Kim. "Corporate First Amendment Rights after *Citizens United*: An Analysis of the Popular Movement to End the Constitutional Personhood of Corporations." 14 *University of Pennsylvania Journal of Business Law* 209 (2011).
Roach, Kent. "Dialogue or Defiance: Legislative Reversals of Supreme Court Decisions in Canada and the United States." 4 *International Journal of Constitutional Law* 347 (2006).
Roberts, Owen J. *The Court and the Constitution: The Oliver Wendell Holmes Lectures*. Cambridge, MA: Harvard University Press, 1951.
Rosen, Jeffrey. "'Rehnquist the Great': Even Liberals May Come to Regard William

Rehnquist as One of the Most Successful Chief Justices of the Century." *Atlantic Monthly*, April, 2005, 84–86; reprinted in Friedman, *Will of the People*, 371.

Rosenberg, Gerald N. *The Hollow Hope: Can Courts Bring about Social Change?* (2d ed.). Chicago: University of Chicago Press, 2008.

———. "The 1964 Civil Rights Act: The Crucial Role of Social Movements in the Enactment and Implementation of Anti-Discrimination Law." 49 *Saint Louis University Law Journal* 1147 (2005).

Rosenbloom, David H. *Federal Service and the Constitution: The Development of the Public Employment Relationship*. Ithaca: Cornell University Press, 1971.

Ross, William G. "Attacks on the Warren Court by State Officials: A Case Study of Why Court-Curbing Movements Fail." 50 *University of Buffalo Law Review* 483 (2002).

———. "The Resilience of *Marbury v. Madison*: Why Judicial Review Has Survived So Many Attacks." 38 *Wake Forest Law Review* 733 (2003).

Russo, Charles J., and Ralph D. Mawdsley. "The United States Supreme Court and Aid to Students Who Attend Religiously-Affiliated Institutions of Higher Education." 14 *Education and Law Journal* 301 (2005).

Schaffer, Ronald. "General Stanley D. Embick: Military Dissenter." 37 *Military Affairs* 89 (1973).

Scheingold, Stuart A., *Politics of Rights: Lawyers, Public Policy, and Political Change*. New Haven, CT: Yale University Press, 1974.

———. Preface to *Politics of Rights: Lawyers, Public Policy, and Political Change* (2d ed.). Ann Arbor: University of Michigan Press, 2004.

Schlesinger, Arthur. *The Imperial Presidency*. Boston: Houghton Mifflin, Harcourt, 2004.

Schubert, Glendon A. "Politics and the Constitution: The Becker Amendment during 1953." 16 *Journal of Politics* 257 (1954).

Schwartz, Bernard. "More Unpublished Warren Court Opinions." 1986 *Supreme Court Review* 317.

Segal, Jeffrey A., and Harold J. Spaeth. *The Supreme Court and the Attitudinal Model Revisited*. New York: Cambridge University Press, 2002.

Shane, Peter M. "Voting Rights and the 'Statutory Constitution.'" 56 *Law and Contemporary Problems* 243 (1993).

Shesol, Jeff. *Supreme Power: Franklin Roosevelt vs. The Supreme Court*. New York: W. W. Norton, 2010.

Siegel, Reva. "Constitutional Culture, Social Movement Conflict and National Change: The Case of the De Facto ERA." 94 *University of California Law Review* 1323 (2006).

Sikorski, Robert. *Prayer in Public Schools and the Constitution, 1961–1992: Government-Sponsored Religious Activities in Public Schools and the Constitution* (Controversies in Constitutional Law). New York: Routledge, 1993.

Simpson, Albert F. "The Political Significance of Slave Representation, 1787–1821." 7 *Journal of Southern History* 315 (1941).

Solomon, Rayman L. "Black Monday," in Kermit L. Hall, ed., *The Oxford Companion to the Supreme Court of the United States* (2d ed.). New York: Oxford University Press, 2005.

Soohoo, Cynthia. "Hyde-Care for All: The Expansion of Abortion-Funding Restrictions under Health Care Reform." 15 *CUNY Law Review* 391(2012).

Sorauf, Frank J. "The Political Potential of an Amending Convention," in Kermit L. Hall, Harold M. Hyman, and Leon V. Sigal, eds., *The Constitutional Convention as an Amending Device*. Washington, DC: The American Historical Association and The American Political Science Association, 1981.

Soule, Sarah A., and Susan Olzak. "When Do Movements Matter? The Politics of Contingency and the Equal Rights Amendment." 69 *American Sociological Review* 473 (2004).

Sparrow, Bartholomew H. *The Insular Cases and Emergence of American Empire*. Lawrence: University Press of Kansas, 2006.

Steiner, Gilbert Y. *Constitutional Inequality: The Political Fortunes of the Equal Rights Amendment*. Washington, DC: Brookings Institution, 1985.

Stephenson, Nathaniel Wright. *Nelson W. Aldrich: A Leader in American Politics*. New York: Charles Scribner's Sons, 1930.

Stevens, John Paul. *Six Amendments: How and Why We Should Change the Constitution*. New York: Little, Brown, 2014.

Stone, Ralph. *The Irreconcilables: The Fight against the League of Nations*. New York: W. W. Norton, 1973.

Strauss, David A. "The Irrelevance of Constitutional Amendments." 114 *Harvard Law Review* 1457 (2001).

Sullivan, Kathleen M. "Constitutional Constancy: Why Congress Should Cure Itself of Amendment Fever." 17 *Cardozo Law Review* 691 (1996).

Tananbaum, Duane. *The Bricker Amendment Controversy: A Test of Eisenhower's Political Leadership*. Ithaca, NY: Cornell University Press, 1988.

Taylor, Alan. *The Civil War of 1812*. New York: Vintage Books, 2011.

Taylor, Verta. "Review of *Sex, Gender, and the Politics of ERA: A State and the Nation*, by Donald G. Matthews and Jane Sherron DeHart." 21 *Contemporary Sociology*, 37 (1992).

Thomas, Evan. *The War Lovers*. New York: Little, Brown, 2010.

Tribe, Laurence H. *Abortion: The Clash of Absolutes* (rev. ed.). New York: W. W. Norton, 1992.

———. "Taking Text and Structure Seriously: Reflections on Free-Form Method in Constitutional Interpretation." 108 *Harvard Law Review* 1221 (1995).

Trimble, Phillip R. *International Law: United States Foreign Relations Law*. New York: Foundation Press, 2002.

Tucker, George. *The Life of Thomas Jefferson*. Philadelphia: Carey, Lea and Blanchard, 1837 (digitized November 27, 2014).

Tushnet, Mark. "The New Deal Constitutional Revolution: Law, Politics, or What?" Review of *Rethinking the New Deal Court* by Barry Cushman. 66 *University of Chicago Law Review* 1061 (1999).

———. *Why the Constitution Matters*. New Haven, CT: Yale University Press, 2010.

Van Riper, Paul P. *History of the United States Civil Service*. Evanston, IL: Row, Peterson, 1958.

Vanberg, Georg. "Establishing and Maintaining Judicial Independence," in Keith E. Whittington, R. Daniel Kelemen, and Gregory A. Caldeira, eds., *The Oxford Handbook of Law and Politics*. New York: Oxford University Press, 2008.

Vile, John R. *Constitutional Change in the United States: A Comparative Study of the Role of Constitutional Amendment, Judicial Interpretations, and Legislative and Executive Actions.* Westport, CT: Praeger, 1994.

———. *Encyclopedia of Constitutional Amendments, Proposed Amendments* (2d ed.). Santa Barbara, CA: ABC-CLIO, 2003.

———. *170 Eccentric, Visionary, and Patriotic Proposals to Rewrite the US Constitution.* Santa Barbara, CA: ABC-CLIO, 2014.

Viteritti, Joseph P. "Choosing Equality: Religious Freedom and Educational Opportunity under Constitutional Federalism." 15 *Yale Law and Policy Review* 113 (1996).

Vose, Clement E. *Constitutional Change: Amendment Politics and Supreme Court Litigation since 1900.* Lexington, MA: Lexington Books, 1972.

Warren, Charles. *The Supreme Court in United States History*, Vol. II. Boston: Little, Brown, 1922.

Wharton, Linda J. "State Equal Rights Amendments Revisited: Evaluating Their Effectiveness in Advancing Protection against Sex Discrimination," 36 *Rutgers Law Journal* 1201 (2005).

White, Edward G. *The Constitution and the New Deal.* Cambridge, MA: Harvard University Press, 2000.

White, James Boyd. *When Words Lose Their Meaning.* Chicago: University of Chicago Press, 1984.

Whittington, Keith E. *Constitutional Construction: Divided Powers and Constitutional Meaning.* Cambridge, MA: Harvard University Press, 1999.

———. *Political Foundations of Judicial Supremacy: The Presidency, the Supreme Court, and Constitutional Leadership in US History.* Princeton, NJ: Princeton University Press, 2007.

Wills, Garry. *Negro President: Jefferson and the Slave Power.* Boston: Houghton Mifflin, 2003.

Winger, Maurice. "Restrictive Wartime Labor Measures in Congress." 9 *Law and Contemporary Problems* 502 (1942).

Wood, Gordon S. *Empire of Liberty: A History of the Early Republic, 1789–1815.* New York: Oxford University Press, 2009.

Woodward, Bob, and Scott Armstrong. *The Brethren: Inside the Supreme Court.* New York: Simon and Schuster, 1979.

Yates, Jeff. *Popular Justice: Presidential Prestige and Executive Success in the Supreme Court.* Albany: State University of New York Press, 2002.

Zemans, Kahn. "Legal Mobilization: The Neglected Role of the Law in the Political System." 77 *American Political Science Review* 690 (1983).

Index

abolitionists, 25, 28, 29. *See also* slavery
abortion, 193n156
    and Congress, 195n173
    and funding restrictions, 194n159
    and legislation, 196n183
    and Nixon, 194n157
    as political issue, 195n177
    regulation of, 45, 60–66, 193n155
    See also *Roe v. Wade*
Ackerman, Bruce, 5, 58, 151–52, 154, 155, 168n27, 190n118
activation, 10–11, 14, 30–31
Adams, John, 92, 93, 94, 205n15
Adams, John Quincy, 27–30, 158, 179n101, 179n106, 179n111
advice and consent role, 134
affirmative action, 12
Affordable Care Act, 3
AFL-CIO, 22
Agricultural Adjustment Act of 1933 (AAA), 51
Alabama, 99
Aldrich, Nelson, 119–20, 161, 214n42
Alien Act, 89–90, 92–94
Alien Land Law, 142, 221n47
aliens, 91–92, 205n20
amendments. *See* Article V; constitutional amendments; proposed amendments; *specific amendments*
American Anti-Slavery Society, 28
American Women (report), 17
Ames, Herman, 26, 100
anti-Federalists, 89
antislavery movement, 25–30, 180n118
Application Clause, 87–108
apportionment, 103–8, 160–61

Armstrong, Scott, 43
Article II Treaty Clause, 152, 162
Article V, 1, 5
    and amendment process, 59
    Application Clause, 94, 103, 106, 107, 160
    and Bill of Rights, 88–89
    congressional influence of, 77
    and contemporary constitutionalism, 6
    and federal legislation, 109–28
    and line-item veto, 113
    and Philippine independence, 120
    political function of, 2, 67, 74, 162
    procedures of, 3, 33
    and Prohibition, 31
    and Roosevelt, 48–60
    and school prayer, 69, 71–73
    as straw man, 118–24, 161, 215n48
Article VI, 122, 141, 143–44, 150
Asakura v. City of Seattle, 142

Back to the People Amendment, 32–33
Baker v. Carr, 103–4
balanced budget amendment, 108–28, 161, 212n21
Balanced Budget and Emergency Deficit Control Act of 1985, 113–16, 161
Balkin, Jack, 46, 193n152
Baltimore, 69
Bankhead, William, 53
Banner, James, 99
Becker, Frank J., 69, 71–72
Becker Amendment, 71–72
Bible in schools, 47, 66–76
bicameralism, 112, 125, 126
Bickel, Alexander, 39

241

Bill of Rights, 1, 3, 88–89
Birkby, Robert, 73
Bituminous Coal Conservation Act, 51
Black, Hugo, 70, 150
Black Monday decisions, 49–50
Blackmun, Harry, 186n54
Blaine, James G., 83–84
Blaine Amendment, 83–84, 160, 203n299
Bone, Homer, 53–55
Bowsher v. Synar, 115
Breedlove v. Suttles, 79–81, 159
Brennan, William J., 42–43, 70, 185n50
Brethren, The (Woodward and Armstrong), 43
Bricker, John, 139–50
Bricker Amendment, 134, 139–50, 162, 220n33
    and conservatives, 142
    defeat of, 146
    goals of, 139–40
    impact of, 146–56
    and individual rights, 143–44
    and judiciary, 149
    and *Missouri v. Holland*, 140–43, 221n48
    and presidential-executive agreements, 144–46
Britain, 96
Buchanan, James, 131
budget authority, 112
budget reduction, 108, 113–16, 161, 212n21
bully pulpit, 35, 39, 47, 123–24, 138
Bumpers, Dale, 157
Burns, James MacGregor, 190n121
Burr, Aaron, 94–95
Bush, George H. W., 76, 77
busing, 12
Butler, Pierce, 167n17

Calhoun, John C., 99
California Alien Land Law, 142, 221n47
campaign finance, 2, 13, 171n20
Cardozo, Benjamin, 37
Carter administration, 61, 147, 194n157
Carter v. Carter Coal. Co., 51
cases cited, 163–64
Casey, 60, 65, 66, 159

cash and carry, 136
Cassell, Paul, 117–18
Catholics, 67, 83, 198n228
catholic view of Constitution, 35
Celler, Emanuel, 71, 80
censorship, 178n99
Chadha, 125–28
Chamberlin v. Dade County Board of Public Instruction, 73
Chemerinsky, Erwin, 2, 172n21
China, 137
Choate, Joseph, 119
Christian American Association, 123, 216n58
church and state, 66–76
Citizen Genet, 90–91, 204n12, 205n17
citizens, 22, 39, 92
Citizen's Advisory Council on the Status of Women, 22
Citizens United v. Federal Election Commission, 34
City of Akron v. Akron Center for Reproductive Health, Inc., 195n177
Civil Rights Act, 17–20, 173n39, 215n48
civil rights legislation, 143
Civil War, 132–33
claim-of-rights struggle, 15
Clark, Tom, 70
classifications, suspect, 42–43, 186n54
Clinton administration, 116
Clinton v. City of New York, 112–13, 212n13
Cold War, 68
Colegrove v. Green, 104
collective action, 10–11
collective bargaining, 121
collective legal mobilization theory, 22–23, 26
Commerce Clause, 143
Commerce Power, 188n86
Committee of Thirteen, 132
Comptroller General, 115
concurrent resolution, 124–25
Congress
    and 1800 presidential election, 94–95
    and abortion restrictions, 195n173
    and administrative agencies, 127
    and balanced budget amendment, 114–15

and Bible, 68
and Black Monday decisions, 49–50
and convention applications, 88
and Court-packing plan, 190n121
and Dirksen constitution effort, 106–7
and disapproval bill, 112
and Embargo of 1807, 98, 99
and *Engel*, 68
and ERA, 43
and failed amendment efforts, 87–108
and federal income tax, 119
first, 88
and foreign policy, 134–56
and high-salience constituents, 195n176
and isolationism, 139
legislative authority of, 140
and line-item-veto legislation, 113
and Ludlow Amendment, 137, 139
and pay raises, 213n23
political pressure on, 124
and post-*Chadha politics*, 127–28
and presidential-executive agreements, 145
and presidential foreign policy, 155–56
and public opinion, 50, 139
and reapportionment, 105
and right-to-work laws, 123
and school prayer, 67, 71–72
and Southern slave power, 25–27
and spending power, 111–12, 211n8
and Supreme Court, 57–58, 188n101
and tariffs, 99–100
and Title VII, 18
and treaty ratification, 155
and veto power, 57–58
and victims' rights, 117–18
and voting districts, 104
and Wheeler-Bone amendment, 48
Congressional Budget and Impoundment Control Act of 1974, 110–12
congressional-executive agreements, 150–56, 162
Connecticut, 26, 93
consciousness raising, 20, 176n77
conservatives, 24, 142
constitutional amendments
and 1936 presidential election, 55–56
anti-poll-tax, 79–81
balanced budget, 108–28, 161, 212n21
and Buchanan, 131
and civil rights legislation, 18
defensive use of, 60–78
and democratic deliberation, 59
failed (*See* failed amendment efforts)
and federal income tax, 119
flag protection, 77–78, 159
and foreign affairs, 134–56
and franchise, 4
and legislative process, 79–80
motivation for, 34
as movement-building resource, 9–33
open-shop, 122–23
and Philippine independence, 121
and proposal process, 1, 5, 87, 191n128
proposed (*See* proposed amendments)
and public pressure, 50
and school prayer, 66–76
and slavery, 27
strategic use of, 21, 61, 200n249
studies of, 165n3
and Three-Fifths Clause, 25
and victims' rights, 116–18
and voter referenda, 181n132
constitutional convention, 210n106
1787, 87–88
applications for, 99–100, 103, 106
calls for, 88–89
fear of, 106
and Southern states, 25
threat of, 95, 160
constitutional crisis of 1937, 4, 48, 59
constitutional culture, 44
constitutional dialectic, 36
Constitutional Equality Amendment (CEA), 23
Constitutional Faith (Levinson), 35
constitutionalism, 6
laissez-faire, 48, 59, 187n75
late twentieth-century, 4
popular, 35–36
protestant ideology of, 39
constitutional jurisprudence, 35, 196n184
constitutional meaning, 34, 36–40, 64, 66, 158, 168n21, 184n38
constitutional norms, 169n1

constitutional values, 168n27
Constitution of the United States
    and congressional-executive
        agreements, 151
    and fiscal policies, 109
    and foreign relations, 134–56
    and limited federal government, 4
    ratification of, 88–89
    and Southern states, 28–29, 125–26
    and voting, 78
    See also specific amendments; specific articles
continuity theory, 153–54
Contract with America, 112, 116
convention
    1858 Illinois Republican Party, 101
    constitutional (*See* constitutional convention)
    national proposing, 3, 87
    of political parties, 101–2
    state, 33
    and state legislatures, 98–99
Convention on the Punishment of the Crime of Genocide, 142, 147, 150, 221n51
Copeland, Royal, 120, 121, 161
corporate abolitionists' Move to Amend, 34–35
corporate personhood, 34, 181n2
corruption, 100–101
Corwin Amendment, 132–33, 162
Council of State Governments, 105–7
countermobilization, 24, 46, 51, 61
Court-curbing efforts, 184n30
Court-packing, 54, 57, 58, 187n80, 190n121, 191n122
credit claiming, 199n242
Creel, George, 51
crime victims, 116–18, 161, 214n35
Crime Victims' Rights Act (CVRA), 118
Crittenden, John J., 132
Cruz, Ted, 3

Dahl, Robert, 37, 183n26
death penalty, 195n174
debt, 113–16
deliberation, 64
    and amendment efforts, 34–84, 66
    and ERA, 40–46, 158

and poll taxes, 159
and school prayer, 69–73
Democrats, 27, 56, 58
depression, 56, 97. *See also* New Deal
desegregation, 12
destroyers-for-bases agreement, 138, 144
Dirksen, Everett, 105–8, 160–61
Dirksen Amendment, 105–6
disability rights legislation, 170n11
disapproval bill, 112
discrimination, 17, 19, 40–46, 158, 186n54
dissent, 34–84
Douglas, Stephen, 101, 198n208
Douglas, William O., 71
dual strategy, 174n50
Dulles, John Foster, 147–48

Eastland, James O., 186n54
Eastwood, Mary, 21
Eighteenth Amendment, 31–33
Eisenhower, Dwight, 22, 144, 146, 149
election
    1800 presidential, 94–95
    and 1858 Illinois Republican Party convention, 101
    1936 presidential, 52, 55–56
    1964 Republican Party platform, 73
    and amendments, 165n2
    eligibility for, 206n27
    federal, 79–80
    judicial retention, 3
    of senators, 100–103, 201n270, 209n75, 209n83
Electoral College, 201n270
elite support, 21, 64
Ely Amendment, 25–26
emancipation, 27–29
Embargo Act, 98
Embargo of 1807, 95–99, 207n43, 207n48, 207n53, 208n65
Embick, Stanley, 137
Engel v. Vitale, 66, 68–71, 75, 159, 198n208
entitlement, 30–31
Equal Access Act, 75
Equal Employment Opportunity Commission, 19
equality, 45

Equal Protection Clause, 12, 40–41, 81, 83, 174n50, 185n44, 185n45
ERA (Equal Rights Amendment), 5, 15–24, 158, 172n26
   in 1920s, 15–16
   and 1930s, 16–17
   backlash against, 10, 24
   congressional history of, 15, 20
   and constitutional doctrine, 41
   and constitutional meaning, 43–46
   and Equal Protection doctrine, 43, 185n44
   and financial contributions, 23
   and Fourteenth Amendment, 185n43
   history of, 15–24
   impact of, 9, 20–24
   and judicial scrutiny, 41–43
   and movement building, 20, 158
   national dialogue on, 44
   and NOW membership, 20, 175n56
   opposition to, 16–17, 45, 196n182
   and politics of rights, 15–24
   pre-1970 support for, 15–20, 173n34
   and President's Commission on the Status of Women, 172n31
   ratification effort of, 41–44
   and social movements, 177n84
   and societal acceptance, 45–46
   and state laws, 82–84, 159–60
   support for, 22, 43
Establishment Clause, 75
establishment of religion, 66
executive branch
   authority of, 111, 149
   and *Chadha*, 128
   and Comptroller General, 115
   and lawmaking, 146
   policy of, 161–62
   and spending power, 211n8
ex post congressional-executive agreement, 154
ex post congressional review, 151

failed amendment efforts
   and balanced budget amendment, 109
   and congressional politics, 87–108
   and constitutional meaning, 42
   effect of, 2–3, 34
   and movement building, 9–10
   political impact of, 14, 41, 47–84
   and pro-life movement, 62
   and state politics, 82–84
fast-track process, 156
Federal Bird Act, 141
federal debt, 113–16
federal government
   and civil rights legislation, 18–19
   and New Deal, 167n16
   role of, 167n16
   spending of, 112, 114, 212n21
   structure of, 4
   See also Congress; president; Senate; Supreme Court of the United States
federal income tax, 109, 118–20, 212n14, 214n37, 214n38
federalism, 140
Federalists
   and 1800 election, 94–95
   amendment proposals of, 206n33
   and bill of rights, 89
   and embargos, 95
   and Jeffersonian Republicans, 91
   New England, 98
   and Three-Fifths Clause, 25
Federalist-Whig political organizations, 27
federal legislation
   and Article V, 109–28
   and civil rights, 18–19
   and *Missouri v. Holland*, 141
   and New Deal, 48, 53–55
   and proposed amendments, 161
   and treaty implementation, 141, 142
   and veto, 126
federal preemption, 216n56
federal ratio, 25–27, 158, 177n89, 179n95
federal regulatory authority, 188n82
feminist movement, 10, 15–24, 158, 173n35. *See also* ERA (Equal Rights Amendment); NOW; women's movement; women's rights
Field v. Clark, 153
Fifteenth Amendment, 119
Fifth Amendment, 41, 150
financial support, 13–15, 23
flag desecration, 47, 76–78, 159, 201n267
Flag Protection Act, 76–78, 159
Ford administration, 61
foreign influence, 91

foreign policy
  and amendment process, 162
  control of, 134–56
  and Eisenhower administration, 149
  and governmental branches, 140
  and House, 151
  and legislative authority, 148
  and presidential-executive agreements, 144–46
  and presidential power, 138–50
Four Horsemen, 167n17
Fourteenth Amendment
  and equal protection, 78, 81, 185n44
  Equal Protection Clause of, 40–41, 46, 79, 174n50
  and gender equality, 43
  and state laws, 83
  and UN Charter, 221n47
framing, 12–14
France, 89–94, 97–98, 206n32
franchise eligibility rules, 80
Frankfurter, Felix, 197n200
freedom of expression, 27–28, 76–77
Free Soil Party, 30
French-American Alliance of 1778, 90
French Directory, 92
French Revolution, 91
Friedan, Betty, 19–20
Friedman, Barry, 37–38, 66
Frontiero v. Richardson, 42–43, 185n50

gag rule, 27–30, 178n99, 178n100, 179n108
Gallatin, Albert, 97
Garner, John Nance, 189n102, 189n107
Garrison, William Lloyd, 29
gender classifications, 43, 185n49, 185n50
gender discrimination, 17, 40–46, 158, 186n54
General Agreement on Tariffs and Trade (GATT), 156
General Treaty for Renunciation of War as an Instrument of National Policy, 136
Genet, Edmund Charles, 90–91, 204n12, 205n17
Genocide Treaty, 142, 147, 150, 221n51
George, Walter, 146
Georgia, 79, 99

Ginsburg, Ruth Bader, 39, 185n43
Goldberg, Arthur J., 71, 81–82, 159
Goldwater, Barry, 24, 215n48
Golove, David, 151–52, 154, 155
Goodell, Charles, 80
Government Accounting Office (GAO), 115
Gramm-Rudman-Hollings Deficit Reduction Act of 1985, 113–16, 161
Grant, Ulysses S., 83, 110
grassroots mobilization, 20, 102
Great Britain, 90, 97–98
great compromise, 100, 152
group cohesion, 14
Guarantee Clause, 78

Hamilton, Alexander, 204n12
handshake deals, 127
Harper v. Virginia State Board of Elections, 81–82, 159, 202n288
Harriman, Mrs. E. Roland, 32
Harrison, William Henry, 27
Harris v. McCrea, 61
Hatch-Eagleton "Human Life Federalism Amendment," 62
Henkin, Louis, 140, 143
Holland, Spessard, 80
homosexuality, 45
Hoover, Herbert, 124, 192n140
House Judiciary Committee, 71–73, 80
Howe, Daniel Walker, 30
Hughes, Charles Evans, 48–49, 51, 54–57
Human Life Amendment, 62, 196n182
human rights movement, 147–48
human rights treaties, 142–43, 147, 221n51
Hyde Amendment, 61

Illinois, 101–2
immigration, 91–93
Imperial Presidency, 139
implementing legislation, 141, 142
impoundment, 110–11, 113, 211n10
income tax, 109, 118–20, 212n14, 214n37, 214n38
individual rights, 143–44
informal side agreements, 127
Insular Cases, 214n44

Index 247

INS v. Chadha, 125–28
International Court of Justice, 148
interstate commerce, 141
Iowa, 106
Irish Catholics, 83
Irish Rebellion, 91
isolationism, 134–39, 154

Jackson, Andrew, 99–100, 208n69
Jefferson, Thomas, 94–97, 108n60, 110, 113, 160
Jeffersonian Republicans, 93, 95
jingoism, 91
John Birch Society, 69
Johnson, 47, 76–77, 159
Johnson, Gregory Lee, 76
Johnson, Lyndon B., 22, 110, 123
joint resolution of disapproval, 126
Jones Act of 1916, 121
Jones and Laughlin, 54, 57, 59-60, 191n128
judicial impact scholarship, 169n5
judicial policy, 35–36
judicial power, 120
judicial precedent, 34
judicial retention elections, 3
judicial scrutiny, 43, 60, 185n49

Kahn, Ronald, 66, 179n106, 184n38
Keck, Thomas, 64
Kellogg-Briand Pact, 136
Kelly, Florence, 16
Kennedy, John F., 16–17, 22, 202n280
Kentucky, 219n12
Kentucky Resolution, 90, 93–94, 206n33
Kirkpatrick v. Preisler, 107, 108

labor laws, 16, 122
labor unions, 121–24
Lain, Corinna Barrett, 69
laissez-faire constitutionalism, 59, 187n75
League of Nations, 135, 219n19
legal category, 12
legal consciousness, 14
legal culture, 32
legal mobilization, 30, 170n7, 170n11
legislation. *See* federal legislation; state law
legislative committee veto, 125
legislative veto, 124–28

Levinson, Sanford, 35
Lincoln, Abraham, 101, 131–34, 218n9
line-item veto, 109, 111–13, 212n14
Line-Item Veto Act, 112–13
litigation
　and movement building, 9–10
　and political legitimacy, 12–13
　as strategy, 42
Litvinov Agreement, 145
lobbying, 101
Lodge, Henry Cabot, 135
Louisiana Purchase, 25
Ludlow, Louis, 136–39
Ludlow Amendment, 134–40, 162

Madison, James, 88, 89, 97–98, 204n7, 208n60
Maher v. Roe, 61
Mansbridge, Jane, 22–23
Marbury v. Madison, 58
Marshall, John, 58
Maryland, 97
Mason, George, 87
Massachusetts, 25–26, 93, 98–99
mass mobilization, 9
Mayeri, Serena, 174n50
Mayhew, David, 74
McCann, Michael, 170n12
McCarthyite Red Hunts, 32
McCloskey, Robert, 37
McCormick, Ellen, 196n182
McKinley Tariff Act of 1890, 153
McReynolds, James Clark, 167n17
Medellin v. Texas, 148
media coverage, 12–15
　of Article V, 1
　and *Engel*, 68, 70
　and ERA, 21
　and Prohibition, 32
　and pro-life movement, 64
　and school prayer, 72, 73
military courts, 149–50
minimum wage statute, 52, 54
Minor v. Happersett, 78
Missouri, 108
Missouri v. Holland, 140–43, 147, 149, 150
mobilization, 14, 30, 46, 170n13, 175n59, 195n175

Morehead v. Tipaldo, 52, 54, 55, 56
movement building, 9–33, 158, 170n13, 172n22
movement dynamics, 24
myth of rights, 10

naming, 12, 14
naming rights, 171n16
National Catholic Welfare Conference, 198n228
National Consumers League, 16, 56
National Day of Prayer, 74
National Governors' Conference, 69
National Industrial Recovery Act (NIRA), 49–50
National Labor Relations Act (Wagner Act), 49, 57, 215n50
    constitutionality of, 54
    and federal preemption, 216n56
    history of, 122, 216n55
    Taft-Hartley Act Amendments to, 123
National Organization for Women (NOW). *See* NOW
National Women's Party (NWP), 15, 18, 173n35, 173n38
Nativist movements, 83–84
Naturalization Act, 83, 92
neutrality, 90
neutrality acts, 136, 139
neutrality principle, 71
New Deal
    and constitutional amendment proposals, 48–51
    constitutional legitimacy of, 190n113
    and economic crisis, 192n142
    and federal government structure, 4, 167n16
    legislation during, 53–55
    majoritarian defiance during, 48–60
    and Supreme Court, 167n17
    and Wheeler-Bone Amendment, 158–59
New England, 95, 97
New Right, 194n165
New York, 97–98
New York Circular Letter, 88
New York public schools, 67–68
Nineteenth Amendment, 15, 32–33, 209n84

Nixon, Richard, 22, 61, 110, 194n157
NLRB v. Jones and Laughlin Corporation, 54, 57, 59–60, 191n128
non-preemption, 123
North American Free Trade Agreement (NAFTA), 151
NOW, 19–21, 23, 41–44, 175n56, 176n74, 176n77
NOW/PAC, 177n79
nullification, 98–100
    and 1832 crisis, 160
    and amendments, 181nn3–4
    controversy about, 208n69
    and New Deal legislation, 48, 49, 53, 56
Nye, Gerald, 136
Nye Committee, 136

O'Connor, Sandra Day, 182n20
O'Daniel, Wilbert "Pappy," 123, 161
one-house veto, 124–25
one person, one vote, 104–5
open-shop constitutional amendment, 122–23
Oregon system, 102
organized labor, 16, 22, 121–24
organizing, 10, 31–32
Otis, Harrison Gray, 92

pacifism, 137
Panay incident, 137
parochial schools, 83–84
Parrish, 54, 56, 190n120, 191n126
party platforms, 78–80
Paul, Alice, 15, 16
pay equity, 14, 170n12
Payne v. Tennessee, 117
Peace Convention, 132
Pennsylvania, 69
Peterson, Esther, 16–17
petitions, 27–28
Philippine Islands, 120–21, 214n44
Philippine Organic Act of 1902 (Cooper Act), 121
Planned Parenthood of Southeastern Pennsylvania v. Casey, 60, 65, 66, 159
plausibility, 46
Pledge of Allegiance, 68
policy impoundment, 110

political consciousness, 15, 30
political education, 172n22
political empowerment, 14
political legacy, 15, 23–24
political mobilization, 10–11
political opportunity structure (POS), 175n59
political party convention system, 101–2
politics of rights, 11, 15–24
Polk, James K., 30
Pollock v. Farmers' Loan and Trust Company, 119, 120, 214n39
poll tax, 78–82, 159, 202n283, 202n288
popular constitutionalism, 35–36
population, 103–8
pork-barrel projects, 110
position taking, 74
Posner, Richard, 37
Powe, Lucas, 69, 208n69
Powell, Lewis F., Jr., 42–43, 185n50
prayer. *See* school prayer
Presentment Clause, 125–28
president
    authority of, 111, 138–39, 153
    and disapproval bill, 112
    and foreign policy, 139–50, 152, 155
    See also individual names
presidential-executive agreements, 140, 144–46
President's Commission on the Status of Women, 16–17, 174n46
press coverage. *See* media coverage
progressivism, 100
Prohibition, 30–33, 158, 180n124, 180n128
pro-life movement, 60–66, 193n152, 196n183
proposed amendments
    and constitutional appeal, 5–6
    and *Engel*, 69
    impact of, 157–58
    number of, 2, 166n4
    and public attention, 193n153
    See also constitutional amendments; failed amendment efforts; *specific amendments*
protestant view of Constitution, 35, 39
public consciousness, 26–27, 193n153
publicity. *See* media coverage

public opinion, 182n14
    and Article V amendment process, 51
    and bully pulpit, 39
    and congressional attitudes, 50
    and constitutional meaning, 36–40, 184n38
    and Court-packing, 55
    and failed amendment efforts, 26
    and political institutions, 37
    and reproductive choice, 62
    and school prayer, 69, 199n233, 199n241
    and sex discrimination law, 46
    and Supreme Court, 36–40, 47, 169n2, 182n20
    and treaty ratification, 223n97
    and women's rights, 176n68
public protest, 15
public schools, 63–69

quarantine speech, 138
Quasi-War, 89–94, 205n22

racial discrimination, 78–82, 142, 143, 221n51
racial tension, 18
ratification, 33, 81, 103, 168n26
rational basis test, 40
Reagan, Ronald, 62, 65, 74–76, 114, 200n246
reapportionment, 103–8, 160–61
recruitment, 14
redistricting, 103–8, 160–61
Reed v. Reed, 40
reform movements, 31–32, 64
reform strategies, 2, 11
Regents' Prayer, 66–68, 197n193
Rehnquist, William, 37, 43
Reid v. Covert, 149–50
Reign of Terror, 90–91
religion, 63–76, 83–84
Religious Right, 60
reproductive choice, 62
Republicans
    in 1800, 94–95
    1964 platform of, 73
    and antislavery movement, 27, 29–30
    and human life amendment, 62
    Jeffersonian, 27, 89–90, 93

Restatement (Third) of the Foreign Relations Law of the United States, 156
Reynolds v. Sims, 104, 107
rights
    claiming of, 10–15, 24, 26–27
    naming of, 171n16
    of victims, 116–18
Right-to-Life movement, 60–66, 193n152
right-to-work amendments, 121–24, 161, 217n61
right-to-work laws, 122–23, 216n55, 217n61
Roberts, Owen, 48–49, 51, 54–57, 191n126
Robinson, Joseph, 53, 189n104, 190n118
Roe v. Wade, 6, 47, 60–66, 158–59, 193n155, 194n162, 200n255
Roman Catholics, 67, 83, 198n228
Roosevelt, Eleanor, 16–17
Roosevelt, Franklin Delano, 137
    and 1936 election, 52
    and Article V, 48–60
    and constitutional amendments, 50–51, 188n101
    and Court-packing plan, 48, 52–55, 189n102, 190n118
    and foreign policy, 155
    and isolationism, 138
    and Litvinov Agreement, 145
    and Ludlow Amendment, 137
    and presidential-executive agreements, 144
    and Reciprocal Trade Agreement Act, 153
    and Supreme Court power, 50
    and Wheeler, 189n107
    and Wheeler-Bone Amendment, 59
Roosevelt, Mrs. Archibald B., 32
RUDs, 148, 222n72
rural dominance, 104

Sabin, Pauline Morton, 32
salience, 21–22, 32, 65
same-sex marriage, 3
Scalia, Antonin, 100, 117
Schechter Poultry, 49
Scheingold, Stuart, 10–11, 30, 169n4
Schempp, 69–71, 75, 159
Schlafly, Phyllis, 24

Schlesinger, Arthur Jr., 139
School District of Abington Township v. Schempp, 69–71, 75, 159
school prayer, 47, 66–76, 169n4, 200n249
    after *Schempp*, 199n234
    and Blaine Amendment, 83–84
    and Catholics, 198n228
    and Congress, 199n231
    and framing, 12
    and public opinion, 69, 199n233, 199n241
    and Reagan administration, 200n245
school segregation, 169n4
secession, 131–34, 161–62, 218n3, 219n11
sectarian education, 83–84
section 14(b), 123
Sedition Act, 89–90, 92–94
self-executing treaties, 141
Senate
    election of, 100–103, 160, 201n270, 209n74, 209n75
    and foreign policy, 152
    and treaty ratification process, 146, 148, 224n102
Senate Foreign Relations Committee, 135
Senate Judiciary Committee, 2, 13, 57, 80, 147
Senate's Special Committee Investigating the Munitions Industry, 136
separation of powers, 115
sequestration, 115
Seventeenth Amendment, 100, 102, 103, 201n270, 209n81, 209n83
Seventh Circuit Court of Appeals, 37
sex discrimination, 16–19, 41–46, 158, 186n54
Shesol, Jeff, 56
side agreements, 127
Siegel, Reva, 44, 187n65
simple resolution, 124–25
Sixteenth Amendment, 118–20, 160, 161, 214n39
Sixth Amendment, 150
slavery, 25–30
    attitude toward, 180n118
    and censorship, 178n99
    and Corwin Amendment, 132–33
    and gag rule, 28

Index   251

and political parties, 180n117
public opinion of, 179n113
Smith, Howard W. "Judge," 18, 173n39
Smith, Young B., 57
social movements
 and constitutional amendment
  proposals, 5–6
 contestation of, 46
 and ERA, 44–45, 177n84
 goals of, 31–32
 growth of, 11–12
 organizers of, 10
 and prohibition, 30–31
 recruiting support for, 11, 20
 and societal values, 36
 See also movement building
social reform agenda, 14–15
Social Security Act, 49, 54, 57
societal values, 39
South Carolina, 99
Southern states
 and constitutional bargain, 28–29
 and school prayer, 73
 and secession, 131–34
 and tariffs, 99
 and Three-Fifths Clause, 25
 and Voting Rights Act of 1965, 81
Spanish-American War, 135
spectrum of plausibility, 46
spending authority, 111, 211n8
state-church relations, 83–84
state commissions on status of women, 16–17, 19–20
state constitutions, 82–84, 117, 159–60
state convention, 33
state law
 and abortion, 61
 bottom-up influence of, 209n84
 discriminatory, 40
 and failed constitutional amendments, 82–84
 and international treaties, 141
 and Litvinov Agreement, 145
 and minimum wage, 52
 and Prohibition, 31, 180n124
 and right-to-work, 122–23
state legislatures
 and Alien and Sedition Acts, 93–94
 candidates for, 101

and Embargo, 98–99
and national proposing convention, 87
party affiliations in, 217n61
and Prohibition, 31
role of, 33
and US senators, 100–103, 209n74
and voting districts, 104, 107
states
 and 1936 election, 58
 and Article V procedures, 33
 and constitutional convention, 87
 and convention threat, 160
 and Ely Amendment, 25–26
 and embargos, 95–99
 and ERA, 82–84
 and national legislation, 208n60
 since New Deal, 4
 and political parties, 102
 power of, 166n14
 and school prayer, 73
 sovereignty of, 78
 and voting districts, 103–4
 and voting practices, 78
states' rights, 100, 114, 140–43, 210n93
stereotyping, 45
Stevens, John Paul, 2
Stewart, Potter, 43, 198n208
Stop ERA PAC, 24
strategy, 45
 Fourteenth Amendment litigation, 42
 and pro-life movement, 61–66
 reform-oriented, 2
 rights-claiming, 10–15
 of women's movement, 41–43
Strauss, David, 5
straw man, 118–24, 215n48
strict judicial scrutiny, 60, 185n49
suffrage amendments, 78, 165n2
suffrage movement, 32–33
supermajorities, 3
Supremacy Clause, 122, 141, 143–44
Supreme Court of the United States
 and Congress, 57–58, 188n101
 and constitutional amendments, 34
 and decision-making process, 38
 and Equal Protection jurisprudence, 41
 and gender discrimination, 40
 and justices' terms, 2
 and legislative veto, 126

Supreme Court, *continued*
   during New Deal, 48–60, 167n17
   and nullification, 181nn3–4
   October 1935 term of, 51–52
   opposition to, 47, 64
   and people's sovereignty, 35–36
   and political branches, 38, 48–49, 183n29, 184n30
   as a political institution, 58
   political nature of, 183n26
   and public opinion, 36–40, 120, 169n2, 182n20, 183n28
   and reapportionment, 103–8, 161
   research about, 37
   and Roosevelt, 52–55
   and school prayer, 66–76
   and socioeconomic legislation, 52
   and switch, 190n115
   and voting districts, 107
suspect classifications, 42–43, 186n54
suspensive veto, 53
Sutherland, George, 167n17
switch-in-time decisions, 4, 48–60, 158, 187n76, 190n115

Taft, William Howard, 37, 120
Taft-Hartley Act, 123, 161
tariffs, 99–100, 153, 156, 160
Task Force on Women's Rights, 22
tax, 109, 118–20, 212n14, 214n37
Tenth Amendment, 141
term limits, 212n13
territories, 214n44
Texas v. Johnson, 47, 76–77, 159
Third National Conference of Commissions on the Status of Women, 19–20
Thirteenth Amendment, 5, 133
Three-Fifths Clause, 25–27, 158, 177n89, 179n95
Thurmond, Strom, 76
Tipaldo, 52, 54, 55, 56
Title VII of 1964 Civil Rights Act, 18–19, 173n38, 173n39, 174n44
trade, 96–98, 153, 207n53, 223n91
Trade Act of 1974, 156
traditional-family-values movement, 45
Train v. City of New York, 111

treaties
   and Bricker Amendment, 139–50
   and congressional-executive agreements, 150–51
   and domestic law, 139–40, 142, 147
   and House of Representatives, 151–52
   human rights, 142–43
   and public opinion, 223n97
   ratification process for, 140, 152
   and self-execution, 141–42, 148–49
   and Senate, 224n102
   and state law, 140–43
   and trade agreements, 223n91
   See also specific treaties
Treaty Clause, 135, 140, 146, 151–54, 156, 162
Treaty of Versailles, 135, 153, 154
Treaty Power, 143–44
Tribe, Laurence, 152
Truman, Harry S., 144, 217n61
Twelfth Amendment, 4–5
Twenty-First Amendment, 33
Twenty-Fourth Amendment, 80–82, 159, 202n280, 202n288
Twenty-Seventh Amendment, 167n20, 213n23
two-house solution, 155
two-house veto, 124–25
Tydings-McDuffe Act of 1934, 121, 161

UN Charter, 142, 155
unions, 121–24, 215n50
United Columbia, 91
United States v. Belmont, 145–46
United States v. Eichman, 77, 201n267
United States v. Pink, 145–46
Universal Declaration of Human Rights, 142
Utah, 106

Vandenberg, Arthur, 54
Van Devanter, Willis, 167n17
Van Renssalaer, Mrs. Coffin, 32
Versailles Treaty, 135, 153, 154
veto, 53, 109, 111–13, 124–28, 212n14
victims' rights, 116–18, 161, 214n35
Victim's Rights Amendment (VRA), 116–18, 214n35

Index   253

Vile, John, 165n3
Virginia, 219n11
Virginia Plan, 87
Virginia Resolution, 90, 93–94, 206n33
voter referenda, 181n132
voting
    and 1787 Constitution, 78
    districts for, 103–8, 160–6`
    eligibility for, 78–80, 202n283
    and poll taxes, 78–82, 159, 202n283, 202n288
    rights of, 78–82
    rural and urban, 104
Voting Rights Act of 1965, 81, 202n283

Wagner Act. *See* National Labor Relations Act (Wagner Act)
war, 135–39, 205n21
War Labor Board, 122
Warren, Earl, 69, 70, 103, 105
warships, 205n21
Washington, George, 90
Wesberry v. Sanders, 104
West Coast Hotel v. Parrish, 54, 56, 190n120, 191n126
Wheeler, Burton, 52–55, 58, 189n104
Wheeler-Bone Amendment, 48, 53–55
    and 1937 Constitutional Revolution, 57
    and Court's switch, 51–60
    and deliberation, 158
    and radio broadcasts, 59
    ratification prospects of, 58
Whigs, 27, 30

White, Byron, 42, 197n200
Whittaker, Charles Evans, 197n200
Whittington, Keith, 38
Wisconsin, 106
Women's Bureau, 16–17
women's movement
    of 1970s and 1980s, 32
    allies of, 22
    development of, 176n63
    early 20th century, 16
    funding of, 23
    and media coverage, 21–22
    and POS, 175n59
    and President's Commission on the Status of Women, 16–17
    strategies of, 41–43
    and Title VII, 18–19
    See also ERA (Equal Rights Amendment); feminist movement; NOW; women's rights
Women's Organization for National Prohibition Reform (WONPR), 32
women's rights, 15–24
    and amendments, 186n57
    and Bricker Amendment, 147
    funding for, 176n75
    and pay equity, 170n12
    and public opinion, 176n68
women's suffrage, 32–33
Wood, Gordon, 96
Wood v. Broom, 104
Woodward, Bob, 43
World Trade Organization (WTO), 151
World War I, 135